The Damndest Radical

GORDON
B. COOKE
DOCTOR
"BEN"

Roger A. Bruns

The Damndest Radical

The Life and World of Ben Reitman, Chicago's Celebrated Social Reformer, Hobo King, and Whorehouse Physician

UNIVERSITY OF ILLINOIS PRESS
Urbana and Chicago

Manufactured in the United States of America
C 5 4 3 2 1

This book is printed on acid-free paper.

LIBRARY OF CONGRESS CATALOGING-IN-PUBLICATION DATA

Bruns, Roger.
The damndest radical.

Bibliography: p.
Includes index.
1. Reitman, Ben L. (Ben Lewis), 1879–1942.
2. Social reformers—Illinois—Chicago—Biography.
3. Physicians—Illinois—Chicago—Biography.
I. Title.
HN80.C5B76 1987 303.4'84 [B] 86-4364
ISBN 0-252-00984-3 (alk. paper)

To Carrie

Contents

Preface

Ben L. Reitman, Chicago's celebrated clap doctor. Physician and lover of prostitutes, a man who hawked treatises on sexual prowess, an inveterate skirt-chaser, he nevertheless fought vigorously for birth control and other women's rights issues. The man who attacked Billy Sunday and other preachers as insipid tools of the capitalists was the same man who carried a Bible in his early days as a hobo and even taught Sunday school classes in Emma Goldman's anarchist offices. The man who spent much time in jail and prison fighting for radical causes was the same man who counted among his friends various law enforcement officials. The man who was abducted by a vigilante mob in San Diego and was stripped, beaten, branded with cigars, tarred and rolled in sagebrush was the same man who, with his well-known flair for crude, off-color remarks, publicly joked about the humiliating attack rather than allow his radical friends to use it to illustrate the viciousness of the conservative establishment. In these and so many other ways Ben Reitman always slapped hard the faces of convention and predictability. Most who crossed his path agreed that he was the damndest radical they had ever known.

I first crossed paths with Ben Reitman while researching my book *Knights of the Road: A Hobo History.* As I ploughed through his formidable collection of papers at the library of the University of Illinois at Chicago, I was soon absorbed with one of the most remarkable lives I had ever encountered. The extraordinary range of his personal experiences; the variety of individuals surrounding him; the mélange of causes, movements, and protests of which he was a part—it was all astonishing. What a life! I hope this book does it justice.

I owe a great deal of gratitude to numerous institutions and individuals who have offered their generous assistance. My appreciation goes to the University of Illinois at Chicago library and its staff. Mary Ann Bamberger, of the Special Collections Department, provided invaluable assistance as I wrestled with the Reitman collection, and she offered her keen insights into Ben's life.

A special thanks goes to Candace Falk, Emma Goldman's best biographer, who shared her knowledge and perceptions of the times and emotions dominating the Goldman-Reitman relationship.

Ben's daughters, Medina Gross and Mecca Carpenter, and his niece, Ruth Highberg, provided much valuable information on Ben's later days. Their support has been especially gratifying.

I salute Herbert Blumer, eminent sociologist; Al Kaufman, con man extraordinaire; Elmer Gertz, respected lawyer and biographer; and Van Allen Bradley, journalist and book dealer—friends of Reitman, all—who shared their memories with me.

My thanks also to Suzanne Poirier, who discovered a valuable cache of letters between Ben Reitman and Anna Martindale and alerted me to them; to James Kenneally of Stonehill College, who found letters between Ben Reitman and Margaret Foley; and to Margaret Fusco of the Regenstein Library, University of Chicago, and Archie Motley of the Chicago Historical Society, both of whom were more than professionally responsive to my requests for assistance.

My friends and fellow workers with the National Historical Publications and Records Commission—Mary Giunta, Richard Sheldon, George Vogt, and Julie Nash—read portions of the manuscript and offered helpful advice. Julie entered the book on the trusty word processor.

My special appreciation goes to Richard Wentworth, director of the University of Illinois Press, who encouraged me throughout the work, and to Terry Sears, a superb editor, who made numerous enlightened suggestions.

Finally, my respect goes out to the hoboes, the men who took on much in life that most of us have never even imagined and toughed it out. Dan O'Brien, road knight of the Thirties, once described the hobo in terms which sum up the life of Doc Reitman: "He is the man in whom the wanderlust is the strongest lust . . . reckless perambulating soldier of fortune . . . He is an avowed optimist, laughs a great deal at the gyrations of men, looks upon politicians as tyrants, the clergy as supreme dodgers of things religious, hopes the human race, like whiskey, will improve with age."

The Damndest Radical

Prologue

Outrageously Byronesque in a cape and flowing Windsor tie, he sauntered down the aisle, confronting the weathered faces of the hoboes one by one, taunting, cajoling, trading quips and barbs. He wanted their nickels and dimes, the very same coins they had so recently solicited outside. "Here comes the damn tax collector," one of them yelled. Many quickly spun stories of their dire economic distress. But he persisted, reminding the shabby gathering of his devotion to the hobo cause. Hadn't he given them free meals and free flops? Hadn't he found jobs for them and intervened on their behalf with the police? Hadn't he hustled theater tickets for them? He chided them for their penury, appealed to their consciences, threatened them with bodily harm, and warded off their good-natured insults. And in the end they filled the hat. The night's entertainment could now begin.

This was Chicago's Hobo College; and the solicitor, its director, Dr. Ben Reitman. Just off the "main stem" of Chicago's transient district, the college occupied a part of the second and third floors of an ancient frame building. The auditorium, in which the hoboes now gathered, featured a small stage adorned with calico curtains, a stove, a piano, and a hundred or so camp chairs.

Although many Chicagoans had assumed that newspaper accounts of the college and its activities were only lighthearted whimsies, this institution was indeed real and its purpose serious. Through the Hobo College, Ben Reitman and others sought to give the workers of the road—the itinerant farm workers, miners, timber beasts, bridge snakes, skinners, ice harvesters, and gandy dancers—an intellectual and spiritual haven, a place where they could seek an education in a variety of subjects from law to economics, where they could make their own voices heard, and where in times of trouble they could find sympathy and concern, not the typical mission's soup and sermon.

A special confrontation lay in store this night at the Hobo College, a battle that made the crusty boxcar veterans in the audience squirm with anticipation. A debating team from the University of Chicago had dared migrate from the Midway on the South Side to challenge the forensic skills of a squad of West Madison Street soapboxers, a group that had matched wits and wisdom with the finest street-corner philosophers in America, from New York's Bowery to Chicago's Bughouse Square. A contingent of university lads also rallied in the grungy skid-road building among its motley collection of wanderers and belted out a few football cheers, confident that their fellows from academe would easily prevail.

The director knew better. As he looked around the barnlike room with its calcimated walls; at the oil painting of "The Blanket Stiff," a pack-carrying hobo; at the stanzas of hobo verse etched on the walls by a variety of vagabond hands—Reitman was aware that this night was only one in a long series of nights at the college. There had been the lectures on English literature and history; the open forum nights on labor problems and public health; the amateur theatrical and musical presentations; the debates on everything from free love to anarchism; the courses on public speaking. Looking now at John Loughman, the king of the soapboxers and captain of the Hobo College debating team, and at team members Scotty Sheridan and Bert Weber, he knew that the academics were destined for defeat.

Hulking, mustached, swarthy, Doc mounted a small platform, gaveled for quiet, and introduced the contestants. Reporters from major Chicago newspapers jockeyed with hard-muscled railroad stiffs for a view. The judges, including an eminent University of Chicago sociologist, prepared to take notes. The stage was set. All eyes were on the director. Ben Reitman was in his element and he loved it.

1. "Following the Monkey"

Ben Reitman. To some, a boorish lout, degenerate, egotistical, un-American, dangerous; to others, compassionate, farsighted, talented, captivating; to no one, dull. Here was the man who for three decades traveled the country as the "King of the Hoboes," the "Master Bum"; who, as an anarchist and Emma Goldman's lover, drew the scorn of federal agents as well as other radicals; who scandalized even Greenwich Village with his outlandish dress, vulgar language, and eccentric bombast. Here was Chicago's infamous clap doctor, who toiled as Al Capone's whorehouse physician and befriended prostitutes, dope fiends, bohemians, con men, thieves, and outcasts of all stripes. Despite an unlettered, uncultivated background, Reitman authored two books praised by sociologists. And in the course of a life filled with countless sexual escapades, tar and sagebrush, jail cells, and days and nights in soapbox parks and avant-garde clubs, he made time to work for significant social reforms to ease the plight of America's downtrodden and homeless. If some thought him the grossest man in America, he was also one of the most ardent champions of the underclass. The man was a charlatan to some, a tireless ally to others.

Reitman was born in 1879, in St. Paul, Minnesota, to poor Russian immigrant Jews. His father, Shockney Reitman, was an itinerant peddler who tramped the state of Minnesota selling dry goods and notions to Swedish farmers. Within a few years, embittered by business failure, Shockney was on his way to New York, leaving behind his wife, Ida, and their two sons, Lew and Ben.[1]

Shepherded by Ida's father, a widower and an itinerant peddler himself, the family was marched through Mississippi, Texas, Louisiana, and then on to places in the East. Later, when her father remarried, Ida Reitman and her two sons were left on their own. Ben was four years old. The family lived a few months in Cleveland then moved on to Chicago. Ida rented a room in a low-class, red-light district on South Clark Street, near the bawdy house run by one of the most notorious madames of them all, Carrie Watson.

Those were the days of open vice in Chicago, the days of gambling parlors and barrelhouse joints, opulent dance halls and whorehouses, dope dens and dime burlesques, voodoo doctors and tawdry penny arcades. A correspondent for the London *Daily Mail Correspondent* noted that Chicago presented more "splendid attractions and hideous repulsions close together than any place known to me . . . it makes a more amazing open display of evil than any other city. . . ."[2]

The brothels were plentiful and imaginative back then. At the French Elm, every wall was a mirror, even the ceilings; at the House of All Nations, women of all colors and dialects awaited, although most were natives of Chicago; at the Park Theatre, jaded sex circuses beckoned those who wanted to watch as well as those who wished to join in. Another visitor from England, an evangelist named Gypsy Smith, later took a look at some of this and pronounced, "A man who visits the red-light district has no right to associate with decent people in daylight."[3]

Some of young Ben's earliest acquaintances were prostitutes. They gave him nickels for running errands, became his confidant, mothered him. He often claimed that he found more life and warmth and human compassion in these ladies of the joy houses than in any other segment of society. "It did not appear to me," he wrote later in life, "that these girls were vicious or immoral. They were kind, jolly, sympathetic, generous—human." On this matter he never changed his mind. Many of these women were his close friends; some, his bedmates.

For several years Ida Reitman moved her family in and out of various cheap rooming houses in Chicago's First Ward, barely existing on occasional jobs and infrequent contributions from other family members. Ben roamed the streets and prowled the railroad yards and the beaches of Lake Michigan. He learned to mooch and steal food and supplied the family in winters with coal from the tracks of the Illinois Central. He ransacked trash heaps for old bottles to sell for a nickel a wagon-load. He hung around free-lunch saloons where customers sometimes offered him scraps of food and maybe even a soda. He sold newspapers and worked as a bootblack.

Because he was the only Jewish boy in an Irish neighborhood, his friends dubbed him "Sheeny Ben," a nickname he accepted but resented. From these early days he developed a decided antipathy for Jews. For a brief time he attended a school operated by the St. John Catholic Church, and he later was enrolled at the Haven School at Fifteenth Street and Wabash Avenue. Ben's most vivid memories of those days at Haven were of his mother's frequent visits to explain her son's unsatisfactory academic progress and habitual truancy.

One day, while still a boy, Reitman walked into the Railroad Chapel, a Presbyterian mission at Fourteenth and State streets. For him it was the beginning of a lifelong attachment to religion. Ben often carried a Bible later in life and taught Sunday school classes. He was an avid believer in the power of prayer, though he admitted that many of his prayers were similar to those uttered by one of his grafter friends, who often implored: "God give me luck and I will beat that fellow out of two hundred dollars."

If, through the years, both friends and detractors were skeptical of and puzzled by the steadfast adherence to protestant religion by a radical, an anarchist, a man noted for vulgarity, licentiousness, and bohemianism, Reitman had a response: "My religious life may be a mystery to others but to me it is perfectly clear. They are mystified because to them religion is piety, morality, and inhibition. To me religion is love and service." He looked back on that night in the Bowery mission as a significant turning point, the night when he answered the call of the mission-house sky pilot to renounce sin, the night when he marched up the aisle to the slow tune of "Jesus Lover of My Soul." The feeling that he was now in the fold, Ben said, gave him an unrivaled sense of exultation.

From his earliest years Ben was intoxicated by the railroad, with its frightening monster locomotives, its beguiling characters, its swirl of excitement and action. Alongside the tracks at Eighteenth and Clark, the boy learned to hop slow-moving freights, slept in box cars, and was overcome by wanderlust.

When he was twelve years old Ben met two tramps named Ohio Skip and Cincinnati Slim, who coaxed him onto an east-bound Lake Shore freight. They fueled his fantasies with talk of the freedom and adventures that lay along the road of steel rails. The next day he was in Ohio. The street kid had become a road kid. While he would always return to Chicago and to his mother after his tramping odysseys, the road world was now before him and he was anxious to seize all of it in his grasp.

During Reitman's youth the railroads had begun to lace the country. By the end of the nineteenth century nearly 200,000 miles of track stretched into every part of the nation, bringing with it not only mobility but romance and legend. The wail of the soot-belching locomotives touched the nerve of restlessness in many Americans, stimulating visions of new places and new fortunes.

In post–Civil War America thousands of young boys, many of whom had ridden freights during the war, hit the road and learned well the tricks of survival. Whatever the personal reasons for their new life—from bitterness over lost jobs and lost families to alcoholism and poverty—many men found relief and escape in the road life. To survive, to roam at will with only wit and guile and muscle as weapons—this was the spirit of the road wanderers.

> We are the True nobility;
> Sons of rest and the outdoor air;
> Knights of the tie and rail are we,
> Lightly meandering everywhere.
>
> Having no gold we buy no care,
> As over the crust of the world we go,
> Stepping in tune to this ditty rare;
> Take up your bundle and beat it, Bo![4]

Harry Kemp, a man who, like Ben Reitman, had run away from home at an early age to hit the freights, later became a poet, composing verse about hooking freights, about the battered stiffs in the boxcars and in the city skid roads, about jail cells in two-bit junctions, about the exhilaration of moving around, unencumbered by convention and social ties. The "Tramp Poet," Kemp was called, bohemian of the tracks, putting into words what many road men had felt, what Ben Reitman would soon feel—the challenge, the frustration, and the independence of the road life:

> The cars lay on a siding through the night;
> The scattered yard lamps winked in green and red;
> I slept upon bare boards with small delight,

My pillow, my two shoes beneath my head;
As hard as my own conscience was my bed;
I lay and listened to my own blood flow;
Outside, I heard the thunder come and go
And glimpsed the golden squares of passing trains,
Or felt the cumbrous freight train rumbling slow;
And yet that life was sweet for all its pain.

I crept with lice that stayed and stayed for spite;
I froze in "jungles" more than can be said;
Dogs tore my clothes, and in a woeful plight
At many a back door for my food I pled
Until I wished to God that I was dead . . .
My shoes broke through and showed an outburst toe;
On every side the world was all my foe,
Threatening me with jibe and jeer and chains,
Hard benches, cells, and woe on endless woe—
And yet that life was sweet for all its pains.[5]

Jack London wrote of being lured into the tramp life: "They were road kids, and with every word they uttered the lure of The Road laid hold of me more imperiously . . . And it all spelled Adventure. Very well; I would tackle this new world. . . ." London would later call his new world a "human cesspool, the shambles and charnel-house of our civilization."[6]

Reitman was now tasting that life, was now a boy tramp, a "punk," one of a growing legion wandering the country on freights, living in "jungles," begging, conning, fighting, running from broken homes and poverty, running through adolescence into that charnel house. Drawn by hardened, older tramps, the "jockers," into a world of petty crime and panhandling, into a society of club and iron and swift retribution and even of pederasty, the road kids looked for excitement and identity. Instead, they often found sordidness and pain and wasted lives.

Ben remembered the first jungle he encountered, a camp near Lima, Ohio, where assorted safe blowers and thieves of the Lake Shore Push, an infamous tramp gang, mingled with other wanderers. As in most jungles, the Lima camp was nestled among the trees, close to a railroad track and a water tank. Lounging around a fire Ben saw notable veterans of the train-jumping fraternity. There was Cleveland Mushy, an umbrella mender, or "mushfakir," a Civil

War veteran who had roamed the West even before there were railroads. Soft-spoken, some distinguished Tolstoyan whiskers giving him a philosophical bearing, he looked to Ben like a character straight out of Maxim Gorkey's "A Night's Lodging." When Mushy began a recitation of his exploits, the hoboes all listened, their imaginations fired by tales of venerable cow towns and rough mining camps.

Denver Red, tall, popular with the other stiffs, racked by a consumptive cough, was also at the Lima camp. Red was one of the many tuberculosis victims who had fled the cities and their congestion and bad air in search of better health on the open road. Everybody knew he had the "Con," but no one in the jungle seemed to be alarmed. Red himself considered the disease a good graft, as it gave him a legitimate excuse and much sympathy for panhandling, or "throwing the feet." He could also walk into any town, declare that he had the dreaded disease, be referred to social agencies, and then get free transportation to another state. It was obvious to all that most charity workers preferred to pass the problem of an infectious tubercular bum to another locale.

Another camp veteran was Irish, an itinerant worker, heavy drinker, tough fighter, and aggressive womanizer. His sagas and songs of Ireland brought tears to the eyes of those compatriots surrounding the mulligan. Irish later tired of the road life and settled down with a wife and family.

New Orleans Slim, a malarial, grizzled Johnny Reb, hated Yankees and blacks, blaming them for his own woes as well as the country's. The South, traditionally a region of terror for hoboes, where weeks on chain gangs and vicious beatings were commonplace, caused no fear in Slim. The old Confederate soldier traveled on the freights as he pleased, in Alabama, Texas, Georgia, and Louisiana; the South was his briar patch. He tramped with his son, Louisiana Blue, who always wore a blue shirt, blue jacket, blue overalls, and blue socks; he even had blue eyes and sang the blues.

There was Sailor Bill, an anchor tattooed on his chest, a bottle of rum in his pocket, an endless stream of seafaring whimsy in his repertoire. "I'm a seafaring man," he would say, "I never work on land." Since he had not been to sea for nearly a decade, Bill and work were strangers.

Blackie, a recent telegraph company lineman on the run from the family of a pregnant girl, was one of several men around the fire that night who mentioned problems with women. Another tramp told how his wife had asked him to leave home, how he had given up his job and hit the freights, how he still sent her money. The bitterness toward women was revealing, Reitman later wrote. "Usually, but not always, whenever a man derides women, it is more than likely he has first deceived or mistreated a woman."

And then there was Rags, massive and lousy, wearing four coats, three pairs of pants, three shirts, no socks, and large, unmatched shoes. Every pocket bulged—pieces of paper, newspapers, pencils, books, scraps of metal, food. "Rags had an immobile face," Ben recalled, "except when someone attempted to take some of his precious belongings and then he would snarl like a dog. The snarl was distinctly effeminate. Beyond the dirt and the matter, you could see soft blue eyes." Some of the hoboes fed Rags in the jungles, and he also salvaged food from garbage cans and the fields.

If the benign snarl of Rags rose from the depths of mental illness, the ferocity of some of the other road characters Ben encountered was more real. He saw men murdered in vicious fights, saw others rolled in their drunken sleep, saw young boys sexually molested. William Aspinwall, a mushfakir like Cleveland Mushy, heard stories of the Lake Shore gang with which Ben had come in close contact: "They do not hesitate as I am told by Hoboes to commit any kind of a crime. They Rob and even murder hoboes that do not belong to their Gang—I was told a young boy probably 16 or 18 years old from Kalamazoo, Michigan happened to jump into a box car to beat his way and there was a number of the above Gang in the Car. They stripped the young fellow of everything but his Pants and Shirt, Committed sodomy on his person and then threw the fellow out while the train was running at full speed. The fellow was found with his shoulder broke and otherwise cut and bruised up more dead than alive."[7]

Young Ben was running with a tough crowd. But he found among many in the tramp fraternity a robust enthusiasm for life, considerable ingenuity, intelligence, and a spirit to leave behind the stifling problems of home and family, to find relief from grinding poverty and wrenching personal problems. As did so many others from the slums, Ben found in the freight train a ticket to change.

In his own tramping days as a youth, Jack London was awed by jungle stiffs arguing philosophy and economic theory. Their forensic skills and erudition on a variety of subjects convinced the fledgling writer that he needed to read more widely.[8] Godfrey Irwin, a veteran tramp who was later recognized as an authority on hobo vernacular and song, remembered one evening beside a western railroad yard listening to the crackling of ties in the fire and the astonishing talk of tramps encircling the mulligan. An old sea stiff quietly spoke verses of John Masefield's "Sea Fever"; another recited "The Gila Monster Route." From literature to railroad stories to the inevitable sex jokes, the conversation ranged wide. Irwin recalled many such nights—hard-muscled road stiffs quoting Kipling and Edgar Guest and Robert Service, and songs and poems "on the rights of man and confusion of the ruling class." There was little lovesick sentimentalism around the jungle fires but much ribald humor, social parody, and ballads of hard life of the road.[9]

Ben listened and dreamed. He could see early on that these men had found camaraderie and some sense of common purpose in their destitution. Their stories were similar, always in stark contrast to the idealized vision of the freedom and independence of the open road that overlooked the hunger, the sickness and violence, the tackling of freights in bitter cold and rain, the grubbing for food. Somehow, all the rhapsodizing about rugged individualism seemed like so much bunk when the gut ached and the spirit sagged. Nonetheless, Ben continued to ride the freights across the country, taking odd jobs and slumming in the skid roads of the major cities. He once remarked, "I can't help batting around the world. I have been everywhere . . . This is my hobby, my sport, my life."[10]

In New York's Bowery, Ben made friends with prostitutes like Truck Horse May and Dopey Liz. He befriended tramps like the Time Kid, a young stiff bent on establishing coast-to-coast traveling records on the freights. The Kid was a dromomaniac, compelled always to move. He and Ben had much in common.

The "Chi Kid," as Reitman now became known, slept in YMCA rooms when he had money and in missions, haystacks, streets, and parks when he didn't. He became completely absorbed in the life of the tracks; for him and other fledgling road knights the train was a rite of passage. To deck a fast express, to ride the brake beams inches from the biting cinders and the knife-edged wheels, to outwit train conductors and railroad police—these were badges of initiation into the train-jumping fraternity. Ben rode the gondolas and the reefers; he whirled through tunnels on top of passenger cars, swaying and jolting with every move, inches away from death or serious injury. Of his first ride atop a baggage car Reitman recalled: "Hot cinders burned my neck. Zzzzzz! came the wind. I have always had faith in God and the Cosmos, but I was frightened . . . I lay on my stomach and tried to dig my toes into the car. I held on to the chimney for dear life. The hot cinders from the engine swept across the train burning my face, ears, and neck but I kept my hold on the little ventilator chimney. I closed my eyes and prayed for the train to stop."

Ben began to learn the tramp argot, much of it an amalgam of prison and railroad terms: for example, "angel food" was a mission-house sermon; a "bone polisher," an unfriendly dog; Jesus Christ was "Jerusalem Slim." He also honed his techniques of panhandling, sometimes devising elaborate stories, often working with other tramps in teams. As one road veteran explained, panhandling was a matter of survival: "If you had spent weeks, perhaps, sleeping in box cars or worse; had traveled many hundreds of weary miles, with little and often no food, unshaved, ill-clothed, swaying on the bumpers, face scarred with flying gravel, on the rods blinded by cinders, half-crazy from looking for places to boil up, would the great driving force of hunger compel you to ask for something to eat?"[11]

Often arrested for vagrancy, Reitman always talked jocularly about his life of crime, carefully pointing out that the laws under which he was apprehended were unjust and reflected the bigotry and inanity of those who framed them. His first visit to jail had been in 1890, at the hands of a railroad clerk in Chicago who saw him picking up coal at Sixteenth Street and the tracks. After being questioned at the Harrison Street Police Station, Ben, aged eleven, was turned loose on society in the custody of his mother. At that moment, he said, a great current in his life was unleashed—an interest in and identification with the outcasts of society.[12]

During his first jail term, a stint in Omaha when he was fifteen, Ben encountered such characters as Chinatown Blinky, a one-eyed moocher from the Bowery; Oakland Slim, habitué of the opium dens on the West Coast; Eddie Mack, stickup and pete man of some fame; and English, prosperous con man and card shark. In the days before the Feds moved against narcotic use, many prisons were like dope dens, with prisoners spreading morphine over slices of bread, openly shooting up, and even using small opium pipes. From this horror the young Reitman managed to stay clean. Later, as a doctor, he would treat men like Oakland Slim.

When his zeal for tramping had cooled temporarily, Ben would return to Chicago to live with his mother. His attachment to her became exceptionally strong, welded by the shared trauma of abandonment by his father and the poverty under which the family had struggled so long. Also, his time on the road, these escapes from the emotional burdens in his young life, brought their own measure of guilt and seemed to make his devotion to his mother stronger when he returned.

Even in Ben's adulthood, Ida Reitman remained the most important woman in his life. Throughout, he labored to forge emotional bonds to other women only to find his ardent attachment to his mother a formidable wall. Other women were merely sex objects, indiscriminate prizes in his game of pursuit. Years later, when he read D. H. Lawrence's *Sons and Lovers* for the first time, he immediately identified with the book's mother-fixated hero. He never shrank from nor attempted to hide these dominant emotions, much to the frustration and sorrow of his many female companions.

While in Chicago, Ben took numerous jobs. For several years he was a part-time office boy for the Cook Remedy Company, which sold Syphelene, a treatment for syphilis. As the boy from Chicago's red-light district once remarked, "Strange how main currents direct our lives. From my earliest childhood I have been associated with syphilis."[13]

Ben Reitman's tramping adventures were not confined to the United States. At Tampa Bay he once boarded the British tramp steamer *Tresco* as a fireman. He had never before been on a tramp steamer and was now passing himself off as an experienced hand at one of the naval world's most testing jobs. After the first few hours of the trip, exhausted, almost asphyxiated in the suffocating stokehole, blackened by coal, Ben grappled up the ladder to the deck and announced to his superiors, at mid-sea, that he was quitting. He was rudely escorted back down to the stokehole. "My hands were blistered, my body was burned, my back was sore, and my pride had received a mortal wound. However, I had not been wholly impervious to the teachings of experience during my six years on the road. I made a speedy recovery, physically and mentally. . . ."

To Antwerp, Cardiff, Liverpool, Malta, and Port Said the *Tresco* sailed with its fatigued but wide-eyed novice fireman aboard. Near Massawa, Italy, Ben saw a compulsory venereal disease hospital, a kind of corral patrolled by armed soldiers who forcibly detained the infected. In the Abyssinian desert he carried on animated conversations in the huts of natives who didn't understand a word he said. In Calcutta he spent time with Christian missionaries working among the destitute. In Ceylon he saw Salvation Army evangelists holding religious services on street corners. In Marseilles he wandered the back streets and the docks where hordes of prostitutes swarmed around every potential customer. In Paris he mooched twenty-five francs at the American consulate, begged more money from American tourists in downtown hotels, and booked passage home. Landing in New York, broke, he hoboed to Chicago, rushed into the Reitman home, and declared, "Mother, I've come home to eat."

In 1898, Ben, through the help of the YMCA, got a job at Chicago's Polyclinic Laboratory as a lab boy under the tutelage of Dr. Maximilian Herzog, a respected pathologist and bacteriologist. Herzog was then working on the etiology of syphilis and was conducting a variety of experiments in which Ben was asked to assist. Impressed by the young man's facility for the work, Herzog encouraged him to consider medicine as a career. In the spring of 1900, Dr. Leo Loeb joined the clinic to assist Herzog, and he, too, quickly warmed to the young lab assistant from the slums. A few months later, when Loeb was offered an assistantship in pathology at the College of Physicians and Surgeons, he encouraged Ben to go with him as a student, offering to pay his tuition. Reitman eagerly accepted.

In October 1900, at the age of twenty-one, Ben entered medical school, despite his woeful lack of a rudimentary education. Just as he had been able to earn a little extra money while at the clinic by selling stray dogs to medical students for use in courses on operative surgery, now fourteen equally unfortunate creatures paid for his copy of *Gray's Anatomy*. A skeleton, which he obtained by "cleaning" one of the cadavers being dissected at the Polyclinic, was sold to pay for his other textbooks. His freshman year was one of much painstaking work and barely passing grades.

During his first year of medical school Ben almost married a girl he met at Bethany Baptist Church where he taught Sunday school. (Curiously, throughout his life Ben made numerous conquests among Sunday school acquaintances.) After a short courtship he soon found himself partner to a scheduled wedding at the girl's home. Twenty minutes before the fateful encounter, however, the young Lothario was beaming into the jet-black eyes and fondling the soft hands of the minister's sister, a flirtatious beauty who was unaware that she was sitting with the imminent groom.

Standing before his fiancée's family and his own mother and brother, Ben got as far as "Do you Ben L. Reitman take . . ."; then he went berserk. "First I let out a wild yell that I [had] heard in an Indian reservation in Arizona. This was followed by a correct immitation of drunken Buffalo Fat when he was trying to lick three men with one hand behind his back. Then I gave a sincere but perfect imitation of an elephant calling his mate, a rooster boasting over the egg his friend's wife [had] laid, a tom cat lamenting the fact that his wife's mistress had locked all the windows, and the Anvil chorus sung in Chinese." He sprang at the preacher, biting him on the neck, at which the preacher pleaded for a doctor, thinking that the crazed young man had probably poisoned him. The bride knelt down and gave thanks to God that He had saved her from marrying a lunatic. The father threatened Ben with death. Ben's mother and brother led their blabbering relative home and put him to bed.

In the summer Ben changed churches but not his habits. While teaching Sunday school at Immanuel Baptist Church, he met May Schwartz, a twenty-one-year-old student at the Chicago Musical College. Beautiful, blue-eyed, born on a farm near Golden, Illinois, May was plagued by emotional troubles and had spent time in a sanatorium in Jacksonville, Illinois. It was her misfortune to fall in love with a man who was most unlikely to bring stability and calm to her life. After what Ben later called a "short moony, spoony romance," the two were married on July 4, 1901, at Judson Memorial Church in New York. "I tried to avoid getting married," Ben later wrote, "but my fiance was apprehensive and insistent . . . I felt at the time it was a sacrifice, and later I had occasion to remark that it was not only stupid, but futile."

After a couple of days in New York, Ben and his new wife took the Hamburg-American Line to Germany on a honeymoon financed by May's parents. The couple traveled to Berlin, Hamburg, Dresden, and Prague, where Ben panicked and deserted May. He wandered on to Antwerp, feeling, as he later wrote, "as fancy free as the day in my childhood when I wandered away from home. . . ." The wife he had left behind was pregnant.

Ben never attempted to justify what he did in Prague, never found a way to explain what inner forces, what psychic upheaval drove him to abandon his wife. His near marriage a few months earlier now seem prophetic, its comical elements contrasted to the terrible psychological assault he committed on May Reitman. Just as he had as a boy along the tracks at Eighteenth Street and Clark, he now ran from the dread of entrapment, from an emotional burden. Later, he lamely talked about how his grandfather and his father were both family deserters, how he himself had been left to "starve or to be lost in that great whirlpool that sucks up deserted mothers and children." Like grandfather, like father, like son.

With no apparent remorse he was again the low-budget American wayfarer in Europe, drinking wine with frauleins in Antwerp, bumming food and money in Frankfurt-on-Main. Several weeks passed before Ben worked his way back to the United States on a tramp steamer. He was in Chicago in time for his sophomore year at the College of Physicians and Surgeons. Still in Europe, May Reitman traveled to Leipzig to study music and, naively, to await her husband's return. The following spring, after delivering a baby girl, May's health broke and she was sent by American consular officials to a sanatorium in Hamburg. Ben, oblivious to all of this, continued his schoolwork, searched for stray dogs, taught Sunday school, and romped to burlesque shows and tenderloin dives.

After his second school year ended, Reitman set out for Europe,[14] slipping between the blind baggage and the engine of a Lake Shore passenger train headed east. Reaching New York three days later, he signed on with a White Star Line ship as a fireman and made Liverpool in a week. Unsure of May's whereabouts, Ben retraced her movements to Leipzig and Hamburg, finally reaching the sanatorium on June 20. Ben, his wife, and their daughter, Helen, departed Hamburg that evening on a boat bound for Liverpool. The next day, May and the baby left for the United States, their passage provided by American authorities. Ben, refused assistance by consular officials, remained in Europe to fend for himself. From Philadelphia, three weeks later, May wrote a pathetic letter to Brainard Warner, the American consul who had befriended and assisted her during her year in Europe: "My husband has left me to my own resources. He is roaming in Scotland now. He does not come back until September 15. I am sometimes terrified to let him lose me. He values me so little."[15]

May Reitman returned to Golden, Illinois, with her infant daughter. She and Ben later divorced. Although they corresponded on occasion, Ben never provided for her or Helen. May's emotional problems continued, and she was again confined to a sanatorium. It would be two decades before Ben again saw his daughter. He later wrote, "I have no excuse to offer. I only know that whoever comes into parenthood, whether by accident as so many do, or by choice as some others do, takes on a great burden . . . How often in my every day life do I see parents failing, though not always as thoughtlessly as I did . . . I admit a child has rights. My daughter, too, has rights. I believe it is the sacred duty of every man to provide for his offspring until they are educated and able to care for themselves." This was a sacred duty the young medical student, on the run, driven by wanderlust, chose not to accept.

Ben Reitman spent his final year as a student at the American College of Medicine and Surgery, graduating on May 17, 1904.[16] He passed the Illinois State Board of Health examinations, obtained a license, and opened an office at Thirty-ninth Street and Cottage Grove Avenue, directly across from Scotty's Gambling Parlor. Underworld types and down-and-outs gravitated to Ben's office, as did prostitutes, pimps, dope addicts, and sexual perverts, all of whom began to call him "Doc." His infant career, unprofitable but entertaining, was mixed with frequent visits to Scotty's crap tables and much boozing and carousing. He nonetheless found time to teach a few courses at local medical colleges.

When the routine became too confining, Ben would quickly suspend his medical practice and head for the rail yards and docks. He took a job cleaning the cattle cars on a ship bound for Liverpool, later lamenting "the amount of excreta that a cow could manufacture in 24 hours." Once in Europe he hit the old haunts with English and French beggars, crooks, and sporting ladies. In Paris he worked for Buffalo Bill's Wild West Show as a general roustabout and physician treating the circus boys who had contracted venereal disease. About the only ones who didn't get the clap, Ben said, were those who already had it.

Mistakenly arrested in Ireland on a murder charge, Ben asked the magistrates if the murderer was an Irishman. When told that he was, the American Jew had a ready alibi: "I showed them the evidence of a rite that had been performed on me by a Jewish Rabbi during my infancy in St. Paul. They were highly amused and roared with delight. I threatened to have the American soldiers come and wipe the village off the map. We compromised, however. They gave me three drinks, a good bed and breakfast."

On a tramp in 1906, Reitman was asleep in a ship's bunk off the coast of San Francisco when that city was struck by a devastating earthquake. After the ship docked at the Fulton Iron Works, Ben walked the streets. "People were acting so strange that it did not seem like life but like a great moving panorama and I was standing on the side watching it all pass . . . They all moved eastward and the flames were following in mad pursuit." He quickly joined an improvised hospital in Golden Gate Park, volunteered for a medical unit at Fort Mason, rode ambulances around the fire-swept city, and later worked under General P. J. Farrell at the Presidio doing lab work. He also learned something about crime, as many of his hobo and underground comrades prowled the city looting at will. "It is a rather interesting thing about the psychology of crooks, that when there is fire and anger, murder and excitement, they work calmly and deliberately. The pain and needs of civilization do not affect them."

On still another tramp the following year Reitman signed on as doctor to a Southern Pacific Railroad gang working in the interior of Mexico. It was here he witnessed a pitched battle between Mexican laborers and 300 Chinese workmen from Manchuria, most of whom had been shanghaied to work in the blistering desert heat. Pickaxes, iron bars, clubs, daggers, and even fingernails tore flesh that day. Several men were buried along the tracks, and Ben helped minister to the rest. He said later that witnessing the horror made him a pacifist.

As he hoboed his way back toward Chicago with a traveling mate named Iowa Red, the two were ditched in Bowie, Arizona, and arrested for illegal train-jumping. They were confined for four days to a "booby-hatch," a six-foot-square building of wooden planks with no lights or toilet facilities. Ben and Iowa Red had been forced to turn over all their cash, which the judge and the sheriff split, the latter immediately getting a shave and haircut with his share. As the sheriff put the two men on an eastbound freight and waved good-bye, Reitman's fury welled. He was determined to fight this kind of "boodle-jail" graft, this cynical, official corruption against the lowest in society.

In February 1907, Ben arrived in Silver City, New Mexico, and made the acquaintance of a young army sergeant, a recruiter named Hugh McComb. The sergeant, who had himself ridden the blind baggage and top decks in earlier years, got along famously with the Chicago hobo doctor. They ate and drank together, all at government expense, while McComb sized up Reitman as a possible recruit. Ben never said no; then again, he never said yes. When McComb suggested that Ben report to the recruiting station in El Paso, the affable wanderer readily accepted. El Paso was east, the direction he was headed, and the government was offering a free ride on the cushions. Ben did contact the recruiting officials in El Paso, but he did not enlist, instead vanishing on an eastbound freight. When a newspaper reporter later confronted him with the story of his brief encounter with the military, Ben commented, "Anything like confinement—the army—the jail—is offensive to me. I wish to be free as a bird to soar where I will. . . ."[17] Although the government later made meek efforts to recover transportation costs, subsistence, and lodging from their recent guest, Ben had not actually enlisted and could not be charged with desertion. But in the months following, the military began an investigative file on Ben Reitman, only one of many in the years to come.[18]

In mid-life Ben Reitman began an autobiography he called "Following the Monkey." A four-year-old street urchin, seduced by the marvels of an organ-grinder and his monkey, trails along impulsively, ignoring time and place and responsibility. The organ-grinders, the monkeys—many of them crossed Reitman's path, each with a compelling call. Ben followed them all.

2. Millionaire Hobo

Ben Reitman continued drifting from big cities to two-bit junctions, from municipal lodging houses to tramp saloons. As he begged and conned and freighted his way to and from "Big Chi," the hoboes home port, his home port, he began to philosophize about life on the road. As he talked with grizzled veterans and upstart punks in the jungles, as he cleared his head of booze binges in flophouses and jail cells, as he faced no-name judges, boodle-jail sheriffs, and sadistic railroad shacks, he tried to find perspective in such insane drifting. The road was both siren and demon, its call a refreshing breeze, its seduction a curse.

In a remarkable, maundering composition written in a hotel during one of his tramps, Reitman revealed his feelings about his life on the road. He wrote clinically of wanderlust, as if it were an infection brought on by an alien virus. St. Paul had it; so did Lewis and Clark, and Stanley and Livingston; hoboes all. No matter what city Reitman visited, no matter how long he had been on the road, the ravenous craving to move on was always there, a thirst never quenched, a perverted delirium, a mania. He knew no day when the yearning was not intense, no day when he was not tortured by it. Geneva, Glascow, Hamburg, Naples, Le Havre—he had seen them all; had traveled on railroads and steamers; eaten in Bowery missions, London soup kitchens, and Colorado jails; shared cornbread and bacon with roving stiffs in Georgia; mooched francs from Americans in Paris. He remembered the deep grass of a southern field; the star-splashed skies of a western desert; the smell of fresh hay in many a barn and the sound of horses munching in their stalls as he bedded down nearby. He quoted Kipling: "I've turned my 'and to most, and turned it good." Yet the delirium of flight was always there, driving him to the brake rods of a midnight train heading west or to the hold of a lake boat gliding into the night. The many jails he had been in were to him respites, not punishment, reminders that the road life was for the rugged and that he had survived. "The band is playing in the hotel," he wrote, "and as the music floats to me I think of Paris, London, Berlin, Rome, Chicago, and a thousand other places I have roamed, feeling as I do now, full of life and hope."[1] Reitman's affinity for the road life, with its characters and challenges and the escape it offered, was never stronger than at this time of his life.

To many men the road had brought disillusionment and despair. Jack London, who tackled the rods and blind baggage as he wandered through the West, who had prided himself in his "blond-beastly" Nietzschean exploits and conquests, had gradually seen the road as a grisly recess of life, its players as "wrenched and distorted and twisted out of shape by toil and hardship and accident, and cast adrift." He saw himself hanging on the edge, strength failing, slipping into the human cellar, the "Social Pit."[2] Josiah Flynt, the foremost writer of the nineteenth century on tramp life, a man who had spent his early years wandering through the hobo haunts as an idealistic sojourner in search of adventure and freedom, later called the road life degrading, debased, and sordid. Instead of the wonders of the open road, he found crime and poverty and disease. Flynt, the recorder of tramp life, later became a railroad detective.[3]

But to Ben Reitman the tramp steamers, waterside rathskellers and dives, and squalid rooming houses were welcome diversions. Unlike the battered stevedores, skinners, ice harvesters, gandy dancers, and other vagabonds he encountered on his odysseys, Ben could, and often did, choose to leave the road, return to Chicago, and resume his medical practice. For him, time on the road was for tasting some of the netherlife. Like Eugene O'Neill, who in his early days also spent periods of time drifting, Reitman was a kind of scenery bum, out for the excitement and drama, charged by the uncertainties, sometimes touched by the pathos. He took that road numerous times but always with the realization that it could never swallow him and that the Windy City, his protective port, awaited.

In February 1907 Reitman was again heading back to Chicago when, in a St. Louis hotel, he noticed an advertisement in the Sunday *Post-Dispatch* for a meeting of hoboes, to be held that afternoon. His curiosity stirred, he marched over to a large vacant store on Olive Street, where about 300 men were gathered to hear various people speak about the unemployed and shelters for homeless men. After a few formal speeches, the chairman of the meeting asked for volunteers to offer remarks. His exhibitionist tendencies prevailing, Ben stood up and declared, "Friends, we ought to do something to stop the police and the sheriffs from picking up men and sending them to jail for vagrancy." The dark, swarthy stranger got no arguments on this point from the tough, bedraggled journeymen in the crowd, most of whom had undoubtedly suffered the fate to which Reitman referred; indeed, they lustily cheered his remarks. Later, the gaunt, bearded leader of the meeting approached Ben and asked him to join a new organization for hoboes. The man was James Eads How; the organization, the Brotherhood Welfare Association. For Ben it was a most fateful encounter. In fact, he said later that it had changed his whole life.[4]

James Eads How was born into wealth in 1874. His father, James F. How, was a vice-president and the general manager of the Wabash Railroad; his grandfather, James Buchanan Eads, was a noted civil engineer, designer of the Eads Bridge, the first network of steel to span the Mississippi River.[5] While a student at Meadville Theological Seminary in Pennsylvania, James Eads How had begun to exhibit some of the singular eccentricities which so characterized his entire life. He sold his expensive suit and gave the money to the poor; he gave away other personal possessions, including money, and lived in a barren room.

How later attended Harvard and Oxford universities. He joined the Fabian Society, a group which nurtured his growing interest in social experiments and reform, and continued to renounce the trappings of the wealth of his family. He began to wear threadbare clothes and also became a vegetarian. Some of his deeds became local lore. On one Sunday morning in St. Louis, How wandered the streets buying all of the newspapers from the newsboys. When asked why, he explained that he wanted the boys off the streets and in Sunday schools.[6]

When his father died How received $20,000 from the estate, which he immediately gave to the mayor of St. Louis, asking that it be turned over to the people who had earned it—the poor. Following the death of his mother, he received over $125,000, which he also gave to the poor, much to the dismay of remaining family members. Then, with additional monies earned from tolls paid at the Eads Bridge, he launced a crusade for social justice. The beneficiary of his work was the American hobo.

At the turn of the century the hobo had many images. To some he was the idealistic dreamer, the iconoclast, the truly free man unbound by convention; to others he was a public nuisance, a dreg, an abject figure of contempt and scorn, a striking example of human failure. His numbers represented an enormous problem to public welfare agencies; to some social reformers he was a tragic symbol of the evils of capitalistic exploitation. American industry viewed the hobo as something of a necessary evil, his labor indispensable, his habits revolting. But in James How's search for a cause with which to identify, a mission to undertake, the hobo was a figure to be embraced, in stark contrast to How's own roots. His new organization, the International Brotherhood Welfare Association, would seek to bring relief to this complex segment of society, these outcasts with so much potential and so little advantage.

To How, the hoboes were a great body of unorganized, uneducated men without plan or purpose. With thousands of them roaming in and out of America's major cities, homeless, most ill clad and ill fed, How saw a clear field for reform, a field relatively untouched by government or private philanthropy. He made the hobo his life's work, giving his time, his talent, and his money.[7] Itinerant miners, berry grabbers and hop pickers, bridge snakes and timber beasts, all saw in the IBWA the chance for shorter workdays, free transportation to and from jobs, and other favorable working conditions, those traditional labor demands sought for skilled workers by various labor organizations. The migratory workers, How knew, had been generally unrepresented in the labor movement, and he now sought to give them voice.

This was not a traditional labor union, however. Although How traveled the country preaching for workers' rights, the IBWA was primarily an educational movement, one which fought to establish social bonds and solidarity for the homeless. One hobo wrote in 1893, "Now I want you to distinctly understand me. I am not a Bum. I'd rather be kicked than go up to a House and ask for something to eat. I have went Hungry many a time almost starve before I would ask. I often wished I was more of a Bum when I was good and hungry."[8] This was the kind of man How hoped to aid—the man on the working fringes of society; the man whose self-esteem and pride were being unfairly maligned. The hobo, How believed, had been driven to the road by industrial conditions over which he had little control. Although part of an important economic class, the class that harvested the grain, picked the fruit, cut the timber, and built the railroads, the hobo was closed out of the social life of the country, despised for his migratory habits, snubbed by polite society, paid unfair wages, and maltreated by the police.[9]

The great key in this reform effort, in How's view, was in educating the road worker, in raising his intellectual sights and preparing him to confront the society that was crushing him underfoot. To achieve this end, How and the IBWA started the "hobo colleges," what he called "the migratory worker's university." Night after night, in several American cities, seasoned veterans of the tracks gathered in dilapidated, skid-road locations to hear lectures on everything from philosophy and industrial law to politics and health. "The laboring man has listened and clapped and cheered the sentiments of people he can not understand," How declared. "He has done all this too long. Now the time has come when he is going to learn about society, and all the rest of it for himself."[10]

How saw the colleges as oases, places where the road stiffs could share ideas, find a sense of belonging; where they could gain a sense of respect and self-esteem. Officers of the IBWA recruited as lecturers academics from local universities, physicians, psychologists, lawyers, social reformers, and radical orators. They encouraged the hobo soapboxers to participate, although few needed much encouragement. The men debated, heckled, argued, expounded, and sang; they talked about Aristotle and clap, the politics of the Hungarian Republic and methods of panhandling. Through it all, these hobo colleges made the harsh winters seem less severe.

How's hobo colleges would continue to grow in the decades after Ben Reitman walked into the St. Louis meeting in 1907. If some pundits and skeptics believed that discussions on economics and political theory were too esoteric for the knights of the rail, How nonetheless remained confident that the colleges had a significant impact. He argued that if a hobo knew industrial law, he would be better equipped to fight for his rights in the courts; if he knew philosophy, he would better understand himself. "You know," How mused, "people laugh at the idea of hoboes getting together to talk politics and labor problems. They think statesmen should have a monopoly in the discussion of these affairs." The hobo, he insisted, was doing fundamental work in society and must be accorded the same rights as other classes. "It is the business of society to recognize this fact. And, remember, a hobo is not ashamed to be a hobo. He is a worker who lives on the sweat of his face."[11] Many hoboes at the turn of the century were avid newspaper readers and held strong opinions on national affairs. From street-corner pulpits to hobo jungle fires, the drifters debated everything from free silver to the single tax to the Open Door (the Orient as well as the boxcar), and the hobo colleges served to ignite their interests and their passions. The men talked anarchism and socialism. Some championed Henry George; others, William Jennings Bryan and Eugene Debs. Most vented their ire at trusts and syndicates and the capitalist system.

Although How's own speeches were heavily tinctured with socialist thought, his colleges were less a political forum than a meeting place and cultural center, a rendezvous at which the hobo could feel some security and fellowship. "If he is penniless we sustain him," How declared. "He always repays the kindness when he finds work. We try to show him that he will play an important part in the coming change and that he must take an interest in the study of industry and social and economic conditions. Needless to say, the kind of education we want him to get is not the kind the Chamber of Commerce or the Bankers' Association are interested in."[12]

"If ever America produced a Christ figure," Ben Reitman once declared, "it was James Eads How. He had a decided Messianic complex, and he took the Scriptures seriously."[13] John Kelley, one of How's lieutenants, once said that the man was a complete puzzle, wholly dedicated to the welfare of the men in the IBWA. "I have been so mad at him at times that I called him all the names that I could think of. At one meeting of the hoboes, I saw the speaker throw the mallet at him, but How never lost his temper, and I have never known him to hold a grudge against anyone." Kelley recalled seeing How follow a bum for a block to apologize for offending him.[14]

Ben Reitman joined the IBWA on that night in 1907, paying the membership dues with a dime given to him by How. The "Millionaire Hobo," somehow dignified in his baggy clothes and shaggy beard, took Ben and several others to a cheap restaurant for coffee and talked about his dreams for the reform movement. Captivated by How's mission and purpose, Reitman immediately enlisted in the cause. Remembering countless nights on freights and in the jungles, Ben identified in a special way with these hoboes, with the forces that drove them to the road, with their plight in American society. This would be his cause, too.

"That visit to the Hobo College," Reitman wrote, "gave me visions and aspirations." As he boarded the train to Chicago, the ebullient hobo doctor was now a man with a purpose: James Eads How had asked him to open a Chicago branch of the International Brotherhood Welfare Association.[15]

3. The Banquet

"I saw new worlds to conquer," Ben Reitman wrote, "and in my mind I began to concoct schemes for meeting the hobo problem. I saw myself as the greatest of hobos, the hobo who would save all the rest of them from their homeless, womanless, jobless lives."[1] As Ben returned to Chicago from St. Louis and his encounter with James Eads How, he carried with him dreams of a new priesthood, a crusade to rescue thousands of drifters from exploitation and personal anguish. Although he had many ideas about vagrancy law reform and municipal programs for the homeless, Reitman wanted to do more than dabble in theories or squander energy in fruitless political debate. His crusade would not slough along in endless legal or political appeals. In his view the hobo war needed public notice, limelight, promotion. And what better gladiator of vision to deliver the goods than Ben Reitman.

After setting up a medical practice on State Street, in Chicago's Stewart Building, Ben eagerly approached merchants and other benefactors for help. He began to pass the word among the denizens of West Madison that the Chicago branch of the International Brotherhood Welfare Association, the Hobo College, was open for business. In the barrelhouses and nickel flops of the transient rooming-house district, along the Clark Street adult playground and the greasy spoons of the hobo corridor, it soon became known that Doc Reitman was good for a touch. Singly, in pairs, in groups, the bums and derelicts made their way to his door for handouts, cheap medical attention, clothing, help in finding jobs, and advice.

One of Ben's first customers was a strapping, mustached actor named G. Covington Symonds, temporarily unemployed, embarrassed, hungry but still eloquent. "I'm going to do you a great honor," G. Covington informed Ben. "There isn't a man in Chicago of whom I'd ask the same thing. Doctor Reitman, my good friend, I'm going to permit you to loan me $50." Ben handed him fifty cents. G. Covington bowed, snatched a cigar out of the good doctor's pocket, lit up, took a puff, accepted the coins graciously, and strode with erect bearing from the office.[2]

In the first few months of the Chicago IBWA, many of the hoboes took to riding the elevator to the top floor of the Stewart Building then descending from floor to floor to solicit financial assistance from all of the tenants. This practice quickly wore thin among the occupants of the building, especially the manager, who complained to Reitman that human vermin were infesting his building like cockroaches. It was obvious that the IBWA would not long retain its present quarters.

All of the storm within this one State Street office complex seemed ephemeral to Reitman, for a weighty plan was dominating his mind, an idea of which Phineas T. Barnum himself would have been proud, something that would bring grand notice and attention and thus launch the Hobo College into national view. The scheme: a lavish Hobo Banquet, hosted by Ben Reitman.

After securing funds from friends and associates and lining up a hotel restaurant, Ben called the press to announce the coming attraction. Kindling the interest not only of Chicago reporters but of others from around the country, Ben declared, "The purpose of the banquet is to learn just what these men need. We have no right to tell of the needs of men whose lives we do not know. We will let them tell their stories. They will tell us the truth and they will tell many new things. Sociologists can learn much from the statements of these fallen men."[3]

The date of the affair was May 20, 1907; the site, the Windsor-Clifton Hotel, Monroe Street and Wabash Avenue; the participants, over 100 panhandlers, dips, tramps, and other social outcasts, a few social workers, and Ben. A couple of recently released inmates from the House of Corrections and County Jail were invited, too, as well as some discharged patients from the County Hospital. Ben also toured the hobo districts on the west and south sides of the city. When he handed out invitations at Hinky Dink Kenna's saloon he was almost mobbed, the limited number of tickets considered a prize by hungry and thirsty vagabonds. The greatest excitement centered along Clark and Van Buren streets, the favorite haunts of such figures as Lazy Luke, Traveling Pete, Dirty Joe, and Peg Leg Wilson, all of whom received invitations.

Reitman scheduled ten speakers, including his old friend Ohio Skip, from the Lake Shore gang, who had given him numerous lessons on the road. Wishing to avert violence, Ben instructed the orators to exclude inflammatory rhetoric and provocative remarks about Chicago's police. Washington Flat, scheduled to preside as toastmaster, sent late word that he was unexpectedly on his way to St. Louis or other places west (Flat was on the lam from the police after an unspecified transgression).

On the night of the affair a vanguard of hoboes ambled through the hotel lobby to the restaurant, creating much commotion as crowds of onlookers chuckled and pointed. Although some of the honored guests wore high-collared shirts for the occasion, most came in their normally tattered condition. Reitman had gathered a notable human miscellany: John the Jocker, Gin Ricky Jack, Dick the Piker (weight with jewelry on, ninety-seven pounds; weight without, ninety), Coffin Nailer, Hot Tamale Kelly, Pierpont Morgan, Dirty Bill of Oklahoma, Black Slim, Fairy Tale Anderson, and One Tooth Scully. The menu for the evening, featuring a Manhattan cocktail, boiled fresh halibut, pommes Parisienne, prime rib of beef au jus, fromage de brie and wafers, cafe noir, and cigars, justified the *New York Times* headline announcing that hoboes were "Dining in State."[4]

The diners came from assorted backgrounds: prosperous businessmen who had fallen because of booze or other misfortunes; skilled mechanics who had lost both jobs and self-esteem; boys who had run away from home on tramping expeditions and settled into a roaming life; men with missing arms or legs who made a few cents each day on Chicago streets; former soldiers on the bum; grizzled tramp sailors up in years and down in usefulness. Most of the men, Reitman said, were penniless and hungry, wary of most charity organizations but enthusiastic about the apparent goals of the IBWA. Although many at the banquet were at first apprehensive, "when they saw that most of the men at the dinner were their comrades and friends," Ben wrote later, "their timidity disappeared . . . And as they drank the liquor and ate the sumptuous meal, they became cheerful and bright. They laughed, they talked, they sang, they made merry. They became their former selves."[5]

The regular program opened with a poem by Chicago Tommy, entitled "The Face on the Bar Room Floor," a long, grave saga of a hobo named Osler Joe, a drifter who had dropped dead in a saloon after drawing a picture in chalk of his angelic wife. Philadelphia Jack Brown then delivered his own composition:

> When an old bum dies, bury him deep,
> Put a link at his head, put a pin at his feet
> Put a solid draw bar across his breast
> For he's only an old timer, gone to his rest.[6]

Some of the guests were great names in the hobo world—Strawberry Shorty, Scranton Pa, Bum Mitt Casey, and Slim and Fat, the Traveling Twins, knights of the road all, quaffing beer in long glasses, sampling cocktails served by twelve waitresses who mingled with the crowd.

The guests listened to Gloomy George complain about the employment picture. "I can't get no work," he said gloomily. "They told me to wash windows but I ain't able to hang five stories above the sidewalk on the end of a rope."[7] Fritz Snyder spoke on the subject, "Why a Man in Rags Cannot Get a Job." "I have been used to doing clerical work," he declared. "When my clothes are all worn out, my collar is dirty, my hat is crushed, I know better to even go around the retail houses looking for work." Ben Reitman and the International Brotherhood Welfare Association had given him better clothes and new hope. Charles Chase spoke on "Fourteen Caret Misery." A one-armed peddler with lung trouble, Chase had been unable to find work and had been sleeping in barns, wagons, and boxcars. The charitable institutions of Chicago, he told the audience, did nothing but make men feel ashamed. "Whose fault is it that I am not working? I want to work!"[8]

The drinking, dining, and orating continued. Dancing Kid and Philadelphia Jack Brown left early to catch the blind baggage of the Chicago, Burlington, and Quincy to Frisco. Other incidents briefly interrupted the speech making. Fred the Bum, who was supposed to address the gathering on the subject, "Why I Hang Around Barrel Houses," had picked up too many drinks before he came to the banquet and was asleep under a table when his name was called. A–No. 1, a hobo whose monicker graced water tanks across the land, threatened to leave the event, claiming that some of the guests were not of the true genus hobo. As one of the less affluent speakers told of his miseries in the city, No. 1 charged that this was a bum at the rostrum, not a hobo. "I wouldn't associate with a snide that carries the banner," No. 1 smirked. Another of the renowned panhandlers in the audience created a minor stir when he began plying his mooching talents among fellow guests during lulls in the festivities.[9]

But the stories, varied in theme and tone from pathos to hilarity, kept most of the audience attentive. Pittsburgh Joe Burley, red-faced, a novice at soapbox oratory, told of his five years in city missions, soup lines, and gutters after an accident in a steel mill had left him crippled. "No one seemed to want me," Joe began haltingly. "I drifted out here and had poor clothes, and no one seemed to want me here, so I had to beg." But Ben Reitman and the IBWA had given him hope and a steady job. "I like to work more than to beg or to bum!"[10]

William Steers, a seventy-six-year-old carpenter, veteran of the tie and rail and countless city skid roads, told of his failure to find steady work in Chicago as a young man and his fatal decision to hit the road on a freight. "I attribute my failure," Steers said, "to the fact that I followed Horace Greeley's advice and came west." Now physically unable to undertake hard labor, he wandered along the West Madison slave auction looking for odd jobs. "I do not want to go to the poor house. What is left for an old man like me to do but to beg?"[11]

The men with the lined, weathered faces in the Windsor-Clifton that night had seen the inside of dank jails, felt the club of railroad dicks, had broken bones on track cinders, worked at hundreds of odd jobs for low pay, shared mulligan with fellow drifters, shivered in city doorways, battled vermin in two-bit flophouses, begged, conned, stole, fought, and sometimes barely survived. Eddie Barscho had served time for vagrancy in jails from Cheyenne to Albuquerque, Yuma to Omaha, a frequent victim of boodle-jail graft. Under state and local vagrancy laws, men with no visible means of support could be locked up for varying lengths of time, and many sheriffs eagerly rounded up men like Eddie. If a sheriff were allotted seventy-five cents a day for the care of a prisoner under his supervision, he might pocket fifty cents and spend only a quarter, a tidy profit.[12]

A hard-bitten man in his twenties, who called himself John Smith, had not only been in boodle jails but in prisons. He told his comrades in the Windsor-Clifton of his fourteen years in and out of correctional facilities. "Living in an unsanitary, dark, miserable cell, I walked up and down, I cried, then I laughed, and finally the bitterness of it all made these lines on my face. Now, I am working, and the hard lines are disappearing and the International Brotherhood Welfare Association did this for me!"[13]

The crowd traded good-natured barbs and insults, joked, swilled copious amounts of liquor, ate large amounts of food, taunted speakers, and occasionally fell into hushed, contemplative silence during heart-rending recitations. This was their night and they made the most of it.

This was also Ben Reitman's night, one which would, he hoped, establish him as hobo king and benefactor. The sociologists and psychiatrists and mission preachers didn't understand the men with wanderlust as he understood them; they hadn't tasted the life of the tracks as he had tasted it. Hobo reform was his calling—he knew that to be a fact—and this the majestic beginning.

Ben's own speech was entitled "Kindness and No Red Tape," a brief discussion of the goals of the IBWA. When a man asks for help, Ben said, he should not be humiliated, force-fed religion, or enlisted into the armed forces. In early April, disguised as a vagrant, Reitman had spent a night at the Municipal Lodging House at 10 Union Street. Questioned, stripped, examined, he choked on the sulphur fumigant sprayed on him. He later said he would rather walk the streets than spend another night in the city facility.[14] The IBWA would not treat men this way, Ben declared. Its aim was to encourage vagrants to work at productive occupations; to enlist tramps, beggars, and released convicts in helping young men reject the life of the road; to accept responsibility; to find faith in themselves. If the veteran drifters set out to help others, Ben said, they would also help themselves.[15]

The speech drew little notice from reporters covering the event. Reitman had created the hoopla and circus atmosphere to entice the press, hoping that, once he had their attention, his concern for the plight of the homeless would be understood and appreciated. But as the reporters mingled with the ragged men that night, they mostly saw the ludicrous trappings of the event. From barrelhouse bums to young boys just out of the House of Corrections, the crowd could have supplied the press with a hundred poignant tales. But the serious purpose in gathering these men together was lost in reports about shabby Weary Willies soiling Windsor-Clifton tablecloths and mutilating the English language. One story in the press the following day told of Pinochle Pete and Ben the Goose staggering away from the hotel at 1 A.M. and into the arms of a policeman on LaSalle Street. They invited him to join the merriment in a nearby groggery, but instead the officer invited them to the Harrison Street Police Station.[16]

Ben Reitman nonetheless considered the banquet a success. The *New York Times* ran a story on it, as did papers in other cities. Referring to Ben's "novel experiments in practical sociology," the *Times* declared that the hobo doctor from Chicago had attracted considerable attention.[17] The Women's Christian Temperance Union and some other reformers blasted Ben for serving liquor to hoboes, but others praised the banquet for the sociological lessons it graphically demonstrated, daring to show the contrast between the upper and lower crusts of society. In St. Petersburg, Florida, Ivan Stavoan, self-styled "King of the Beggars," was so inspired by Reitman's dinner that he hosted one of his own.[18]

As Doc knew so well from his many tramping odysseys, the hobo was seen by most of the American public as a figure of ridicule and comedy, of scorn and contempt. At a distance, the homeless wanderer and panhandler was a clown figure, his broken language and threadbare clothes a poor-soul stereotype. Up close he was a threat, his reputation for vandalism and violence unnerving, his rejection of American customs and mores an affront. The *Chicago Daily News,* in its coverage of the Reitman banquet, displayed the usual ambivalence toward the hobo figure, offering a typical narration of the comedic events of the banquet: inebriated soldiers of misfortune made kings for a night. But the *Daily News* editorialists were uneasy about Reitman's purpose in all of this. The spirit of the hobo oratory, they said, was chiefly a glorification of irresponsibility. "This community is well educated to a disbelief in indiscriminate charity."[19]

None of them seem to have heard the words of Charles Day, one of the speakers at the banquet and a college graduate who had been on the tramp for several years. Day was an embittered man. "Once I was in society. I got down and out and it doesn't make any difference whose fault it is. Society looks down on me, society finds fault with me, they pity me, they give me advice, they give me unkind words." He asked for a community that would help the homeless man find a place to sleep, a hungry man something to eat, and a jobless man employment.[20]

Ben Reitman was ready to take on this work, to accept Charles Day's challenge. The banquet had brought the hobo doctor notoriety. Some of the papers even began to call him "King of the Hoboes," an appellation he eagerly embraced. Let the crusade roll on!

4. King of the Hoboes

A tale of tramps and railroad ties,
  of old clay pipes and rum,
Of broken heads and blackened eyes,
  And "Thirty days" to come.[1]

Hamlin Garland, while operating his father's farm near Osage, Iowa, in the 1870s, hired large numbers of itinerant field hands—former soldiers, sons of poor farmers, mechanics from the East—all on the road to find fortune and adventure. Swarming into the Midwest in the harvest season, disappearing in September as mysteriously as they first appeared, the drifters seemed to the young Garland like "a flight of alien unclean birds." From these men Garland "acquired a desolating fund of information concerning South Clark Street in Chicago and the river front in St. Louis." The talk was not alluring, Garland said, but base and sordid. A few years later, however, he himself was on the road, taking odd jobs, sleeping in barns and abandoned buildings, hungry, shocked at the hostility and contempt of suspicious farmers. "To plod on and on into the dusk, rejected of comfortable folk, to couch at last with pole-cats in a shock of grain is a liberal education in sociology."[2]

Like Garland, Ben Reitman had achieved that liberal education, had been among those in the alien swarms. He knew well those drifters lurking in the railroad yards, pounding on back doors. He had seen ding-bats, old professional tramp beggars, putting on the touch; the elderly stew bums wasting themselves on rot booze; jack-rollers, sneaking around lumber and mining camps, angling for wallets on paydays; road yeggs, planning safe-blowing jobs and gang holdups; mushfakirs, their umbrella-mending kits strapped to their shoulders, looking for honest work; gandy dancers, hobo shovel stiffs, working the railroad construction sites. He had seen young, tenderfoot gay cats, new to the road and its perils; pathetic jungle buzzards, feeding off the leavings after hobo feasts; hoop-chislers, peddling their fake rings. With them he had mooched, flipped freights, boiled up clothes in the jungles, ridden the rods, carried the banner in no-name towns, chalked his moniker on water tanks, listened to the sky pilots in the missions drone their angel-food sermons, and done time in jerkwater jails. He had spent at least four months on the road each year, flopping in municipal lodging houses in almost every state, hanging around tramp saloons for weeks at a time, roaming with tramp gangs. He had been arrested over forty times in the United States for vagrancy as well as several times in foreign countries. He had been to sea as a stowaway. "There is," he wrote, "scarcely any phase of vagrancy in which I had not had a practical experience."[3]

Ben's experience had taught him a deep and bitter lesson: the tramp in American society was despised, feared, mistrusted, abused. Well before the day he had first slid onto an open boxcar in Chicago, the spectre of a tramp menace had inflamed public debate all across the United States. Newspapers emblazoned story after story about train robberies and hijackings; of marauding gangs of rioting young punks setting fire to trains and waging pitched battles with police; of hordes of Hun-like invaders infesting small towns and terrifying the citizens; of safe-blowers and murderers. It made little difference that many of the wandering men of the road were hobo workers moving from job to job, filling the labor needs of mine owners, railroad magnates, and farmers. To most of American society the road wanderers were a single mass of men, both deviant and dangerous. Editorialists, law enforcement officials, railroad spokesmen, government leaders, all called for a campaign against the tramp peril. One writer in 1886 declared that the tramp had no more rights than "the sow that wallows in the gutter, or the lost dog that hovers around the city squares. He is no more to be consulted, in his wishes or his will . . . than if he were a bullock in a corral."[4]

Concerned citizens zealously combed English precedents for dealing with the army of homeless men wandering the country. They discovered that the tramp laws enacted some 300 years earlier in England provided that a beggar could be driven back to his birthplace for the first offense, deprived of the gristle of his right ear for the second, and executed for the third. Some zealots saw a more modest solution in Washington Irving's 1809 burlesque, *The History of New York.* Governor William the Testy, according to Irving, had solved the vagrant problem with a gibbet, from which he dangled the offenders: "It is incredible how the little governor chuckled at beholding caitiff vagrants and sturdy beggars thus swinging by the crupper, and cutting antic gambols in the air. He had a thousand pleasantries and mirthful conceits to utter upon these occasions. He called them his dandelions—his wildfowl—his high-flyers—his spread-eagles—his goshawks—his scarecrows—and finally, his gallows-birds."[5]

Just as William the Testy found sport in tormenting captured wayfarers, entire communities sometimes enjoyed similar revelry in the late 1800s. In one Iowa community the townspeople stoned and whipped tramps and beggars as they ran a gauntlet. In Elizabeth, New Jersey, town officials created a "tramp-trap," an inviting, open boxcar placed on a switch of the Pennsylvania Railroad. At about ten o'clock each night the trap was usually filled with at least a few of the prey, lured like rats to cheese. Another New Jersey constable went a few steps further in later years. He chained tramps to trees in the center of the village, where they became feasts for swarms of mosquitoes from nearby lowlands.[6]

Mostly the states relied on new vagrancy laws. Ben Reitman wrote, "No one can tramp about the country without feeling the effect of the vagrancy law. If a boy keeps going, he will be arrested for vagrancy on an average of once every six weeks; and it is during one of these stays in jail that he makes up his mind to go home or become a criminal. It is much easier to do the latter . . . the vagrancy law makes many tramps criminals."[7] The Pennsylvania vagrancy law, enacted in 1876, defined tramps and vagrants as persons who loiter with "no labor, trade, occupation, or business, and have no visible means of subsistence, and can give no reasonable account of themselves. . . ." Such an offense called for hard labor for no less than thirty days nor more than six months. In Ohio a tramp could be imprisoned for three years for kindling a fire on a highway or railroad track.[8]

Ill defined, with a hurried, hysterical quality, the vagrancy laws gave city officials broad license. Besides herding men in and out of jail, judges began to exercise the option of deportation. A typical sentence meted out to a penniless drifter was an injunction to leave town immediately. Judicial purists might have questioned the legality of such sentences, yet thousands of homeless men were shuffled back and forth in streams, from town to town, by courts and law enforcement officials anxious to pass the problem on to some other location.

With recurring depressions and economic hard times in the late 1800s, the tramp problem did not abate. The *Railroad Gazette* declared in 1894, "Like potato bugs and English sparrows it is an evil which has arisen quickly, but which can be exterminated only at prodigious pains." Only through rigid enforcement of the vagrancy laws, the *Gazette* concluded, could the plague be eradicated.[9] Those in that plague, those "potato bugs and English sparrows," were finding the road a harrowing place, as Ben Reitman knew well. Hoboes and tramps suffered a grisly slaughter on the tracks: jolted from insecurely fastened hopper cars; mangled by sliding boxcar doors; crushed by shifting loads on gondolas; suffocated or frozen in reefers when trapdoors locked shut; rolled off decks of passenger cars; pitched from rods and gunnels to the track bed and the grinding wheels; robbed, beaten, and killed by fellow drifters and train dicks.

At a national conference of charities and corrections held in Minneapolis in 1907, several sociologists, charity workers, and railroad officials who were examining the national tramp problem lamented the violence that infested railroad operations and the frightening increase in the number of tramps robbing stations and shipments, building fires in boxcars, interfering with signals, stoning railroad equipment, and sometimes inflicting injury or death on railroad employees. But they also provided the grim statistics of the fate of many of the train-jumpers: between 1901 and 1905 the toll of maimed and killed vagrants discovered along cinder beds across the country was a national disgrace, with over 23,000 trespassers losing their lives, more individuals than populated Bangor, Maine. Some of the railroad companies maintained private tramp graveyards where anonymous drifters were quickly laid to rest without an inquest. James J. Hill of the Great Northern wrote, "Tramps attempt to secret themselves on every train at any risk. A considerable number of these are killed or injured each year. They get on or off trains while in motion, and some suffer in life or limb. Others fall off trains while asleep. It would be difficult to gather reliable statistics on this point, because a large percentage of the tramps reported as killed on the railroads are really murdered. Men returning from the harvest fields with their wages are killed for their money by their more vicious and criminal fellows."[10]

As Ben Reitman launched his hobo crusade, the nation's sympathies were not with the thousands of stiffs trudging along the roadbeds. The *Philadelphia Press* in 1907 called the marauding tramp population "The Shadow on the Roadside," picturing innocent women on country roads fleeing from aggressive railroad bums, ominous hordes of miscreant vagrants invading the sanctity of rural America. The *New York Times* in the same year referred to Chicago as a "drainage basin" of vagrant and criminal types and called for vigorous prosecution of the dangerous predators. Jail the ne're-do-wells, spread the word that the sin city of the Midwest would no longer tolerate undesirable, decadent tramps, those "terrors of burglary, sneak-thievery, highway robbery, and pocket-picking." In Chicago itself, an editorialist for the *Herald* wrote, "There are several great American jokes but none is more reliable than Weary Willie. It seems however that he is not all joke." Through his treachery and violence, the *Herald* continued, the "funny hobo thus elevates himself to the loftier position of robber and murderer."[11]

As the swelling call for retribution dominated debate on the tramp problem, Chicago's own hobo doctor appealed for understanding and constructive reform. A few days after the Windsor-Clifton banquet, Reitman decided to sponsor another public affair, a "sociological clinic," where knights of the tie and rail could tell their own stories. "I want to show the people of Chicago what these men are like," he told a reporter on May 26. "I believe it would be a good thing if the people found out that these are real men. . . ." Bum Mitt Casey would be there, he promised, along with Rocky Mountain Lemon, the Banjo-Eyed Kid, and Olaf the Unwashed, who had cleaned himself up recently and was in the process of changing his monicker as well as his clothes.[12] Ben stressed that the typical road wayfarer was not the Happy Hooligan caricature of the cartoon strip or the criminal portrayed in the press. Tramps and hoboes did not carry their valuables in tomato cans as pictured in the comics and on stage. Most were not simple-minded boobs, as much of the American public believed; nor were they the vicious desperados imagined by many others.

On May 31, at Handel Hall, twenty-five gentlemen of the road told of their escapades and travails to a group of reporters, social workers, and fellow vagabonds. A hobo from Cincinnati opened the program with a piano solo, which he characterized as a combination of Beethoven's melody in F major and "There'll Be a Hot Time in the Old Town Tonight." Those who heard it characterized it in less flattering terms. Another gent wailed the old hobo standard, "Where Is My Wandering Boy Tonight?" Ben then paraded onto the stage several homeless men who represented various backgrounds—doctor, lawyer, pharmacist, criminal, soldier, and sailor. All of the participants were asked to explain how wanderlust had affected their lives. The *Tribune* reported that "a good deal of stage effect was lost through not turning the lights low to slow music."

The tramps were allotted only five minutes to speak, and some loquacious types had to be restrained from rambling on. When they were done, Ben mounted the stage to give his own address, not limited, of course, to five minutes. Steaming into a heady tirade, he attacked the practices of such charitable institutions as the social settlement houses and the YMCA. To the charity workers in the audience, host Reitman was anything but charitable. "You people," he charged, "would be all right if you would have a lot more kindness and not try to separate the sheep from the goats. The first thing you ask is 'Are you worthy?' You ought to ask, 'Are you hungry?'"

Charity officials, Ben argued, were baffled by the enigmatic vagrom men and their puzzling migratory habits. "They come from the somewhere and vanish into the nowhere," a favorite saying among social workers, was a charming but unsatisfactory explanation of the tramp life, he scolded. Tramps come from the division stations and terminal points of the railroad lines, the favorite haunts of young boys just learning to flip freights. The boy who successfully decks a rattler for a five- or ten-mile excursion could very easily succumb to the bewitching train-jumping habit and find himself taking hundred- or thousand-mile journeys.

Reitman told the audience that many of the young boys who stayed on the road and suffered its privations became hardened track ruffians. The only answer to the tramp problem was to police adequately the railroad yards, and toward this end he proposed that the government impose fines on those railroads that allowed trespassing. Blind baggage and deck-riding tourists must be forced off the freights for the good of the country and for the good of the train-jumpers themselves, Ben said. He didn't elaborate on how such a law could be enforced. But as long as homeless men needed shelter and food, as long as the road exacted its toll of human misery, there must be individuals and institutions willing to lend a hand, preferably one not holding red tape. "Everyone wants to give the tramp a bath," Ben bristled. "Now, who wants a bath? The hobo simply asks for food, a place to sleep, and sometimes a job."[13]

Four days after the tramp symposium, the *Chicago Daily News* ran an editorial supporting Reitman's call for increased supervision of the railroads. "Superintendents," the paper charged, "have it in their power to check the spread of the tramp evil, of which their lines are the chief agencies." Although the editorial characterized the May 31 meeting at Handel Hall as "bizarre," Ben had at last evoked serious newspaper response on the tramp question.[14]

Less than two weeks later, however, Reitman's controversial social experiment was temporarily squelched. On June 15 the *Tribune* announced that a deep gloom had descended on suite 610 of the Stewart Building, the Chicago home of the International Brotherhood Welfare Association, haven for bums, yeggmen, and cadgers of all stripes. Doc Reitman, president of the organization, had been evicted. If sorrow and melancholy clouded the spirits of those in 610, the other tenants appeared collectively relieved. For them, the past few weeks had been harrowing indeed.

Miss Jessie Verneta, owner of a beauty shop next to the infamous doctor's office, revealed that a tramp had recently invaded her salon, brandishing a cane and harassing her customers until they purchased some collar buttons. "The man frightened me very much," attested Miss Verneta. "There were only girls in the parlors. I tried to pass him to get to the door, but he barred the way with his cane and insisted that we assist him by buying some collar buttons. He frightened us so that we bought." Similar chilling tales came from other parts of the building. One woman reported that as she waited in a doctor's reception room on another floor, a hobo walked in and proclaimed, "'Scuse me, lady, but I'd like a little financial assistance." The lady was, the *Tribune* noted, suffering from a case of nerves.

"I believe Dr. Reitman is sincere," one of the physicians in the

Stewart Building admitted, "but we could not stand for the tramps." They would invade the premises at all hours of the night, subjecting the tenants to all sorts of indignities and inconveniences. Reitman would always give the beggars something, whether they were drunk or not, the physician said. "He must have given away from $6 to $8 a day in dimes and quarters to bums. He would never question them, but put his hand in his pocket."

Unshaven, his crumpled clothes and tossled black hair giving him a gypsy-like appearance, Reitman met the press outside his former office. "I feel like a bum myself," Ben said. "Where I'll go I don't know . . . This was purely a charitable enterprise."[15]

With his base of operations lost but his reputation as a hobo benefactor established, with the spring weather and open boxcars calling him, Ben decided to head out on another tramping expedition. But this trek would be unlike his usual frivolous outings, he decided. This one would have a grand purpose: a fact-finding tour for the IBWA; a careful, firsthand investigation of the present conditions in American trampdom. It would provide him with potent ammunition, he thought, for his continuing campaign for the downtrodden.

El Paso, Albuquerque, Detroit, Philadelphia. Reitman freighted across the country as "King of the Hoboes" and the "Master Bum," speaking before groups of fellow road knights, reformers, and invited members of the fourth estate. He told how he had given up a potentially lucrative medical practice to devote time to his charitable crusade; how the charity agencies had failed to deal effectively with the needs of the homeless; how the International Brotherhood Welfare Association was inaugurating a remarkable experiment in social reform.

In Philadelphia Ben met with the mayor on the same afternoon that a trained baboon and his keeper also appeared at city hall. In Toledo he met with the nationally respected reform mayor, Brand Whitlock, and spoke at Golden Rule Hall on the plight of the American tramp. In New York he met the sociologist Orlando Lewis of the Charity Society, a leading authority on the subject of the tramp. Lewis was convinced, along with most other reformers and students of the wayfaring society, that homeless men were products of their own moral inadequacies, not of outside economic influences. All jobless men could find employment if they really wanted it. To Lewis and others unemployment was a problem of motivation, not of the currents of the country's economic waters.[16]

In an article in *Atlantic Monthly* the following spring, Lewis, recounting Reitman's side of the argument, quoted "a thinking tramp . . . a man who indeed has frequently 'hit the road' as a hobo." Vagrancy, Ben told the sociologist, "is not a national problem in the sense in which you describe it to be; it is a railroad problem." Penalize the railroad companies for allowing trespassing and the companies would solve the vagrancy problem. As for the drifters themselves, pay them for the work they perform in jail so that they would not be forced to return to petty thievery and train-hopping upon release. Reitman argued that more than 50 percent of the men riding freights and idling in skid roads would take jobs if they could get them.[17]

While in New York, Ben also met Edmund Kelly, an influential lawyer and humanitarian who was writing a book called *The Elimination of the Tramp.* Kelly, who was quite ill, spent most of one night with Ben on the Bowery, in Union Square, and down at the Battery mingling with the hoboes. At four o'clock in the morning Kelly approached about fifty men in the Square and invited them to feed at an all-night restaurant. After the long night had ended, Kelly told Reitman that he didn't want to die in bed, that he was beginning to see ways in which the world could be changed for the better, and that he wanted to be part of a new revolution that could make people such as those on the Bowery conscious of their own worth and possibilities. "Yes," he told Ben, "start a revolution."[18]

Reitman left Lewis and Kelly in New York and headed back to Chicago in the fall, having gained a new perspective on the American tramp. In 1907, when he had met James Eads How in St. Louis, Ben had been inspired by the idea of a reform movement but was basically ignorant of the history and politics of the tramp question. Through bluff and blunder and brashness, through a dogged effort to fill newspaper columns with his schemes and notions, driven by a waxing confidence that he could become the leading figure in America on the subject, he had achieved the notoriety that he insatiably craved. But he had now become more than the tawdry grandstander, the coxcomb. Filling page after page with notes and statistics, interviewing sociologists and government officials, debating charity workers, Reitman had gained extensive information which he began to sift and analyze. Ben Reitman the reform dandy was now Ben Reitman the researcher.

In a paper entitled "The American Tramp," Ben revealed that the typical road drifter was not a middle-aged alcoholic fleeing marital or economic distress, nor was he a hardened criminal escaping from the law, as most Americans suspected. The typical tramp, Reitman claimed, was a young boy. His conclusions about the road in 1907 were similar to the findings of such researchers as Thomas Minehan and Edwin Sutherland nearly thirty years later, during the Great Depression. The horrifying portrait sketched by them of packs of wild youth, forced to the road by poverty and neglect, was a testament, most sociologists agreed, to the volcanic scoria of economic collapse. In 1907 Reitman found much of the same social desolation. Those hordes of wastrels stealthily slinking around freight cars, terrorizing society's good citizens, were America's youth.

After interviewing railroad detectives and railroad employees, pouring over police records in more than 100 towns, talking to mission directors and sociological investigators, and tallying his own informal observations from railroad yards and jungles, Reitman concluded that approximately 75 percent of the road wanderers were under twenty-one years of age, some as young as eight. One example from his own experience was typical. Among eighteen tramps with whom he shared a boxcar near Washington, D.C., not one was over twenty-one. "My estimate that 75 percent of the tramps in America are boys I have shown to many railroad policemen, railroad brakemen, conductors and station agents (these men see more real tramps than any other class of men in the world) and they stated that this figure was *too low.*"

In assessing the causes of the large numbers of drifters on the road, Ben looked to his own past as well as to the country's economic and social conditions. Young boys succumb, as he did, to the alluring enticements of places never seen. They begin to flip freights and to make friends with veteran tramps and jockers, who entrance them with stories of wild deeds and swashbuckling adventure. Driven by wanderlust, given opportunity of movement by easy access to the freights, taught the lessons of the road by those who know its ways, hardened by stints in jail, these young boys age quickly, their lives becoming a habitual succession of hazardous, insensate ventures, odd jobs, and petty crimes. "They go to jail, penniless and ragged," Ben wrote, "penniless and ragged they depart. Finally in self-defense they prey upon society."[19] Those on the road were victims more than villains, he believed, prodded by their own restlessness, plagued by poverty, and exploited by a legal system that exacerbated their plight. The only difference between a drifter and a man with a regular job was "a change in the social geography; not a change in his heart, in his mind, or in his attitude toward the world."[20]

But even as Chicago's hobo doctor gained greater insight and understanding of the tramp question, his proposals remained the same as they had been before: force the railroads to take better measures to prevent train trespassing; and amend the vagrancy laws to allow the segregation (in jail) of young drifters from seasoned criminals and to provide money to them upon release. Only in this way might the vicious cycle that created the tramp class be broken.

Reitman began to prepare articles and papers on the road life and in doing so developed classifications of tramp and hobo types based on the men he had known on the freights. The division was essentially of three classes: the tramp, the hobo, and the bum. "A tramp is a man who doesn't work, who apparently doesn't want to work, who lives without working and who is constantly travelling. A hobo is a non-skilled, non-employed laborer without money, looking for work. A bum is a man who hangs around a low-class saloon, and begs or earns a few pennies a day in order to obtain drink. He is usually an inebriate."[21] Ben's classification was a more elaborate version of a simple definition shared by many men on the road. The hobo, the saying went, was a migratory worker, the tramp a migratory nonworker, and the bum a nonmigratory nonworker.

In a conversation with Ben, General Jacob Coxey claimed, "The trouble with these movements of the unemployed is that people fail to recognize that there are men honestly seeking employment. They think they are a lot of ruffians and property destroyers. They call all out of work, hobos." "A lot you know about hobos," Reitman gently shot back. "When you led your army of three thousand to the lawns of Washington to pay your respects to President Cleveland, you were at the head of a mob of unemployed hobos. A hobo is a man tramping around looking for work." "That's not the way I've heard the term used," Coxey responded, "and I have been hearing the word for forty years. A hobo is a good-for-nothing fellow who would rather beg or steal, or even starve than work. I never led hobos to Washington." Ben told Coxey that the parasites described by the general were tramps, not hoboes, and he continued to insist to reporters, sociologists, and anyone else who would listen that the men of the road were not a single, invidious mass but were of different types and motivations. He even wrote a paper on the subject, "A Plea for a Proper Classification of the Itinerant Vagrant."[22]

After his summer of tramping, interviewing, and public speaking, Reitman began to sketch specific plans for the organization of Chicago's Hobo College, whose infancy in the Stewart Building had been so ignominiously cut short in June. The Chicago chapter of the IBWA would be much more than a succession of vagrants making their unsteady way to suite 610 to panhandle dimes and quarters from a sympathetic hobo doctor.

Ben once described to a wealthy Chicagoan the kind of charitable institution for social outcasts he would establish if he had the capital.

In the basement I'd have a first-class bathroom and laundry; I'd equip the place with modern laundry machinery where a man could come in raggedy, lousy and dirty and by the time he took a bath and manicured his toes, got a shave and a haircut, his clothes would not only have been laundered but they would have gone through the mending department and have been mended, patched and had buttons sewed on. His shoes would have gone to the shoe shop, have been soled and repaired and shined so that when he came upstairs to the desk to register he would be looking like a real human being. Then we'd have a clearinghouse upstairs. After he had had a good breakfast with the proper amount of calories and vitamins I would have him pass through the hands of a doctor who would examine him carefully, detect any infection or physical ailment, and, if necessary, send him to a hospital or to a clinic for treatment. Then I'd have a psychiatrist examine him, see what his mental capacity and fitness for work was. If necessary we would treat him. Then we'd pass him on to the employment department to find out what his vocation was and try to get him a job. Then I'd give him a guest card for one week and provide for all of his needs until he got a job. If, at the end of the week, he was unable to find a job, I would send him to our banking department and loan him money enough to take care of him until he found work. While under our supervision it would not be necessary for the man to beg or to steal; he would not be a menace or a danger to the community. I'd make special provision to receive men the minute they got out of jail. I would father and help and guide them until they adjusted themselves.[23]

If this was only a wistful vision of a tramp Shangri-La, Ben's plans for the Hobo College were not.

The object of the college, he wrote, would be "to teach the vagrant the truth about himself, what his duty is to society . . . to teach him that labor is man's lot and that education will restore him to habits of industry and contentment." In his early plans, Reitman conceived of the college as a structured institution, one which would offer room and board, a fixed two-week term, and a series of lectures all designed to encourage young boys of the road to leave the lairs of the homeless and the slum Rialtos and to achieve respectability. He planned an intense assault on the tramp life-style, a detoxification of fledgling drifters from the road life. His aim was to recruit physicians to describe the deleterious effects of a tramping existence; psychologists, to talk about the roots of wanderlust and dromomania; judges, to explain the vagrancy laws and the liability of railroad bums to arrest and incarceration; and business representatives, to talk about job opportunities. Reitman even thought of presenting a physiologist to demonstrate the comparative amounts of energy expended by an individual holding a regular job and by one who was "idle." On the main stem, Ben knew, there was no real idleness or leisure.

"There'll be work for all," Reitman said of the college, "but first we'll ask: 'Have you had your dinner?' Having it, how easy comes the work when we can say, 'I wish you'd do a little over here; these windows need a washing; this floor has not been scrubbed for several days.'" The Hobo College would be "The Whole Meal Hull House for Hoboes," a place of respect and fraternity, an oasis for all those infected, like Reitman himself, with the mania for roaming. "No ghost will be hovering to the background of the place. No sermons will be on the program. No woodyard will be just around the corner . . . and once a week we'll send one boy back home to mother; we'll settle ten hoboes a week to steady work who the day before had no work and settled place of existence farthest from their soberest thoughts; and, greater than these, we'll give to 10 per cent—15—perhaps 20 per cent of Chicago's 500 incoming wanderers daily a new, refreshing touch and reminder that they are still human in a world that has not lost all humanity."[24]

In early December 1907 Ben again traveled to New York to spread the gospel of hobo reform. He checked into the Occidental Hotel in the Bowery and notified the *New York Times* of his continuing research on the lives of drifters. He carefully explained to a *Times* reporter the difference between the city bum, the tramp, and the hobo. His mission in New York, Ben said, was to expose the evils of society's treatment of these men—from the hopeless street derelict of the Bowery to the hard-muscled hobo who worked the wheat fields of the Dakotas, the orange groves of California, and the fruit farms of Michigan.

Ben also prepared to host another dinner for homeless men, much in the manner of earlier dinners in Chicago. He invited "the cream of the world of itinerant vagrants," notables of the road he had befriended over the years: Flat-Head Horatio of Comanche, Texas; Pittsburgh Spider Leg; Pessimistic Bernheimer, dean of the Madison Square park benchers; and Blue-Eyed Perce, rod-riding paladin of the East. "It would be wrong," the *Times* observed, "to get the idea that 'Doc' Reitman resembles in any way the vaudeville Happy Hooligan. He is a broad-shouldered, black-eyed, black-haired man . . . he wears his hair just a little long and it curls. He affects a loose tie of the artist's style. His face is big and open. A fine Roman nose helps his picture. He seems to have taken a bath within his memory. His vocabulary is quite ample."[25]

On December 4, Reitman stood before a crowded Bowery mission audience, trading hobo truths and insights with his motley comrades. One of the great underlying causes of the vagrancy problem, he declared, "is the fact that the men who are on the road lie to those who are not. When I was a boy I ran away. When I got back, I would lie to the other boys, telling them what a good time I had had. Well, I hadn't had any good time and you men know that you don't have any good time on the road. Am I right?" A chorus of voices resounded, "You're right." He went on to assail the conditions of the municipal lodging houses, railed at the country's system of labor which worked individuals twelve and fourteen hours a day and kept other thousands unemployed, and attacked the inefficiencies and motives of the charity societies, the insipid soup and sermon emporiums which robbed the drifters of their dignity. The *Times* reporter who covered the event was impressed more by the fancy sartorial appearance of the speaker than he was by his message, referring to Reitman as the "Millionaire Hobo." Ben's reputation, at least to this one reporter, had preceded him to New York; but the writer obviously had confused him with James Eads How.[26]

Ben persevered in his mission. Ten days later he hosted another meeting, this one specifically for young boy tramps. More than 500 teenage runaways filled the Bowery mission house. "The youth and flower of New York trampdom convened," the *Times* announced. "Practically all the boys were homeless, but none the less they presented a surprisingly clean appearance. A few linen collars glistened among the sweaters, and many of the boys seemed capable of better things." In his speech Ben sought to convince them of that very fact. "You're all young boys," he lectured, "and I want to tell you that you're on the wrong track. There is no part of the country where you can live idly and without doing something for the community . . . You know how many of you are happy? What's the use of going around like you are. Panhandling plays itself out. You can't be a tramp and stay out of the jug for longer than six weeks . . . We're going to do our best for you boys. But you must help us. Go back to your homes. Keep away from the Bowery."

Chicago's celebrated hobo doctor talked of his own life on the road, of his arrests and humiliations, of the pitiful sights of the wasted men he had met. When he concluded his talk, a sickly-looking kid named Jackson rose with tears lining his face and in a trembling, halting voice said, "I thought it would be fun to tramp, but it ain't." Later that night Jackson left the Bowery and its brokenness and headed back to his home in New England.[27]

Once again Ben Reitman returned to the Windy City. He negotiated for a storefront hall in a building on Harrison Street, to house the Chicago Hobo College, and continued to make headlines. On New Year's Day, 1908, he hosted an exclusive dinner for boy tramps—no hoboes, bums, or town boys allowed, only road kids like Omaha Red and Boston Slim were given sanctuary that night at 180 Washington Street. Along with food and music the boys were treated to the usual remarks on the ignominy of the road life. Ben now saw himself as a champion of misguided youth on the run.

Shortly after the feed for young tramps, Reitman received an angry, sorrowful letter, one that charged the hobo crusader with indirect complicity in the death of a young boy. Mrs. F. J. McBain-Evans told Ben that the publicity of his hobo meetings and the tales of his road exploits had impelled her son William to take to the freights, only to meet a tragic end. In the flaming wreckage of a boxcar near Niles, Michigan, the boy and a friend were burned beyond recognition. Mrs. McBain-Evans wrote that her son had wanted to taste some of the adventures and face some of the risks heralded in the stories about the legendary Ben Reitman. "That is what these stories have cost me. I will spend my life trying to off-set the mischief they have done to other boys. I am going to get in touch with boys all over the country. I may not be able to accomplish much but if I can save one mother from the agony that I have suffered through the loss of my boy I shall feel my work has not been in vain." The grim irony was not lost on Ben. Even as he had been traveling the country encouraging teenagers on the road to give up their hot-spur foolishness, William McBain had taken that message not as counsel but as a fateful challenge.[28]

Burdened by the letter but still confident that he was making a significant, positive contribution, Reitman continued to provide the Chicago press, local charity officials, and sociologists with eccentric but stimulating grist for the debate on vagrancy. In one venture he shed his cape, Windsor tie, and walking stick, disguised himself as a grimy down-and-out, and, accompanied by a well-known Chicago panhandler, made the rounds of local missions, churches, and saloons asking for handouts. For several days the investigative duo tramped through Chicago's underclass areas mooching food and money. They visited over 100 downtown saloons and came away with only three nickels. Twenty-two well-known gamblers in some of the vice dens donated seven dimes, one quarter, and twenty-two nickels. The churches and missions were a bit more generous, at least in providing food, if not hard cash. Reitman also knocked on the doors of several hundred doctors to test the generosity of those of his own profession. His conclusion: the parsimony of Chicago's medical profession equalled that of gamblers and saloonkeepers. The entire expedition netted only $4.21.

Ben also went in disguise to Chicago's Municipal Lodging House. "The men sleep on steel cots," he reported, "with no mattress and with only one blanket to wrap up in. These blankets are used night after night, are passed from one man to another without being washed. They are as foul-smelling and vermin-infested as the building itself." The International Brotherhood Welfare Association, he vowed, would fight to clean the place up.[29]

Since his meeting with James Eads How months before, Ben had achieved a curious prominence. His travels around the country had created sparkling copy for the newspapers, ignited the wrath of some charity workers who felt unjustly maligned, stimulated debate among sociologists and other researchers over some of his findings, and attracted a wary eye from police officials who saw his infant campaign as a possible source of trouble. He had also gained genuine respect among those in the underclasses, for unlike many of the sky pilots of the missions, the street-corner bell ringers in the Salvation Army, and the charity innkeepers, Chicago's hobo doctor had firsthand knowledge of the road life and a sincere feeling for the plight of those who tackled it. As he looked around at the huddled men on West Madison Street and North Clark, as he consorted with the tomato-can vags as well as the profesh of the rails, he became more convinced than ever that his work could make a difference.

Nineteenth-century gentlemen of the road. *Top:* Providence Bob and Philadelphia Shorty riding the rails, 1894; *bottom:* a hobo jungle, 1895.
(Courtesy Butler-McCook Homestead Collection, The Antiquarian and Landmarks Society, Inc., of Hartford, Conn.)

Hard days in the cities. *Top:* Chopping wood in exchange for breakfast at the Wayfarer's Lodge, Boston, January 1895; *bottom:* washing up at the Lodge. (Courtesy Butler-McCook Homestead Collection, The Antiquarian and Landmarks Society, Inc., of Hartford, Conn.)

Jungling in Downer's Grove, Illinois.
(Courtesy Chicago Historical Society)

Roving Bill Aspinwall, a mushfakir (umbrella mender), 1890s.
(Courtesy Butler-McCook Homestead Collection, The Antiquarian and Landmarks Society, Inc., of Hartford, Conn.)

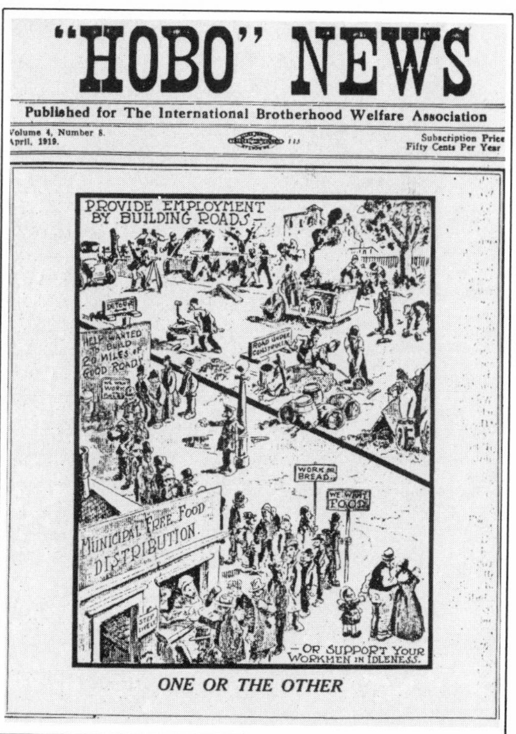

"HOBO" NEWS

Published for The International Brotherhood Welfare Association

Volume 4, Number 8.
April, 1919.

Subscription Price
Fifty Cents Per Year

ONE OR THE OTHER

James Eads How, the "Millionaire Hobo," founder of the International Brotherhood Welfare Association, publisher of *The Hobo News,* and mentor of Ben Reitman.

(How photograph in *Collier's,* vol. 77, June 26, 1926; *Hobo News* cover in the National Archives)

Ben Reitman, ca. 1912.
(Courtesy International Institute of Social History)

5. To the Streets

Rocked by the fall of the stock market in March 1907, shaken further in October by a run on the Knickerbocker Trust Company of New York, many banks failed as another "financial panic" hit the country. Once again economists, government officials, and businessmen fine-tuned the distinctions between "depression" and "panic," debated inflationary and deflationary policies, pointed to the ramifications of investment downturn and shifts in international flows of credit, and pored over the stream of facts and figures about labor productivity, per capita products, long-term accelerated growth patterns, and self-regulating markets. To the jobless, of course, it was so much blather. They needed help and were not getting it. Neither municipal governments nor private charity organizations could cope with the large numbers of desperate men wandering aimlessly from city to city in search of jobs.

Some business giants did assume some civic responsibility in the new year. John D. Rockefeller, noting the large number of unemployed Americans around his estate in Tarrytown, New York, fired all of the Italians then toiling in his Pocantico Hills mansion and replaced them with local unemployed laborers. The *New York Times* told of resounding praise from all quarters for Mr. Rockefeller's resourcefulness, his actions being especially timely because of the heavy snowstorm which threatened the well-being of his jobless neighbors. Some of the Italians, the *Times* reported, "may go back to Italy." That same issue of the paper told of a man who wasn't as lucky as Rockefeller's neighbors. Francis Joseph Smith, a tramp who won fame by slipping into the house of John Jacob Astor and falling asleep on a downy bed, was found dead in the snow in front of the Columbia Lodging House.[1]

In Chicago, the papers filled their columns with stories of distress fund drives by local tycoons, the problems of the city's bureau of charities and relief aid societies, statistics on the "real" unemployed as opposed to the chronic loafers and moochers, and bankruptcy actions, which even felled a well-respected home for the aged. The *Tribune* established its own relief fund and opened a lodging house at 59 Canal Street which served as an emergency annex to the Municipal Lodging House. Frank Solon, assistant superintendent of streets, advised the commissioner of public works, John Hanberg, that the homeless men receiving assistance at the lodging house demonstrated surprising gratitude. "Unfortunately," he wrote, "many people are of the opinion that those men are tramps who will not work, but such is not the case, as the majority showed their willingness to work in the streets as remuneration for the help given them."[2] To the shivering homeless of Chicago's streets, Malcolm McDowell's coffee wagon was perhaps the most visible sign of private philanthropy. Each night McDowell rolled his wagon along the West Madison Street hobo district as hundreds of men, many without overcoats, lined up in the biting winds for free coffee and rolls. One derelict waiting in line on New Year's night said, "That cart there is the finest church, the best church I ever saw. That's the true religion."[3]

Assorted socialist and other left-wing and radical movements pressed their causes vigorously in this period of social discontent and dislocation. To a political neophyte such as Ben Reitman, this mélange of industrial unionists, Socialist party centrists, Fabians, anarchists, and communists presented a baffling but intriguing force of alienation, a strange but exciting chorus of opposition to the existing order of things. As he roamed the country promoting the International Brotherhood Welfare Association, Reitman met numerous reformers and agitators and saw in them a kinship of spirit. And, as he gathered support for his hobo ventures in Chicago, he could see in the local left-wing organizers and soapboxers some of his own fire for agitation and ferment, the same thirst for notoriety and action.

In early January Ben began to hang around the offices of Chicago's *Daily Socialist,* discussing with assorted party leaders and labor union officials their plans for a massive march. As a protest against the impotence of the government in meeting the needs of the unemployed, a demonstration was being planned to petition the mayor and city officials to provide jobs. The date set for the march was January 23, 1908; the time, 2:00 P.M. In a meeting at Brant Hall, radicals, including labor firebrand Mary ("Mother") Jones, denounced capitalist exploitation of the workers and police violence. Lucy Parsons, widow of anarchist Albert Parsons, told about the demonstration of unemployed workers at the Haymarket in 1886 and the police violence and machinations which led to the hanging of her husband. Ben listened intently to all of this.[4]

As the day of the march approached, Chicago Police Chief George Shippy, seeing the possible magnitude of the demonstration and haunted by the spectre of the Haymarket violence more than twenty years earlier, declared, "There will be no parade. The conditions today are not the same as they were in 1886 and the police department is well able to maintain the peace of the city . . . We will not permit any display of the red flag on the streets of Chicago." Some of Shippy's men had managed to infiltrate several radical meetings in preceding months. He, like other Chicago officials, regarded the radicals as alien dogs, violent, un-American, a threat to traditional values, and he promised that a crack police department drill company would enforce the peace on January 23.[5]

Shippy's order intimidated some of the officials of the Socialist party, including the state secretary, James S. Smith; it did not intimidate others. Dr. M. Knopfnagel, in defiance of higher party officials, said that the march would go on. "I propose the name of Chief of Police Shippy as a member of the Socialist Party," Knopfnagel quipped, "because he has made more socialists within the last few days than our workers." The socialists decided to refer to the chief of police as "Comrade."[6] However, at emergency meetings of the march planners on January 22, it became apparent that the threats of police violence had unnerved the less adventuresome, and many others suggested postponement. But after protracted debate the organizers decided to send their lieutenants to the groggeries and skid row lodging houses to spread the word, via 20,000 handbills, that the march was on.

On January 23 groups of men began to wander the streets as early as 8:00 A.M., talking about the momentous event scheduled for that afternoon. Chief Shippy, arriving early at his office, carefully brushed his uniform coat, attached his gold star to it, fondled a club of polished rosewood trimmed with ivory, and declared, "We're ready for 'em." At 11:00 A.M. socialist leaders of the parade once again debated the wisdom of defying Chief Shippy. By this time Dr. Knopfnagel also had reconsidered. "They will have thugs," he declared nervously, "and then there will be trouble and they will shoot us dead and crack our heads. There will be widows and orphans, and I for one will not be responsible." He counseled postponement, others agreed, and a resolution to call off the march carried easily. The socialists decided to petition the city council for permission to hold a march one month later.[7]

Into this sudden breach of leadership leaped Ben Reitman. With the streets now filling with hundreds of marchers, he enthusiastically announced, "There'll be a parade anyway. If the unemployed are there and want to parade, I'll lead them. I'm not afraid. These socialists have cold feet. They are bluffers. I'm not a socialist. I have just been away getting my will made."[8]

Swinging his walking stick at his side, a petition to the mayor and city council stuffed in his pocket, Ben strode over to the lakefront alone, just before two o'clock, to take command of the demonstrators. Dressed in a long black coat and slouch hat, smoking one cigarette after another, he hustled through the crowd giving instructions. Mustering his troops at Michigan Avenue near the Art Institute, Ben faced several hundred policemen, including the crack drill squad promised by Chief Shippy. Firemen at the engine house at Washington Street and Michigan Avenue prepared to use their hoses on the demonstrators if the marchers turned violent. Seven protesters wearing crimson neckties stood on the steps of the public library and unfurled a red flag embroidered with the words "Unemployed Workers." Shippy pointed out to his men that numerous anarchists were in the crowd, along with Russians wearing astrakhen caps and puffing on long cigarettes.

At Reitman's signal, given shortly after two o'clock, several hundred marchers formed a line and began to walk, two abreast, down Michigan Avenue. They picked up large numbers of additional recruits along the way, and newspaper cameramen ran to the front of the line to take pictures of their leader. The *Tribune* reported that Ben quickly thrust back his shoulders and adopted a Bonapartist pose.[9]

At State Street, in an attempt to evade the approaching police, the hobo doctor led the marchers south, away from their proposed destination, city hall. As they neared Adams, the police charged through the ragged formation with billies flying. Ben defiantly pushed forward, his bearing erect, his walking stick still at his side, as the ranks behind him scattered in disarray, many bleeding from fresh wounds. Several policemen, including Chief Shippy, began ominously to encircle him, at which Reitman wailed, "This is an outrage." As they closed in, Ben, trying to fend off his attackers, took more than a few solid blows to the head. Several officers formed a cordon around the dazed protest leader and led him off.

At the Harrison Street police station, an emotionally and physically battered Ben Reitman, his hat and coat torn, his face cut, emptied from his pockets eight boxes of Turkish cigarettes, eleven cents, a package of papers on the subject of tramps, and his petition. It read in part: "We, the unemployed and destitute, call your attention to the fact that we are anxious, able and willing to work; that our only means of existence is to sell our powers of wealth creation. We do not own our homes and must pay rent. Without employment there are but two avenues open for us, suicide or crime."[10]

Charged with disorderly conduct, Ben called his mother and was later released on bond. Curiously, he told one interviewer, "I'd like to settle down, get married and earn a decent living. Guess I'll go out to California for about six months and rest up."[11] He told another, "I'm glad to be free. I've seen too much of the inside of jails and moreover I have been through hell today." He denied that he was an anarchist or a troublemaker and said that he felt it a duty to protest against injustices wracking the lowly of society.[12] But he told still another reporter, "I'm through with it all. I am not going to try to do good anymore. I am going back to my profession. I will not try to help the hobos anymore. I thought that I was doing a good thing until this afternoon. Now, I begin to think that I was mistaken. I got a crack on the head today and I've wakened from an ugly dream, ugh!"[13]

Chief Shippy expressed regret over the arrest of Ben Reitman, because it had given notoriety to a notoriety-seeker. "But I did not intend to allow any anarchist gathering," he blustered. In the parade were only a handful of honest unemployed men, he claimed; the rest were filthy radicals and hoboes. "I took the precautions I did merely to be sure of preventing anything worse occurring." The chief was content that he had saved the city of Chicago from another Haymarket riot.[14]

Chicago newspapers swiftly extolled Chief Shippy's actions and made mockery of those of his protagonist, Ben Reitman. The *Inter-Ocean* proclaimed, "Well Done, Mr. Shippy!" Calling the demonstrators "habitual rioters" and the parade an excuse for anarchists and no-accounts to create public havoc and disorder, the editorial declared that such a dangerous aggregation of chronic loafers and malcontents had to be smashed, that lawlessness must be met with necessary force. Chicago was fortunate in having the kind of government willing to suppress anarchy, the kind of government it did not have in years past. Ben Reitman, the paper charged, was a misguided lunatic infatuated with a ravenous pursuit of publicity and distorted notions of reform. The blows on his head were fit medicine to clear his clouded intellect.[15]

Once again Ben basked in national attention. As police and journalists derided this self-proclaimed reformer, with stories about his eccentricities and mad escapades emblazoned in headlines, his craving for excitement, his passion for the whirl and flurry of the limelight, of happenings, swelled even more. His protestations to the police and newspapers about giving up the hobo reform effort were soon disavowed. He would fight on.

Arraigned on a charge of disorderly conduct, Ben demanded a jury trial; his case was set for the following week. Chief Shippy, determined to give him as little further publicity as possible and to send him from Chicago's midst, said he would recommend to the judge that Reitman be fined only two dollars and costs but be ordered to leave the city on the next passenger train or fast freight, whichever suited him best.[16]

If Shippy wanted no martyrdom for Reitman, the court went even further, acquiting him on January 28. When the verdict was announced, a number of Ben's friends in the crowd cheered and clapped, prompting a warning from the judge that he would impose fines. Ben said afterward, "I have won the fight for my friends and they now will be able to carry on the battle more easily. The trial has been a matter of interest to me more than of concern. I have found much food for psychological study through it."[17]

All of this commotion over anarchism, socialism, all the -isms now charging the social and political atmosphere in Chicago was confounding but stirring to Ben Reitman. Sincere in his impulse toward reform, he nevertheless knew little about the fine distinctions of political and legal theory. For the first time he had encountered the fury and anger that political advocacy can engender, and if anarchism now meant little more to him than a pejorative word, he was rapidly being identified in police and public circles as a leftist radical. Chicago's celebrated hobo doctor was quickly moving into a more perilous arena.

6. Emma

She was the high priestess of anarchy, a firebrand, a disturber of the peace. She was the most dangerous woman on the loose in the United States—or that was what many Americans concluded. Her name had blazed in headlines across the country, always linked with visions of bombs, red flags, terrorism, destruction, assassination, violence, subversion, and revolution. Naturally, she was captivating to Ben Reitman.

Emma Goldman was born in 1869 in Kovno, Russia, to Jewish parents. Although her formal schooling was sporadic and generally inadequate, she credited a German teacher in Königsberg with instilling in her a love of literature and music. As a teenager living in St. Petersburg, she developed an interest in radical literature through friendships with nihilist university students.

Emigrating to America with a half-sister in 1885, Emma took a job in a clothing factory in Rochester, New York. After a brief, unhappy marriage to a fellow factory worker, Jacob Kershner, and after living for a time in New Haven, Connecticut, where she worked in a corset factory, she headed for New York City in 1889. For Emma Goldman the move to New York opened up a new world of intellect and excitement, for it was there that she met Johann Most, editor of the fiery radical paper *Die Freiheit,* and Alexander Berkman, an impassioned, young Russian revolutionary. Both men became her lovers and comrades.

Emma's road to anarchism started with her early acquaintances in Russia and resumed in New Haven, where she had befriended a group of young Russian socialists and anarchists, as well as in Rochester, where, stirred by publicity surrounding the Chicago Haymarket riot, she had avidly read Most's paper and other anarchist literature. Now, in New York, she soon was reveling in the torrent of radical ideas espoused by a wide circle of leftist thinkers. Emma was drawn to the social humanism of the Russian scientist and philosopher Peter Kropotkin, who with his followers talked of a new day when social and religious authoritarianism and coercive political power would surrender to a society of free, equal individuals organized in small cooperatives, dedicated to humanity and justice.

Working in sweatshops to support herself, Emma fervidly joined radical activities. When Johann Most discovered that she had a robust, magnetic speaking ability, he began to arrange tours for her in various cities. The career of the notorious "Red Emma," the grenadier of anarchy, was thus launched.

In 1892, enraged over the brutal suppression of the Homestead strike, Emma aided Berkman in his attempted assassination of industrialist Henry Clay Frick, an act which cost Berkman fourteen years in Pennsylvania's Western Penitentiary. A year later, Emma herself began a short stay on New York's Blackwell's Island for inciting the unemployed to defy authority. She reputedly encouraged the starving to take bread if it were not given.

After her release from prison, Emma traveled to Vienna to study midwifery and nursing, an interest whetted by her experience as a nurse on Blackwell's Island. While in Europe she continued lecturing and later made a return trip, meeting some of the greatest anarchist leaders in the world, including Kropotkin and Enrico Malatesta. Her trips to Europe further inspired her love of contemporary social theater and literature, a love which would lead her to become one of America's foremost popularizers of the arts at the same time she was blistering lecture halls with stormy political invective.

By the early 1900s Emma Goldman was a powerful revolutionary orator, lecturing not only on anarchism but on European drama, women's freedom, free speech, and a host of other social and political issues. She founded the radical monthly *Mother Earth* to provide a forum for the anarchist message. She was also widely suspected of complicity in the assassination of President McKinley, although laborious investigations failed to unearth a shred of evidence that she even knew the assassin.[1]

Preaching a vague idealism of absolute, untrammeled freedom, Emma attacked all forms of government and their laws as wrong and unnecessary. More an expression of human values than a philosophical system, anarchism extolled personal expression, the free association of individuals, and human liberty. Goldman and other anarchists called for direct action against and open defiance of all laws and external restraints—economic, social, and moral. Their aim was to uplift the underclasses from grinding poverty and official repression, to free the masses from the subjugation of governmental and economic tyranny. She declared in a speech in 1901: "Anarchism aims at a new and complete freedom. It strives to bring about the freedom . . . which will prevent any man from having a desire to interfere in any way with the liberty of his neighbor . . . We merely desire complete individual liberty, and this can never be obtained as long as there is an existing government."[2] Frank Harris wrote that Emma's ideal "is based on the assumption that the majority of individuals constituting the State are intelligent and reasonable,"[3] a proposition which, in light of her treatment by many ill-wishing crowds and police over the years, might seem surprising.

Among other things, Emma called for the final abolition of the class structure; political, economic, and social equality for both sexes; and the international solidarity of the working classes. "Tell all friends that we will not waver," she once wrote, "that we will not compromise, and that if the worst comes we shall go to prison in the proud consciousness that we have remained faithful to the spirit of internationalism and to the solidarity of all the people of the world."[4] She spoke out forcefully for women's equality, an area in which, she confessed, she often felt closer to the traditional mothers of a previous generation than to the emancipated women flocking into the business and professional circles who seemed ashamed of their deepest maternal and sexual instincts. The anarchist creed, Emma insisted, did not sublimate these feelings; with its emphasis on equality and personal freedom, anarchism opened the way for a full expression of them. "A true conception of the relation of the sexes will not admit of conqueror and conquered," Emma wrote. "It knows of but one great thing: to give of one's self boundlessly, in order to find oneself richer, deeper, better."[5]

Eugene Debs wrote, "During all her years of service in this country, Emma Goldman stood staunchly always on the side of the struggling workers in every battle and for this she was hated, feared, and persecuted by the exploiting capitalists, their prostituted newspaper scribblers, their tools in public office, and all the rest of their minions and mercenaries."[6] William Reedy, editor of the *St. Louis Mirror,* wrote of a woman 8,000 years ahead of her time: vibrant; a fount of ideas on arts, science, economics, philosophy, poetry; free from truculence and coarseness and swagger; holding out the vision of a noble humanity rescued from cant and tyranny and free from the restraint of convention, ceremony, gods, rulers, and stifling institutions. Through it all, Reedy said, Emma had endured misrepresentation, ridicule, and abuse with a remarkable serenity born of the conviction that she was right in a world of madness. "Her vision is of every truly great-souled man or woman who has ever lived."[7]

To politicians, law-enforcement officials, businessmen, and others in positions of authority, however, Emma Goldman was a despicable wretch, an affront to all things good and pure and American. Her challenge of American institutions and customs and values was contemptible and villainous. She had to be silenced.

In early March 1908, Emma planned to deliver a series of lectures in Chicago, the city which, since the Haymarket riot, was most symbolically tied in anarchist minds to police repression. Circulars announced a "Paris Commune" celebration in Metropolitan Hall, at Maxwell and Jefferson streets, for Sunday, March 8. Emma was to be the principal speaker, along with several leading socialists. Meetings were also tentatively scheduled for the German Hod Carriers Hall and the Lessing Clubhouse. One of those distributing the circulars was an emotionally troubled twenty-year-old Russian Jew named Lazarus Averbuch.

When word reached the authorities that Emma was preparing to leave Springfield, Missouri, to travel to Chicago, police officials took great pains to assure citizens that the "Queen of Anarchy" would be muted in their city. "Miss Goldman will not be permitted to address any open meetings," Assistant Police Chief Herman Schuettler announced to the press. "There will be no more open anarchist meetings permitted in Chicago. By an open meeting I refer to one the general public is permitted to attend." Asked if Emma would be arrested, Schuettler declared, "The trouble with Emma is she misbehaves herself."[8]

On March 2, two days before Emma's scheduled arrival, Lazarus Averbuch walked to the home of Police Chief George Shippy with a revolver and a knife purchased from a Clark Street pawnshop. At approximately 9:00 A.M. he forced his way into the vestibule of Shippy's home and attempted to murder the chief. There was a vicious death struggle, which Shippy survived; Averbuch did not. The chief was saved by his son, Henry, a student at the Culver Military Academy, who rushed downstairs on hearing the shouting and scuffling. Averbuch was struck in the head and chest by at least five bullets, according to the coroner's report. Henry Shippy was shot in the chest and knifed in the arm, but he recovered. The chief was wounded only slightly.

After rounding up and interrogating scores of citizens, Chicago police reported that Averbuch was a "camp follower" of Ben Reitman and his unemployed demonstrators, that Averbuch regularly attended meetings of Chicago anarchists led by Dr. R. Miriam Yampolsky and William Nathason, and that he apparently acted alone in the assassination attempt. The act of the depressed youth, police declared, had sprung from the influence of the incendiary anarchists with whom he had been in company.[9]

Emma Goldman thus arrived in Chicago on March 4 at the very time that city authorities were most determined to exterminate anarchist societies, root and branch. The mayor and police pledged that sedition would be punished to the letter of the law, that undesirable foreigners who had been in the country less than three years would be weeded out for deportation, as allowed by federal law, and that street gatherings of malcontents spreading inflammatory propaganda would be absolutely prohibited.

On the night of March 6, about the time the body of Lazarus Averbuch was being lowered into a rain-soaked grave at the potter's field, Emma talked with a *Tribune* reporter about the upcoming meetings. Obviously amused that her presence in the city had stirred such panic among law enforcement officials, she declared, "I intend to speak. I intend to insist on my right of free speech. If the police stop me then it is up to them to explain why."

With both her picture and a caricature showing up all over Chicago, with editorialists and politicians and religious leaders calling her the "Priestess of Reds" and pleading for her suppression, Emma had made herself a public menace—and she enjoyed it. "I see no reason why the police should want to arrest me," she dryly observed. Her recent lectures in St. Louis and Springfield had left society still intact. Indeed, many listeners actually agreed with her message. "One of my lectures was on 'Why Emancipation Has Not Freed Women.' You ought to have seen those staid old farmers when I said I believed every woman should have the right to say when and by whom she would have a child."[10]

In the days ahead the police of Chicago were determined to close all halls willing to give Emma Goldman a forum, and in this they succeeded. At every turn her comrades were suddenly spurned. In a matter of days the police had intimidated all the landlords inclined to rent space to the anarchists, and Emma's scheduled rallies were all canceled.[11]

Once again Ben Reitman, who had followed these events with increasing fascination, seized a chance for notoriety. If Emma Goldman needed a hall, he would offer the building he used for hobo meetings at 392 Dearborn Street. Ben got word to local anarchists that the hall was available; then he visited Hinky Dink's Saloon to enlist hobo labor to clean it up. Finally, he called several newspapers with the scoop that Emma would, after all, deliver a lecture on March 13. Ben was assured by the newspapermen that they would not reveal the plan to the police. He also asked his anarchist acquaintances for a personal meeting with Emma.

"How shall I describe Emma Goldman," he wrote later. "I have seen fully five hundred writers attempt to do it. She was short, about five feet, and weighed about 140 pounds. She had a powerful face, beautiful, strong, clear blue eyes, a nose that was not Jewish, and a strong, firm jaw. She was somewhat nearsighted and wore heavy glasses. Her hair was blond and silken and she wore it in a simple knot at the back of her head." Cordially shaking Ben's hand, Emma said that it was most unusual for a physician in America to offer assistance to an anarchist.[12] "So this is the little lady, Emma Goldman," Ben greeted her jauntily, dressed in his cowboy hat and silk tie, walking stick in hand. "I have always wanted to know you." His voice was deep and ingratiating, Emma remembered. She noted his finely shaped head and unwashed tangle of black hair; his large, dreamy brown eyes and beautiful teeth. "He was a handsome brute. His hands, narrow and white, exerted a peculiar fascination . . . I could not take my eyes off his hands. A strange charm seemed to emanate from them, caressing and stirring."[13] Ben and Emma talked about the planned meeting at the hobo hall and about each other for several hours. "When he went away," she wrote, "I remained restless and disturbed, under the spell of the man's hands."[14]

Ben's trust in the newspapermen to conceal his plans for the meeting was, of course, misplaced. As he and his hobo friends worked in the hall on the morning of the scheduled festivities, police and fire inspectors suddenly appeared to notify him that they had condemned the building as a fire trap. It was clear that at least one of the reporters had gone straight to the authorities with the story Ben had so generously offered. A confrontation between anarchists and the police would, the press surmised, make a more delectable story than a simple anarchist meeting. The reporters got their wish, for Ben and Emma decided to hold the meeting in spite of the injunction.

On the evening of March 13 nearly 200 anarchists, socialists, and other leftists mingled in front of the hobo hall as Ben Reitman argued with a force of about fifty policemen. "The building has been condemned for assemblages," an inspector barked. "The front door isn't safe and the doors don't open outward." Ben, wielding a hatchet, offered to hack down the offending doors. The police were not impressed. Then he offered to mobilize hobo carpenters to construct a new floor, a project that could be completed, he claimed, in a few hours. The police were again unimpressed. Shortly after 8:00 P.M. Ben reluctantly dismissed the crowd. "The police didn't seem to want any meeting held," he observed, a perception not requiring extraordinary acuity.[15]

In the next few days Chicago's police followed Emma all over the city as if its very survival were at stake. On March 15 she and Ben attended a meeting of Chicago's Anthropological Society along with a number of local radicals, including Lucy Parsons. Subject of the meeting: The Use of Vaccination and Anti-Toxin. Also attending were approximately forty policemen, many of whom refused to pay the standard entry fee of five cents. Reports from the meeting revealed a distinct lack of interest by Chicago's finest in vaccination. Instead, eighty eyes fixed on a lady seated at the front of the auditorium, described by the *Tribune* as having pink cheeks, wearing rimless glasses, a black silk dress with neat white cuffs, escalloped at the edges, and a dark green felt hat. She also wore a bemused look, especially when the fourth reserve of police entered the hall. Following the presentation of the formal papers by the several speakers, Emma and Ben rose to leave. As the two walked out, police shadows were close behind. The Anthropological Society had lost half its audience.[16]

The following day the anarchists tried again to hoodwink Chicago authorities. They scheduled a "social and concert" at Workingman's Hall for the ostensible purpose of raising funds for the anarchist cause. Behind the charade of announced music and poetry and other hoopla was a plot to smuggle Emma Goldman into the auditorium, where she would unexpectedly appear to give a lecture. Only a few in the anarchist ranks were privy to the covert operation; Ben Reitman was among them.

Several hundred persons gathered that night at the hall, the same building in which Lazarus Averbuch had in earlier days listened to local anarchists decry capitalist oppression. Suddenly, much to the chagrin of the radicals, detectives appeared and began to line the walls of the room. Emma nevertheless managed to get inside undetected and hide behind the stage. As a violin solo neared its conclusion, she walked in the half-light toward the front of the platform. No sooner had she been hurriedly introduced by William Nathason and appeared in view to the shouting hundreds in the audience than a phalanx of police pressed forward to spirit her away. While being dragged off, her dress almost ripping open, Emma loudly called for calm from the audience, many of whom seemed ready to charge the stage in defense of their leader. "Don't mind it, friends," she cried out. "Keep your seats. Be quiet." Emma was not arrested but she was forced to leave the hall. Afterward she traded barbs with the police as reporters listened:

> "Thought you'd come here and make trouble, eh?" said the captain.
>
> "Behave yourself," Emma shot back. "Talk like a man even if you are a policeman."
>
> "Much you care about the police! You'd like to get a chance to abuse them. You can't talk here!"
>
> "I'll talk when I damned please!"[17]

Ben Reitman had come to the meeting dressed in his rail-riding garb, unshaven, a cloth cap pulled down over his eyes. During the tussling on stage, Emma noticed Ben also being dragged down the stairs and into the street by the police. Later, he showed up at the flat of Miriam Yampolsky along with Emma and told reporters that the police had not kept good faith. Ben claimed that Assistant Chief

Schuettler had promised to allow Emma to speak if the anarchists secured a hall that met local building standards, which this building did. "It just shows that the police do not keep their words," Ben observed, a statement against which no anarchist would argue.[18]

Many of the radicals in Emma Goldman's coterie, sorely vexed in seeing their careful plans compromised, suspected treachery in the outsider among them who had knowledge of the scheme—Ben Reitman. Emma brushed off their suspicions, insisting that he had made an admirable gesture in first offering the hobo hall and had himself been treated roughly at the Workingman's Hall fiasco. But by this time Emma's words of support for Ben had more personal and intimate implications. "I had been profoundly stirred by him," she wrote. "Our being much together . . . had strengthened his physical appeal for me. I was aware that he also had been aroused; he had shown it in every look, and one day he had suddenly seized me in an effort to embrace me. I had resented his presumption, though his touch had thrilled me. In the quiet of the night, alone with my thoughts, I became aware of a growing passion for the wild-looking handsome creature, whose hands exerted such fascination."[19]

Later that week Emma traveled to Milwaukee with her comrades to fulfill speaking commitments. The stories of assassination and police repression coming out of Chicago fired interest in Emma's scheduled rallies and great numbers engulfed the meeting halls. But the success of the meetings in Milwaukee still left her unfulfilled and restless, craving the company of the hobo doctor. "I wired for him to come, but once he was there, I fought desperately against an inner barrier I could neither explain nor overcome."[20]

When they returned to Chicago, Ben and Emma had time to talk about their pasts. She saw in the dashing yet uncouth Reitman a figure straight out of Dostoyevski or Gorky, a man from society's underside, spinning tales of train flipping, of journeys on tramp steamers, of nights in flophouses and two-bit jails, of whores and pimps and mission stiffs and yeggs. He told her of his road life and his disease of wanderlust; he talked of his devotion to his mother, his early marriage, his friends in the back alleys and dives of Chicago. "I was enthralled," she wrote. "I was caught in the torrent of an elemental passion I had never dreamed any man could rouse in me. I responded shamelessly to its primitive call, its naked beauty, its ecstatic joy."[21]

As no man had before, Ben Reitman now sexually mesmerized Emma Goldman. She had never given herself to anyone in the kind of frenzy with which she gave herself to Ben. He muttered words of the street and brothel as they made love and experimented with a variety of techniques learned from scores of prostitute friends. If Emma's world was the world of intellect, Ben's was of the flesh. He saw himself as a sexual engine, always at the ready. Emma later wrote, "You have opened up the prison gates of my womanhood. And all the passion, that was fettered and unsatisfied in me for so many years, leaped into a wild reckless storm boundless, as the sea . . . I am famished, do you hear the woman in me is famished, what else is there for me to do where to hide, but to follow the call of the wild, the savage, the master lover?"[22]

Shortly before Emma's planned departure for Minneapolis and another speaking engagement, the two lovers, along with anarchist friends, dined at the Bismark Cafe. Seated nearby was a group of men, one of whom Emma immediately recognized as Captain Schuettler, arch-nemesis of radicals. To her horror and acute embarrassment, Ben breezily ambled over to Schuettler's table and engaged the man in friendly repartee. Emma squirmed with anger and disgust. The hands that had burned her with passion were now shaking those of the enemy, the beasts who had suppressed free speech and executed anarchist martyrs. Emma rushed to the train station, dazed and disillusioned, and left Chicago.

That night, haunted by feelings of humiliation and betrayal, Emma realized that the suspicions of her anarchist comrades were probably on the mark, that Ben had likely informed either the police or reporters about the Workingman's Hall meeting. But why? Treachery? Carelessness?

Ben sent several telegrams to Emma pleading for the opportunity to explain his actions at the Bismark. "I love you, I want you," he wired. "Please let me come." Several days later, tormented by a dream in which she saw Ben "bending over me, his face close to mine, his hands on my chest," Emma relented. She wired, "Come."[23]

In Minneapolis, Ben swept away Emma's doubts. He was not

friends with the police, he insisted, but his work among the hoboes and prostitutes often brought him in close contact with the authorities. He bantered and matched wits with them, played the gadfly, but he was not their friend. His sympathies were with the underclasses, the derelicts, the lost. He was a link between those on the fringe and the respectables of society. "It was never anything else," Ben assured Emma, "please believe me and let me prove it to you." She wilted. "Whatever might be at stake," Emma later wrote, "I had to believe in him with an all-embracing faith."[24]

In the flush of excitement for this older woman he began to call "Mommy," and dazed by the aura of filled lecture halls, the press of newspapermen, and the intrigue of radical politics, Ben knew he must leave Chicago with Emma. "Little blue-eyed lover, I want to go with you," he implored. He offered to become the pitchman of the revolution: to arrange meetings, hawk anarchist pamphlets, manage Emma's affairs on the road.[25] Although worried about the reaction of her comrades who considered him an interloper, Emma, totally entranced by her strange new man of the road, agreed to Ben's offer. "It would be wonderful to have someone with me on the long and weary tramps through the country," she knew; "someone who was lover, companion, and manager."[26]

Ben returned briefly to Chicago to bid farewell to his mother, his hoboes, and his patients. His decision to hit the lecture trail with Emma Goldman convulsed the International Brotherhood Welfare Association of Chicago. At one of the hobo haunts on West Madison, fifty of the men who had helped him found the IBWA and who had followed him in the unemployed workers' parade met to denounce their former leader for abandoning their cause to this new wanderlust, anarchism. They passed resolutions:

> *Whereas,* Dr. Ben L. Reitman, self-styled king of the hoboes has conducted himself in a manner unbecoming any member of the hobo party in allying himself with the anarchist movement; and,
>
> *Whereas,* Dr. Reitman has now deserted us and is hitting the road openly with Emma Goldman, the anarchist queen; therefore, be it
>
> *Resolved,* that we, the regular representatives of the hobo unemployed, do hereby renounce forever our allegiance to said Reitman, and the public is hereby notified that he is no longer recognized as our leader.

Cincinnati Fat, one of Chicago's most notable overland travelers, was beside himself. "What is he doin' bumming around Minneapolis with this Goldman woman," Fat fumed. "This anarchist graft is pretty good, it seems. He don't have to chop any more railroad ties for a handout."[27]

As he rode with Emma on a train bound for California, Ben recited a stanza he thought he remembered from Kipling: "I leans and looks across the sea until it seems, / There's no one left alive but you and me . . . ." Circumstance and his own brazenness had suddenly brought Chicago's notorious hobo doctor together with one of the world's most remarkable women. He was intoxicated by her fame, spellbound by her intellect and drive, astonished by her power. He had seen this woman, through the force of words and personality, make an entire city quiver with fear and controversy. He wanted to follow her, to join the heady swirl of radical protest, to taste once again new excitement.

"You and me, my blue-eyed Mommy," he whispered.[28]

7. On Tour

The hobo doctor was now in the anarchist ranks. As Ben Reitman headed west on his first tour with Emma Goldman, a new world of politics, protest, and hostility was opening before him, a world of fiery speeches and venomous crowds and confrontation, of issues with far-reaching significance. His comrade-lover became his teacher. As a mere neophyte in the political arena, a man with a woefully limited grasp of philosophy and literature, Ben's new life with Emma offered an extraordinary opportunity. She began to teach him anarchist theory and other political and social systems and doctrines. Together they read novels, poetry, and essays. Her lectures on anarchism, women's rights, labor problems, and modern drama were as new to Ben as they were to many of her audiences. He was an intellectual ragamuffin, a challenge to her patience and perseverance. But she set to work determined to mold her primitive lover, to provide an intellectual grounding that would make him acceptable to the anarchist philosophes around her.

Reitman was entering her world in turbulent times. Anarchism in the spring of 1908 had wrung from the American people a kind of national hysteria. On March 28 it intensified. A young, idealistic Russian named Selig Cohen, seen frequently at radical anarchist and socialist meetings in New York, took a ball from atop a brass bed, half-filled it with broken nails, added nitroglycerin and gunpowder, put in a short fuse, and walked to New York's Union Square where the socialists were protesting the unemployment then wracking the country. As he excitedly tried to light the fuse with a cigarette, Cohen put the fire to the wrong hole, blowing apart a bystander and seriously maiming himself.[1] Lazarus Averbuch in Chicago, Selig Cohen in New York, both in the same month—it all brought stories to the newspapers and frenzied talk in the bars about the not-forgotten Haymarket riot and the frightful ascendancy of the bomb-throwers.

The mayor of Paterson, New Jersey, was especially disturbed. Andrew McBride pleaded with President Theodore Roosevelt for authority to suppress a local anarchist paper, *La Questione Sociale.* "I appeal to you," he begged, "as mayor of a law-abiding community, proud of their kinship with the American people, for your forceful influence . . . relieve us by excluding from the United States mails this publication and you will earn the deepest gratitude from a thankful people." Directing the postmaster general to investigate the possibilities, the president declared that anarchist publishers were enemies and that "every effort should be made to hold them accountable for an offense far more infamous than that of any ordinary murder." Publishing a newspaper, the president of the United States was telling the mayor of Paterson and the American people, was worse than homicide.

When the attorney general found no law under which criminal prosecution could be made through the federal courts, Roosevelt, in a special message to Congress, asked for such legislation. No immigrant anarchist should be allowed on American shores, the president insisted; no anarchist paper should be published within its borders; no foreign anarchist literature should be permitted circulation among its people.[2]

Thus the image of the anarchist as a dark, menacing, stealthy alien, slinking from subterranean meetings to plant bombs among peaceful citizens, gained official credence. All across the country, city officials, encouraged by the Roosevelt administration, undertook vigorous new efforts to uncover anarchist elements in their midst, to drive them out of their cities, disrupt their meetings, photograph, interrogate, harrass, and arrest them. It made no difference that Emma Goldman and other anarchists publicly repudiated the kind of violence displayed in Chicago and at Union Square; all anarchists were held in mutual opprobrium, not only by the public but by the country's leaders. If Emma delivered learned lectures on everything from Social Darwinism to the plays of Anton Chekov, she was seen nevertheless only as a fanatical Cossack. Although some newspaper editors and civic officials cautioned against the subversion of free speech and assembly in dealing with the anarchists, most observers favored a policy of the iron heel.

To most Americans anarchist theory was not just an ephemeral abstraction, it was dangerous. The abolition of all law and government, the faith in a society resting on complete freedom and individual goodness—all of this seemed, as one newspaper editorialist wrote in 1908, an effort to undermine the whole social fabric, to negate civilization. Referring to Emma, the writer charged, "She would produce chaos. She is an outlaw and she is at war with society."[3] Put into practice, those principles advanced by Emma and a vulnerable society would crumble. To the casual observer there was no difference between the philosophy of anarchism and violent lawlessness. Quite simply, Emma Goldman wanted to turn the country over to criminals.

On April 10, Emma and her traveling party reached Salt Lake City, where she was scheduled to deliver several weekend lectures. That evening reporters clustered at the Wilson Hotel to interview the infamous radical, the apostle of disorder. They were surprised by the woman who greeted them. "Miss Goldman certainly does not look like the dangerous person she is reputed to be, and as numerous people have regarded her," one reporter noted. "She is a little woman, medium in height, quiet in manner, and impresses one as being rather meek, although her eyes flash in conversation and she becomes animated as she talks of the improved conditions which she hopes to have brought about by the establishment of her doctrines through the education of the people."[4]

Anarchism did not promote violence or crime, Emma declared to the assembled press, but stood for an end to tyranny and unjust laws and for the abolition of those conditions in society which oppressed the American working class. It stood for the right of all persons to act according to their desires, untrammeled by those outside forces seeking to enslave them. Marshaling the views of such thinkers as Godwin, Tolstoy, and Kropotkin, Emma dazzled her guests that night with her erudition and conviction. She did not, however, convince them of the efficacy of anarchist principles.

Emma talked of the right to revolt against any government that unjustly interfered with personal liberty. "Very good," one skeptical reporter remarked, "but how about that man who wishes to oppose us? Would we not soon be compelled to take the law into our own hands and fight among ourselves for our rights as they used to do in olden times?" The question was problematic. To fight would be unnecessary, Emma responded lamely, because under anarchism the conditions prompting people to violence would not be present. Violence was rooted in oppression; without oppression there would be few or no criminals.

Anarchism seemed to be a vacuous fiction and Emma Goldman a zealous visionary, a reporter said after the meeting. Although there was much good intention surrounding her crusade, he thought, her wispy notions were so removed from reality as to be virtually worthless.[5] The *Salt Lake Tribune* suggested that Emma's sowing of freedom's seeds would find more virgin ground in Russia than in the United States, where there was already a fine harvest. She should take her anarchism elsewhere.[6] The depiction of Emma Goldman in the Salt Lake press had thus dramatically shifted from that of a dangerous fanatic to one of a matronly fool. For Emma, this was obviously not progress.

Undaunted as always, she delivered several lectures in the Mormon capital. If the press, public officials, and conservative groups sneered at her message, many allies, including Ben Reitman, did not. They admired her vision and her tenacity. She spoke, for example, on the deteriorating relations between labor and capital and the futility of the labor movement in bringing necessary relief to the masses of workers. Holding up the specter of a civil war between the capitalists and workers, she talked of a time not far distant when the world would be swallowed up in the anarchist movement.[7]

From the size of the crowds in Salt Lake City, less than 300 for each of the speeches, it was obvious to Ben Reitman that the swallowing was not imminent. Emma needed more promotional bravura and flair, better advance planning, bigger halls. As the Goldman party left Utah for California and other speaking engagements, the P. T. Barnum of the hobo world began to fashion fresh ideas to bring the principles of Emma Goldman to the American public.

On April 17 the anarchist's train rolled into San Francisco. The *Examiner* heralded their arrival, announcing that Emma was being escorted by the "King of Tramps."[8] The radicals hit San Francisco at about the same time that the U.S. Pacific Squadron steamed into port, a fortuitous combination for Bay City wags: the symbol of anarchy and disorder and disloyalty meets the symbol of patriotism and martial might. City officials played the event to the hilt, dispatching a large retinue of officers, led by their chief, to the train station to meet the invaders. The Red Queen and her court would not wreck havoc on this fair city. Reporters swarmed around Emma as she left the train, asking whether the rumors were true that she intended to blow up the fleet. "Why waste a bomb," she retorted. "What I should like to do with the fleet, with the entire Navy, and the Army too, would be to dump them in the bay."[9]

On the following day, at Emma's appearance at Walton's Pavilion, an old prizefight ring on Golden Gate Avenue, thirty policemen and twenty detectives mingled with the crowd, patrolling the sidewalks and street. A police spokesman declared the obvious: "She is being carefully watched. . . ."[10] At the residence of friends where she stayed during the visit, two mounted officers paraded around the cottage and through the neighborhood. Whenever she delivered a speech, a light brigade surrounded the hall, sometimes more than 100 of San Francisco's bluecoats, on horseback, in squad cars, on foot, all with billies at the ready. Each day, Ben pointed out, the police department was dipping into the city treasury for several hundred dollars to keep watch over Emma. His concern for fiscal responsibility notwithstanding, the surveillance continued. "In years to come," Emma quipped, a young generation would read the story of how 150 brave policemen "helped to spread the ideas which paved the way for a free society."[11]

Emma and Ben did find an afternoon's sanctuary from the constant police harrassment at an unlikely place, the Presidio, military encampment of San Francisco. Ben knew the Presidio's chief physician from those terrible days after the earthquake when he had assisted in caring for the victims. Emma wrote later that the shadowing detectives were kept outside the Presidio walls as Ben and she, "the foe of militarism, [were] entertained by the physician in charge and shown through the wards." The irony was delicious.[12]

Reitman had always craved attention and was now getting it in copious amounts. But his promotional activity had only begun. He printed meeting announcements by the thousands and scattered them everywhere he went. He mounted soapboxes in public squares to deliver spirited, often lewd orations, finishing each performance with an invitation to Emma's next meeting. He hawked anarchist pamphlets and recruited new workers for the cause. He sold cheap reprints of books about which Emma lectured:

I have another little pamphlet here, friends. It is by Ibsen. He was a Swedish dramatist. The book is called "The Doll's House." It's a play. It's about a woman named Nora. Nora got tired of living with her husband and taking care of the kids. One day she said to her old man, "You are just like the rest of the men, always trying to boss me and never giving me an even break. I am going to get the hell out of here and leave you to take care of the kids." Now, if there is anybody in this audience who wishes his wife to leave him let him take this pamphlet home and give it to her. Who'll be the next? Thank you. I have only six more of these left, friends.[13]

Ben's promotional campaign, fanned by police overkill, worked magic on attendance at Emma's lectures. One hall seating over 5,000 proved too small as lines formed hours before the scheduled addresses. Never had Emma seen such enthusiasm. At one Sunday afternoon lecture on "Patriotism," a speech which VFW members and army generals might have dubbed "Anti-Patriotism," the listeners became so annoyed at police interference that the chief of police implored Emma to become a peacemaker. "I promised," she wrote, "on condition that he would reduce the number of men in the hall . . . Out they marched, like guilty schoolboys, accompanied by the jeering and hooting of the crowd."[14]

It was at the "Patriotism" lecture that a young soldier named William Buwalda, who had attended the meeting, or so he claimed, to practice his stenographic skills, was seen shaking the hand of Emma at the conclusion of her speech. Buwalda was courtmartialed for that handshake, dismissed from the Army, and sentenced to five years at Alcatraz, a fitting punishment, the Army concluded, for anyone consorting with un-Americans. This was too much even for Theodore Roosevelt, who later asked for a reduced sentence. After all, the publicity surrounding the case might engender public support for the accursed radicals.[15]

With the April 27 departure of the notorious Emma Goldman, the flaunter of convention and disrupter of the peace, San Francisco authorities breathed a collective sigh of relief. The Bay City had survived. But the city's problems with uppity women in general did not abate. On the day Emma boarded a train for Los Angeles, two fashionably dressed women, one a former belle of Sausalito and a member of its "smart set," entered the St. Francis Hotel, reclined in its luxurious chairs, and in violation of city ordinances began to puff on cigarettes.[16]

On April 28 Ben and Emma entered Los Angeles for another series of lectures. After Emma's first address, the conservative *Los Angeles Times* scoffed at the "Prophetess of Confusion" and her heavy-sounding, fake classicism, her contorted references to Huxley, and her lament that people had to work. Emma's anarchism, the *Times* reported, amounted to telling roughneck ne'er-do-wells that they were all geniuses in disguise with only the police and the law standing in their way to fame and success. She was nothing but a "virago" and a "she-scold."[17]

Even as Ben traveled through the West with Emma, her manager during the day, her bedmate at night, his pursuit of others of her sex did not slacken. He seemed to acquire women with the same casual regularity that some men picked up packages of cigarettes. In fact, the time most men spent with single packs was usually longer than the relationships Ben had with most women. Obsessive, compulsive, he would somehow slip away at any moment, stirred by the slightest whim, to hotels, vice districts, private homes, wherever his newest fleeting acquaintance led. Although undoubtedly suspicious about his frequent absences, Emma never imagined the extent of his extracurricular sexual activity in their first months together. When Ben heard Emma lecture on freedom and independence of spirit, it seemed to give license to the kind of sexual hyperactivity and experimentation that drove him constantly, intensely. But to Emma such licentiousness was as disgusting as it was incomprehensible. On Ben's first tour Emma was oblivious to his philanderings; later, it would be different.

From California they headed north. In Portland, Emma joked with reporters, "Do not be alarmed. I have no dynamite in my pocket. . . . "[18] Education, she said, was the only bomb sanctioned by true anarchism. But her brand of education was unpalatable to most Portlanders, especially to the Young Men's Christian Association.

On May 19, various directors of the Portland YMCA awoke to read in the local paper that their auditorium had been leased to Emma Goldman's advance agent, Alexander Horr. Most of the directors were shocked, and by afternoon the lease had been canceled. Several members of the YMCA expressed the view that to allow Emma's radical road show into their hall would have created the impression that they endorsed murder, bomb-throwing, terror, revolution, and other crimes generally associated with Emma and the anarchists.

The *Portland Oregonian*, on May 21, applauded the YMCA's action, reminding its readers that anarchists throughout history had been murdering sovereigns and citizens alike with impunity. It was unfortunate, the editorialist continued, that the system of government in the United States did not allow for extermination of such "disease spots" as anarchism. As the orchardist exterminates the codling moth, as the rose-grower the cutworm and the stock-grower the tubercular cattle, the American people should find ways to eradicate sick people with treasonous theories.[19]

Horr, Reitman, and others scurried around Portland looking for a new location, finally renting a small hall from an owner who was unimpressed by the anarchists' supposed peril to the community. On May 23, Emma delivered a lecture on women's rights entitled, "Why Emancipation Has Failed to Free Women." "Not until woman divorces herself from the false gods she now worships and asserts her individuality as a human being and as a member of society will she ever be able to work out her emancipation," Emma declared. The drive for women's equality, she predicted, would be frustrated at every turn—by legislators who draft unjust laws; by males with vested interests in keeping women economically dependent; by established social and cultural norms which prescribe that women be wives and mothers and little more; by the Christian church which relegates women to inferior status as the progeny of Adam and his ridiculous rib. Emma deprecated the suffrage movement as useless and its proponents as foolish. "I fail to see how political equality can assist in accomplishing women's emancipation. Man has been enjoying it for years, but he has made the world no better. . . ." Only by asserting themselves as human beings and equal members of society, not as wives, mothers, or things useful to the state, would women rise above their present, ignominious state of servitude. Women must have the vision to see the tremendous opportunities that await and to seize them. Only then would they realize individuality.[20] As did Salt Lake City, San Francisco, and Los Angeles, Portland survived these subversive utterances.

From Portland it was on to other cities in the Northwest. During a meeting in Seattle, Ben's past mixed with his future. Outside the entrance to one of the lecture halls a man asked to see Doc Reitman. He was Chicago's "Delicate Dan," a pickpocket artist as nimble as his name implied. "Glad I saw you, Ben," the old dip whispered. "Heard you was in town and I couldn't pass up a chance to say hello. Law is after me. Got some stuff in 'Chi' and had to skip. Better not come in, might get spotted. Radical meeting is no place for a guy with a price on his bean. See you after the meeting." Following Emma's address, Ben found Dan idling in the shadows of the building, marked only by the faint light of his cigarette. Reminding his old friend of the time in Chicago when Ben had come to his aid in a crisis, Dan slipped a package into the doctor's hand and disappeared into the night. At his hotel, Ben opened the parcel and found six purses containing about seventy dollars and four watches. The master thief from Chicago had hustled Emma's audience and then made his own contribution to the anarchist cause. Ben appreciated the gesture; Emma was furious. Her own followers had been ripped off at the very time she was lecturing to them. "Don't you see, Hobo," she scolded, "that's the way the common people hurt their cause."[21]

Ben's first tour with Emma closed with meetings in Montana. Emma did not care much for Helena, calling it the "smuggest, most self-conceited, bigoted, and mentally decrepit little town I have ever visited." The city council was "malicious and stupid," its politicians "old fossils," and its police and newspaper reporters "hayseeds."[22] In the rough mining town of Butte, Reitman decided to end the trip with a flourish. He made some loud-colored posters and handbills and stood with a couple of boys at a crossroads where miners passed on their way home. Seeing his large hat, black coat, flowing tie, and walking cane, the miners must have thought the circus had hit town.[23] The anarchists, of course, drew big crowds.

"My tour, more eventful than any previous one, was at an end," Emma wrote. "It was a painful wrench to separate after the intimacy of four months. Only four months since that strange being had come so unexpectedly into my life." She longed for Ben's presence, felt him in every pore, was absorbed with this person so unlike any she had ever known. She said she could not explain the appeal he held for her, for in habits, tastes, temperaments, backgrounds, and interests they were worlds apart. He was socially crude and intellectually naive, and his love of publicity and show was repugnant to her. But he had an honest sympathy for society's victims and a genuine taste and instinct for reform. Also, he had quickly shown a deep enthusiasm for directing her business affairs. Even in these first months Emma could see that the publicity for the meetings had increased tremendously and that the sale of anarchist literature was unprecedented, thanks largely to Ben, the master showman. Most of all he had become a new, elemental force in her life. "Nothing mattered now," she wrote, "except the realization that Ben had become an essential part of myself. I would have him in my life and in my work, whatever the cost."[24]

Leaving the West behind, Ben stopped off in Chicago to stay with his mother during the summer; Emma returned to New York, where he would join her in a few months. Soon he would meet Alexander Berkman and the other noted anarchists close to Emma, a meeting about which Ben and Emma were both apprehensive. "Some of my comrades sensed Ben's possibilities and his value to the movement," she wrote. "Others, however, were antagonistic to him."[25] In New York their unlikely relationship would be severely tested.

8. "210"

The leftist journalist Hutchins Hapgood once told Ben Reitman that he planned to write a history of 210 East Thirteenth Street. It is a loss to literature and history that he never did. "210": the hub of American anarchism, the home of Emma Goldman and of *Mother Earth,* a haven for her family of radicals. Bounded by the ghetto and the tenderloin, near Greenwich Village and the Bowery, the little flat on Thirteenth Street was a nexus of radical activity, birthplace of major protest movements and campaigns.

Emma had moved into the five-room flat in 1903 and was one of the building's first tenants. Even in the face of stern police harassment over the years, the landlord steadfastly refused to evict the famous anarchist, for which Emma remained grateful. Heated in the winter only by the kitchen stove, the buzz of linotypes from a nearby printing house always an irritation, the flat nevertheless held a special place in many hearts. As Emma wrote later, it saw within its walls "men and women famous in the annals of life." Or, as Hapgood put it, the flat was a "home of lost dogs." In the fall of 1908, Ben Reitman joined the "210" family.[1]

The regulars there were all long-time friends of Emma. They included Alexander Berkman, her most intimate comrade, who had been born in the same Russian town. The two were lovers, fellow radicals, survivors of a reckless assassination attempt, the *Attentat,* in 1892, an act that had cost Berkman fourteen years in a Pennsylvania penitentiary. Sober, highly intellectual, possessed by a red-hot revolutionary fervor, he wrote in his *Prison Memoirs* that murder and *Attentat* were very much different, that the killing of a tyrant was an act of liberation and moral certitude. Berkman was the consummate revolutionary. Ben remembered his appearance: "He was a short man about five feet, six, well built, with dark hair and eyes, an oval countenance and large lips. He had a good face, a bald head and could have passed easily for a business or professional man."[2]

Hippolyte Havel, an exotic, bohemian Czech dandy of gypsy background whom Emma had met in London, was also a frequent visitor. Short, dark, an encyclopedic mind often muddled by liquor, veteran of numerous anarchist wars and of many jails, Havel had been one of Emma's early lovers. "He thought in German," Ben remembered, "spoke in English, swore in Bohemian and drank in all languages." Profane, wild-haired, Havel became something of a legend in Greenwich Village with his oft-uttered phrase, "Goddamned bourgeoisie!" "Havel is one of those men who ought to be supported by the community," Theodore Dreiser once said to Hutchins Hapgood. "He is a valuable person for life, but can't take care of himself. If I ever have any money, I'll certainly settle some of it on Hippolyte."[3]

Max Baginski was another regular, the first editor of *Mother Earth,* former editor of the Chicago anarchist publication *Arbeiter Zeitung,* a native of Siberia who met Emma in 1893 in Philadelphia shortly after he had come to America. Although an experienced writer and a man with refined literary tastes, Baginski was not especially fluent in English and spoke German most of the time. Stout, with thin blond hair and thick glasses, he did not live at "210" as some of the others did but stayed nearby with his wife and child. Baginski was one of Emma's closest, most loyal friends who, she once said, had a "soothing effect on me like a mother's touch to a sick child."[4]

There was also Harry Kelly, a self-educated Irish printer from St. Louis who had helped publish an anarchist newspaper in Boston and later worked in England, where he cultivated a friendship with Peter Kropotkin. Kelly had close ties with organized labor, unusual for an anarchist. Generous and practical, he would later offer to marry Emma Goldman to make her a naturalized citizen and thus ward off the government's deportation proceedings.

Several others joined the group, including Leonard Abbott, an American anarchist and journalist who took part in numerous reform activities, and Eleanor Fitzgerald, a tall, red-haired, early friend of Ben from Chicago who everyone began to call "Lioness"; she later ran a radical newspaper in San Francisco with Berkman.

There was also Emma's niece, Stella Ballantine, and Becky Edelson, a friend of Berkman.[5]

Intense, fervidly loyal, the anarchists of "210" were a tight-knit cadre on a crusade for Emma and her beliefs. Ben marveled at the extraordinary amount of work the small group produced, mostly because of their passion for the cause, though they were, as a rule, rather somber. At one of the "Mother Earth Balls," small parties hosted by Emma, amid the music and dance, with tables laden with Russian samovar pastries and fresh fruit, a visitor remarked to one of the regulars, "Well, being anarchists doesn't seem to make these people very happy." "Happy?" the woman answered. "Of course not. For the anarchist is always at war with society—and often against himself." The visitor realized just how incongruous a phenomenon an anarchist ball was.[6]

From the earliest days of his association with the radicals at "210" it was clear that Ben simply did not fit in. A political neophyte with suspect background and allegiances, unlearned, fun-loving, with atrocious manners and few social graces, Ben bulled his way into the *Mother Earth* fold with the same lack of decorum that he usually exhibited when approaching women. He was loud and boorish and outlandish, much of it, of course, a screen, a pathetic effort to shield feelings of inferiority and restiveness. He was intimidated by the intellectualism around him, repulsed by the daintiness of much of the parlor-room radicalism. His bombast and crudity now reached new heights; his womanizing lacked any pretense of subtlety; his language was of tramp-steamer vintage. Emma's compatriots could never accept her attraction to the lout from Chicago, and most assumed, fairly correctly, that lust had clouded this middle-aged woman's senses, had brought on a dreadful myopia that threatened her life, her career.

Emma's comrades treated Ben with silent contempt and waited for her deluded fascination with him to wear thin. Ben inwardly seethed at their arrogance and outwardly continued to play the showman, to which they reacted with disgust. He saw the salon and coffeehouse radicals as mostly "¼ ass poets with dreamy eyes and contempt for the world," overcome with tremendous egos, lacking social conscience or understanding. "To hell with them," he once told Emma. Ben assumed that most of these men had never experienced the life of the common men as he had done, had never worked at grinding jobs, begged for food, suffered from legal discrimination, been at the end of a policeman's club in two-bit towns. They were insipid essayists and inconsequential sonnet makers. To hell with them all.[7]

Elmer Gertz, well-known lawyer and biographer of Clarence Darrow and Frank Harris, knew Ben Reitman well, knew that he had a natural sensitivity toward the underclasses. "That's what attracted him to Emma," Gertz said. "He probably had a greater, a more innate sympathy for the downtrodden, the unfortunate, than Emma. Emma was basically an intellectual; by an intellectual process she became an anarchist and became committed to the overthrow of capitalism. But he, by an emotional process, reached the same conclusion."[8] In truth, Ben never felt that Emma or her comrades had respect for those people who had been closest to him all his life, the "dregs" of society as Emma sometimes referred to them. The anarchists, on the other hand, saw his affinity for such people as somewhat base and degrading.

The greatest tension was with Berkman, however. In Reitman's early days at "210" Berkman, through a friend, wrote to the Chicago College of Medicine and Surgery: "Dear Sirs: May we kindly request you to favor us with the information as to the date or year of Dr. Benjamin Reitman's graduation?" He strongly suspected that Reitman was not a doctor at all but a charlatan. Although the reply confirmed Ben's medical pedigree, Berkman remained cool and aloof from the wild interloper, a man he regarded as repulsive and ignorant.[9]

For his part, Reitman looked at Berkman as a classic example of the "anti-mind," a personality characterized by a disdain for authority, a zealous attachment to an unpopular and minority cause, and blinded self-denial and self-sacrifice to the point of martyrdom; someone more concerned with stirring controversy than advancing the causes for which he was working, more interested in asserting his immense ego and in intellectual conquest than in helping others. The two men never did reach an accommodation.

But even with his troubles with the anarchists in New York, Ben never minimized the critical influence Emma and her associates had on his intellectual development. "The significance of history, the meaning of literature and the beauty of art all came to me while I nestled securely under the tutelage of Emma . . . I may say that

'210' was the greatest school room that I ever attended. . . ." He did not return again and again to "210" because of the new intellectual delights it afforded, however. The hobo doctor had joined the world of anarchists because it was the world of Emma Goldman, to whom he remained powerfully attached.[10]

The match between Ben and Emma was a bizarre one indeed. A man who had never known a mature relationship with a woman, whose interest in the opposite sex seemed almost exclusively limited to frolic and sport, was now involved with an erudite, passionate woman who had been newly opened to the joys of sexual energy. It was both exhilarating and enervating. At times they seemed like anguished adolescents.

Emma was often astonished at her own dependency on the relationship: "Fool, lovesick fool that I was, blinded by passion . . . I, Emma Goldman, to be carried away like any ordinary woman of forty by a mad attraction for a young man, a stranger picked up at a chance meeting, an alien to my every thought and feeling. . . . "[11] By the end of 1908 she had grasped the dimensions of Ben's philandering and was shaken. Humiliation, jealously, deep feelings of betrayal—all the base but commonplace emotions the public Emma Goldman stood above, the private Emma suffered. "I am so bruised from the wounds of the lack of stability in your love," she wrote to him. He had come into her life, she confessed, with a force that gripped her soul, paralyzed her nerves, silenced her principles. Pride and self-respect had been blotted out by a terrible hunger for love, an insatiable thirst for sexual expression. She who had never clung to anyone was now lapping at his heels "like a dog." She feared for her work: "It will never again amount to anything, the spirit of it was killed . . . What good does it do? Myself? I can earn more through scrubbing floors."[12]

Soon, however, all was right again. Ben's assurances of his love, his promises to change, his apologies—all brought a new wave of joy and elation. Emma wrote, "Two weeks ago today, I was the poorest most dejected creature on Earth. All life, hope, faith were gone, I was simply stranded. Indeed, I was so terribly poor, that I even lacked the strength to end it all, to throw myself in front of the train . . . all was dead and still in me, like in a graveyard. Today, I feel regenerated, reborn, new. What has performed the miracle? My love, only love."[13] Indeed, that love had brought to her an eroticism and sexual fulfillment which before was unimaginable. Ben had opened up to Emma new kinds of sexual pleasure which satisfied, as she said, her "deepest yearning" and had given her a freedom to "love with a madness, an abandonment, a longing, that excludes everything and everyone else in the World." He had come into her world "like a cyclone, sweeping all ideas, notions, convictions, and consideration aside, taking hold of me, as nothing ever has. . . . "[14]

When apart the two exchanged letters that gloried in this sexual abandon, even using abbreviations of words straight from Victorian eroticism—treasure box, mountains, and the like. In this remarkable stream of correspondence, Ben and Emma wrote of sex as they had never done before and never would again:

> Come close to me precious mine, the t-b is calling, all aglow and red with the setting Sun. Mount Blanc and Juno have raised their heads peeping across the Sea, where no one left behind, except Hobo.[15]

> You are such a powerful creature it is difficult to be a simple lover to you. Your passion is so strong, so glorious . . . Oh lover I come to you full of hope and life, full of burning desire for the big long mountains . . . for the sweet tasting treasure box . . . Willie is starved.[16]

> I will have your love, if I have to drink it through your blood if I have to suck it out of W-, if I have to tear it out of you. It's mine! . . . how long until I can spread the t-b over you, the red, red rose, red with my blood, so that you can take its perfume and the m- how they hurt now, with the fullness of passion for you. Hobo, I am mad, mad, mad.[17]

In her writings and oratory Emma Goldman brought sexuality to the center of anarchist theory, railing against the inner oppressions of social and ethical convention, those oppressions which for so long had served to inhibit women. The relationship with Reitman seemed at first to weld her own public and private worlds even more closely. With Ben she could perhaps achieve that idealized love of which she spoke so often. With Ben she could perhaps free herself from stifling inner tensions and conflicts, abandon them to the buoyancy of sexual freedom. It just never worked out quite that way.

Much of the problem was Ben's infidelity. Emma called it sordid and demeaning, cruel not only to her but to the women he pursued. "Your complete lack of justice, of common humanity, of consideration for the rights of another, is simply killing me," she wrote. His indiscriminate prowling was abhorrent and unscrupulous. He was draining the life blood out of innocent victims and thrusting them aside like used toys.[18]

Ben's other women were not the only competition Emma faced for her lover's attentions, however. He freely admitted that a strange emotional bond tied him to his mother, that she had been and would continue to be the most vital woman in his life. Freud himself would probably have enjoyed analyzing Ben, a man whose father ran away and left an emotionally immature young boy to provide for his mother. Had Reitman chosen to explore his emotional life through psychoanalysis, he might have discovered reasons behind his fear of intimacy, a fear rooted in his troubled relationship with his mother.

While Freud may have been fascinated by Ben's instincts toward his mother, Emma was not enjoying them at all. Ben lived with Ida Reitman at various times, and she doted on him, living her life through his. He spent holidays in Chicago and provided as much money for her as he could afford, some of it from gate receipts from Emma's lectures. For a time she moved to New York and lived with Reitman and Emma under the same roof, an aberrant arrangement which made miserable all concerned.

Reitman's early life had been a succession of tramps followed by periods of rather conventional life at home, a pattern of flight and escape matched by a longing for security. He was the errant child breaking away, with all the guilt attached to such separation, only to return for comfort and assurance. With Emma he now had the recklessness that their torrid affair offered, a kind of erotic incestual fantasy; he also had in her a mother figure to teach, scold, and nurture him. Emma was the "blue-eyed Mommy"; he was the "Hobo."

If Ben filled Emma's need for mothering, a need she expressed often in letters and which was even reflected in the choice of the name for her magazine, *Mother Earth,* she filled his need for sexual emotion. Skipping from escapade to escapade, he had never had an intense attachment to a woman, had never been able to cross the chasm between devotion to his mother and deep sexual passion. With Emma he found the bridge. At the same time, playing a mother role, Emma forged a deeply emotional and sexual bond with Ben that he had never before known. Unlike his numerous bedmates, the sexual playthings in his life, Emma touched something elemental in him. Although he would never give up the one-night trysts, although his obsession with carnal pleasures never cooled, he did, with Emma, find himself in a profoundly moving relationship. He even began to talk of marriage and children. When the break from Emma finally came, years later, it was Ben who settled down with a family in a long-term relationship. In opening Ben to a world of women beyond mother and beyond the whorehouse, Emma thus made possible for him romantic experiences that would prove more mature and enduring.

But all this came at a great cost to them both. They were petulant and bitter and resentful. Emma upbraided Ben often, not only for his womanizing but for various habits she found repugnant. She once wrote that his lack of cleanliness had revolted her for a time, but love had overwhelmed her revulsion; his pandering to the press had enraged her, but love had overcome her rage; his slothful eating habits had sickened her, but love had overcome her sickness. She despaired, however, that he had done nothing for the sake of their love: he continued his skirt chasing, his demeaning chase after notoriety, and all the habits she despised. For his part, Ben endured Emma's frequent fusillades against his character. He continued to profess his love and worked tirelessly in her anarchist campaigns. He also offered Emma the intimacy she craved. He couldn't, however, offer her peace of mind.

The anarchist and the hobo doctor nonetheless stayed together, each finding in the other warmth and caring and passion and unforgettable moments. Ben tolerated, as best he could, the aloofness and barely hidden scorn of the intelligentsia of "210," while Emma tolerated, as best she could, Ben's foibles. And even if some at "210" had not realized the influence that Reitman had brought to Emma's work, others did. In 1914 the fiery IWW orator Elizabeth Gurley Flynn, furious over the sorry outcome of the Paterson silkworkers strike, told Emma that the Wobblies had broken her heart. Emma responded, "You are bigger than the IWW and can do the work without their backing." Flynn's reply: "Yes, if I had someone like Ben."[19]

9. Free Speech

Even for Emma Goldman, the veteran agitator whose career fed off the zealous overreaction of public authorities, this period in history was remarkable. As she, Ben Reitman, and fellow American radicals and labor organizers gained supporters, the enemy struck back, burying with a vengeance the constitutional guarantees of free speech and assembly, making it all, as Emma said, an adventure in the desert of American liberty. These were not tales from darkest Russia but from such respectable, all-American burgs as Everett, Washington, and such cosmopolitan, worldly metropolises as San Francisco.[1] Much was amiss.

From the harassment of street-corner soapboxers to the violence against labor recruiters in the fields and at construction sites, even to the intimidation of owners of auditoriums and halls willing to rent to radical orators, the counter-revolution intensified. Pressured by big business representatives, chambers of commerce, and patriotic and religious groups—the "respectable" society—city and state officials acted swiftly to suppress the radical menace. They broke up meetings, censored the mails, passed anti-street-speaking ordinances, herded to jail assorted Wobblies, socialists, single-taxers, and those from the American Federation of Labor.[2] Especially, they went after the anarchists. Hippolyte Havel even saw policemen hold lighted matches to newspapers in a crowded hall trying to create a panic among anarchists gathered inside. The warfare, Havel wrote, had entered a new phase.[3]

On Labor Day 1908, James Eads How's International Brotherhood Welfare Association sponsored a meeting on the problem of the unemployed at New York's Cooper Union. How's old lieutenant, Ben Reitman, was there to deliver an address. In the days before the meeting, Ben, suffering from a severe cold, had fumbled with a few drafts of a speech before finally asking Emma to prepare the remarks. To a large crowd made up of labor groups as well as a few anarchists, including Alexander Berkman, who entered the hall inconspicuously, Ben read Emma's speech, an attack on American capitalism and a plea for the rights of the workers and the underclasses. He concluded with an admission that the words were not his. "Friends," he said, "I am sure you will be glad that this speech was prepared for me by Emma Goldman." With that a small riot ensued. Many in the audience shouted approval; others hissed. Scuffling broke out on the platform among some of the speakers, and one of them, a man characterized by Emma as a trade union yellow-dog and lickspittle, launched into an impassioned assault on Reitman, Goldman, and the whole anarchist crowd, boasting that on his way into the hall he had knocked down a young boy handing out their sick literature.

All of this was too much for Alexander Berkman. As he leaped to his feet to respond to the antianarchist venom, Berkman, along with friend Becky Edelson, was wrestled away by several New York detectives assigned as anarchist watchdogs. At the station house one of the detectives, echoing the feelings of most of America's law enforcement officials, remarked to his captives, "You ought to be brought here on a stretcher." Berkman got five days at Blackwell's Island for disorderly conduct; Edelson was fined ten dollars for vagrancy after refusing to reveal her address.

The Cooper Union melee prompted a number of handwringing accounts in the press about the anarchist threat and the noble actions of the police in warding off possible violence. But to Ben's friend, James Eads How, the incident was only another example of official, unwarranted suppression of those fighting for the rights of the oppressed. "I am an Anarchist in principle," he declared, "because I believe in as much personal liberty as possible. . . . "[4]

In October, Emma and Ben once again headed west for speaking engagements in Rochester, Pittsburgh, Cleveland, Cincinnati, Indianapolis, and other cities. With the exception of Cleveland, where the liberal influence of Mayor Tom Johnson held sway, police harassment reached new heights of absurdity. The arrival of the anarchists was usually greeted by the kind of panic more appropriately reserved for an infectious plague or an invading army.

Some reporters were astonished to find that Emma Goldman and her paramour were not execrable maniacs. One Kansas City scribe was surprised by Emma's appearance: "Her defiance of the existing order includes corsets. She dresses plainly—a brown skirt, loose waist and a flowing tie." Astonished by the content of her speeches on the tour—poetry, philosophy, and drama—the reporter also enjoyed the talents of Emma's hobo advance man. Ben explained that his promotion job was usually made easy, for when word spread from the press that Red Emma, the destroyer, was about to hit town, the police could be counted on to do the rest.[5] Everyone, it seemed, wanted to hoist by the neck Emma and her ilk, those "dirty, unwashed, unkept traitors" who, as the *Portland Oregonian* editorialized, "have cursed this country with their presence."[6] From the "bear hunter in the White House," as Emma characterized the president, to the police on the beat, all of American officialdom wanted a part in the crusade to cleanse society of these alien curs.

In Seattle, Emma and Ben were arrested for violating property rights after holding a meeting in an unrented hall. In Everett, Washington, police stopped a scheduled meeting after informing the anarchists that they were in danger of being tarred and feathered, drawn and quartered. In Bellingham, Washington, Police Chief Cade, protecting his community from "treason, conspiracy, and outlawry," arrested the two on charges of conspiring to hold an unlawful assembly. Offered the choice of taking a midnight train out of Bellingham or spending time in its jail, they opted for jail. "Many of our radical friends still fondly cherish the belief that we enjoy free speech in this country," Emma wrote. The West Coast trip was making a mockery of that belief.[7]

In San Francisco the police badgering continued. At the Victory Theatre on January 14, club-wielding authorities herded a large crowd out into the street, arresting Emma and Ben on charges of "conspiracy to riot" and "disturbing the public peace." They joined behind bars Alexander Horr, a leading spirit of the Social Science League, already in custody for his efforts in advertising the planned anarchist lectures. Additional charges were levied against Emma and Ben in the days following: "unlawful assemblage, denouncing as unnecessary all organized government, and preaching Anarchist doctrine."[8]

William Buwalda, the soldier who had the previous year been court-martialed at the Presidio, dishonorably discharged, and imprisoned at Alcatraz for consorting with anarchists, was once again arrested, this time for denouncing the treatment of Emma and Ben at the Victory Theatre. Buwalda, who had been reluctantly pardoned by President Roosevelt from a five-year prison term, later sent to the secretary of war a medal he had earned for service in the Philippines. "It speaks of raids and burnings," he wrote, "of many prisoners taken and like vile beasts thrown in the foulest of prisons . . . of a country laid waste with fire and sword; of animals useful to man wantonly killed; of men, women, and children hunted like wild beasts, and all this in the name of Liberty, Humanity and Civilization."[9] To Ben and Emma, William Buwalda was a testament to the power of anarchist teaching, a soul freed from the debasement of military indoctrination and the simplistic notions of patriotism and national pride. To others, however, he was a prime example of the corrupting influence of dangerous fanatics.

With the announcement of the San Francisco arrests, monies began to pour into the coffers of the Free Speech League, a loosely knit organization designed to provide relief to radicals throttled by police and legal authorities. From Los Angeles and New York, from Portland and Seattle, even from friends in Canada, contributions mounted. Cassius Cook, secretary of the League, talked of the remarkable response that the San Francisco case had elicited, "awakening the liberty-loving people to the danger and making them conscious of the evils that lie in the wake of repression of free speech and free assembly."[10]

On January 19 the anarchists appeared before the San Francisco police court. As defense attorney Ernest Kirk grilled 100 prospective jurors, Emma and Ben heard firsthand what most Americans thought of anarchism ("The paper say it teaches bombs and dynamite") and of Emma Goldman ("The papers say she induces people to kill"). Blaming the press for this abysmal distortion, Emma found even the police "as white and virtuous as the proverbial angels" compared to most of the damnable reporters.

During the trial a fidgety prosecuting attorney, attempting to show that Emma Goldman endangered society, was reduced to linking the anarchists with the IWW, pointing out that members of both groups wore red shirts and neckties. The point seemed overdrawn to three men in the jury box who shifted uneasily, red draped from their necks. The anarchists were acquitted, and within two days Emma was addressing a massive reception of 2,000 people in the largest hall in the city. The radicals settled down for several weeks of nightly meetings.

Although the trip had been grueling and a financial disaster, at least from Emma's perspective, she looked on the San Francisco acquittal as a vindication of the anarchist message and a warm demonstration of solidarity by comrades across the country. The letters of support, the money, and the personal involvement of men such as Cassius Cook, Ernest Kirk, and William Buwalda invigorated Emma with a new sense of mission. And as for the manager-lover at her side: "He has been locked up many times for vagrancy. But so long as a man is not an Anarchist, he is still considered respectable. It is the Doctor's first experience to be arrested for such an awful crime as 'denouncing, as unnecessary, all organized government.' But he stood his ground handsomely. He is rather disappointed that he missed the chance to swing between two thieves."[11]

Ben loved San Francisco and took the opportunity to visit many of his old haunts. He especially liked Nathan Greist's bohemian salon, where he could trade iconoclastic musings with West Coast intellectuals. Doc once argued in Greist's Market Street apartment that society should take a more liberal and sensible view toward rape. "The rape of the Sabine women by the old Romans," Ben surmised, "was the real beginning of the Roman Empire." After hearing Ben's novel historical interpretation, Jack London claimed he picked up a volume on Roman history with renewed interest.[12]

London, although usually warm and gracious to Reitman and Goldman, had little use for their anarchist philosophies, however, regarding them as soft and unconstructive. Ben and Emma once visited London and his wife, Charmian, at their home outside San Francisco. Admitting to an admiration of the "big souls" and martyr-sincerity of the anarchists, the socialist London nevertheless considered them misguided dreamers. "I believe in law," he said, "you can see it in my books—all down in black and white." The dreamer Reitman attempted to engage London in intellectual combat a number of times, but the renowned author seemed more amused than challenged. After Ben continued to banter with his host, at one point inferring that London, who had spent a number of years on the road, knew little about tramps, the latter got his revenge. As Ben sat down to dinner at the end of the visit, he confronted a little red volume on his plate. When he, himself a consummate practical joker, opened the book, it exploded. "Never did anyone jump so high as that red anarchist!" London later remarked. In his view, when it came to actual violence the anarchists were mere bluffers, unaccustomed to the practical ways of carrying out the things they preached so vehemently.[13]

Emma and Ben had originally planned to follow their West Coast trip with a journey to Australia, a visit which, they hoped, would not only break new ground in the anarchist crusade but offer some relief from the grind of the American tour. But the Australian venture was now a shaky proposition, given the meager proceeds garnered from the winter tour. Soon the trip was no longer possible, the final death blow delivered by a federal judge in Buffalo, New York. He revoked the citizenship of Jacob Kershner, a man whose true identity was known not only among Emma Goldman's closest intimates but among federal investigators. "Through this order," the *New York Times* reported, "all rights of citizenship also are taken from Kershner's wife, who is none other than Emma Goldman, the woman leader of the anarchists of this country, whose fiery teachings, it was charged by many, incited Leon Czolgosz to the assassination of President McKinley."[14]

Federal warfare against the anarchists had taken an ominous turn, one of jackboot intimidation, and anarchists correctly saw the citizenship revocation as the government's first serious move to rid the country of an arch-nemesis. Emma could now ill afford to leave the United States because any request for a return visa would probably be denied. With the federal noose further tightening, as Emma and her comrades scotched all plans for Australia and began to weigh the implications of the escalating war with the authorities, the ultimate threat now loomed: deportation.

Emma and Ben headed east, making stops in several Texas cities; she finally returned to New York, he to Chicago. "Reviewing the struggle of the last six months, I can say that but for Perseverance it would have been impossible," Emma wrote—perseverance and her friends, especially Ben Reitman, whose "unfaltering optimism" and "great zeal" had made the many ordeals bearable.[15]

Ben stayed only a few weeks in Chicago, for the lure of battle was compelling, the limelight intoxicating. All across the country police now concerned themselves with his peregrinations; newspapers craved his words. If his personal relationship with Emma oscillated wildly between passion and bitterness, the heady notoriety was a constant, and he basked in it. His commitment to the anarchist cause became ever stronger as he saw glaring instances of official injustice, legal contempt for human rights, and police violence. If he remained an outsider in the anarchist ranks, he had nevertheless become a more dedicated convert to anarchist beliefs.

In the spring of 1909 the fight over free speech mounted. The issue was clear enough: Under what authority did the police and other civil authorities assume responsibility for public censorship in denying the anarchists and their audiences the use of lecture halls and other forums? The answer was also clear: They acted from force, not legal sanction. Emma Goldman was being prevented from speaking not because of the objectionable content of her addresses but merely because she was Emma Goldman. Police pressure on hallkeepers was now common in many cities. When anarchists were able to secure places to hold meetings, audiences were sometimes driven forcibly into the streets as if they were rioters. Anarchist speakers were routinely arrested on charges of disorderly conduct or incitement to riot even before they had uttered a single inflammatory word. Much of the American press now began to question this law of the thug, and from the pens of editorialists, most of whom were anything but enamored of Emma's teachings, came a call for reason, for respect of law and constitutional guarantees.[16] For the most part, the calls went unheeded.

On May 15, Emma and Ben were in New Haven, Connecticut, for a meeting at Colonial Hall. Police Chief Henry Cowles, himself not one to interfere with an individual's right to free speech, allowed the two anarchists to enter the hall. Cowles's cheshire grin betrayed his scheme, however. Once Emma and Ben were inside, police lined the doors, thus separating the speakers from their listeners. The *New York Times* headline the next day read, "Police Trick Emma Goldman!" The *New Haven Union* was not so amused:

> It cannot be denied that law-abiding citizens have a right peaceably to assemble to hear her if they so desire. It cannot be denied that Chief Cowles, by an abuse of his power, can stop citizens doing so, because he did it last

night. But it must be said that in doing this Chief Cowles is violating the most sacred rights of men, that he is the real and only law violator, that he is the one who is engendering hatred born of police persecution in the public mind, that he is teaching the people that might makes right, that he is advertising Miss Goldman and gaining for her public sympathy, that he is doing, in short, all that a chief of police with a spark of common sense would not do.[17]

Henry Cowles was unruffled. He wrote to the attorney general of the United States on May 15, 1909, that he had prevented Emma and Ben from making their foul speeches, that Emma was probably the instigator of Czolgosz's murder of President McKinley, and that the good and respectable people of New Haven had no use for such undesirables. "I also wish to call to your attention," Cowles wrote, "that President Taft . . . will be in this city again in the near future, and there may be a few more Czolgosz' in our vicinity, who might be influenced by Emma Goldman, and who under such influence might attempt to do bodily harm to President Taft."[18]

On May 23, Emma and Ben were back in New York for a meeting in Lexington Hall on East 116th Street. Emma's Sunday morning speech to an audience of approximately 400 was on "Modern Drama, the Strongest Disseminator of Radical Thought." In the audience was a central office police detective named Rafsky, charged by his superiors with monitoring the talk to ensure that Emma did not stray too far afield into the forbidden zone of anarchism.

Things went well for Emma, the police later reported, until she brought up Joan of Arc and other martyrs. Detective Rafsky, sniffing in the talk the strong scent of revolution, bounded to the front of the hall demanding that Emma stick to Ibsen or whatever. As Emma continued her speech, the detective remained close by her side, waiting to pounce should the need again arise. Predictably, the unrepentent anarchist ventured once more into the channels of radical politics. Rafsky raised his hand toward Emma, a movement of "gesticulation" the police said later. Many in the audience, thinking that the detective was about to attack the speaker, overturned tables and chairs as they surged to the front. The frightened Rafsky turned tail, scurrying out the back of the building toward safety and reinforcements.

From the East 126th Station they came, some forty men led by Captain Walsh. Emma had vanished, but an angry crowd milled in the street, including Becky Edelson, who leaped on one of the policemen, authorities claimed, grabbing his nightstick. She and a companion were arrested for disorderly conduct. One of the men in the crowd wrote to the *New York Evening Sun,* "And what has become of our much-praised 'freedom of speech'?"[19]

Another in the crowd at Lexington Hall that morning was Alden Freeman, son of a prominent Standard Oil stockholder and a man who traced his ancestry to the pilgrims, thus entitling him to membership in the exclusive Mayflower Society and the Sons of the American Revolution—an unlikely ally of Emma Goldman. Freeman was genuinely shocked by the blatant police action he saw that day and invited Emma to speak in his hometown of East Orange, New Jersey, and to be a guest at a luncheon of his fellow members of the Mayflower Society. "Once people see that you are not as you have been described in the papers," he told her, "they will be glad to come and hear you." Freeman was quite wrong. At the luncheon, some of the matronly folk smirked while many others disdainfully marched out. Freeman was later asked to resign as deputy governor of the organization.

With even more vigor than the Mayflowerites, the civic leaders of East Orange challenged the heretics of Alden Freeman. On the night of June 8 police closed the doors to English's Hall, where Freeman had scheduled Emma's appearance. Undaunted, Freeman mustered close to 1,000 people at the hall and paraded them across town, past the stately homes of East Orange to a large barn he owned at the corner of Central and Main avenues. There, by the light of oil lamps, standing on a chair, to an audience sitting in wagons and on the floor, others peering in through the windows, Emma spoke. "As I drove here," she declared, "it came to me that those Russians battling for freedom could not have believed possible what happened in your town tonight. They think this country is the cradle of liberty. . . ." Emma completed the speech without interference from the police, who squirmed among the others in the barn for a view. Her host jocularly pointed out that Emma had no horns or hoofs, that she had not swooped into the fair city of Orange on a broomstick. She was, he said, the most powerful force for free speech and thought in America. Alden Freeman had hosted what anarchists later fondly called "The Orange Barn Party."[20]

On June 30 Freeman was among a throng of 2,000 that jammed the Great Hall of Cooper Union for a protest meeting called by the Free Speech League. Aristocratic, bulldog-jawed, humorous, a man who in the space of a few weeks had suddenly become a knight errant to the left and turncoat to his fellow pilgrim descendants, Freeman regaled the audience with the story of "Spotless City," his own East Orange, spotless because such topics as Ibsen had been beaten away by the energetic town patriots. He was joined by others that night, sweltering in the Union's confines: radical writer Harry Kelly; Congressman Robert Baker, known as "Anti-Pass Baker" because of his fight against the bribery of free railroad passes; and Voltairine de Cleyre, anarchist philosophe of Philadelphia, an eloquent writer and a stirring speaker.

De Cleyre decried the censorship of the times, that creature of "large biceps, large necks, large stomachs, and pyramidal foreheads" sitting in judgment of things moral, social, scientific, and artistic. "Ah, when Emma Goldman shall next lecture upon the Modern Drama, let her not forget this drama of the censorship, wherein avoirdupois is the hero, and the people of America—if you please, the scientists, the artists, the teachers, the literateurs—are the pitiful clowns." The power of the police to divine what words may be dangerous to society and to suppress them, de Cleyre said, was not only ignorant but invidious.

Eugene Debs, Socialist candidate for president, added his voice. In a letter read at the meeting Debs said, "Emma Goldman has been persecuted and outraged by the police. She has a right to be heard, and that she has repeatedly been suppressed by force is the shame of us all. If she has no right to be heard, neither have we; and if we suffer her to be silenced, we ought to be silenced. Cowardice deserves no hearing, but only contempt, and we are certainly guilty of cowardice if we do not fight for the preservation of free speech."[21]

Despite the growth of free speech committees, the support from disparate labor groups, and favorable editorial comment, Emma Goldman still found most minds (as well as doors) closed to her. A pariah to civic and political leaders, Emma was seen as such a threat to established values that arguments about constitutional liberties of free speech and charges of censorship carried little force. The power was in the grasp of those who wanted her silent.

Ben Reitman plugged ahead, seeking building owners willing to rent to anarchists, softening up the galloping paranoia of mayors and police chiefs. In late summer and fall the anarchists were in Rhode Island, Massachusetts, and Vermont. With many large halls off-limits, they held meetings in abandoned and half-constructed buildings and out-of-doors. Chased out of such towns as Burlington, Vermont, and Molden, Massachusetts, Ben and Emma thought they had found the American Lourdes when they reached Lynn, Massachusetts. There, the mayor shocked everyone, including the anarchists, by declaring, "If the people want to hear Miss Goldman and she wants to talk, she is entitled to go ahead."[22] The mayor of Lynn was a notable exception, however, for most officials parroted the words of James E. Burke, mayor of Burlington: "In the name of peace, of society . . . you can not speak here tonight." "Thus runs the tale of two weary wanderers," Emma wrote, "in quest of the thing that everybody worships and which, like all idols is non-existent—free speech."[23]

In late September the wanderers seized on a different strategy. They decided to take the free-speech war to a single, major city, to concentrate all efforts on winning a decisive victory. To this end, they hunkered down in the City of Brotherly Love.

10. Cradle of Liberty

James Madison, principal architect of the Bill of Rights, to Thomas Jefferson, 1788: ". . . experience proves the inefficacy of a bill of rights on those occasions when its control is most needed. Repeated violations of these parchment barriers have been committed by overbearing majorities in every State . . . wherever the real power in Government lies, there is the danger of oppression."[1] Philadelphia: birthplace of the United States; "Cradle of Liberty"; colonial center for art, science, education, and commerce; hub of statesmen, philosophers, and writers; heir of William Penn's vision of personal freedom and tolerance. Here, on the bluffs overlooking the Schuylkill and Delaware rivers, where seventeen-year-old Benjamin Franklin arrived in 1723 with hardly a shilling to his name, and where, over a half century later, in the feverish heat of the summer of 1787, an older and wiser Benjamin Franklin presided over the constitutional convention, American history breathed. From the fading, yellowed parchments and crystal inkwells of Independence Hall to a cracked bell, the symbol of liberty, to the cobblestone walks, ancient taverns, ivy-covered courtyards, and austere Quaker meetinghouses, Philadelphia in the early twentieth century still made Americans think about their past.

As tourists visited places made almost sacred by Jefferson and Madison and Hamilton, they talked knowingly of liberty and freedom and constitutional rights. But for some visitors to Philadelphia in the brisk October of 1909, all of this was so much bunk. City leaders had decided that for certain individuals freedom of speech was not a right. Emma Goldman and Ben Reitman were prepared to make Philadelphia a battleground over the free speech issue, and the city's civil leaders were determined to take up the challenge. When asked whether Philadelphia would allow Miss

Goldman to deliver a speech, a police spokesman replied, "Not if a fire hose can prevent her." Such devices were most distasteful to anarchists, he went on, so "she had better put on a rubber suit."[2]

In late September Ben scurried around Philadelphia generating newspaper copy, arranging for meetings, attempting to enlist supporters from other labor and radical groups, all this in the face of the police commissioner's announced declaration that the ears of his city would not hear the poisonous sounds of Emma Goldman and her ilk. On September 26 Ben addressed the Central Labor Union, encouraging the members to attend the anarchists' scheduled meeting at the Odd Fellows Hall the following day. He called for an outpouring of support from all those who believed in the right of freedom of speech, whether socialists, single-taxers, or labor leaders. "The Constitution of this state allows free speech," Ben declared. "I believe in free speech, and so do all fair-minded men. The idea of attempting to stop Emma Goldman before they know what she is going to talk about is out of all human reason."[3]

On the night of September 28 the Odd Fellows Hall was jammed to the doors. Outside, several hundred policemen lined all sides of the building as nearly 5,000 people along Broad Street waited for the expected confrontation between the anarchists and the authorities. Leisurely, a little after eight o'clock, Emma stepped out of her hotel alone and headed on foot toward the Hall, immersing herself inconspicuously in the crowd of onlookers, thinking that perhaps in all of this hubbub and the press of people she could quietly slip unnoticed through the cordon of police and into the packed building. She didn't succeed. As Emma edged toward the Hall, Philadelphia's police, thoroughly briefed on the features of the hated little woman, warned about possible ploys and dodges, rose to the occasion. She was spotted and forced away from the scene, back to her hotel.

Inside the Odd Fellows Hall Ben took over. "The greatest crime of the century has taken place," he screeched, his excitement exceeded only by his exaggeration. "Miss Goldman has been insulted and held up by a ruffian who rules this city." The mayor, Ben predicted, would soon be driving a wagon, and his minion, the police chief, would be tending bar.

Stridently vowing that the anarchists would prevail in this struggle, Ben warned that such bluecoat repression usually leads to violence. His words soon seemed prophetic. As Voltairine de Cleyre entered the hall to a rousing reception, a photographer snapped a flash, startling a few individuals standing nearby. One cried out, "A bomb! A bomb!" With many in the crowd rushing to the doors, overturning chairs, with several women falling to their knees, Reitman bounded to the lecturn and roared out that there was no danger. Remarkably, the crowd quieted and no one was injured. Ben then concluded the meeting with an announcement: the anarchists would seek redress in the courts. This was certainly a novel tactic for a group whose antipathy toward legal processes was pronounced. Into the den would go Daniel for help from the lion.[4]

True to their word the anarchists, accompanied by attorney John Henry Nelson, marched to Common Pleas Court No. 3 on September 30 and filed an injunction to restrain city hall and the police department from interfering with free speech.[5] In the days following, Emma and Ben hosted several small gatherings of radicals to raise money for what they assumed would be a protracted legal struggle. "Emma Goldman will address a public meeting in this town," Ben told a reporter at one of the gatherings, "unless death prevents. You are skeptical? Well, the sun may not rise tomorrow, and in the same parallel Emma Goldman may not speak."

The publicity surrounding the anarchists was not endearing them to large segments of Philadelphia society, and they soon were kicked out of the Hotel Wilmot and refused quarters at the Windsor Hotel. After temporarily piling their baggage in the offices of their lawyer, Ben finally was able to rent a room on Arch Street, to serve as battle headquarters for the coming campaign. "I shall remain here," Emma declared, "until I have seen my purpose accomplished or be placed under such restraint that work for the immediate future is impossible."[6] As events were unfolding, the latter possibility seemed more likely.

A reporter for the *Ledger* was shocked to find that Emma was such "a very little woman" to have created such a stir. The high priestess of anarchy was "almost good looking," he wrote, with a magnetic personality, a rich and pleasant voice, and a reservoir of ideas on a number of subjects. She had a peaceful face, the reporter noted, suggesting a well-ordered life rather than the anarchy she preached. Emma even confessed to being proud of her age—forty years: "When we women have something in our heads we cease to care about being young. It's only the empty-headed that want to keep up the farce." Asked if she supported women's suffrage, Emma said that the ballot would not free women anymore than it had freed men. "But I, of course, think that women should be entitled to all the privileges men enjoy, and, indeed, more, since they populate the world and therefore perform the greatest service to mankind."[7]

Many of the visitors who made their way to Emma's Arch Street flat during those days were young, local factory girls infused with her vision of the new woman—self-reliant, independent, freethinking, uninhibited. But it was more than Emma's words and ideas that were compelling; she was a personal figure of defiance and agitation, a symbol of resistance to hoary barriers, the archetype of modern womanhood. From her open attacks on traditional family structure to her advocacy of free love, from openly puffing on cigarettes with men in barrooms to talking about contraceptives, Emma was the consummate rebel, personally taking on established customs at great risk. Harlot, devil, alien, traitor: the biting epithets from much of society always followed, but she nevertheless brought new spirit to many who were tired of institutions that, like those insufferable steel corsets, had for too long crushed the American woman.

Emma was seen by her enemies as a wretched Fagin, leading innocent youth along wayward paths. But it was startling, one newspaper reporter noted, to see many of these girls, some of whom had never spent two consecutive years in school, quoting Ibsen and Tolstoy. Some of her followers even pushed Emma toward more extremist positions. "Be violent," one of the factory girls said to her in the Arch Street room. "Why be called a destroyer and then be peaceful." Smiling, Emma replied, "We will gain nothing that way, Lena."[8]

On October 1 Emma wrote an open letter to the *Ledger.* Recalling the words and deeds of Thoreau and Emerson and William Lloyd Garrison, individuals who had raised their voices for justice and dignity, she promised a ceaseless struggle against the unwarranted governmental invasion of liberty being displayed in Philadelphia. Personal freedom must not be subject to the whims of ignorant and misguided mayors and police chiefs who wielded the power of censorship through physical force. "The club may be a mighty weapon but it sinks into insignificance before reason and human integrity. Therefore, I shall speak in Philadelphia."[9]

On October 8 the anarchists, various members of the Free Speech League, and other supporters held an exuberant demonstration at the Labor Lyceum. In attendance were four police lieutenants and a force of fifty. Still awaiting the decision of the court in her injunction against Philadelphia authorities, Emma Goldman did not join her comrades. Several speakers, including Voltairine de Cleyre, Leonard Abbott, and Ben Reitman, mixed sneering remarks about the gentlemen standing guard at the back of the hall with lilting expressions about the blood of martyrs and the principles for which the nation's forefathers sacrificed their lives and fortunes. But the high spot of the evening was a letter from Emma, which received such an enthusiastic response that it was read twice. With each phrase of their Jeanne d'Arc the crowd thundered. She wrote, "I register my protest not against the gagging of my voice. Silence is more powerful than speech. I protest with all the ardor of my soul against the perpetuation of the majority lie. Liberty fettered by law! Independence at the behest of gold! Freedom of expression at the mercy of the club!"[10]

The anarchists certainly were under no illusions that the courts of Philadelphia were likely to leap to their rescue against the city leadership. In appealing to the legal system, however, the radicals had made an adroit move. A court ruling in their favor would be an eye-popping victory and vindication; a defeat would add fuel to anarchist charges about public harassment, censorship, and denial of constitutional rights.

The court acted as expected. On October 15 it upheld the right of public officers to deny free speech when they suspected "that dangerous and disturbing sentiments, tending to disturb the peace, would be uttered." The court said that all anarchists, believing as they did in the right of individuals to regulate their own conduct according to their own notions of right and wrong, stood for the overthrow of the government, presumably by force. Public pronouncement of such a philosophy would likely inflame the populace and lead to civil unrest, the court claimed. In denying free speech in Philadelphia, the government and its agents had acted in a necessary posture of self-defense.

Beyond the basic right of the government to preserve order, the court continued, was the unfavorable position of anarchists under federal law. Anarchists had no rights of naturalization and, indeed, when their identity was known beforehand they were denied entrance into the United States. The federal government, therefore, had indelibly cast its shadow of opprobrium over anarchist beliefs. The court in Philadelphia was not about to offer a forum for individuals held in such contempt by federal law. Emma Goldman, Ben Reitman, and the other anarchists had come to seek redress with dirty hands. The constitutional right of free speech in this case was "necessarily subject to limitation and restriction, arising out of its abuse. . . . "[11]

Shortly after the decision was announced, the radicals learned that the Spanish revolutionist Francisco Ferrer, founder of the nonsectarian, open-education, "modern school" movement, had been executed in Barcelona, convicted of inciting a general strike. Emma, who had strongly supported the Spaniard's liberal ideas of eliminating church-state indoctrination from the educational process, left Philadelphia to attend meetings in New York commemorating Ferrer.

Back in Philadelphia, Ben organized a protest meeting. On October 17, as he had done in the streets of Chicago with hoboes, he led a band of radicals down Broad Street toward Industrial Hall. Barred from the building by a large force of police, Ben led the crowd to the Radical Library at Fifth and Pine, a haven for socialists and free thinkers. Although the police allowed the crowd to enter the library, they quickly stopped attempts by the radicals to hold a meeting, even gently roughing up Reitman. The *Ledger* reported that Ben had gotten what he wanted—martyrdom. His only regret, the paper claimed, was that he had not been arrested.

The Philadelphia campaign was now playing to Reitman's beat. He eagerly approached a newspaper reporter to ask whether he wanted some good copy. "Does a flower want sunshine?" the reporter replied. The next day, reporter in tow and shadowed by plainclothes detectives, Ben started down Chestnut Street. Suddenly he yelled, "Let's run." Into Wanamakers he sprinted, charging through the aisles, up and over a counter or two, down some stairs, and out a side door to the street, then into and out of a saloon, his huge bulk, flying cape, and flailing walking stick drawing all manner of attention. With the reporter and the detectives laboring to keep up, the surprisingly sprightly anarchist charged into grocery stores, corset shops, and beauty parlors. After a sufficiently teasing romp, Ben went for the finale: the artful train-jumper, the hobo extraordinaire, hopped a speeding streetcar with grace and savoir faire, substantiating his reputation earned long ago as a profesh of the rails. The reporter just managed to scramble aboard; one detective tried it and was almost crunched, and Ben hopped off to assist his wounded pursuer. With little more than his pride severely injured, the detective pleaded, "Reitman cut it out. You're killing me. I can't help it. I got to follow you. The chief don't want you locked up. He only wants us to follow you." Ben escorted the detective, his partner, and the reporter to the nearest bar, where they all hoisted a few.

The story of his escapade through downtown Philadelphia made the papers, as he knew it would. Emma, just returned from New York and some somber meetings of radicals paying homage to the memory of a fallen comrade, was not amused. Neither was Voltairine de Cleyre, the introspective anarchist philosopher. Both women scolded Ben for turning the free-speech fight into a tawdry sideshow. Voltairine, Ben said, never forgave him for this and other childish demonstrations.[12]

Police gagging of the anarchists reached the outer edges of the absurd on October 20. Reitman had issued thirteen letters of invitation to free-speech advocates for a social evening at the Arch Street apartment. At about 7:00 P.M. a squad of detectives, alerted to this private gathering, invaded the house, informed the landlady that no meeting was to take place, and positioned themselves at the bottom of the stairs to prevent visitors from reaching Emma upstairs. "My room is private," Emma complained, "and I fortunately have the privilege of having the choice of my visitors." But in Philadelphia she had no such privilege. One by one the guests arrived, only to be turned away by the police. Meanwhile, the husband of the landlady returned home to find his apartment house in a state of siege. After a hurried, excited huddle with the authorities, he decided to ask Emma and her companions to leave for good. All of this commotion was dreadful for business.

Ben lividly heaped scorn on the police, likening their conduct to that of the Russian autocracy. Emma remarked, "This was not a public meeting, nor did the public know what we were to talk about."[13] All of which was true; none of which made any difference. Not only did the anarchists lack the right of freedom of speech for public meetings, they now lacked the right to assemble a small group of individuals for a strictly private affair. In addition, they were without living quarters. This free-speech campaign in Philadelphia was clearly at an end.

Nearly broke, wearied by the extended stay and constant police surveillance, Emma and Ben left brotherly love behind and returned to New York. They had been successful in marshaling some public opinion in their favor, and even the Philadelphia newspapers, which abhorred the anarchist message, sided with them on this particular issue. Positioning themselves, for a change, in a favorable political stance, the anarchists in later speaking tours were able to win a number of free-speech battles, especially in 1910 and 1911 in such cities as Buffalo, Indianapolis, Columbus, Cheyenne, and Chicago. But the war, the conflict between power and liberty, between majority rule and minority rights, was another matter. Constitutional provisions, no matter how entrenched in law, have never been self-enforcing; rather, they have always depended on the spirit of tolerance at work in society. In 1909 the spirit of tolerance toward anarchists and other radicals was at a low level and sinking even lower.

In the famous 1918 "sedition" amendment to the Espionage Act of the previous year, Justice Oliver Wendell Holmes, in *Schenck* v. *United States,* enunciated the doctrine of "clear and present danger" in the matter of free speech: "The question in every case is whether the words used aroused in such circumstances and are of such a nature as to create a clear and present danger that they will bring about . . . substantive evils. . . . "[14] Echoes of Philadelphia in 1909, when many feared the "substantive evils" that an unleashed Emma Goldman, Ben Reitman, and their comrades might bear. The Liberty Bell's crack, to the anarchists at least, held a measure of symbolism not normally ascribed to it. For their part, the radicals preferred instead to recall the words of Milton in his *Areopagitica* of 1644: "Give me the liberty to know, to utter, and to argue freely according to conscience, above all liberties."[15]

11. Village Sex

Although alive with atheists, cubists, poets, free-thinkers, free-lovers, women with bobbed hair, and assorted intellectuals, Greenwich Village flinched with the arrival of Ben Reitman. In Chicago's bohemian circles on the Near North Side and its nightlife on State Street, Reitman's eccentricities and bizarre behavior were legendary. In Greenwich Village he would also make his mark.

Lincoln Steffens once told two students at Harvard, Walter Lippmann and John ("Jack") Reed, "There is not enough intellectual curiosity in your college."[1] By 1910 the three were all in New York, as were Hutchins Hapgood, author of *Types from City Streets,* chronicler of urban lives and dialects; Max Eastman, a young philosophy instructor at Columbia University, who would soon become editor of the socialist publication *The Masses;* Carl Van Vechten, apostle of Harlem's jazz, author of *Nigger Heaven,* experimenter with hallucinatory drugs; and Harry Kemp, the tramp poet.

"Within a block of my house," Jack Reed wrote, "was all the adventure in the world; within a mile was every foreign country."[2] Ben Reitman, as he had in Chicago and other cities, marched those streets, from the Bowery flophouses to the tenderloin dives, to the enclaves of the Chinese, Italians, Jews, and Germans, to the musty gambling parlors and low-class dance halls. On those excursions he flourished; at other times, among many of Emma Goldman's friends, he was troubled. In these people Ben saw much pretension that repulsed him, much intellectualism that was intimidating.

When Jack Reed joined *The Masses* he dreamed of attacking old, crusty systems and morals, the legacies of dead men, and of lunging at "spectres . . . with a rapier," of being arrogant and impertinent in the name of reform.[3] Such insurgence and the bohemianism of the Village as well as its spirit of radical commitment and social ferment, should have charged Ben. But the kind of outcasts and social misfits and protesters with whom he had mingled on the road and in Chicago generally were not of the Village type. Here, many of the radical thinkers came from bourgeois backgrounds and carried university diplomas; many of them displayed an intellectual arrogance that incensed the Chicago newcomer.

The cultural movements in pre–World War I New York were dizzying, stamped by realism in arts and letters, the advent of modern drama and dance, new theories of education and psychology, a startling array of -isms advanced by zealous proselytizers. Iconoclasm was in; genteelism was out. The intellectuals embraced, often uncritically, avant-garde European philosophers, especially Nietzsche, invoking certain of his ideas to bolster their own preconceived notions and ignoring many of his prejudices. Emma Goldman, for example, praised his attacks on Christianity but said little about his antifeminism.

The choice gathering spot for the spear-carriers of the social revolution was the chandeliered salon of Mabel Dodge on Fifth Avenue. At Mabel's, the parlor poets, artists, philosophers, and political writers could lounge on the white bearskin rug and talk of the new day. Lincoln Steffens recalled a stream of "poor and rich, labor skates, scabs, strikers and unemployed, painters, musicians, reporters, editors," all arguing and pontificating. Mabel had evenings set aside for various issues and themes: the Psychoanalytic Evening, the Family Planning Evening, the Anarchist Evening. Wealthy, cultured, twice-divorced, Mabel Dodge had grown tired of littering her villa in Tuscany with treasured pieces of art. In New York she found passion and excitement. She also found John Reed, with whom she carried on an impetuous, if tenuous, affair.[4]

Mabel, whom some people swore could haunt houses and induce other psychic phenomena, hosted the important "Heads"—of newspapers, movements, groups. She was, she said, a "Species of Head Hunter." The philosophers, artists, reporters, and musicians streamed into the fabulous apartment to taste not only the midnight feasts of turkey, veal, ham, cheese, and expensive wines but also the stimulating intellectual fare. On one occasion, Emma, Alexander Berkman, and Ben defended anarchism; Big Bill Haywood, Carlo Tresca, and Elizabeth Gurley Flynn spoke for the Wobblies; and William English Walling and Walter Lippmann talked socialism.[5]

Sinclair Lewis, making light of some of the Village's intellectual pursuits, talked of the inhabitants sampling new urges and the latest keys to self-realization. They talked of independence, he wrote, and of nature and direct action; they formed little theaters and political leagues. In "Jesse Saffron's" parlor they wrestled with issues of "war, sex, Zuprushin, Mr. Max Pincus' paintings, birth control, eugenics, psycho-analysis, the Hobohemian Players, biological research, Nona Barnes' new way of dressing, her hair, sex, H. G. Wells, the lowness of the popular magazines, Zuprushin, Mr. Max Pincus' poetry, and a few new aspects of sex."[6] All of the Village was talking about a few new aspects of sex.

The all-night discussions of Freudianism at Mabel Dodge's and other Village retreats revealed the glories of free expression and self-awareness and the dangers of suppressed desire. Throughout the Village resounded the rallying cries for sexual freedom. Walter Lippmann argued that repression of pleasure could wreak havoc and recalled the Puritans with their lack of theaters, dances, and festivals, and their plethora of burning witches.[7]

The sexual experimentation and liberation of the Village were, at least on the surface, signs of philosophical advancement, attacks on convention and moral silliness. Monogamy was for the uptown bourgeoisie. "We all had a rationale about sex," one of Jack Reed's friends once observed. "We had discovered Freud—and we considered being libidinous a kind of sacred duty." Such theoretical commitment to sexual freedom, however, often broke down in the face of specific application. Gossip and jealousy infected the Village just as much as it did uptown New York and the Bronx. Village restaurants and saloons often rocked with Hippolyte Havel's rages when his lover, Polly Holliday, made a new conquest.[8] Both Max Eastman, herald for the socialist revolution and free thought, and Harry Kemp, the vagabond poet, singer of praise for the open road and freedom of personal choice, admitted in their autobiographical novels that jealousy was an ingrained instinct outside the bounds of psychoanalytic treatment.[9]

In the Village they spoke about free love, an idea that was not new. Victoria Woodhull and Tennessee Claflin, sisters and co-editors of *Woodhull and Claflin's Weekly,* shocked contemporaries in the late nineteenth century with talk about inherent rights of sexual choice; about the outmoded institution of marriage; about the need for revolutionary changes in the dominant-submissive relationships between men and women. Proudly admitting they were "Free Lovers," the sisters scared off most reformers and suffragists who were afraid of being linked to a politically damaging cause. Then, early in the twentieth century, Ellen Key, a Swede, and Edward Carpenter, an Englishman, both called on women to break the shackles of sexual slavery and seize the freedom of self-expression. Ellen Key even advocated childbearing outside of marriage.[10]

Not surprisingly, many anarchists embraced the free-love philosophy. Enlightened, free-thinking adults, they believed, must be accorded the right to choose the nature and duration of sexual associations. Free love was mutual caring and respect. Although the anarchists divided over such issues as birth control and the value of monogamy, they agreed that sexual relationships must be outside the control of church and state.

Ideas of women's liberation and spontaneity were at the center of Emma Goldman's anarchist creed, one which decried artificial and contrived barriers to individual freedom. "Slavery, submission, poverty, all misery, all social iniquities result from discipline and restraint," she wrote. Love must be outside economic, social, and legal dictates. Women must be released from bondage as sex commodities, whether as prostitutes or as wives.[11]

It was not only the Village that had sex on its mind; such magazines as *Life, The Forum, Leslie's Weekly,* and *The Smart Set* now carried articles on prostitution, white slavery, vice, birth control, and the "New Woman." William Marion Reedy, liberal editor of the *St. Louis Mirror,* was alarmed by this trend. It had struck "sex o'clock" in America, Reedy remarked. But in the long run, he predicted, birth control and the women's rights movements should not lead to a general laxity in sex manners, because women were not subject to the same passion as men; their desires and lusts were mostly pretense. Dr. Cecile L. Creil, a socialist, although applauding the fact that women had pulled their ostrich heads from the sands of prudery, feared a wave of female sexual license. Furiously, she went on at length warning women about myriad temptations lurking in the forest of eroticism, lurid literature, suggestive songs, and primitive rhythm, all of which was exposing young, innocent girls to "pulsating desire" until "the senses are throbbing with leased-in physical passion." So much for William Reedy's understanding of the psyche of women![12]

To Ben Reitman all of this intellectual probing about lust, all of the interminable conversations about psychology, was mystifying. Sex was sex. To a man who for years had been having sex well outside the control of church, state, or anything else, the idea of free love sounded perfectly reasonable, desirable, even advantageous. This new idea of free love, new at least to Ben, took him by surprise. He first confronted the concept at one of the colonies established by the free-love movement's most ardent supporters, a kind of utopian, communal oasis dedicated to freedom, fellowship, and male-female equality. As one of Doc's friends drove him to the colony for a weekend, his expectations were nothing less than feverish. Maybe the problem was the term, *free love.* To the likes of Ben it naturally conjured up visions of easy pickings, delights indiscriminately and freely given. He recalled driving into the woods to the colony's farmhouse, seeing a group of fine, healthy girls in simple dress, congratulating himself on finding a lecher's Nirvana. The folks were nice enough, offering the visitor dinner, even if he was asked to chop wood for two hours. After a sumptuous meal and delightful conversation around a log fire in the library, spiced undoubtedly by Ben's usual lewd remarks, his attention riveted on a magnificent blond, tall, refined. Doc suggested a walk in the woods. She agreed.

It was all too easy. "So you believe in free love?" Ben blurted out. "Have you ever had any experience?" Unfazed, the blond responded, "Yes, I believe in free love, but it isn't the kind of love that you imagine in your dirty little mind . . . I don't want you. You are a stupid, vulgar man and you are very ignorant . . . You think because we women call ourselves free that you can put your dirty hands on us and use us as a sewer. There is nothing in your dirty minds or your corrupt bodies that a clean woman wants. Men like you must understand that free love means beauty, means freedom, means choice." Fazed, Ben meekly said something about the natural inclination for men to want adventure with all the women they could have. She responded with a lecture on the sacredness of sex and the carnality of much of mankind, including her present company.

Women, she declared, were fighting for their self-respect and for their rights. The two walked back to the farmhouse in silence.[13]

Reitman did not take the woman's lesson to heart. Margaret Anderson, editor of *The Little Review,* later remarked that Ben's social behavior "wasn't so bad if you could hastily drop all your ideas as to how human beings should look and act."[14] The man ravaged social settings and took particular delight in introducing crudity at dinner parties. To young, married women he was want to offer the query, "How old was the baby before you were married?" The remark usually drew appropriate anger, righteous indignation, and shock from the victim, and laughter from the group. On one occasion though, he got more than he bargained for. In an exceptionally loud voice, even for him, Ben asked a young matron the oft-used question. Pale and stammering, the woman yelled at her husband across the table, "Sam, why did you tell him that?" Sam hit Ben in the jaw.

Emma was constantly embarrassed and exasperated by such situations. "Hobo, dear," she would plead, "please give more thought about what you say in company . . . Every time you get into a group of people new to the anarchist philosophy you begin to tell some smutty or risque story. The way you talk outrages the sense of niceness and decency of good women and sensitive men. Please don't do it."[15] But Ben never backed off.

At one party hosted by Emma at her uptown Lenox Avenue apartment, amid the tables of Russian food and wine, Ben, as usual, played the hunter. Theodore Dreiser, himself a philanderer of some renown, had escorted an alluring actress and amateur painter named Kirah Markham to the party. Ben stalked her from room to room, and the annoyed woman finally took refuge in the embrace of Dreiser. "Don't be afraid of Ben," whispered the celebrated writer. "He may ask you to sleep with him but you can just tell him that you are sleeping with me." Dreiser, too, had a libido of dominant proportions. He once penned a line with which Ben easily identified: "The coward sips little of life, the strong man drinks deep."[16]

Sometimes Ben's antics gave new meaning to the world "vulgar." During a single speech in 1912 he mentioned, among other things, teenage incest, sex between ministers and their parishioners, masturbation orgies, and sex between women and dogs. Among the natural rights of man, Ben declared, was the right to be passionate or "as a man, I would put it, the right to have a hard on." "Ben," one of his friends told him, "you're bug-house . . . you're all right, but you're degenerate in regard to the sex question. You've got balls in your brains."[17]

All the philosophizing and agonizing over the sex question, Ben thought, betrayed much personal tension among the Village leftists. Their intellects cried out for freedom; their residual moral codes demanded caution. Ben had, since his boyhood days, mingled freely with whores and pimps in a world where sex was bartered and flaunted openly, not a world of free love but of easy love. His gutter language and sexual abandon were part of his past, part of the people among whom he had moved. To many in the Village, however, sex was an awakening. They read Freud, wrote tracts, engaged in seemingly endless café conversations, and then experimented, whereas Ben had always just experimented. At least in the universe of sex he was comfortable, his mind uncluttered by Freudian theory, his spirit unfettered by guilt. To him lust was not a subject for dilettantish debate; it was simple, uncomplicated pleasure.

When in New York Ben did try on occasion to meld his old hobo and underside world with the Village. In November 1910 he organized a rollicking night at Pacific Hall on East Broadway. Promising to shock everyone who dared attend, Ben hosted an evening of merriment and confession by "social outcasts" of all stripes—the radical and the bum, the junker and the grafter and the bohemian. He persuaded several intellectuals in Emma's crowd to join selected road types in delivering orations on unconventionality, lawlessness, sexual aberration, and other subjects of wide interest, especially to the large contingent of well-to-do uptowners venturing forth for a night of titillation. Emma was there in the overflow crowd and so was the press—Ben saw to that.

This kind of affair was hardly new to the slum showman who had hosted numerous outcast nights with hobo jockers and soapboxers in Chicago and New York, but this particular night was extraordinary. Here were Village regulars Hutchins Hapgood reading a letter from Alexander Berkman, Hippolyte Havel declaring that Adam and Eve were the first outcasts and that Jesus Christ was one too, and Sadakichi Hartmann reading a play called "Mohammed," which he surmised could not be published because of a "certain freedom in language." Ben's old friend Chuck Connors, the Irish philosopher of the slums and opium cellars, was there, his small derby perched over his eyes, preaching a sermon against the foolishness of being a "good feller" and the joys for the bloke who spends his coin on alcohol. Pittsburgh Joe, an English beggarman, assailed the trusts and defended as ethical his vocation of not working. And Mickey the Farmer, erstwhile itinerant, talked of his fruit-picking days on the road. Since he got little of the fruit of his labors, Mickey punned, he had decided to retire to a station in life similar to that of Pittsburgh Joe.

During the evening Reitman unveiled his masterpiece, a large map called "Outcast Island," with such familiar territories as the "Sea of Isolation," the "Gulf of Doubt," and "Radical Island," all adrift from the "Land of Respect." Two mountains, floating on the waters and looking very much like female breasts, were labeled "Utopia" and "Freedom." In his address Ben duly cursed the police, the newspapers, the law, and "everything respectable." This prompted Emma, who was not scheduled to speak, to stride to the front of the hall and declare that the audience had been buncoed. These other outcasts in the room were nothing compared to her, she joked. The "Sea of Isolation," the "Gulf of Doubt"—to Emma Goldman they were all very familiar waters.[18]

The relationship between Ben and Emma had reached a state of turbulent constancy. At one moment she was castigating his unfaithfulness and outlandish public behavior; at another she was waxing about the heights of her primitive desires for him. "Never in all my life," she wrote, "was a man so terribly in my blood, scourging my flesh, tearing my soul, as you are doing." At times her words sounded much the same as Ben's when he talked of the wanderlust driving him to the road, a kind of alien obsession, unexplained, uncontrolled, beyond reason. Passion "sweeps me off my feet," she wrote, ". . . carrys me along in a mad fury."[19]

Ben continued to feel genuine love and passion for Emma, and he was still lured by the limelight, but her demands for conformity were exasperating. She anguished over his lack of sexual fidelity, acceptable political sophistication, and civilized social habits. For all the talk of freedom and liberty and anarchist philosophy, Emma held Ben up to standards of convention that he wasn't able to meet. He was now falling victim to the kind of introspection that plagued his new Greenwich Village acquaintances. He spent time agonizing, questioning his own motives and standards, assessing and reassessing his feelings. The rambler of the open road, the tenderloin iconoclast, was now emotionally caged.

Responding to Emma's passion with equal passion he wrote, "Oh lover I come to you full of hope and life, full of burning desire . . . take the Mountains and Treasure Box, Willie is starved and wants Mommy. I love you." Reacting to her scorn, he was self-denigrating: "I can't see how you can attach yourself to a worthless Hobo. . . . " Sometimes he was self-pitying: "Four years ago today was the parade of the unemployed. I was a 'Hero' for a day. Tonight I sit down sad and gloomy. Your letters have done their work."[20] Yet Ben's naive, sometimes comedic openness with Emma often exacerbated their problems. At one point, trying to assure Emma that his thoughts were on her and not on other women, he reported that his "Will shrank up" while he was attempting to consummate yet another affair. Given his enormous pride in the realm of sex, this was a major admission, one meant to demonstrate his love. Instead, Emma was understandably furious. "Your affairs . . . nauseate me," she fumed, "because they are so common. . . . "[21]

Ben was now so absorbed in Emma's attacks that he even wrote an essay on the subject of sex and civilization, casting himself as a victim of lust, powerless against the black demons and devils dancing before him, the heat in his blood. "I cry for water, for a cooling thought, but only breasts, legs, and eyes float before me." He damned his newly discovered conscience and the moral restraints of society which brought him, in his promiscuity, a measure of guilt and regret. "What is life if one cannot respond freely to his passion. If civilization means that a man must stop and think when he desires another man's wife, it is time to do away with it." To Ben, his philandering seemed to be an extension of anarchism's demands for freedom and choice. To Emma, all of this was just prattle, feeble rationalization masking a lack of respect for women and a complete misunderstanding of anarchism. She had to agree with a friend that her lover's anarchism began "with [his] sex organ." But soon, her anger and despair lifting, she once again began "to bloom . . . my whole being Dear Hobo . . . I want to be with you, in love, in work, in everything."[22]

In 1911, when Ben Reitman looked back on his first years with Emma Goldman, the best memories were not of their time in New

York but of the months on the road. In theaters, opera houses, Elks and Masonic halls, armories, barns, even vacant lots, the anarchists had delivered their message. Sometimes to crowds numbering several hundred or even thousands, at other times to small groups, Emma and her comrades had made many Americans think hard about a host of issues, from war to women's rights to government tyranny. Since Ben had taken charge of the advance planning and promotion of the tours, the anarchists were getting substantial press coverage and selling and distributing an astonishing amount of literature. He even prodded local libraries to purchase works by Kropotkin, Bakunin, and Goldman.

The grueling schedules, frequent harassment, and constant shortage of money only seemed to fuel Ben's enthusiasm in the early years with Emma, and it was this peripatetic, frenzied activity that he now craved. Away from New York, away from what he regarded as inane discussion about sex and other intellectual niceties, Ben and Emma would draw closer. Always there were new escapades, gambles, close calls. In Spokane, in 1912, they were in a car that was struck by a locomotive. Neither was seriously injured, but they knew that the anarchist odyssey had nearly ended that day. And there were the little victories. In Seattle, in 1911, the anarchists rented a church and placarded the building with signs reading, "E.G. will speak." If many in the crowd on lecture day had expected a revival meeting, Emma gave them another message. "Think of it," she wrote, "E.G. in the house of the Lord. . . . "

The work and influence of Chicago's hobo doctor was not lost to the anarchist queen. Telling *Mother Earth* readers of the tremendous momentum of the campaign, Emma wrote, "The credit for the difference is due chiefly to the zeal, the devotion, and skill of Ben Reitman." Even some of her comrades in New York came to realize the impact that Ben had in spreading the message. Discussing plans for a possible new speaking sortie, Hippolyte Havel told Emma, "No one but Ben can do it, you must send for Ben."[23]

Neither was the importance of Emma and her work lost to Ben. In a speech in Detroit in 1911 he called her the greatest woman in the world, the most important force fighting for the freedom of man, the George Sand, the Mary Wollstonecraft, and the Louise Michel of the twentieth century. On the road with Emma, seeing the crowds, basking in the attention, Greenwich Village seemed a long way away. But the tension surrounding his affair with Emma, much of it caused by the "sex question," was still very much with him. To the Detroit crowd Ben gave his own thoughts on free love: "Only imbeciles, afraid to die and too weak to live, will admit that morality as society preaches it is right and natural." All the laws of prohibition were vicious, he charged. "Life would be a dull, stupid monstrosity without all those pleasures which a normal man admits he thinks much of."[24]

12. San Diego

The city of San Diego in the spring of 1912 was suffering from a dreaded infestation, a plague, an army of human locusts. It was enough to nettle every city official and upright citizen of that quiet southern California community. The Wobblies were in town.

The first major labor organization to take up the fight for the rights of unskilled migratory laborers, the Industrial Workers of the World was carrying on an intensive organizing campaign among itinerant harvesters, gandy dancers, miners, and timber beasts, all those excluded from craft-union membership. Holding out the vision of a new society, the rising of the "wage slaves," the Wobblies sought to strike down the master-class oppressors, control the means of production, and bind workers together under the banner of the One Big Union—the "International Industrial Commonwealth." The rhetoric of the Wobblies was tough, calling for direct action and sabotage; the symbol was the black cat, mysterious, defiant, ominous.

Although the IWW made early inroads among low-paid factory workers of the industrial East with strikes at the Lawrence, Massachusetts, textile factories and in other cities, the lasting base would be among the camp workers of the West. Big Bill Haywood, the IWW leader, proclaimed that the Wobblies would go to the hobo jungles, weed out the scissorbills, organize camp committees, and weld a fraternity among those workers for whom no one before had fought. "All peace so long as the wage system lasts is but an armed truce," an IWW leaflet announced: "Onward, Christian soldiers, rip, tear and smite! / Let the gentle Jesus bless your dynamite!"[1] One wandering stiff of the road remembered hearing the message one night in Seattle, drinking in the words of hope, a "plan of freeing the world from economic slavery, so amazing in its simplicity that it dazzled me."[2] To sit back and take the oppression from the employers was no longer tolerable; organize, attack! "The bum on the rods is a social flea / Who gets an occasional bite, / The bum on the plush is a social leach, / Bloodsucking day and night."[3]

The Wobblies' strength was not in violence, as the rhetoric implied, but in their spirit, much of it mobilized in song, soapbox oratory, and rough poetry. By 1910 the IWW street-corner preachers and red-card delegates had spread the word through much of the West. Although they could not claim large numbers of fee-paying recruits, they had demonstrated through strikes and aggressive membership drives in the cities and the labor fields that an organization stood ready to fight "the bum on the plush."

But those on the plush were ready. City authorities, prodded by business interests, began to enact ordinances denying IWW members the right to speak in the streets, to hold meetings, or otherwise to agitate for union organization. The laws seriously threatened the recruiting of migratory workers who gathered in western cities in the off-seasons.

The Wobblies responded with a nonviolent, passive-resistance tactic that bewildered many local officials: the agitators courted arrest. Deliberately violating the new ordinances denying free speech, Wobblies marched off to jail and called for new recruits to take their places in the street. Arrested by the hundreds in some towns, the protesters, singing, taunting the arresting officers, filled the jails and the improvised bull pens, causing the city politicians intolerable expense and embarrassment. In many cases the perplexed officials relented, lifting the bans against free speech and assembly.

In Missoula, Montana, in 1909 and in Spokane, Washington, in 1910, Wobblies won prolonged confrontations. The Spokane struggle saw Frank Little, an American Indian IWW organizer, jailed for thirty days for reading the Declaration of Independence. In one month over 600 Wobblies squeezed into crowded cells in Spokane. Many suffered the "hot-box" torture in which prisoners were packed into unventilated rooms, given a large dose of forced steam heat, and then placed in ice-cold cells. Yet even with the death of a number of Wobblies in Spokane, in San Francisco and Fresno, Kansas City and Des Moines, Denver and Omaha, the Wobblies carried on their free-speech battles.[4]

It was in San Diego that the free speech movement garnered extensive notoriety, not because of the gains achieved by the demonstrators, but because of the brutality inflicted on them. Antiunion feeling in southern California had reached near hysterical dimensions following the dynamiting of the Los Angeles Times Building in 1910. With such conservative newspapers as the *Times* and the *San Diego Union* branding labor leaders as traitors and subversives, with business, civic, and fraternal organizations fanning the fears among southern California citizens of an imminent invasion and takeover by humanity's scum, the authorities enjoyed a license for repression. A Wobbly verse lamented: "In that town called San Diego when the workers try to talk / The cops will smash them with a say and tell 'em 'take a walk.' / They throw them in a bull pen and they feed them rotten beans, / And they call that 'law and order' in that city, so it seems."[5]

But the IWW and other labor groups refused to back off. When the San Diego city council barred street meetings and speeches, 2,000 members of the Free Speech League—Wobblies, socialists, anarchists, single-taxers, and even some AFL members—defied the order. As hundreds were herded to jail, several thousand other free-speech fighters swarmed into the city, and the IWW called for even more. A Wobbly poet appealed to working stiffs across the country to come to the new battlefield: "Come on the cushions; Ride up on top; / Stick to the breakbeams; Let nothing stop. / Come in great numbers; This we beseech; / Help San Diego to win / *Free Speech!*"[6]

In early May, various city officials and influential citizens of San Diego appealed to the Justice Department in Washington for assistance in combating the invasion. F. C. Spalding, president of the Chamber of Commerce, sent an urgent telegram to U.S. Attorney General George Wickersham depicting an armed insurrection aimed at the assassination of the mayor, chief of police, plots to destroy the waterworks and other public utilities, and the ultimate goal of overthrowing the legally constituted government. San Deigo Police Superintendent John Sehon, in concert with John McCormick, a federal attorney, and with private detectives appointed by a citizen's group controlled by John Spreckels, sugar king, and Harrison Grey Otis, antiunion owner of the *Los Angeles Times,* also appealed for help. The Wobblies and their traitorous ilk were heavily armed, they charged, and were bent on looting and murdering law-abiding citizens, demoralizing respectable business enterprises, and defying the laws of the country. If that were not enough, some intelligence information suggested that left-wing insurgents aimed for the grand design of conquering all of lower California and establishing a separate community of anarchists and IWW members. At the call of national Wobbly leaders, the rods and blinds of freight cars from all over the country were carrying hobo trash, dynamiters, toward San Diego. The Honorable Leroy Wright, Member of the State Senate of California, wrote from his home in San Diego to James Needham of the U.S. House of Representatives: "Situation much more serious than general public appreciates. It is not San Diego society alone that is being threatened but organized society everywhere." Armageddon was on its way to lower California.[7]

With no sign from the Justice Department that help would be forthcoming, vigilante groups took over in San Diego. The forces of law and order—retired bankers and army officers, doctors, lawyers, real estate men—drove prisoners into the desert for flag-kissing ceremonies. One victim remembered being herded into a truck with about fourteen other Wobblies and taken to a spot near Sorrento, about fifteen miles from San Diego. There, with nearly seventy-five men brandishing knives, blackjacks, and revolvers, all wearing white handkerchiefs tied at the elbow as insignias of the vigilante band, the Wobblies were dragged to a platform at the base of a flagpole and forced to kiss the flag and sing the national anthem. They were slugged and blacksnaked, run through a gauntlet, deposited on cattle cars headed away from the city, and told never to return. The scene was repeated numerous times in the California desert in the spring of 1912.[8]

Into this charged atmosphere came Emma Goldman and Ben Reitman. They arrived in Los Angeles in April to hold several meetings in support of IWW members and other left-wing comrades carrying on the California fight. On May 7, Joseph Mikolasek, an IWW soapboxer, was killed, riddled by police bullets while in his San Diego home. Mikolasek's body was shipped to Los Angeles where Emma and other radicals arranged a public demonstration. Along with other left-wing women, Emma also organized a feeding station at Wobbly headquarters to care for the embattled from San Diego who had returned from skirmishes with the police and the vigilantes.[9]

On May 14, Goldman and Reitman traveled to the war zone. Some friends in San Diego had arranged a meeting where Emma planned to speak on Henrik Ibsen's *An Enemy of the People.* To most San Diegans the theme was quite appropriate, but not for the reasons Emma might have wished: in their minds, no greater enemy of the people than Emma Goldman could have entered their city.

Many turned out at the San Diego depot to hiss at the renowned anarchists. Later that night several pillars of the community visited the U.S. Grant Hotel where Emma and Ben had taken rooms. The mission of the townsfolk was to deliver a spirited vigilante welcome to the un-American trash invading their fair city. Being men of respectable habits, they planned no special greetings for the despised Emma Goldman because she was, after all, a woman. But her lover. . . .

The hotel manager came to Emma's room at about 10:30 P.M., announcing that the chief of police wished to talk with her. She was escorted away. Then, six gun-toting visitors confronted Ben and hauled him down a corridor, past a uniformed policeman, out to the street, and into a waiting automobile for a ride he didn't want to take. As the car moved slowly down San Diego's main thoroughfare it was joined by another carrying about seven additional citizens. As the two cars moved out of the city into the California desert, Reitman's companions began to amuse themselves by gouging and biting their guest, pulling his long hair and poking their fingers into his eyes. During the scuffling he overheard one of the men remark that the doctor in the other car had left specific instructions that the anarchist's nose was to remain unbroken: that doctor wanted to break it himself. One of Ben's hosts sneered, "We could kill you and tear out your guts and no one would know who did it, but we promised the Chief of Police that we wouldn't kill you. . . . " Another informed Ben that this little party, which had just begun, was designed to send a message to dago anarchists and IWW hoboes that the city of San Diego intended to protect its property and money from outlaws and political swine.

Twenty miles from downtown San Diego the two autos pulled off the road and stopped in the desert. With the headlights providing a sickly stage setting, Reitman was dragged front and center, encircled by fourteen men, and stripped. They stuck pencils up his nostrils, more fingers in his eyes, and filth in his mouth. Patriots all, the men had brought along an American flag, which they asked the traitorous anarchist to kiss. When he refused, they kicked him to the ground. The ensuing moments were, Ben remembered later, something straight out of lynch party history and tales of the Spanish inquisition:

> When I lay naked on the ground, my tormentors kicked and beat me until I was almost insensible. With a lighted cigar they burned I.W.W. on my buttocks; then they poured a can of tar over my head and body, and, in the absence of feathers, they rubbed handfuls of sage brush on my body. One very gentle business man, who is active in church work, deliberately attempted to push my cane into my rectum. One unassuming banker twisted my testicles. These and many other things they did to me, until I forgot "whether I had done a great or little thing." When these business men were tired of their fun, they gave me my underwear for fear I should meet some women. These respectable citizens are very considerate of their women. They also gave me back my vest, in order that I might carry money, railroad ticket, and watch. The rest of my clothes they stole from me in highwayman fashion. I was ordered to make a speech, and then they commanded me to run the gauntlet. The fourteen vigilantes were lined up, and as I ran past them, each one, in a businesslike manner, gave me a parting blow or kick.[10]

Doc stumbled in the general direction of San Diego, through the rolling hills and canyons, a bizarre-looking creature. He reached the small village of Bernardo around daybreak, then waited for a couple of hours for the local general store to open, fought off embarrassment at his appearance, and bought a pair of overalls, a shirt, some turpentine, and tar soap. Under a bridge the infamous hobo anarchist tried to wash off the evidence of his humiliation. He later walked on to Oceanside, spent several hours rolling in the sand and surf, and then wired friends in Los Angeles that he was alive and heading there on the next train.

All through the previous night Emma had been wracked with fear that Ben was dead. After town officials insisted that the vigilantes had put him on a train to Los Angeles, Emma left San Diego at around 3 A.M. When she arrived in Los Angeles in the early morning Ben was not at the station or at the apartment where the two usually stayed. Later, an anonymous phone caller reported that Ben was on the next train and would need a stretcher.

Emma recalled the ghastly sight of her lover as he arrived, huddled in a rear car, face pale, terror in his eyes, hair still sticky with tar.

"Oh, Mommy, I'm with you at last!" he muttered on seeing her. "Take me away, take me home!" When she later helped him undress, she was horrified at the mass of wounds and the grotesque letters branded on his flesh.[11]

The bitter animosity fueled by the anarchists and other radical and labor groups could be measured by reports in the *Los Angeles Times* the next day on the Reitman abduction. The cynical *Times* reporter described the hobo doctor stepping off the train in Los Angeles looking like a "Mexican peon," tar still clinging to his seared features. Welcomed by a large following of "undesirable human parasites," including "the Goldman woman," Reitman appeared forlorn and crestfallen. His face, the reporter noted, was covered with deep burns; the vigilantes had done their work well; the radical was marked forever.[12]

A *Times* editorial declared that the lynch law was deplorable but better than no law at all. The "I-Won't-Workers" and their hundreds of journeymen tramps had provoked a natural response. "The *Times* does not commend the fowl treatment accorded by the San Diegans to the anarchist doctor, but it does not attempt to sit in judgment upon those who discouraged his longer stay in the city . . . Maybe he got, on the whole, about what was coming to him."[13] Even the *New York Times* scoffed at Reitman's piddling martyrdom and lamented that the malcontent anarchists should not have been given such publicity. And besides, the tarring and sagebrushing was a hopelessly amateurish production, not close to the standards of excellence achieved against the con men in *The Adventures of Huckleberry Finn.* After all, Reitman was able to remove most of the tar the very day it was administered. Poor work indeed![14]

The view from the left was, as might be expected, different. Eugene Debs declared, "The cannibals who tarred and tortured Ben Reitman in the name of 'law and order' are below the moral level of a tribe of head-hunters . . . and the time will come when their children will blush with shame to hear their names."[15]

The day after he returned to Los Angeles, Ben, along with Emma and a number of other radicals, held a mass meeting to protest the San Diego outrage. After the speakers had roused the audience into a frenzy, portraying Ben's torture as an abominable affront to the working classes and to free speech, the victim himself mounted the podium. As Ben made crude allusions to his abused anatomy, his story of the pathetic, late-night desert crossing drew laughter instead of passion. The political storm in the room subsided. One of the earlier speakers, Charlie Sprading, later said to Ben, "You're the damndest martyr I ever saw in my life. You made your experience so ridiculous that a lot of these people will be wanting to go over to San Deigo and meet the same friendly mob. It was the cleverest speech you ever made." A furious Emma didn't think it was clever at all. Ben had, she thought, sacrificed much of the mobilizing spirit engendered by the San Diego incident for the sake of a few cheap laughs.[16]

But Ben's humor was only camouflage. He was never psychologically the same after May 16, 1912, for he had entered a new dimension of political violence, a world of club and iron that he had before only imagined. This was not a two-bit sheriff filling a vagrancy quota or the Chicago police quelling an innocuous unemployment march. These people in San Diego, these respectable community leaders, men of principle and means, under siege, their city invaded by people they didn't understand, their business interests threatened by strike actions, their hatred stirred by newspapers reporting imminent disasters, had reacted with startling force and vengeance. Never before had he felt this kind of human fury. The men in the desert that night just as easily could have poured that boiling tar down his throat. His death, in their minds, would have been satisfying and justified. And although Ben continued to tour with Emma in the coming months, back up the coast and on to Denver, he was tormented by the San Diego experience. It was a demon he would never completely exorcise.

In San Diego the furor over labor troubles continued. Colonel Harris Weinstock, a special commissioner appointed by Governor Hiram Johnson to investigate the San Diego hostilities, issued a report in mid-May that was critical of city officials and vigilantes. Weinstock noted that of the hundreds of arrests made by San Diego authorities, no prisoner had been charged with violence and none had carried weapons. "Their plan," Weinstock said, "was purely one of passive resistance; annoying, aggravating, burdensome, but not inimical to life and property."[17]

The report was not favorably received by the citizens of San Diego; indeed, influential groups continued to press Washington for federal intervention against the left-wing menace. But despite this pressure from conservative organizations and from Republican politicians, Attorney General Wickersham insisted that the labor troubles in southern California were of state and local concern. To mollify political pressures, however, Wickersham allowed Federal Attorney McCormick to impanel a Los Angeles grand jury to investigate the Wobblies for possible criminal conspiracy. The proceedings, which uncovered no plots of national import, were later dropped.

In the summer of 1912 other Republicans went over the head of the unsympathetic Wickersham to President Taft. Comparing the San Diego uprising to the Chicago Pullman strike of 1894, when President Cleveland dispatched troops to crush laborites, the California Republicans continued to spin their tale that the Wobblies planned to establish a revolutionary territory north of Mexico. Taft believed much of it. From the White House in September came the same kind of alarm and panic trumpeted by the San Diego officials. A formidable conspiracy of anarchists and other undesirables, headed by Emma Goldman and Ben Reitman, was enlisting thousands of armed invaders for a major assault on lower California to set up "a new form of government, or non-government," Taft wrote to his attorney general. There was no doubt that the San Diego area was a cauldron of troubles for the nation, the president claimed, and that it attracted "all the lawless flotsom and jetsam that proximity to the Mexican border thrusts into these two cities of San Diego and Los Angeles. Even with the president's support, however, the private investigators hired by Republican business and political interests were not able to marshal enough evidence to support federal intervention. The subversive IWW rascals would not be totally crushed.[18]

Neither would they be victorious. The unrelenting vigilante and police repression had taken much of the fire from the San Diego free-speech fight. The injuries and jailings had exacted a serious toll. In October 1912 San Diego was mostly lonely and deserted at night, with no street-corner rallies or curbstone singing to shatter the tranquility. One leftist observer noted glumly, "The sacred spot where so many I.W.W.'s were clubbed and arrested last winter lies safe and secure from the unhallowed tread of the hated anarchist. . . ." The civic authorities and business types "have the courts, the jails and funds."[19]

Jack Whyte, a Wobbly sentenced to six months in jail and a $300 fine for conspiracy to violate the city ordinance banning free speech, declared to the judge at his trial, "You have become blind and deaf to the rights of men to pursue life and happiness, and you have crushed these rights so that the sacred rights of property should be preserved. Then you tell me to respect 'the law' . . . My right to life is far more sacred than the sacred right of property that you and your kind so ably defend."[20]

Following the summer tour, Ben and Emma separated for several months, as they had done in previous years, he returning to Chicago to spend time with his mother and his friends, she to New York to catch up on *Mother Earth* business and prepare for future speaking excursions. San Diego remained very much in their thoughts. The experience had driven between them a great psychological wedge, revealing a wide gulf of temperament and passion. Now, in New York, Emma began to edit for Alexander Berkman his prison memoirs, writings that once again rekindled in her mind the fire of revolutionary zeal which had cemented their relationship. As she read his charge to true revolutionaries, to those willing to sacrifice their lives for the Grand Cause, her beloved Ben seemed even more the coward.

Later that year Emma, disillusioned with Ben's continued references in his speeches to the San Diego humiliation, references which seemed to her childish and lacking in radical ardor, upbraided her manager-lover as a feckless excuse for a revolutionary: "I hope Hobo dear that if you ever face another S.D. you may not have to herald your action as cowardly, or at least if you feel it to be such, that you will keep it to yourself. It certainly can not be indifferent to the woman, who loves a man, especially the woman who has all her life faced persecution to hear that man shout from the house tops, he is a coward."[21] How different, she would write years later, was Reitman in the face of danger, how different his commitment to anarchism, than Alexander Berkman, that consummate rebel, who was willing to lay down his life.

For Doc, the kind of heroism represented by Berkman, the kind that led to his *Attentat* twenty years earlier, was ill conceived and futile. Especially after San Diego, Ben's aversion to violence became increasingly pronounced. In 1914 he wrote to Emma about the stupidity of some of those in the anarchist ranks who were calling on their comrades to fight the master class with homemade bombs. The terrorists were giving the cause a bad name, he charged, submerging the strength of the anarchist message in a sink of inflammable invective. "Now why in the hell should I take my stand with a lot of temperamental boys and men," he wrote. "Violence is a matter of sex and emotion."[22] The hobo doctor would much rather prove his manhood in the bedroom than in cottage-industry bomb making.

To Emma the issue of violence was not a simple one. Even though she had played a close part in Berkman's attempted assassination of Henry Clay Frick two decades earlier, she had consistently counseled against violence in her letters and from the platform. In most of the physical confrontations between leftist demonstrators and the upholders of the status quo, Emma noted, the upholders nearly always prevailed. She continued to argue that violence was counterproductive to the anarchist cause.

Yet in her more reflective moments Emma betrayed an ambivalence toward the issue. She realized that the venom spewed at the master class by anarchist agitators would inevitably lead to crazed individual acts; and she believed that capitalist oppression in America would drive the frustrated underclasses to rebellion. At a party attended by several writers and political thinkers, the poet Harry Kemp heard Emma liken the condition of society to that of a swampy ground. "If you step in one place," she observed, "the pressure of the foot will cause water to spurt up in another; just as naturally, violence pressing down from above, in social and economic disputes—is inevitably answered by violence from below, by mere force of the pressure. . . ."[23]

For Emma and Ben, San Diego had brought the issue of political radicalism and violence much more to the center of their relationship. Emma's political life was dedicated to stirring and fomenting those social pressures that naturally led to violence. Ben was now one of the hunted, the target of right-wing retribution. Unlike Alexander Berkman, he had no desire whatsoever to sacrifice his life for some grand political ideology. Now, as he tried to put his life together after the physical and emotional trauma in San Diego, his anarchist lover was challenging his courage and manhood.

Ben reacted with a strange mix of fear, resentment, and purpose. He became obsessed with returning to San Diego to expunge the wrongs done to him, to show his mettle under fire. Unable to sleep, he brooded, his usual buoyancy sapped by that one night in the desert. He badgered Emma to plan a return trip the following spring. "His whole being was centered on San Diego," Emma wrote, "and it became almost a hallucination with him. He taxed my affection, by his constant insistence on starting for the Coast."

Although California radicals cautioned Emma against another attempt to speak in San Diego, she decided to go. "I was certain that Ben would not be freed from the hold of that city unless he returned to the scene of the May outrage." Emma and Ben once again advertised through an advance agent that they would hold a meeting in San Diego where she would speak on the subject "An Enemy of the People."[24]

On May 20, 1913, a little over a year after their first San Diego adventure, Reitman and Goldman once again entered the "City of the Silver Gate." As they stepped from a Santa Fe parlor car at daybreak, a trio of law enforcement officials immediately took them into custody, whisking them from the station to the city jail. Quickly, the two visitors realized their good fortune, for even in these early morning hours the San Diego jail was drawing an ominous crowd. The phones of vigilante committee members all over the city were ringing, and the dedicated were responding in great numbers. Hour by hour, growing numbers of serious-looking men with hip-pockets bulging with billies surrounded the jail, shouting to the anarchists inside. Most in the throng wore little American flags in their buttonholes. One man was nearly killed when someone attempted to pin a flag on him and he refused it. "The crowd surged around him and he was knocked down," the *Sun* reported. "Twenty policemen rushed into the crowd and rescued the man. . . ."

When a vigilante telephoned the Spreckels plant and asked the engineer to blow the militia alarm, the signal for the gathering of the troops, additional hundreds of men appeared. The crowd, shouting obscenities, grew larger, many calling for Reitman. Inside, nerves were taut. As Ben wiped his face with a towel, he shook noticeably; Emma seemed pale. Police Chief J. Keno Wilson, returning from an interview with the superintendent of the police department, H. N. Manney, told reporters that the arrest of the two anarchists was for their own protection. If they were allowed to remain at large, Wilson said grimly, the vigilantes would swing the two by their necks within an hour.

Inside the jail Chief Wilson approached Reitman and suggested a police escort to the train station. Emma agreed, very reluctantly. The thought of anarchists needing police protection was almost too much to accept. But after witnessing the mob and seeing "the pale horror staring at me out of Ben's eyes," she shelved principles for the moment in favor of staying alive. Theatrically playing the scene to its limits, Wilson then made a dramatic speech to the crowd, announcing that the anarchists would be led out of town. When the two appeared the crowd roared. "Miss Goldman was plainly frightened and clung to Chief Wilson's arm," the *Sun* reported. "When someone cried: 'There she is; get her!' the woman winced and her lip trembled. Reitman was the least disturbed. He scowled and pulled his broad-brimmed black hat down over his eyes."

A dozen policemen carrying shotguns marched at the head of the procession, driving a wedge through the hooting thousands. The jostling, jeering mob pressed toward the prisoners, howling, spitting, and otherwise demonstrating its lack of affection for the two anarchists. Goldman and Reitman finally made their way to a waiting car bedecked in American flags (everything in San Diego seemed to be covered by flags). Chief Wilson, who along with his riflemen and detectives mounted the running boards of the cars, posed for pictures, shotgun upraised.

At the station a cordon of police lined the platform to protect the infamous duo, who prepared to board the 1 : 10 train to Los Angeles. The *Times* reported that "Emma, still a little pale, made the ascent from platform to platform almost in a bound, so eager was she to be inside, and Reitman, albeit a little more dignified in his movements, was considerably more agile than the ordinary passenger." Emma declared to the police and reporters as she climbed aboard the train, "I will return to San Diego when San Diego has free speech." As the train pulled out, J. M. Porter, a successful realtor, boarded the car briefly, walked over to Reitman, and spat in his face. Porter was familiar to Reitman—he was one of the men who had taken Ben on his late-night ride a year earlier. Once again the city of San Diego had delivered to Ben and Emma devastating, humiliating rebuke.[25] "I thought of the savagery of the mob," Emma later wrote, "terrifying yet fascinating at the same time. I realized why Ben's previous experience had so obsessed him. . . ."[26] Like Ben a year before, Emma now felt a driving compulsion to return, to face again the power of the crowd's overwhelming hatred, to face it again and win.

The following morning the conservative press of southern California had a field day. The *San Diego Union* trumpeted, "City Purges Itself of Anarchists, Drives Out Goldman and Her Pal." The *Los Angeles Times* derisively announced, "The Shrew Is Tamed."[27] Featuring a cartoon depicting Emma and Ben heading out of San Diego, the *Times* declared that "the human vulperine and her wolf-mate" had shown to the world the barrenness of anarchist philosophy. The two, "firebrands and swordswallowers" of American anarchism, those wicked opponents of constitutional liberty and law and order, had cowered behind the peace officers they routinely denounced. "Well Done, San Diego!"[28]

As she had promised, Emma did return to San Diego—in 1915. She went without Ben, whom she believed lacked the strength of will and a sense of responsibility to face political upheaval. Although the vigilance committee was still active then, the city was less threatened by labor troubles and had recently elected a more liberal mayor. Assisted by Berkman, the musician George Edwards, and a loose free-speech organization called the Open Forum, founded by Baptist minister A. Lyle de Jarnette, Emma finally delivered the lecture "An Enemy of the People," as well as a speech on birth control.[29] Years later Ben also returned to San Diego—without Emma. Accompanied by his mother and several friends, he arrived with no fanfare and walked the streets unnoticed. He even visited the office of the *San Diego Union,* the paper that had so viciously attacked him years earlier.

But in 1913, as Ben looked at his recent San Diego experiences, he saw them as "no different from what hundreds of others at different times have suffered for some cause." He could also see, however, that for him San Diego was a turning point. Although still powerfully attracted to Emma and her ideals, Ben was now bitterly disillusioned. Emma's self-righteous attacks on his character just at the time he most needed her support, his own self-doubts, his deepening alienation from many of the radicals surrounding Emma, especially Alexander Berkman—all served to cloud his future as an anarchist. But he tried, as always, to keep up a good front. When friends would speak jokingly about a possible lecture in San Diego, Ben would remind them of a bit of advice he received from a hobo during his boyhood wanderings: "Kid, my friend Jesus used to have a standing rule that if he went into a town and the town received him not he would wash its dust off his feet and tell it to go to hell."[30]

13. Ludlow

The lot of the political agitator, Emma Goldman and Ben Reitman knew well, is shaped by unforeseen events. In the spring of 1913 Emma's appearances in various cities were devoted largely to lectures on modern drama and its potential for influencing social change. But the flames of war in Mexico and the stories of horror from Colorado's mine fields soon made lectures on modern drama seem like so much pabulum.

In the winter of 1913 the dashing correspondent John Reed, who had lounged with Emma and Ben on Mabel Dodge's bearskin rug to talk of revolution, had made his way to Mexico to cover the real thing. To some, the Mexican revolution was just another sombrero riot which threatened American business interests; to others, such as the muckraker Lincoln Steffens, it was the vision of the new order, the uprising of the underclasses who were taking control of their own destinies. Four years had passed since Emiliano Zapata raised the cry of "Land and Liberty" and overthrew the Mexican dictator Diaz. Now, half a dozen military ruffians still jousted for power, with poverty, hunger, and death their only legacies to the battered country.

Arriving at Ojinaga, John Reed saw roofless, bullet-riddled houses and streets overflowing with sick and starving people, refugees from the interior fleeing the approaching rebels. By Christmas Day he was in Chihuahua, its mosque-like churches and soft, yellow-brown cathedrals standing in contrast to the overwhelming confusion and devastation. It was here he met Francisco ("Pancho") Villa, the peon Robin Hood. If Villa was little more than a chicken thief and bandit to some, to Reed he was a man of extraordinary native shrewdness and reckless and romantic bravery.[1] For several weeks

Reed traveled with Villa's ragged troops and saw the admiration that the ruthless revolutionary commanded in much of the countryside. To Reed, Villa was the best hope for the Mexican poor, the one leader who could marshal enough support to take on the machine-slavery imposed on the Mexicans by Wall Street exploiters and their Mexican businesses.

In Chihuahua, Reed spent a day at a mining camp controlled by American capitalists. As he rode with an American mine manager through the mountain passes to the lead and silver deposits, he heard the refrain common among American businessmen there. American capital had made Mexico, the manager told Reed. The revolution, however, had made the peon more uppity, had spoiled him. The American mine interests had provided opportunity for these low-lifes. Now there were strikes all the time. The only thing to do with strikers, the manager concluded, was to shoot them down.[2]

On April 21 United States marines shelled and occupied Vera Cruz. John Reed's worst fears were confirmed. He could conceive of no more disastrous a blow to Mexican liberty than to inflict upon it "our grand democratic institutions—trust government, unemployment, and wage slavery."[3]

As newspapers across the country ran front-page stories on the Mexican situation, Emma Goldman, Ben Reitman, and other leftist speakers and writers began to decry American intervention in Mexican affairs and the evils of capitalist exploitation. Soon they did not have to look south of the Mexican border for such crimes, however. At the very time United States forces entered Vera Cruz, a small town in southern Colorado was also becoming a symbol of the terrible times. Just as the mine manager in Chihuahua had told John Reed that strikers should be shot, in Ludlow, Colorado, such instincts were now law.

On April 21 Red Cross workers and reporters wandered through the devastation that had been a tent colony of striking miners. A day earlier Ludlow had been just one of many nothing towns in the isolated mine fields, towns with names like Guy's Spur and Primrose and Rugby Junction; now Ludlow had identity. A quiet, eerie scene of charred debris was made more grotesque by still-smoldering fires. Bodies, many of them quite small, lay covered with blankets. Glassy-eyed, hard-muscled miners, mostly Italians and Greeks, wept openly and vowed revenge.[4]

David Stewart had seen it all happen. A homesteader living in Forbes, Colorado, a few miles from Ludlow, Stewart had visited the striking miners on Sunday, April 20, to play baseball and had stayed overnight. The next morning, at about nine o'clock, he wandered over to the camp store, about 200 yards from the rows of tents housing the mining families. Suddenly he heard rifle and machine-gun fire from the direction of railroad cars near the colony. Behind those cars were the soldiers of fortune and plug-uglies brought west by the Rockefeller-controlled Colorado Fuel and Iron Company to deal with the strikers. David Stewart thought they had gone mad.[5]

For several hours steel-jacketed bullets raked the makeshift village as women and children huddled in rows of pits dug inside the tents for protection. Most of the miners had not been inside the tents when the attack began, and those who ran across the area were easy targets for the coal company troops, their machine guns pumping out 400 bullets a minute. By late afternoon what little resistance the strikers mustered had been overwhelmed by the company army. Over thirty men, women, and children lay dead. The gunmen were now free to set fire to the tents with coal-oil torches and to begin an orgy of looting that included the store inside which David Stewart had hidden. The terrified homesteader stayed in the cellar all night, finally emerging the next morning to witness the carnage.[6]

Frank Didano, a miner, had hidden in an arroyo during much of the shooting. He saw the train from Trinidad, Colorado, bringing in the machine guns, saw the mine owners' army line up close to the camp, saw the families crawling in the shallow pits trying to escape the hailstorm of bullets, saw several men take machine guns to the top of a hill to shoot down into the pits. The soldiers tried to kill everybody and everything, Frank Didano said. They even massacred a dog.[7]

Godfrey Irwin, a young electrical engineer working for a local gas company, witnessed the killing of Louis Tikas, Greek miner and leading organizer of the strike. Irwin and a friend were on a tramp in the low hills outside Ludlow when they heard the intense fusillade from below. From a rock shelter the two watched as Tikas attempted to lead a group of women away from the tents to an arroyo. The unarmed Greek leader walked out into the open to plead for the lives of the women and children. Bullets tore through his body. "It was," Godfrey Irwin said, "the first murder I had ever seen."[8]

Socialist writer Max Eastman called it a "black orgy," a degenerate blood-lust instigated by the moneyed interests against organized labor. "I put that crime, not upon the perpetrators who are savage, but upon the gentlemen of noble leisure who hired them to this service."[9] Even the conservative *New York Post,* comparing Colorado with Mexico, observed, "Victoriano Huerta might well prefer to sever relations with a Government under which it is possible for women and children to be mowed down by machine-guns in a frenzy of civil war." A local Colorado paper decried the barbarity as beyond anything seen in the Mexican revolution. Pancho Villa, the paper noted, had never burned tents over the heads of nursing mothers and helpless infants. A political cartoon in the *New York World* pictured the miner families withering under the shower of gunfire. The caption read: "Not in Mexico but in Colorado!"[10]

John Reed, the chronicler of Mexico's turmoil, went to Ludlow. During his weeks in Mexico he had abhorred the aggressive American capitalists exploiting cheap labor and meddling in Mexican political affairs, all in the name of democracy. So intensely did he respect the struggles of the Mexican peasant, so passionately did he despise American businessmen there, that he told friends he would join the peon army against the United States if it invaded Mexico. Now, in Colorado, the naked hatred between labor and capital had led to outright butchery. Reed remembered the words of the mine owner in Mexico as he surveyed the scarred little tent colony in his own country ten days after the massacre. At the Trades Assembly Hall in Trinidad, just a few miles from Ludlow, children sang: "There's a strike in Colorado for to set the miners free / From the tyrants and the money-kings and all the powers that be."[11]

Reed talked with grieving women in black shawls and heard their stories of terror. In the remains of the tent colony, now called the "death hole" by the miners, were the stoves and pots still half-filled with food that had been cooking that morning, along with the scorched, bullet-scarred baby carriages and children's toys. In the days that followed, the journalist began to piece together for himself the story of Ludlow, a story which, he thought, revealed in stark dimensions the great cleavage in American society between the exploiters and the producers, a class war in its most vicious terms.

Southern Colorado, Reed discovered, was ruled economically by three coal companies, the largest controlled by the Rockefeller interests. Most of the incorporated towns were run by these companies, which virtually owned the mayors, the sheriffs, the houses, and the stores. Most of the miners and their families, representing over twenty nationalities, spoke little or no English. They were forced to pay "taxes" to the company, were charged preachers' fees, school fees, and blacksmithing fees, and were made to trade at the company stores, which sometimes charged prices 100 percent higher than outside the camps. Most of the miners made little more than two dollars a day. Scores of workers died in accidents, yet the companies did virtually nothing to improve safety conditions.[12]

Most of the demands of the strikers, including the right of the union to exist and the eight-hour day, were already part of Colorado's mining laws, stored away safely in the capital. Thus, the strike was largely a battle to force the mining companies to obey the law. Economist E. R. Seligman wrote, "Is it not a remarkable commentary on the state of American civilization that individuals should be compelled to strike in order to enforce a series of laws which it is the obligation of the employers to obey and of the state to enforce."[13]

To the miners, however, the strike was more than a list of formal demands; it was a protest against a grinding system of peonage. A woman who ran a boardinghouse near one of the mines told how personally invasive that peonage was. "Well, it was everything," she said. "It was dirt, water, scrip, robbery. They kept everybody in debt all the time." Men were fired because they didn't trade at the company store. Their mining loads were consistently underweighed. The water, polluted with hay, alfalfa, and manure, was dark green in color.[14]

Into Colorado had come the United Mine Workers. Despite intimidation by the companies and language differences with the miners, the union had established an infant organization in the state. The coal operators retaliated with imported mercenaries assigned to ward off the threat of a strike. Not surprisingly, violence erupted, with company thugs frequently shooting at strikers, several of whom were killed.

In September 1913 the miners had gone on strike, and the violence had increased. The Colorado mine fields threatened to become a war zone as miners began to collect arms. A congressional committee visited Colorado, and afterward some of the miners who had testified against the company were beaten with rawhide strips and speared with bayonets. At a hearing in Washington, D.C., John D. Rockefeller, Jr., argued that the hired troops brought to Colorado to enforce law and order were acting in the best interests not only of the company but of nonunion workers. In a spirited defense of the open shop and of the actions of his company's troops, Rockefeller declared, "My conscience entirely aquits me. We would rather that the unfortunate conditions should continue, and that we should lose all the millions invested, than that American workmen should be deprived of their right, under the Constitution, to work for whom they please. That is the great principle at stake. It is a national issue."[15]

On April 20 Ludlow itself became a national issue. The massacre, reported in bold newspaper headlines across the country, ignited a furor of protest. In New York, Alexander Berkman led anarchist protesters through the streets. A young anarchist firebrand named Marie Ganz was taken into custody for threatening the life of J. D. Rockefeller, Jr. Upton Sinclair, arrested in a march, began a hunger strike in New York's Tombs prison. IWW picketers surrounded the Rockefeller home in Tarrytown, New York. Various committees began to raise funds for the striking Colorado miners.[16] In Colorado, John Reed helped set up relief organizations and spoke at protest meetings. He later returned to New York to write a blistering article for *Metropolitan* magazine. There was no word for the Colorado situation, he wrote, but war.[17]

In late April Ben Reitman and Emma Goldman arrived in Colorado. Neither the local authorities nor the miners and their spokesmen welcomed the two. The sheriffs and mine officials feared that the anarchists would incite further violent resistance from the miners, and labor leaders feared that the miners' cause would be compromised by a close association with radicals of unsavory reputations. Even some of the local anarchists asked Emma and Ben to keep a low profile. "It was painful to know," she wrote, "that I was not wanted by the very people for whom I had worked all my life!"[18]

But despite the cool reception from both sides, Emma and Ben went to work with their usual zeal. Emma scheduled several lectures on drama, lectures which gave her visit to Colorado an outward appearance of legitimacy beyond the labor dispute. Indeed, several reviewers in the social pages of local newspapers praised Emma's erudition on the subject. But her attention and that of her manager were riveted on the events of the previous days in the desolate southern coalfields. The two organized several mass meetings to protest the outrages of American business interests and their lackeys, the local police authorities. Ben even became chairman of a Colorado "Anti-Militarist League" and, with Emma, addressed several audiences reaching into the thousands. Although labor leaders did not publicly acknowledge the efforts of the anarchists, they did accept monies raised by Emma and Ben to further the cause of the miners. Linking the Ludlow massacre and the American involvement in Mexico as products of American capitalist greed and exploitation, as did John Reed, Emma declared them both "streams from the same source."[19]

IWW soapboxers had also traveled to Colorado to show their solidarity with the miners. Shortly before the arrival of Emma and Ben, numerous Wobblies had been thrown into Denver's jails for disorderly conduct, vagrancy, and other such charges. The IWW boys, as usual, were quickly becoming more obnoxious in jail than they had been on the outside. They refused to work on the rock pile, even after sweat-box torture; instead, they sang—loudly. As word of the IWW lockups spread to the hinterlands, hundreds more Wobblies began to arrive on the freights. Street-corner oratory quickly reached new heights in Denver during these days as hundreds of veteran migrants and hoboes filled the roads, held impromptu meetings, denounced civil authority, and generally made local leaders extremely uncomfortable.[20]

With the jails packed with Wobblies, it was clear that the mayor and chief of police were rapidly reaching a state of panic. For Ben

Reitman this was a delicious opportunity. Always convinced of his savoir faire in delicate situations, he soon made diplomatic overtures and later remembered the mayor's perplexed musings:

> "Reitman, I don't want to lock up those I.W.W.'s but what will I do? If they have meetings on the street the preachers and businessmen complain. If I lock them up the news gets out and more of them come to town. What will I do?"
>
> "If you keep up these strong-arm tactics," Ben warned, "you will have a thousand men in jail instead of a hundred. It's better to have the businessmen and the preachers on your neck than to have a revolution."
>
> "Reitman," the mayor said, "if you'll promise there won't be any serious trouble and these boys won't have their meetings in the center of town, I'll parole them all to you."

At the county jail a pale, nervous warden greeted the anarchist emissary. "Doctor, listen to that noise. Do you know what that is? That's the I.W.W. singing—they're singing all the time. They make more trouble than any prisoners I ever had in my life. I got a couple of men here waiting to be hung and these radicals are teaching them to sing too. I haven't had any rest since they came to jail. You can have them!"

Doc was stirred as he heard the protest song from inside: "The workers' flag is deepest red, beneath its folds we live and die." He remembered seeing young, rough Wobbly hoboes on Chicago's main stem taking on the Salvation Army bands, matching every pious refrain with a call for revolution. He remembered several years earlier sitting in an IWW meeting listening to ragged workers singing "How the hell can we work when there's no work to do?" Here was an organization, a man in the hall told Ben then, that was vibrant, alive with spirit, living on nothing but faith and muscle and the songs of Joe Hill. It was a group of men, Ben knew, that was to be reckoned with. And now, years later, he saw the power of peaceful protest in action, the intimidation of numbers. The authorities were scared in Denver, not because the Wobblies had busted heads, but because they were filling the town, filling the jails, all the time singing those damned radical songs.

Ben told the Wobbly prisoners in Denver of the offer of freedom made by the mayor. To a man they opposed making any concessions to the authorities, and some even accused Ben of being an unwitting mouthpiece of the system. "To hell with you," one yelled at him. "To hell with the mayor. We'll rot in jail before we'll agree not to start a revolution." Up against such resistance it took all of Ben's considerable persuasiveness to convince the men to leave the jail. But he finally prevailed, and to the great relief of Denver's jailer and his guards, a pack of Wobblies marched out of jail and down Sixteenth Street, singing and howling, led by the infamous hobo doctor cum anarchist, swinging his walking stick.[21]

At the Wobbly hall the anarchists hosted a big feed, and Emma delivered a spirited lecture. She later wrote that the efforts of the anarchists, despite the cool reception by organized labor, had demonstrated once again the influence that could be marshaled by a few militants imbued with idealism. At the hall, with their banners waving, singing lustily, the anarchists and the Wobblies were, she said, united in comradeship and solidarity.[22]

The radical protests in Denver continued for several weeks as the mine war dragged on. Only the intervention of federal troops prevented a loss of life unprecedented in America's bloody history of labor struggles. The fiery labor organizer Mother Jones, who had been active in the early days of the Colorado strike, returned to Denver from Washington. "Well, here I am again boys," she shouted, fists clenched, from a platform erected at the statehouse. "You aren't licked by a whole lot . . . Just keep your heads level and don't do anything foolish . . . We'll win out. They'll never crush a principle."[23]

In spite of the efforts of nationally prominent figures such as Mother Jones, John Reed, and the anarchists, however, the deaths of the women and children in the Ludlow pits went relatively unavenged. With the governor and most of the state's politicians and jurists in the hip-pocket of the coal interests, most of the prominent arrests made in subsequent weeks were against the strikers. Indeed, one of the state judges who took an especially aggressive role in prosecuting the miners was a former coal company attorney.[24]

For Emma Goldman the Ludlow strike represented a significant turning point in the struggles of American labor to assert its power and determination. She wrote to Margaret Sanger that the resistance mounted by the striking miners and the support extended to them by the unions was "the most wonderful thing that has happened in this country." The fact was demonstrated, she declared, "that the only way the workers can command respect is when they are ready to fight." Emma even gloated that a surprising amount of company property had been destroyed by miner sabotage in the days following the massacre.[25]

If Emma applauded the miners' resistance, their refusal to be crushed underfoot by company thugs, if she saw hope in sabotage, news from New York, ugly news, quickly dashed her spirit. While in California, where Emma and Ben had traveled to continue their speaking tour, they learned of an explosion in a tenement house on New York's Lexington Avenue which had taken the lives of three men—Karl Hansen, Charles Berg, and Arthur Carson—and of an unidentified woman. Although the names were unfamiliar to Emma and Ben, press reports indicated that the four individuals were anarchists. The explosion was caused by a bomb which accidently detonated, a bomb apparently intended for John D. Rockefeller, Jr. Not surprisingly, Alexander Berkman became the principal target of police investigation. He quickly wrote Emma that the dead anarchists had worked with him in the Tarrytown protests against the Ludlow massacre and that they could very well have been plotting a terrorist attack on the swine Rockefeller. But the men had kept their intentions to themselves, Berkman wrote; he denied any knowledge of or culpability in the bomb factory on Lexington Avenue.

Emma later wrote, "Comrades, idealists, manufacturing gas bombs in a congested tenement-house. I was aghast at such irresponsibility."[26] But she remembered a day years before, in a tenement room on Fifth Avenue, the drawn blinds shielding another bomb maker—Alexander Berkman. She had watched him that day, silencing her fears and aversion by repeating over and over again that the ends justified the means. She still believed that capitalist evil would inevitably lead to acts of desperate retribution, that injustice would breed vengeance. But Emma now saw the futility of the kind of *Attentat* her comrade had carried out years before. Indeed, the publicity surrounding such violence was a devastating blow to the peaceful campaign she was waging, the lecture tours, the uncompromising but reasoned editorial stance of her magazine, *Mother Earth.* As Emma and Ben traveled the country they were constantly warding off charges that anarchists were nothing more than mad, bomb-wielding maniacs bent on subverting American society and values. The bomb makers on Lexington Avenue had given powerful credence to those charges.

Berkman did little to renounce the violent intentions of the suspected bomb makers and, in fact, promoted their martyrdom. With all the radical troops, including the IWW, warning the old anarchist warrior of the likely negative effect of a public funeral and mass demonstration, he charged ahead undeterred. Union Square was seething with a mob of 20,000 when Berkman delivered an incendiary speech. He later wrote Emma that he had deposited an urn containing the ashes of the dead anarchists in the office of *Mother Earth.* The urn, decorated in wreaths and red and black banners, was specially designed in the shape of a clenched fist.

As if all of this news from New York was not enough, the July issue of *Mother Earth,* put together by Berkman in Emma's absence, sent her into a rage. Lamenting that the entire issue was filled with "prattle about force and dynamite," Emma was particularly furious over an article written by one Charles Plunkett, a man she didn't even know, who had in the pages of her own magazine trumpeted inanely the glory and majesty of dynamite. If the ruling class had guns, the anarchists had dynamite. If the ruling class had soldiers, the anarchists had dynamite. To all oppression, and tyranny, and injustice, to jails and armies and navies, there was, for Charles Plunkett, one answer—dynamite. In all of the years Emma had published *Mother Earth* she had avoided this kind of frenzied harangue which so obviously played into the hands of political enemies and law enforcement officials. "I wanted the entire issue thrown into the fire," she wrote later.[27]

In early May the Ludlow tragedy had focused the country's attention on the plight of immigrant miners, the extent to which moneyed interests had exploited their labor, and the depths of barbarity to which the capitalists had sunk in maintaining power. Emma delivered lectures on Ludlow, and many newspaper reporters were favorably disposed to her side. But by summer all that had changed. The anarchists were again on the defensive. As Emma and Ben toured California the old questions about violence loomed even larger. The Lexington Avenue bomb had destroyed more than the lives of the anarchists in the tenement; it had grievously hurt the image of reform that Emma Goldman was trying to cultivate, an image that said that anarchists and other radicals were not murderers, that the callous purveyors of violence and injustice were not found in Greenwich Village tea parlors but in corporate boardrooms.

From San Francisco Emma wrote Margaret Sanger in late June that the radical movement in America was now mired in apathy, uninspired, helpless in the clutches of increased reactionary pressures. "It is hell," she wrote, "to be confronted with such a state of affairs."[28]

14. Billy Sunday

If Billy Sunday had been able to hit, he would surely have been one of baseball's greats. Discovered by the legendary Adrian ("Pop") Anson, signed to a Chicago White Stockings contract in 1883, Sunday played in the major leagues for eight years. Baseball observers raved about his lightning speed, acrobatic fielding, and his flair for the game. But at a time when batting averages often reached .400, Billy's lifetime mark was a mere .254. After striking out his first thirteen times at bat in the majors, Sunday drew this alleged remark from one fan: "If only he could steal first!" Billy Sunday would not make it to the Hall of Fame.

Early in his sporting career, however, Sunday wandered into the Pacific Garden Mission in Chicago and was genuinely moved by a revival service. "I have followed Jesus from that day," he wrote, "to this very second, like the hound on the trail of the fox, and will continue until he leads me through the pearly gate into the presence of God and it closes on its jeweled hinges." After a few more frustrating years at the plate he left baseball and joined the YMCA as an assistant secretary. Under the guidance of evangelist J. Wilbur Chapman, Sunday developed the unique speaking abilities and stage mannerisms which propelled his remarkable evangelistic career. He quickly discovered that swinging at the devil was much more lucrative than swinging at those exasperating curve balls.

Ordained by the Chicago Presbytery in 1903, Billy Sunday began his preaching career in small churches and tents, quickly graduating to large tabernacles in major cities. His performances were strikingly unconventional, even in the world of revival hoopla. With a huge supporting cast of choirs and skilled musicians, Billy was a commanding presence, leaping about the stage, slapping his hands, crashing his fists on chairs and other accessories. A photographic memory enabled him to reel off long sermons which were always punctuated by colorful homilies and common slang. At the close of his services, large numbers of converts would parade up the aisles to testify to their spiritual rebirth, a phenomenon known as "hitting the sawdust trail" (from the substance covering the tabernacle floors).

Sunday's conservative theology venerated hard work, godly living, the holiness of motherhood, and divine love; it condemned sin, vanity, the devil, scientists, liberals and radicals, booze, novel reading, theaters, and many other amusements, though not baseball. The most popular and influential evangelical minister of his day, Sunday paved the way for such later figures as Billy Graham and Oral Roberts.[1]

Ben Reitman, Emma Goldman, and other radicals were convinced that the Billy Sunday crusade was a serious menace to the labor movement and the rights of workingmen. His message of repentance, conversion, moral uplift, and righteous living was, they believed, pabulum fed to the worker to induce passivity. Just as plantation owners in the Old South encouraged slaves to endure their troubles and look toward Jordan and the next life, so too were the industrialists bent on making the working classes docile. Championed by the Chamber of Commerce, the Rotary, and other business and fraternal groups, Sunday was telling workers to be loyal, industrious, thankful for those few blessings they had, and, most of all, fearful of the Lord's wrath. From such a message few social revolutions are born, at least not the type favored by Ben Reitman. If too many workers were lured down the sawdust trail, the radicals feared, the drive for reform would be crippled.

Now, in the spring of 1915, Paterson, New Jersey, prepared to welcome Billy Sunday. Paterson, scene of the bloody millworkers strike of 1913, where industrialists had strong-armed 25,000 workers and their families with goon squads, where working conditions remained pitiful and paychecks inadequate. Paterson, symbol of repression and capitalist exploitation to labor and left-wing groups, greeted Billy Sunday, a symbol of religious hypocrisy.

On March 17, several days before Sunday's scheduled arrival, the electrifying IWW orator Elizabeth Gurley Flynn addressed a labor audience in Paterson, calling the famous evangelist a tool of the manufacturers, a union-breaker hired to distract the minds of the workers from their sufferings with simple-minded visions of heaven and threats of hell. Billy Sunday was coming to tell the workers how many glasses of beer they drank and how many cigarettes they smoked, Flynn said; he was not coming to talk about layoffs and blacklists and wretched working conditions. He also was not coming without a guarantee of lucre. "The promoters of Sunday," Flynn declared, "ought to pay more attention to material affairs instead of spiritual matters. If the ministers who are bringing Sunday to Paterson had your welfare at heart, they would take the money they are paying to this agitator and stick it in your pay envelopes."[2]

On April 3 the preacher and his entourage arrived in Paterson during a heavy snowstorm and went immediately to inspect the great revival tabernacle where he would wage a seven-week war on hell. The snow had wiped out a scheduled parade but not his spirits. "Of course we expect to accomplish great things here," he declared to a small crowd. "If you people are as good as the silk you make, you are all right."[3]

Easter Sunday, 1915. Nearly 8,000 people crowded the Paterson tabernacle to hear the renowned evangelist; hundreds of others were turned away, disappointed. A choir of 1,000 sat on a stage decorated by American flags wrapped around pillars. Each member of the choir held a hymnal with a large cross on the back. Sporting a $1,000, dark gray morning coat given to him by the department store magnate John Wanamaker, patent-leather shoes, a diamond scarfpin, and a gold chain, Billy Sunday leaped onto the stage, darted from side to side in a remarkable display of agility, and thrashed his arms. If an angel came to earth and associated with most human beings, he shouted, the angel would have to be fumigated, sterilized, and washed in carbolic acid. Too many lily-livered Christians allowed "cheap four-flushers" and "blatant old beer-soaked infidels" to laugh and smirk them out of their religion. Some Christians, those with no guts and stamina, were "excess baggage." Billy shadowboxed with the devil, hopped around the stage, threw himself prostrate on the floor, all the while slinging at the crowd his exhortations on sin. Shaking a threatening finger, he warned of the eternal damnation facing those who gave any quarter to the devil and his handmaidens. "I do not believe in this brotherhood of man," he roared. "We are not the children of God unless we are Christians. There are people in this world who are the children of the devil." He ran about the stage again, at one point leaping onto the pulpit, gesturing wildly.[4]

The first two weeks of the Paterson crusade were not happy ones for Billy Sunday. The number of new converts was disappointing, revenues were low, and costs were excessive. The ministers and other locals who had invited the evangelist were expected to roam among the audience during the meetings, encouraging wavering souls to come forward and open their wallets. So far the workers had failed to produce the kind of results the evangelist expected. On April 16 a flushed and excited Sunday gathered the troops aside after the close of the service and admonished, "You're not doing enough. You preachers must get down off the stage and mingle in with the crowd. If you think I'm going to wear out my life for a lot of dead ones you're very much mistaken." He was clearly upset. There should have been 500 converts that night, he fumed, instead of a paltry 300. The evangelist's troops, humbled by his rage, promised to do better.[5]

Adding to the Reverend Billy's pique that day was the arrival from New York of one of the enemy, one of the dangerous sin-and-gin-soaked radicals so inimical to the Way of the Light. Ben Reitman came to Paterson around noon, met with Frank Whitman of the Jewish Anarchist Committee and other radical leaders, and announced to the press his plans for an anti–Billy Sunday rally, to be held in Turn Hall on Monday, April 19. The radicals in New York, Ben said, had grown tired of waiting for the Paterson IWW crowd and other left-wing groups to take action against the evangelical invasion. The anarchists would step into the breach, led by Ben.

That evening at the tabernacle, Ben stood at an obscure spot beside the choir seated on the platform and watched Billy Sunday in action. Later, at the door of the press room, he confronted Edward Emmett, Sunday's personal representative. As a *New York Times* reporter listened in, Ben asked Emmett, "Is any man who has been converted ever bettered himself in any way?" "Yes, lots of them," Emmett responded. "They have increased their efficiency as employees." "Ah, that is just what I wanted you to say," Ben shot back. "They have been able to give more to the bosses." To Ben's various other labor-related questions Emmett offered silence.[6] Sunday had a simple rejoinder, however. To critics such as Reitman he said, "If you want to live in sin, all right, live in sin, and go to hell in the end. But you can't live in sin and go to heaven, too." Those people who were decent people agreed with his philosophy and message, Sunday said; those who didn't "give three whoops this side of perdition."[7]

On April 20 Billy Sunday addressed an audience of 9,000 at the tabernacle on the subject of "Repentance." He also paid a tribute to his wife, whom everyone called "Ma Sunday." "She wouldn't win any prize at a beauty show," Billy remarked, "but for good, common horse sense she's got anybody I ever met beat a mile."[8]

Across town in Turn Hall, a building in the Italian section of Paterson which had been used for labor rallies during the 1913 strike, Ben Reitman's anti–Billy Sunday rally had attracted a crowd of nearly 1,000. Ben was also accompanied by a close woman friend, one he often called "Mommy." Emma quickly attacked Ma Sunday's husband, calling the evangelist a "poor, screeching clown," an "empty barrel." If Christianity had Billy Sunday to represent it, then she felt sorry for Christianity. "He preaches hell," Emma declared. "Why, the poor people have lived so long in hell here that if they went to heaven they'd be kicked out for disorderly conduct. They wouldn't know how to behave on a cloud with a harp and no grub to eat."

After Emma finished her stock lecture on "The Failure of Christianity," Carlo Tresca, anarchism's most notable Italian, spoke to his many compatriots in the hall in their own language. Then Ben was ready for his contribution, an anti–Billy Sunday prayer. By way of introduction he declared that the purpose of the rally was not to abuse Sunday but to awaken the workers in the silk mills to the false doctrine now spewing forth from the tabernacle.[9] Ben Reitman, the man who had carried a Bible while hoboing across America and Europe, the man who on occasion had taught Sunday school lessons in Emma Goldman's *Mother Earth* offices, much to the shock and disgust of his fellow anarchists, now offered a prayer.

> Oh, Mr. God, the God of Billy Sunday, The German Emperor, Moody and Sankey, King George, Jonathan Edwards and the Russian Czar, if you are really on the square and live way up there in the skies; if you are not a bluffer and if you have a little power, won't you please, sir, for the love of brother Jesus and the deacons in the churches do something to help the poor working people of Paterson?
>
> Oh, dear Mr. God, if Billy Sunday is right and you know everything and

you do care a little, please make the bosses in the silk mills kinder to the workingmen; touch their hearts so that they will shorten the hours and raise the pay of the workers; fix it so that the owners of the mills will send the old women and the young children out of the factories and replace them with some of the able-bodied men who are looking for work.

Oh, dear Mr. God, please, dear Mr. God! Won't you do something to stop this war and prevent the workingmen from getting shot to pieces? Ain't you got enough sense and power to show all the ammunition manufacturers that it's wicked to sell bullets and cannon to European nations which will result in breaking your commandments?

Please, Mr. God, if you don't mind and if it ain't too much trouble, would you just as soon strike dead all the kings and diplomats and capitalists who are prolonging this war for the benefit of their own power and gain?

Dear Mr. God, you sent your very lovely son into the world to save it, but he didn't do very well. Men and women have been fourflushing and saying they believed in him, but everything in their lives has shown that they didn't care any more about him than they did about Mohammed, Socrates, or Proudhon.

Now Mr. God, I don't want to make you tired by asking too much. Some of us who do not want to meet you face to face and walk on the golden streets want to get the full product of our labor. We want to build a world where we can live in beauty, harmony and freedom. If you can help us, Mr. God, we will be much obliged and if you don't we will help ourselves and you can devote more of your time to Billy Sunday. Amen![10]

After Ben concluded the prayer he did a thriving business selling anarchist pamphlets. He also handed out free a printed sheet bearing the jingle "Live and Let Live." The last stanza read:

Every city has its easy marks, and
  evangelists are getting stale,
There are thousands who will fall for it,
  that's how Billy gets the kale.
There's lots of money in baseball, some
  players are in soft,
When asked to explain why he quit the
  game, just to help the man aloft.
If you want to queer this fellow just
  listen to what I say,
Keep your nickels and dimes in these
  hard times and he won't stay here one day.
There are lots of people worried, but
  they shouldn't be annoyed,
Keep the money home and feed our own,
  for there is plenty unemployed.[11]

The anti–Billy Sunday rally broke up around 10:30 P.M. Shortly before midnight a fire destroyed Turn Hall, leaving only the walls standing. The entire Paterson Fire Department futilely battled the spectacular blaze for several hours, as over 6,000 people jammed nearby streets to watch. One of the frenzied women in the crowd cried, "They say 'No Christ,' Heh look! Look! He speaks from Heaven."

The following day leading clergymen echoed the woman's assessment of the fire. "The judgment of God, surely," said John Callahan, chaplain of the Tombs prison in New York. "It is most singular," added Mrs. Garret Hobart, widow of the former vice-president and one of Billy Sunday's most ardent supporters. "I believe God has shown that he is pleased with the work Mr. Sunday is doing." Reverend A. Lincoln Moore of the Park Avenue Baptist Church concluded that the anarchist rally "gave God his opportunity and he answered by showering his fire on the scene of the blasphemy." Billy Sunday declined to comment. Few remembered that God had apparently done this before to Turn Hall: a fire had consumed much of the building in 1913 after a labor rally.[12]

On May 23, the great day of the Pentecost of biblical times, when Peter brought 3,000 souls to Christ, the Reverend Billy Sunday gave his farewell sermon of the Paterson crusade. A massive outpouring of 12,000 people jammed the tabernacle, with several thousand turned away. People sat on the sawdust trail aisles, on the back of the platform, even on the edge of the grand piano. A dozen nurses administered to some sixty people who suffered fainting spells. After his sermon Billy said that he would regret leaving Paterson and its people; Paterson's citizens had become more entangled in his heart strings than any others. Late that evening, Arthur H. Dey, treasurer of the Billy Sunday Committee for Paterson, handed the evangelist a check for $25,000. Total collections for the seven-week campaign were $62,741; expenses totaled $31,482. The revival netted local charities $6,258 and Sunday pocketed the rest. The following day he left Paterson for Philadelphia to see a ball game and plan another crusade.[13]

Cartoonist Robert Minor depicted on the cover of the May 1915 issue of *Mother Earth* a sprightly Billy Sunday tangoing with a forlorn, bleeding Jesus Christ, just removed from the cross. The lead article in the issue was Ben Reitman's prayer. The editors, commenting on the moral cant, religious hysteria, and social slavery alive in the land, declared that Sunday was a huckster mouthpiece of the church, press, and money interests. "His job is to make the workers content and satisfied with their misery, as that is the only safety valve against rebellion, which the powers that be fear even more than Billy's hell."[14]

Ben and Emma prepared for another cross-country tour, one which would take them to such cities as Los Angeles, San Francisco, Portland, Denver, and Cleveland. When Doc looked back years later to the confrontation with the Sunday crusade and his controversial prayer, he realized that most listeners assumed he was only delivering a mocking parody and that he himself must have been a confirmed atheist. They would have been astonished to learn that he wasn't. "I don't think I blasphemed in that prayer," Ben wrote. "I think God will understand. I am not certain who God is nor where he is, yet I believe in prayer. I don't care what the modernists and the scientists with their notions of evolution do to our Bible, but I hope they don't take prayer from the human race."[15]

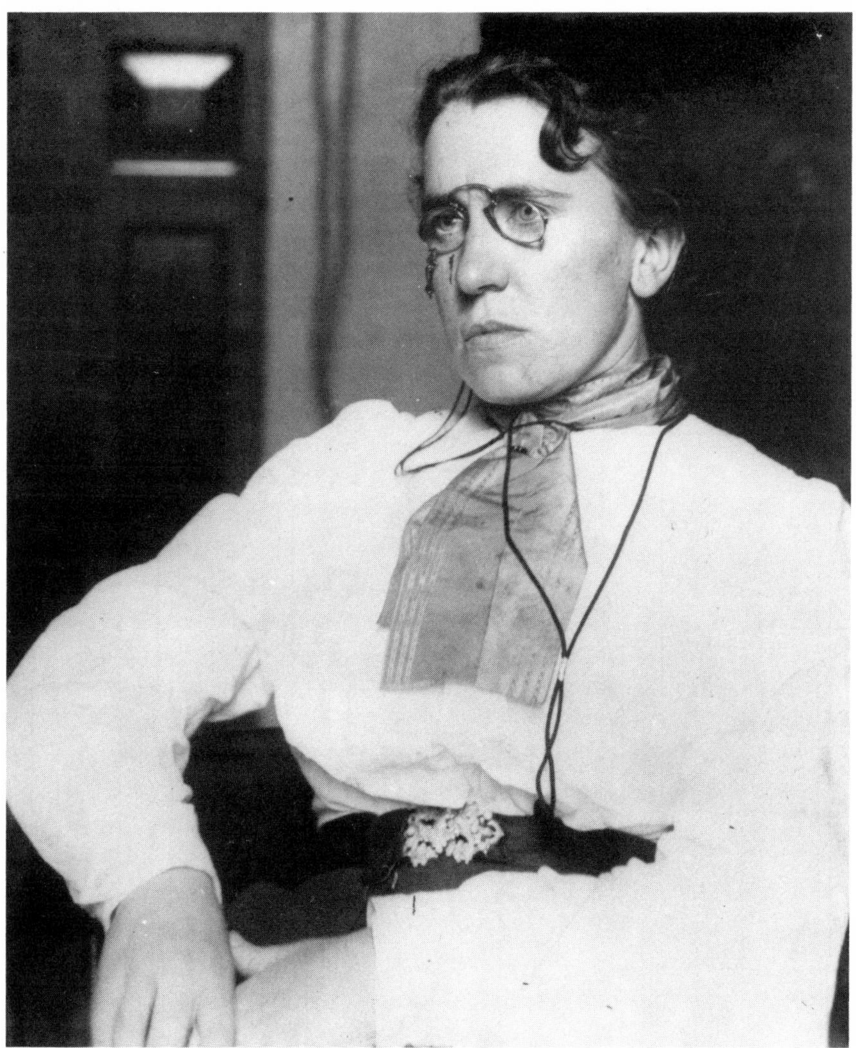

Emma Goldman, the "Queen of Anarchy."
(National Archives)

Ben Reitman, the "Main Stem Dandy," ca. 1918.
(Ben L. Reitman Papers, Special Collections, University Library, University of Illinois at Chicago)

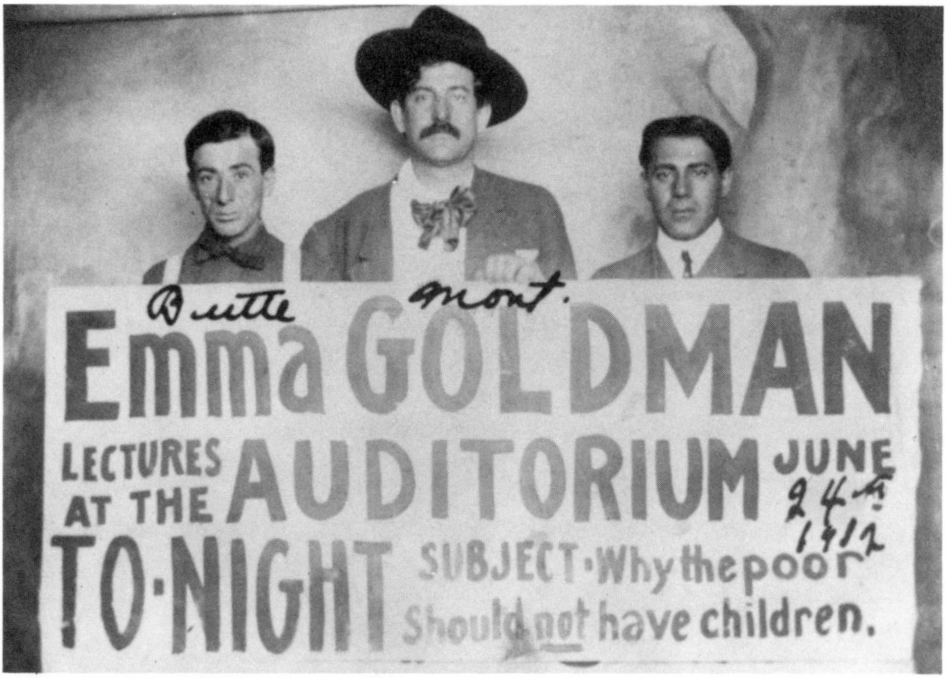

Disturbers of the peace.
Top: Ben Reitman and allies at a birth control rally, Butte, Montana, June 1912.
(Ben L. Reitman Papers, Special Collections, University Library,
University of Illinois at Chicago)
Bottom: Emma Goldman and Alexander Berkman, New York City, 1917.
(National Archives).

Friend and foe.
Top: John Reed, journalist and fellow radical; *bottom:* Evangelist Billy Sunday, as portrayed by painter George Bellows.
(Courtesy National Portrait Gallery, Smithsonian Institution)

15. The Poison Banquet

The early days of February 1916 were pivotal ones for George Mundelein and the American Catholic church. It was then that Mundelein, appointed two months earlier by Rome to head the Chicago archdiocese, arrived for the pageantry of his inaugural. Amid the pomp of elaborate ceremonies and banquets, the new archbishop whirled around the city, flushed with excitement over the exuberant welcome. "Chicago has received me with a cordiality which has completely won my heart," he exclaimed. "But this friendliness, kindness and hospitality are just what I expected of Chicago."[1]

Ordained in 1895, George Mundelein had risen swiftly in the diocese of Brooklyn, first as priest, then chancellor, then monsignor at age thirty-four, and auxiliary bishop at thirty-seven. Under his leadership the parish erected an elegant church and school, designed in the French Gothic style, an accomplishment noted both for the architectural excellence of the edifice and the extraordinary fund-raising skills of Mundelein. The New York cleric had gained considerable notoriety in Catholic circles, and no one in the religious hierarchy was surprised at his promotion in 1915. The particular assignment to Chicago, however, was something of a shock. The ascendancy of such a young clergyman to a position of this importance was highly unusual. The Catholic community in Chicago was surprised, to say the least. Mundelein himself was in a kind of euphoric disbelief, basking in the warm adulation always reserved for Chicago's religious premier.[2]

On February 10 Mundelein attended a magnificent civic reception at the University Club, an event sponsored by the board of governors of the Catholic Church Extension Society, featuring as speakers Richmond Dean of the Pullman Company and well-known diplomat William J. Calhoun. The guest list boasted 300 of the elite of Chicago's business, academic, political, and religious communities, including Governor Edward Dunne, former mayor Carter Harrison, business magnate Samuel Insull, and assorted judges, bank presidents, and military figures. To the young prelate this was heady stuff.

As the guests sat down to dinner that evening, Monsignor Luke Evers, pastor of Chicago's St. Andrews Church, was so deep in conversation that he didn't touch his chicken soup. Lucky for him, for the soup had been poisoned. The first intimation of trouble came when a gray-haired man seated at a table in the center of the room rose from his chair gripping his waist, staggered, and fell full-length. As men rushed to his side, others in the room began to swoon and groan, several falling about. "Men rushed here and there," Monsignor Evers said, "attempting to do something to alleviate the suffering of their fellows but they, too, soon were overcome by the poison."[3] Diners lay on chairs, leaned against walls, reeled up and down the halls, moaning and crying. Fortunately for the banquet guests a physician, Dr. J. B. Murphy, although himself mildly stricken, mixed a large quantity of mustard with water and wandered around the floor administering the emetic. Although nearly 100 guests suffered serious nausea, vomiting, and vertigo, all of them survived.

With many of the guests leaving the hall, and the governor sitting "as pale as a ghost," according to one reporter, the new archbishop carried off the rest of the night with marked aplomb. "While we have seen 100 or more of the great men here tonight falter and fall by the wayside," Mundelein declared, "it is to be noted that the church and state remained serene. It augurs well for Illinois." Mundelein later told a *Chicago Tribune* reporter that it would take something stronger than bad soup to put him out.[4]

It was first believed that the banqueters had been stricken with ptomaine poisoning, but by the following day investigators had discovered the true cause—arsenic. The University Club had very nearly been the scene of mass murder, and it didn't take long to identify the poisoner:

WANTED—For attempted homicide, Jean Crones, about 24 years old; 5 feet 7 inches tall; 150 pounds; dark, crisp, bushy hair, brushed back; pale complexion; high cheek bones; piercing look. When greeted he always smiles. May have small dark spot above right eye. Continually smiles when talking and when so smiling shows a depression on both cheeks and chin. When last seen wore a dark suit and gray overcoat, and he may wear a cap or soft hat. His shoulders are stooped, and he walks fast, with a long, swinging gait. Wears a ring designed with a wolf's or lion's head, with a small diamond in the mouth; cost $320. Is a great reader. Very quiet, neat in appearance, and usually travels alone, and when sitting his knees shake, as though from nervousness. Born in Urdingen or Cologne, Germany. Speaks French, German, and English with a German accent.[5]

Jean Crones was a cook at the University Club. He was also an anarchist. Crones's former landlord said that his now infamous boarder displayed no unusual characteristics when he first moved into the apartment. "Then he went bugs on the subject of anarchy and Emma Goldman. My wife told me I had better get him out or we would get into some sort of trouble." Crones, the landlord said, later moved out, saying that he felt guilty living in such a good room when so many individuals in the world were impoverished.[6]

Police found in Crones's room a veritable chemical laboratory—numerous bottles and vials, test tubes, gas plates, batteries, cans of asbestos, nitroglycerin, and fuses. Several of the bottles contained arsenic, cyanide of potassium mercury, and other poisons. They also found a rifle and other weapons, as well as various anarchist writings, including copies of *Mother Earth*. The *Tribune* was careful to point out that one of the issues of Emma Goldman's magazine commanded "Don't Submit."[7] In the rooming houses of two of Crones's friends police found photographs of forty churches and various public buildings in Chicago and other major cities, among them the First National Bank of Chicago and the Cathedral of St. John the Divine in New York. One of the uncovered letters talked of a plan to blow up the state penitentiary at Joliet, Illinois.

With local police now beginning to fear a nationwide anarchist plot, federal authorities, under the direction of Hinton Claybaugh, head of the Chicago Department of Justice, joined the investigation. They found that Crones had enrolled in the chemistry department of the International Correspondence School of Scranton, Pennsylvania, in October 1915. Officials of the school revealed that Crones was a remarkable student, never receiving exam marks lower than ninety-two. On January 18 he had submitted his fourteenth lesson, the last he ever sent. It dealt with arsenic and other poisons.[8]

Wearied by a barrage of questions from reporters, Chicago's disgruntled mayor denied that his city was a nest for organized assassins and plotters and bombers of churches. "I'll be glad when the newspapers . . . print something good about the city," Thompson snapped, "instead of heralding it from one end of the country to the other as the headquarters of the murderers and criminals of the world." But police and federal investigators found enough evidence in the homes of local anarchists to convince them that something was afoot. Several police spokesmen painted a sordid picture of an anarchist criminal underground ready to strike violent terror. "That these anarchists operating in Chicago are desperate men is unquestioned," Police Chief Healey declared. "That they took their first desperate step at the banquet is undoubted." One of the anarchists whose room yielded up a stock of dynamite had some months earlier lost an eye and one finger in an accidental explosion. These were, Chief Healey warned, dangerous men,[9] and many believed that only a small part of the anticlerical, antiestablishment plot had been unearthed, a plot to bring a holocaust to Chicago, New York, and other cities; to hurl bombs in the midst of churchgoers; to destroy city skyscrapers, hotels, federal buildings; to poison the soup of the nation's leaders. Jean Crones was indeed a foreboding specter.

If the authorities needed additional evidence that Crones was the villain in the "Poison Banquet," that came on February 17 in a letter he wrote to the *New York Times*, telling all. In a mocking, almost jocular tone Crones detailed his arrival in America in 1913; his various jobs in restaurants in New York, Cleveland, and Chicago; his studies in chemistry and astronomy from the Scranton correspondence school; his interest in radical politics. "As I love science I hate religion," he wrote, "and as I have seen the menue for that dinner 12 days before I thought that it a sanitary thing to make a good clean up and I started right away to Work." He was sorry, he said, that his poison had not killed everyone at the banquet, or at least a hundred or so. Then, in a second letter to the *Times*, Crones talked of thousands tramping the streets without food or shelter while church prelates hosted sumptuous dinners of Beluga caviar and champagne with money taken from the poor. "That is the failure of Christianity," he charged, "an insult toward honesty and a challenge to Humanity."[10]

Chief of Detectives Nicholas Hunt concluded that Crones's

brazen and reckless effrontery in sending letters to the press was only a reflection of typical anarchist fatalism, a loyalty to a dogma that recognizes ideal before life, a state of mind that seeks martyrdom. Crones, like the Haymarket fiends of another generation, would just as soon die taking out a few policemen in a dazzling gesture for the radical cause. The terrorist, Hunt said, was probably at that moment carrying "some sort of an infernal machine" or some nitroglycerin.[11]

In yet another scornful missive to the *Times* on February 19, Crones said that he had become an anarchist after the atrocities of the Ludlow massacre. Ridiculing the futility of the massive dragnet now on his trail, the fugitive said he had recently walked into police headquarters in New York and sauntered around amid detectives, talking with a few and all the time snickering.

As the investigation of the near-tragedy proceeded, it became clear that Jean Crones had originally believed that 200 guests would dine at the banquet. When 300 attended, the arsenic in the soup he had prepared the previous day had been thinned to one and two-tenths grains per guest, or about three-fifths of the minimal fatal dosage. Crones was not at the University Club when the soup was served. If he had known of the expanded guest list, he likely would have increased the amount of poison, and February 10, 1916, would have been forever remembered as one of the most sensational and odious days in the history of American radicalism.[12]

On February 23 Archbishop Mundelein attended a public dinner at the Knights of Columbus, his first since the University Club banquet two weeks earlier. As he dipped a spoon into a bowl of soup and brought it to his lips, hushed guests peered uneasily in his direction. When the prelate announced, "It's all right," a rousing cheer echoed through the hall.[13]

In the next few weeks anonymous letters and phone tips flooded police headquarters in cities across the country. Most everybody, it seemed, had seen the prisoner or at least knew somebody who had. On a single day in late February, New York police dragged three men into custody on suspicion of being the elusive anarchist. Meanwhile, Crones merrily played the fox. He crashed a dinner at the Annunciation Club in Buffalo, an occasion at which none other than Governor Dunne of Illinois was a guest. In a picture published in a local paper the following morning, a number of men at the dinner, including Dunne, are shown smiling broadly. Jean Crones is among them.[14]

Ben Reitman met Jean Crones in the summer of 1916, after the twenty-two-year-old fugitive had eluded the manhunt for several months. "Tell me," Ben asked the cocky, feverish radical, "why did you do such a thing?" "I'll tell you why—Archbishop Mundelein represents the Catholic Church. The Catholic Church is against science and against the working class. The priests keep the poor people in ignorance. In Italy and in Spain the working people don't get any education and the Catholic Church is responsible for it." The rich people at the University Club banquet, Crones continued, were unscrupulous agents for a capitalist system that starved and crushed the poor; they were fat, wine drinkers slobbering over their seven-dollar-a-plate dinners; they were craven enemies of working classes. The church, the politicians, the army, the police, the businessmen—all were there at the banquet; all deserved punishment, even death. "When you scare them like I did," Crones bragged, "they'll think; then things will be better for the working class."[15]

In the succeeding months the paths of Reitman and Crones crossed on several occasions, as the fugitive worked first in a factory in Brooklyn and lived in a room in one of its best residential districts. His picture may have graced wanted posters offering a reward of $10,000, yet Jean Crones delighted in strolling around Times Square chatting with policemen. His audaciousness seemed to be his shield.

The hunt continued. In early January 1917 a man was arrested in Watertown, South Dakota—five feet, eight inches tall, 155 pounds, stoop-shouldered, black hair inclined to be curly, piercing stare, continuous smile, ability to speak both French and German. Federal investigators rushed to Watertown, where they met Carl Ackerman, a German-born hobo dishwasher. The following month they scurried to Middletown, Connecticut, where local authorities had in custody another stoop-shouldered, foreign-born drifter with a broad smile. More disappointment—they found Nicholas Klutz, a Dutchman who worked as a night watchman. Several months later, postal officials in Grand Rapids, Michigan, turned over to federal agents an envelope addressed to Woodrow Wilson. It had on the flap an American flag with the following words written, appropriately, in red ink: "War Is Hell: Those That Want War Can Go to Hell." It was signed "Jean Crones." In Washington, D.C., the Crones investigative file bulged. But the poisoner remained on the loose.[16]

In the summer of 1917 the limping manhunt suddenly gained new life. In a casual conversation with Dr. William Evans, a medical columnist for the *Chicago Tribune,* Ben Reitman mentioned that he had talked to Jean Crones. As Doc should have guessed, the information traveled quickly through Evans's reporters at the *Tribune* and on to the Chicago police and the federal agents. Once again, with a bit of offhand braggadocio, Ben had managed to entangle himself in a nationally sensational affair.

On Saturday, October 6, Herman Schuettler, general superintendent of police, City of Chicago, Ben Reitman's friendly nemesis since the days of the hobo demonstrations a decade earlier, arrived at Grand Central Station in New York. There he met Captain W. K. Evans of the United States Army Intelligence Service. The mission: to interrogate Reitman as to the whereabouts of Jean Crones. After checking into the inconspicuous Long Acre Hotel, Schuettler telephoned the offices of *Mother Earth.*

"This you, Ben?"

"Yes, Dr. Ben Reitman speaking."

"Reitman, don't repeat anything I say and I will tell you who this is. You listen to what I have to say and you say nothing, at least don't let anyone know who is talking to you. This is Schuettler."

"Chief, I recognize your voice."

"You are a damn fool; you had to spill the beans immediately. I told you not to mention my name."

Schuettler asked Ben to meet him in front of the hotel to talk over an important matter.

"Is everything on the square?" Reitman asked.

"I never told you anything that was not on the square, have I?" the Chief responded. "You come on and you need not fear anything, everything is allright. I never told you any lies."

Although Emma, supported by Alexander Berkman, argued that Ben should not voluntarily meet with Schuettler, Ben decided to go. In Schuettler's room at the Long Acre the chief told Doc that he believed him to be a philosophical anarchist, not of the same stripe as some of his fire-spitting, bomb-making, monomaniac comrades; that Ben could not possibly condone the type of insane act of horror perpetrated by the poisoner Crones; and that a large reward awaited anyone who turned Crones in. Ben replied that Crones's attempt at mass murder was completely repugnant; that during the years he had been in the anarchist movement he had tried to soften the violent predilections of some of the principal spokesmen of the radicals. Perhaps his influence had made a difference, even saving some lives. As for Crones, Doc said that he had not seen him for many months. If not dead, he might have fled to another country.

At a second meeting, W. K. Evans joined Schuettler in pressing Ben further, Evans accusing the hobo doctor of knowing more than he had revealed. Evans tried to persuade him to be a general informant, insisting that he must surely be privy to the insidious plots being hatched by the radicals. Schuettler then said,

> "Ben, I'm an old man. I have been in the police game for thirty-five years. I want to get out of it. My son's grown up and is going to practice medicine; and I've got a little farm and I want to settle down. Also, I'm ill and I don't think I'll live very long. Before I die I want to achieve the ambition of my lifetime. I want to get Jean Crones . . . Now, Ben, I've got a lot of things on you. There are a lot of things we could do to you. I'm not going to mention that. I'm not trying to bluff you nor to scare you . . . I'm not trying to bribe you, but here's a thousand dollars cash that I want to give you for your trouble. Now, don't try to say that you don't know where Jean Crones is—we know you do."

Reitman once again denied that he knew the whereabouts of Crones. He told the chief that after ten years in the anarchist movement he was weary, dissatisfied, and unhappy, anxious to go back to Chicago, practice medicine, and raise a family. He had never betrayed a comrade or a trust, he said. "I want to go back to Chicago clean." He had told Crones never to give him his address; he didn't know where to find him. "I want to be able to have the respect of Emma Goldman and the comrades I have worked with for ten years; and I want to be able to hold my head up and respect myself. If there's anything that is honorable that I can do to help you I'll be glad to do it—you know that. I can't betray my friends. I'd rather go to jail or die than to be a traitor."

Schuettler and Reitman shook hands. "That's all right, Ben," the chief said. "I don't want you to do anything you can't do." With that Schuettler returned to Chicago, and after the abysmal failure to elicit a single piece of information on Crones from Ben Reitman, the federal investigation whimpered to a close as well. W. K. Evans and his colleagues turned to other matters.[17]

What of the fate of the principal actors in the "Poison Banquet"? Archbishop Mundelein became Cardinal Mundelein on March 24, 1924. His leadership epitomized the big city cardinals of the first half of this century, men such as Cardinal O'Donnell in Boston and Cardinal Spellman in New York, men who consolidated and centralized the administrative structure of the Catholic church in America, tying it more closely to Rome; men who gave the church self-confidence and clout, businesslike administration and political influence. Jean Crones, the hunted, was never found, disappearing into the recesses of the radical underground. Although for a time he taunted and publicly reviled the federal and local law enforcement agencies with impunity, a quirk of fate had guaranteed for the young anarchist a sentence of anonymity. For the lack of a little more poison, the man who craved attention and martyrdom was soon forgotten.

And what of Ben Reitman? From the beginning of his association with Emma Goldman and the anarchist movement, many of the radicals were chagrined that the flamboyant Chicago hobo doctor nestled too closely with men like Herman Schuettler. Some even suspected Ben of being an informant. The story of the Crones affair typifies many of Doc's wanderings through the world of American radicalism. Never an ideologue, always the boisterous jester, he made nervous both the committed leftists, who feared betrayal, and the hardened right-wing enthusiasts, who considered all anarchists filth and scum. Both sides were wrong about Ben. Evans, the zealous federal agent, had been convinced that he would break under pressure, that intimidation or bribery would further loosen his already loose lip and bring forth a rich garden of facts about Crones and other anarchist activities. Schuettler knew better. He had told Evans early in the investigation that Ben, though loud and coarse, had his own ideals, to which Evans had responded, "Oh, he will tell me all about it . . . I have handled such fellows before."

A few days after the meetings between the three men, Doc sent a letter to the Chicago police chief, an individual for whom he had great respect and personal affection. Ben told him again, as he had in the meetings, that he couldn't betray his friends.[18] Evans was surprised at his sincerity. Most of the anarchists would have been too.

16. Birth Control

In October 1915 the chief of police of Portland, Oregon, confronted Ben Reitman after an Emma Goldman speech on birth control. "What is this birth control, anyway," the chief asked. "Is it anything like self-abuse?"[1]

Perhaps no other issue advanced by anarchists and other radicals in the late nineteenth and early twentieth centuries was so wrapped in misunderstanding and confusion as that of birth control. To many Americans, including the Portland police chief, birth control was illicit and morally wrong, whatever it was. To others, such as Emma Goldman and Ben Reitman, birth control was vitally important in the battle against poverty in the major cities. Opposition to it touched such basic issues as women's rights, free speech, and government censorship.

As early as the 1820s the English radical Francis Place shocked many of his contemporaries by including family limitation in his proposals to strengthen the position of the laboring classes. Englishmen gasped when the eminent libertarian thinker John Stuart Mill distributed a pamphlet that encouraged *coitus interruptus* and the use of vaginal sponges, an act that landed him in jail for several days. But by the latter decades of the nineteenth century, public opinion and legal interpretation in England had so changed that the Malthusian League, founded in 1877 to furnish advice on family limitation, was openly advertising birth control information in its journal. Any married or about-to-be married individual could sign a printed form and receive a packet of contraceptive advice—any individual, that is, except an American. The Malthusian League reported that it was "unable to comply with applications for this leaflet from the United States," the home territory of Anthony Comstock.[2]

Born to pious, fundamentalist parents in Pennsylvania, as a boy Comstock attended daily prayer sessions on his family's farm and dutifully listened to the admonition that sex was sinful, a proposition he not only accepted but later made his personal crusade. His favorite biblical quotation was, "Whosoever looks on a woman to lust after her has already committed adultery in his heart." After serving in the Union Army and working as a clerk in a store in New Canaan, Connecticut, Comstock moved to New York City and became active in the Young Men's Christian Association. Soliciting support from a number of financial backers of the YMCA, he launched a campaign against his favorite obsession, commercial vice.

By March 1873 the zealous purity spokesman had marshaled enough support around the country to push through the U.S. Congress a bill whose main purpose was to close the mails to obscene material. The law vested in the Post Office the power to suppress "every filthy book, pamphlet, picture, paper, letter, writing, print, or other publication of an indecent character, and every article or thing designed, adapted, or intended for preventing conception or producing abortion. . . ." Thus federal legislation for the first time defined information on birth control as obscene. A number of state legislatures enacted laws modeled on Comstock's handiwork, and Congress appointed the fundamentalist reformer as a special agent of the Post Office, with the authority to arrest those who used the mails in violation of the law.

Comstock relished his considerable power, even persuading the courts to convict owners of dress shops who displayed naked wax dummies. He used decoy letters and false signatures to entrap physicians who dispensed contraceptive information and even entrapped victims by impersonating loose women and sexually depraved men. He went after painters who worked from nude models and instituted legal proceedings against George Bernard Shaw's play *Mrs. Warren's Profession.* Comstock and his allies associated birth control devices with "vice emporiums," because condoms were, as one physician explained, "suggestive of licentiousness and the brothel, and their employment degrades to bestiality the true feelings of manhood and the holy state of matrimony."

One leftist observer remembered seeing Comstock talk in New York's Labor Church at Third Avenue and Fourteenth Street for almost two hours about the carloads of pictures, devices, periodicals, and other forms of filthy expression he had confiscated. "He told how many men and women he'd forced into prison, how many had committed suicide, and how many he had served well in the work of glorifying His Holy Name." Comstock anchored himself solidly on the side of censoring much of classical literature. "The country must be cleansed of sin and immorality," he declared, "and if the classics stand in the way they should be destroyed. Think of all the adolescent boys who have been led to masturbation by these writers. . . ."[3]

Before the advent of Comstockery and the 1873 law, the middle and upper classes in post–Civil War America had little difficulty obtaining birth control information and devices. The well-to-do business and professional classes could simply secure such materials from their favorite physicians or druggists. In light of the growing number of available contraceptives such as pessaries and suppositories, the *New York Medical Journal* ran a parody entitled "A Raid on the Uterus." The article detailed 123 different varieties of pessaries on the market, from a simple plug to a "patent threshing machine, which can be worn with the largest hoops." This proliferation far outweighed the need, the author insisted. "I do think that this filling the vagina with such traps, making a Chinese toyshop of it, is outrageous."[4]

But under the new federal and state laws, diligently monitored by Comstock and his lieutenants, dispensing birth control information was now illegal. Like those infamous, dirty French postcards, contraceptives had become a brown-paper-bag purchase. For middle- and upper-class women, however, the law didn't end the supply. Although most of the medical profession obeyed the new statutes, some physicians and druggists continued to provide information to their friends. Those women told others and the illicit knowledge spread, much to the dismay of Anthony Comstock. But for masses of poor, immigrant families in America's large cities, those who had no physician or druggist friends, the lack of contraceptive advice often meant economic disaster and personal anguish.

Earlier, as a nurse and midwife, Emma Goldman had ministered to poor immigrant mothers living in shabby tenements who were struggling to feed and protect large families; she also had counseled many who pleaded for the secrets of family limitation. To Emma the issue was an extension of the anarchist philosophy of human liberation and the right of all individuals to control their own destinies, free from artificially proscribed dictums of government or convention. All cultures, she believed, were restrictive, their demands on personal growth inhibitory. In the United States thousands of women, submerged by ignorance, prejudice, and exploitation, were being denied control over their own bodies.

Emma talked often of the masses of poor women butchered by the economic grinding wheel, deprived of information to which they, above all others, should have access. The whole idea was criminal, she believed, a product of politicians and wealthy industrialists anxious to maintain a necessary supply of hapless workers for their factories and soldiers for their wars. Keep the underclasses in poverty, keep them breeding, ensure a bountiful supply of industrial slaves and cannon fodder.[5]

But in fitting the birth control issue into the confines of a worldview of class exploitation, Emma was giving too much credit to the power groups for pulling off what she saw as an orchestrated policy. In fact, many in those groups feared the alarming population increase among immigrants, feared that the western European stock in America would soon be overwhelmed by inferior sorts. Race suicide, many called it. If birth control could have been directed only toward the masses of recent immigrants in the cities, much of the "master class" would have tolerated it. What so many feared, however, was that birth control would be only a middle-class phenomenon, embraced by the very women in society who should be encouraged to have more babies, not fewer.

In March 1905 Theodore Roosevelt declared that the desire among women for smaller families was a decadent, moral disease. Those women who avoided having children were, the president said, criminals against the race, "the object of contemptuous abhorrence by healthy people." The women to whom he referred were, of course, America's Yankee stock, and he was not alone in his sentiments. By the turn of the century a chorus of politicians, sociologists, and other academics had lamented that the traditional American population was giving way numerically to recent immigrants, nonwhites, and the poor. Even strict immigration laws did not seem to stop the galloping increase of those of the meaner sort.

The respected economist Francis Walker had published findings in 1891 showing a steadily increasing birthrate among foreign-born Americans and a corresponding decline among native-born Americans. A decade later, Robert Hunter, in his book *Poverty,* concluded that this ominous trend would eventually result in the complete substitution throughout the United States of one kind of people, presumably the best, for another kind, presumably the worst. The president of Harvard added his own gloomy statistic—Harvard graduates, Lord help them, were not even replenishing their own numbers. To observers such as Roosevelt and many others of traditional American heritage, this was social degeneration. The president despaired for a country now losing its fundamental virtues and "strong, racial qualities without which there can be no strong races." Birth control, he and others argued, was destroying America's racial integrity.[6]

Emma Goldman was right in declaring that the lack of birth control information was resulting in large families among the immigrants and the attendant tragic social and personal repercussions that those large families produced. But those of the "master class," men like Teddy Roosevelt, did not rejoice any more than Emma over those large numbers and, in fact, were afraid of them.

Birth control was far more complicated than an issue of capitalist exploitation. It involved vague assumptions held by much of the American public about the movement and its implications: birth control, many said, was sinful; it was an attack on the family, the bedrock national institution; it was a rebellion by middle- and upper-class women against their primary social responsibility, motherhood; it encouraged promiscuity among women; its tools were the tools of prostitution and therefore were immoral; it was another perfidious, left-wing assault against the American Way. As radicals like Emma Goldman and Ben Reitman pressed the birth control issue, these assorted notions and prejudices stood as formidable challenges.

In the early 1900s Emma had often discussed birth control in speeches. She also had worked with the free-speech warrior Moses Harman in arranging joint-subscription offers for *Mother Earth* and Harman's *American Journal of Eugenics.* Harman, an aging, embattled foe of Comstockery, had spent much time in jail for his attempts to spread birth control information in the late nineteenth century. Emma, in a 1910 article, hailed him as the pioneer of the free-motherhood movement in America.

Although birth control was only one issue addressed by Emma in her work, it nevertheless made an especially keen impression on one young woman who had recently arrived in New York—a woman who would profoundly change the debate over birth control in the United States.[7] Margaret Sanger began to learn many of the propaganda tactics employed by the radical left when her husband introduced her to his socialist and anarchist friends in Greenwich Village in 1911. A daughter of poor Irish parents in Corning, New York, married in 1902 to a young architect, the mother of three children in less than ten years, Sanger had been restless under the constraining bonds of suburban life. When William Sanger occasionally took his young wife to hear Big Bill Haywood, the Wobbly chief, socialists Eugene Debs and Morris Hillquit, and the New York anarchists, she reveled in the excitement and spirit of rebellion and defiance. She spent long evenings with Alexander Berkman in little Russian restaurants along Second Avenue, chain-smoking cigarettes, sipping tea, and talking about revolution and anarchist philosophy. And at Emma's home on East Thirteenth Street, while discussing the emancipation of women, Margaret received her first exposure to contraceptive information. The issue knifed her conscience as no other had before.

Years later, when Margaret Sanger was an international figure, she chose, in the interest of placating her more respectable supporters, to forget those nights in Russian restaurants and anarchist havens. But the days in 1911 were exhilarating ones: lectures by Leonard Abbott of the Free Speech League; intimate discussions with the journalist Lincoln Steffens; street-corner orations by a wide assortment of radicals and proselytizers. She joined the Socialist party and actively worked in labor strikes. She began to make speeches and write articles on sex, reproduction, and contraception. In one of her pieces, called "How Six Little Children Learned the Truth," Sanger decried "the deprived childhoods of children whose mothers are forced to abandon them to earn money" and charged the capitalist system with "fiendish exploitation, and ultimate murder." In other articles she lashed out at a system that forced underclass women to slink off to quack abortionists to limit their families, visits which often killed more than the unwanted fetuses.[8]

In 1914 Sanger founded a new journal, *The Woman Rebel,* dedicated to carrying the banner of the birth control movement, to mobilizing a mass demand for the legalization of contraception. Postal authorities ruled the *Rebel* unfit for pure eyes and thus unmailable. Sanger ignored their injunctions, was charged with violating the obscenity laws, and fled to Europe in October 1914 to avoid arrest. Ever on the prowl, the New York Society for the Suppression of Vice dispatched one of its agents to entrap Sanger's husband, who was still in the United States, into handing over a copy of a how-to-do-it pamphlet called *Family Limitation.* William Sanger was arrested.[9]

The threats of legal reprisals against the Sangers convinced Emma Goldman that the time had come to provoke confrontation, that she "must either stop lecturing on the subject or do it practical justice." On March 28, 1915, to an audience of 600 at New York's Sunrise Club, Emma publicly explained how to use a contraceptive. She was so certain of being arrested that she took a book along to read in jail. Surprisingly, she was not apprehended; capricious were the fates of lawbreakers, she thought. Emma continued to lecture in major cities, convinced that the work was important but annoyed by some of the women in the audiences who giggled and tittered and snickered at the subject matter. After one particularly annoying night of watching her remarks draw blushes and feigned shock from well-heeled society types, Emma wrote, "It's just been hell to speak on Birth Control with many women present." But she, along with others, persevered.[10]

For the ninth time in their tempestuous relationship, Ben and Emma toured the country: six weeks in Chicago, stops in Minneapolis, Cleveland, Pittsburgh, Denver, and on to the West Coast. "O Brave Margaret Sanger!" Reitman wrote. "You can be glad even if they hang you or send you to the penitentiary for life." The anarchists had spread birth control literature across the country, and Anthony Comstock, "though aided by all the powers of government or hell, cannot stop this stupendous movement."[11]

Led by women socialists and Wobblies, local birth control organizations appeared in 1915 in several major cities. Leading radicals such as Elizabeth Gurley Flynn and Eugene Debs joined Emma Goldman in flailing at the obscenity laws, Debs promising Margaret

Sanger a "pretty good-sized bunch of revolutionists" to spread the gospel. Liberal and radical periodicals such as *The New Republic* and *The Masses* began to carry articles on the movement, the latter featuring on one of its covers an illustration of a shrouded woman in the dark of night carrying a baby toward a waterfront. The caption read: "Family Limitation—Old Style."[12]

In September 1915 William Sanger was convicted in a dramatic trial that saw radicals evicted from the courtroom for shouting at a judge who called the distribution of birth control information a violation not only of the laws of man but of God. Too many people, he said, were attempting to prevent motherhood. "If some persons would go around and urge Christian women to bear children, instead of wasting their time on woman suffrage, this city and society would be better off." Anthony Comstock testified against William Sanger, the last time the old crusader appeared in public. When he died on September 21, 1915,[13] Floyd Dell remarked, "The infamous Anthony Comstock died and went to hell."

The general of the moral purity movement had left a remarkable legacy. Comstock, in his war against the poison of pornography and vice, had destroyed enough books, films, and obscene magazines to fill a building. And Comstock's death did not dampen the war effort. The mantle of leadership was now seized by the mild but earnest son of a Navy admiral who had been shocked in his youth by dirty pictures circulating around his Brooklyn high school. John S. Sumner, forty years old and a member of the YMCA, now became New York's top filth spy, confiscating books, films, postcards, and periodicals just like his predecessor, editing out "damns" and rewriting love scenes from manuscripts submitted by authors to New York publishers. As writers such as Theodore Dreiser found to their disgust, and as Margaret Sanger, Emma Goldman, and Ben Reitman would discover, the New York Society for the Suppression of Vice had a new leader just as driven as the hated Comstock. Birth control champions had ahead of them much more harassment and many more days in jail.[14]

To Ben Reitman, the celebrated clap doctor from Chicago, the birth control movement was familiar intellectual terrain, not some mine field of abstract philosophical reasoning. Here he could explain a few things to the tearoom and parlor thinkers. Here, in the world of spermicidal jellies, he could provide a wealth of experience.

Writing and peddling pamphlets regarded by many to be slightly lascivious; speaking to large numbers of people on his favorite subject, sex; lecturing women on the function of their bodies; using forbidden words like "vagina" and "uterus" and "intercourse" to serious intellectual purpose, Reitman marched into this reform effort like the gynecological trooper he was. And in this work Ben was no less serious and dedicated than the other radicals. He too despised the cant and hypocrisy of government officials and the tyranny of the law over this issue. He had known and treated many hundreds of underclass women, knew their suffering like few others in the ranks of radical leaders.

On October 6, 1915, Ben and Emma were arrested in Portland, Oregon, for circulating a birth control pamphlet. The publicity surrounding the arrest drew an immense crowd to the municipal building the following day, so much so that the *Oregon Journal* observed that such a throng had seldom gathered for a trial in Portland. When the deputy city attorney, L. E. Latourette, declined to read aloud the contents of the tainted circular that had caused all the trouble, the expectant audience gave forth sighs of disappointment.

Dressed in his Stetson hat, flowing black tie, blue suit, and ruffled shirt, Ben strode to the stand and accepted responsibility for handing out the literature. "We are anarchist propagandists," he said, "and the proceeds of our sales go to further the cause of anarchism." Acting Municipal Judge Stadter held that the circular violated the obscenity ordinance and fined both Emma and Ben $100.

H. C. Uthoff, president of the Portland Birth Control League, one of the strongest new organizations of its kind in the country, remarked after the verdict that the information in the pamphlet was no more obscene than a lecture at the Oregon Medical College. Portland officialdom, he charged, had made the city appear foolish in the eyes of the world. One observer at the trial, Mrs. J. R. Oatman, said that if city officials themselves had to undergo unwanted childbirth they might welcome contraceptive information. "Even as it is," she noted, "a good many officials in the courtroom did not find the alleged objectionable pamphlet too obscene to pass around and read themselves."

A week later the anarchist celebrities faced Judge William Gatens in an appellate court proceeding. During the entire hearing Emma sat idly playing with a rose, occasionally smiling at some of the testimony. Gatens, a supporter of women's suffrage and other liberal causes, seemed embarrassed for the city. Sympathetic to the anarchists' birth control work, he bristled at a young, cocky district attorney who flourished sheets of the offensive literature before the courtroom. "Ignorance and prudery are the millstones about the neck of progress," the judge scolded. "Everyone knows that we are all shocked by things publicly stated that we know privately ourselves." He dismissed the case.[15] Louise Bryant, writing in *The Masses,* said of Gatens, "He has made people in Oregon think. He looks pretty tired sometimes, but he stays on the job."[16]

Emma and Ben also stayed on the job, hitting new cities, inspiring local advocates of birth control to organize. Shortly after the Portland trial Ben met a woman he later characterized as "very unusual." Considering his varied associations with the opposite sex, that was saying a great deal. Following one of his lectures in Everett, Washington, this tall, thin woman approached him wearing an expensive brown dress and, as Ben observed, looking through hungry eyes. "Doctor, you delivered a very interesting lecture tonight. I feel that you have said many things that I don't understand. I do wish you would come to my home and chat with me for a little while." Always willing to oblige a woman in need, always dedicated to the cause of education, Ben arrived at her fashionable home early the next day. After pouring her guest a glass of whiskey, she began to pour out her soul. She was twenty-seven years old, an only child, a graduate of the University of Colorado, plagued by a "narrow, conventional, dull, stupid life." Her parents had dominated her, she said. After hearing Ben talk of sex and liberation, she knew that he was a person who could help her discover life's mysteries and fascinations. Ben listened sympathetically. "I hope you won't think it unladylike, or terrible of me, if I ask you to help me. If I asked my few male friends they would think I was a vulgar person, but you are an anarchist and a big man—you will understand." Ben understood. He took her cold hand. As tears came to her eyes and quivers to her body, Ben put his arms around her, tight enough to notice that her breasts were rather undeveloped. No matter. "I am in a hurry," he said, "but if it doesn't take too long I will be glad to do anything I can to help you." "Are you sure you won't hate me and think me a bad girl?" He gave assurances. Biting her lip, looking her eager guest in the eye, she said, "Doctor, will you teach me to smoke a cigarette?"[17]

By the end of 1915 Margaret Sanger had returned to the United States; birth control was now a burgeoning national issue. She made repeated headlines by demanding a trial on the earlier charge from which she had fled to Europe. In November the Sangers' youngest child, Peggy, died of pneumonia. Already a sympathetic figure, Margaret Sanger now became a tragic one as well. A group of British intellectuals wired President Wilson that "such work as that of Mrs. Sanger receives appreciation and circulation in every civilized country except the United States of America." In such an atmosphere federal officials realized that prosecuting Mrs. Sanger would be counter-productive and they dropped the charges.[18]

What the world saw in the press and in the lecture halls in early 1916 was a growing, united front in the drive for birth control legalization; what it didn't see were the tensions among its disparate advocates. Emma Goldman's slashing speeches and her tactics of nonviolent confrontation, provoking debate, and courting arrest had always angered some radicals. Voltairine de Cleyre said, "I have never liked Emma Goldman or her speeches; I don't like fishwifery or billingsgate." Emma also knew that other radicals were disenchanted with her focus on contraception because many on the left looked "upon Birth Control only as a very small phase in a much larger social setting: namely the freedom of expression in life, labor and art which is constantly being interfered with and curtailed by the reactionary forces." Concentrating intensely on birth control, some radicals believed, could weaken the larger program of reform.

On the other side, Margaret Sanger, who adopted birth control as a single reform issue, claimed that the commitment of Emma and the anarchists to birth control was questionable, that the anarchists were only using the issue in a larger political context of free speech and women's rights. Only through a vigorous, concentrated assault on the laws prohibiting the spread of contraceptive information, she now believed, would true reform be possible. She wrote later that "Emma Goldman and her campaign manager, Ben Reitman, belatedly advocated birth control, not to further it but strategically to utilize in their own program of anarchism the publicity value it had achieved." Margaret Sanger had long since chosen to forget those nights in Emma's home years earlier.[19] As she marshaled support for her campaign, her identification with the anarchists, who were held in such obloquy by large segments of the American public, was a formidable albatross from which she was determined to cut loose. She disassociated herself and her cause from the radicals.

The anarchists had collected money for Margaret Sanger and distributed her literature widely. Emma had written long letters to her in Europe, encouraging her to fight indictment in the courts. But her ambitious personality grated on the headstrong Emma, who resented the increasing publicity given to the Sangers as the foremost champions of the birth control movement. She wrote to a friend that she and the anarchists had "started out on birth control agitation long before the Sangers thought of it."[20] Emma and Ben aggressively marched forward in the work.

In February Emma was arrested in New York City for a speech at the New Star Casino, a speech she had given many times in cities across the country and eight times previously in New York. At the jail Emma was revolted by a search done on her person "in the most vulgar manner by a coarse looking matron in the presence of two detectives, a thing which would outrage the most hardened criminal."[21] In the days ahead she and Ben decided to use the occasion of the impending trial to launch an even more vigorous national publicity drive.

On March 1, 1916, birth control advocates filled Carnegie Hall to hear speeches on what Emma called "the greatest social problem confronting the United States today." The journalist John Reed, prominent radical Bolton Hall, Dr. William Robinson, and others joined Emma in calling for a "birth strike." A letter from Margaret Sanger was read from the platform and several speakers talked of letters from Rudyard Kipling and H. G. Wells to President Wilson on the right to freely disseminate knowledge. Robinson declared that an observer from Mars would be dumbfounded to find that Earth creatures in America would make it illegal to impart vital knowledge among themselves concerning health and economic well-being.[22]

William Sanger had not been asked to speak at the rally and was angry. The Sangers, William insisted in a bitter letter to Emma, had borne the major share of the birth control fight, had taken on Comstockery, the silence of the press, and "the Chinese Wall of bigotry and prudery in this city." The anarchists, he charged, were now trying to preempt them on the issue. "Margaret's work stands out clear cut and revolutionary," he wrote to Emma. "She was the first one to my mind to attack the statutes *involving long terms of imprisonment.* Your arrests have been based on only misdemeanors and disorderly conduct . . . It is only when the pioneers have done their work and when results are achieved that others come in for the applause . . . between anarchist judges and Capitalist judges, I might prefer the latter. Truly, Emma you are SOME Squeeze."[23]

At her trial in April Emma protested that the law under which she had been arrested was originally framed to protect the public from fake patent medicines and their vendors, not social reformers and humanitarians providing vital information. "The information connected with this movement," she declared at the trial, "is not for personal gain or profit, but for the education of the working and professional classes who, harassed by economic conditions, by the high cost of living, by the terrible congestion of our large cities, cannot decently provide for a large brood of children, as a result of which their children are born weak, are ill cared for and ill nourished." If it constituted a crime to be for happier childhood and happier motherhood, she was proud to be a criminal. The crowd in the courtroom erupted into applause. The judges gave her the choice of a $100 fine or fifteen days in the workhouse; she chose the latter.[24] Margaret Anderson, editor of *The Little Review,* wrote after Emma's arrest, "Emma Goldman was sent to prison for advocating that women need not always keep their mouths shut and their wombs open."[25]

As Emma donned her blue prison uniform and bid a sad farewell to matzo and fish and other favorite foods, Ben worked to increase the momentum of the birth control drive. At a meeting at the Harlem Masonic Temple on April 23 he recruited volunteers to distribute a pamphlet containing the very information on birth control methods that had landed Emma in jail. He subsequently was arrested and ordered to appear in court on May 8. "They are not going to hang me, are they?" Ben quipped to reporters. "Well, boys, if they send me to jail for six months, don't forget to send me some cigarettes."[26]

A few days before his trial Ben organized a rally at Carnegie Hall to celebrate Emma's release from prison. She wrote later, "The most wonderful speech was made by Ben, as in fact the meeting was made possible only through his marvelous energy."[27] One conspicuous leftist absent from the rally was Max Eastman, socialist editor of *The Masses.* He had at first agreed to speak at the rally, but when he learned that Ben was also scheduled to address the crowd, the socialist canceled his appearance. Reitman was, Eastman wrote, "a white-fleshed, waxy-looking doctor, who thought it radical to shock people with crude allusions to their sexual physiology. I did not want to associate my feminism with this juvenile diversion, and I told the committee I would not preside." The fact that one of the most influential intellectuals in the country was deflected from appearing in public by Doc's crudity was remarkable. To Emma it was a startling example of the vacuous commitment and infantile pettiness infecting much of the left. "The incident once more proved," she wrote, "how poorly some alleged radicals in America have grasped the true meaning of freedom."[28]

On May 8 Ben Reitman appeared before the Court of Special Sessions in New York on the charge of unlawfully possessing and distributing printed matter of indecent character. One of the three judges sitting for the trial had prosecuted William Sanger and had advised Christian women to have more children to better society. Conducting his own defense, Ben said he was responsible for the distribution of the birth control literature at the April 23 protest meeting. Admitting that he knew at the time that the transfer of contraception information was illegal, he said that he purposefully broke the law to provoke arrest and test the judicial application of the obscenity statutes. "I can't do anything but honor the law by breaking it," Doc said. "There is no evil intent to commit a crime. We want to help the human race. We believe by birth control the human race will be better, that we will have better and happier babies."

Reitman spoke of over 8,000 letters which had been written to him asking for birth control information. He spoke of a Danish man from Connecticut who had ridden on his motorcycle to the anarchist offices in Manhattan to get the literature. Poor, out of work, the father of three children and husband of an ailing wife, the man was desperate, Ben said. He wanted no more children. Doc told the court, "I did what might be properly called 'inciting to rebellion against the State'"—he gave the man a pamphlet. "The people want Birth Control and I am glad to be one of those who gladly give it to them." He hoped for a "modern judge" who would give him a favorable ruling and permit the birth control advocates to proceed with their important work.

Ben found no modern judge that day in New York City, and he got no favorable ruling. He did get sixty days in the workhouse.[29]

On May 20, 1916, birth control and free-speech advocates held an open-air demonstration at Union Square to protest Ben's conviction. Emma Goldman, Anna Sloan, Leonard Abbott, Bolton Hall, Jessie Ashley, and Ida Rauh all addressed the crowd from an open car and handed out pamphlets. There were no arrests. Ida Rauh made perhaps the most eloquent statement:

> It is not in order to defy the law and the authorities that I shall distribute information about birth control, but because it is more moral that an old, ignorant law should be violated than that the right of the people should be violated to get information of vital importance to them and their families . . . Under the ghastly competitive system of today the child born to the poor who survives infancy is confronted by a childhood of work and drudgery, a manhood, or womanhood of work, drudgery and anxiety, and poverty-eaten old age . . . Therefore one of the most important and fundamental things we can do today to lighten the burden of women and strengthen the hands of laboring people is to distribute information which will teach them how to limit their families.[30]

There was a certain irony about Ida Rauh, the wife of Max Eastman, delivering an impassioned speech at a rally protesting the arrest of Ben Reitman.

For a man who had crossed the Red Sea in the stokehole of a tramp steamer, Blackwell's Island seemed like a sixty-day summer retreat, Ben said later. As a matter of fact, he claimed that jail was never an agonizing experience, a statement that seems strange for a man whose thirst for movement was unquenchable. But the arrests and convictions whetted his appetite for notoriety and excitement. In jails and prisons, while taking special pains to stay out of trouble and solitary confinement, Doc hustled extra food, entertained fellow inmates with fanciful stories, and kept regular hours, a practice in which he rarely engaged on the outside. The time in jail also gave him the opportunity to hear stories of the underworld. "Oh, the profitable hours I spent listening to real criminals tell of their activities. They told me of all the safes they cracked, and all the lies they knew." The jails were like postgraduate courses on the underlife: intimate revelations of pickpockets and thieves, jack-rollers and pimps, con men and vice kings. Ben listened, took notes, penned articles, and made plans to write books.[31]

Doc stayed on Blackwell's Island for a week and then was transferred to the Queen's County Jail on Long Island, a much more comfortable facility. His only special request was for some bats and balls for his fellow inmates and an apple pie for himself. When the pie was delivered to the prison the officials advised Ben not to eat it because the other prisoners would regard it as a special privilege. He asked merely to kiss the pie, and the warden granted his request only after Ben promised not to stick his tongue into it. He recalled, "I gave the pie a very chaste kiss."[32]

Emma published several of Ben's letters from prison in *Mother Earth.* In one he wrote, "I feel humble that I am permitted to be a part in the great work. I have no regrets. We have shown them how to work, how to have big meetings, and how to face the music. Now let us show how to go on with our work even when I am in jail. . . ."[33]

For the first time in eight years Emma Goldman set off on a tour to the West Coast without Ben Reitman. She wrote to Alice Inglis, "I always used to look forward with great intensity to my visits in Los Angeles and San Francisco, but so far it has been disappointing here . . . I think, of course, it is Ben. He always manages to give the audiences his spirit and nervous anticipation. You will appreciate it, since you have attended meetings which he has conducted. . . ."[34]

Ben had a frequent visitor during his stay at the Queens County Jail, a tall, blond, blue-eyed English suffragist named Anna Martindale. Ben had met Anna over a year earlier at the *Mother Earth* offices on 119th Street and had seen her frequently at anarchist meetings. "We had a sort of strange romance," Ben wrote. "All this time I was living and working with Emma Goldman . . . During the birth control trial in New York, Anna stood by me, and in the sixty days that I lived in the New York jail her letters and love helped sustain me." For the first time in his life Ben longed for a wife, children, and a home. Of Anna he wrote, ". . . if ever I did I think I can say I fell desperately in love with her."[35]

Ben also received letters from other female admirers. The volume that poured into the jail from assorted women astonished the prison trustees who were in charge of checking the mail. A couple of the inmates, noting the content of the correspondence, began to send their own letters to Ben's female acquaintances, much to his annoyance.

One of Ben's correspondents was Margaret Foley, a prominent member of the Women's Trade Union League of Boston. A former hat trimmer and teacher of swimming and gymnastics at California resorts, Foley became an energetic open-air orator for women's suffrage in the early 1900s at a time "when people ran away from the speakers as if they had the plague, and peeked around the streetcorners at an empty square with crazy women talking to the empty air in the middle of it."[36] She later made speaking tours in the South and Midwest, and in one of her more noted exploits ascended in a balloon to distribute suffrage leaflets. Such unconventionality, not surprisingly, attracted Ben Reitman. The two had liaisons in numerous places—Minnesota, Chicago, New York, Boston. In January 1916 Ben had written on *Mother Earth* stationery to Margaret: "Wish we could take a long walk in the park and talk about life and work, then we could go to a comfortable home and I could put my head on your beautiful breast and weep for joy. Write me, love me, want me. Ben."[37]

And now, from Queen's County Jail, Doc reported that his health and spirits had revived and that he had learned to enjoy useful work, even cleaning toilets and spittoons. Discussing their respective reform efforts, he pleaded with Margaret Foley for more support for birth control from other radicals and progressive elements in America. "If you suffragetts don't stand behind the Birth Controllers, I don't see what good your emancipation is doing."[38] Ben was frustrated by the intellectual arrogance and petty rivalries infecting the various leftist reform drives, with many reformers zealously pushing single causes. They were, he thought, like racehorses with blinders, oblivious to the larger issues. Suffrage and birth control, he knew, were both expressions of a total feminist revolution. But it was now a fragmented revolution. Ben envisioned a united drive of political and reform groups that would crush the exploiters of American society. But at the same time he was lamenting the splintered reform efforts at work in the United States. Margaret Sanger, blinders firmly in place, was trying very hard to make the cause of birth control an even more potent single issue.

In early August Ben completed his jail term on Long Island and soon gave a speech at New York's Lenox Hall, calling on radicals to continue the birth control fight. For every agitator who was arrested, he said, hundreds of thousands of pamphlets were being distributed to the poor. It was a small price to pay. And never mind the Society for the Suppression of Vice or "that little bed-bug Sumner." He and his society were dying a slow death.[39] A slow death indeed. It would not be until 1936 that doctors were exempted from the 1873 federal law prohibiting the dissemination and importation of contraceptives (U.S. vs. one package of Japanese pessaries), and not until 1965 that the U.S. Supreme Court ruled that the right of privacy embraced the right of individuals to use birth control devices.

In an unpublished paper, Chicago's clap doctor talked of the Sisyphean labor that faced the reformer in America: "There's still almost no understanding in the United States for social ideals and their exponents, no conception of the forces that irrevocably divide the classes, no contact with the vital issues of social life. Robust, exuberant, over-flowing with physical energy, America considers cultural values as so much waste. It has no patience with the social pioneer. It treats him with scorn, contempt, and bitter opposition."[40]

17. Two Cities, Two Trials

"Birth control is getting to be terribly respectable," Ben Reitman remarked to *Mother Earth* readers in October 1916. Although the anarchists were not the pioneers of the movement—that distinction belonged to Moses Harman and others—Emma Goldman and her coterie had done more to popularize the issue than any other group. Birth control pamphlets now circulated with little interference in such cities as Denver, Los Angeles, Portland, Seattle, San Francisco, Chicago, and Cleveland. Margaret Sanger had just finished a successful cross-country tour, enjoying the support of numerous groups of people who had been attracted to the subject by Emma's lectures years earlier. Even if Sanger was now the last to admit it, the birth control issue was rooted in political radicalism, given life and force by those early anarchist and socialist agitators first willing to challenge the champions of moral purity. Things had gone so well, Ben noted, that a judge in Des Moines had recently instructed two juvenile delinquents to study and use birth control methods.[1]

Doc Reitman's effervescence was short-lived. On December 12 he was arrested in Cleveland at Moose Hall after Emma—or the "Lady of Sorrows," as Ben now called her—had delivered a lecture on "The Educational and Sexual Dwarfing of the Child." Ben had distributed a number of pamphlets at the close of meeting, which had been attended by over 100 people, mostly women. After the arrest, most of the crowd trailed Ben and his captors to Central Police Station, where David Gibson, owner of a local building company and a Reitman supporter, declared to the crowd, "Take your literature on Birth Control with you and don't be afraid to show it, either." Gibson signed Doc's bail bond of $1,000 and led the cheers as he reappeared on the street. A number of women presented the good doctor with a bouquet of roses.[2]

Three days later Ben was arrested again, this time in the Fine Arts Building in Rochester, New York, on the charge of selling Margaret Sanger's "What Every Girl Should Know" and Dr. William Robinson's "Limitation of Offspring." He was also charged with having in his possession a copy of his own birth control leaflet, "Why and How the Poor Should Not Have Children," a four-page work which, among other things, advised that condoms be checked before using by blowing them up like balloons. It also described rubber cervical caps, diaphragms (then called pessaries, or womb veils), douches, and other homemade contraceptive methods, and argued that the rhythm method was unreliable. The world was a wretched place for poor children, the pamphlet declared. "If you think that the teaching of the prevention of conception will help working men and women, spread the glad tidings." The pamphlet had been distributed free in hundreds of cities, copied and recopied, and translated into several languages. More than any other piece of literature, this pamphlet, Ben claimed, had made a significant impact in reducing the birthrate in various parts of the country. But in 1916 many courts still held that the information it contained was obscene, antimarriage, antifamily, anti-American. The trials that lay ahead in Cleveland and Rochester would test the prevailing sentiment.[3]

Cleveland, noted for its municipal reforms and a tradition of liberalism fostered by the late Mayor Tom Johnson, seemed to Ben Reitman an unlikely place for birth control advocates to suffer harassment. It was one of the few cities that had a decent reputation among radicals on the issues of free speech and freedom of the press. It was also the home of the first major birth control organization. In the center of Cleveland was a monument in honor of Tom Johnson, who had died in 1911. It was inscribed with such tributes as, "He gave the city a soul" and "He gave Cleveland a civic mind." To Ben, Cleveland was not San Diego.

Rochester, by contrast, was an unknown quantity. Home of George Eastman's Kodak Company and hub of the rich agricultural area around Lake Ontario, Rochester was proud of its appellation as the "Flower City." Now, into the garden had come the weeds—anarchist agitators spreading indecent literature. Ben was understandably nervous about the possible attitude of Rochester's judges and other city officials.

On January 10 his trial opened in Cleveland. A large number of women active in birth control efforts pressed to get inside to see the renowned radical from Chicago take on the locals. The *Plain Dealer* ran large pictures of the crowd and of Ben with the headline, "Women Throng Courtroom as Birth Control Trial Begins."[4]

After listening to the prosecuting attorney promptly denounce him as "an Anarchist who comes to our fair city to defy our laws" and then declare that the community's property, wives, and daughters were endangered by such sleazy lawbreakers, Doc sensed trouble. When the judge, Dan Cull, nodded approvingly as the prosecutor pleaded in the good name of Cleveland to save its citizens from "dirty, filthy, stinking" birth control literature, Ben reconsidered Cleveland's reputation.[5]

The prosecution called three witnesses before the jury, two police officers and a physician. Ben's lawyer, Herman Eisler, badgered the doctor for nearly a half hour, trying to show that the pamphlets which had landed Ben in court were not obscene but contained valuable medical advice. The defense wanted to know what was obscene about such declarations as: "Until Society is prepared to offer every child that is born proper food, shelter and care and to every adult desirable employment, liberty and an opportunity to express himself, poor people should have as few children as possible."[6]

Testifying in Reitman's behalf, two women who had been at the meeting in December said that he had not distributed the pamphlets himself; that, instead, thirty volunteers from the audience had handed them out. Ben then marched to the witness box and took responsibility for bringing the literature to the hall, though not for its distribution. As he began to explain his anarchist position on birth control, Judge Cull ruled him out of order and forced him off the stand. Eisler, in his summation, told the jury that free speech was far more important than the possible fine and imprisonment of Ben Reitman and that a decision against his client would strike a damaging and unconscionable blow at all the progress that had been made in Cleveland and across the country on the free-speech issue.

Shortly after the jury retired to discuss the case one of the members requested a large supply of paper. Ben later claimed that several of the jurors had laboriously copied for their own enlightenment much of the information contained in the pamphlets presented as evidence. After all, he noted, the material contained important advice.

After deliberating for over seven hours, the jury members sent word that they could not agree on a verdict. The judge ordered them back to the tiny jury room, where they argued for another six hours. At midnight they agreed: Reitman was guilty. Ben wrote, "A jury of twelve average Cleveland men decided that women should bear children whether they want to or not; that little babies must come into a world and fight against disease and poverty and obstacles which many of them will never be able to overcome; and that the jails, insane asylums, and other institutions should not want for victims."

Before pronouncing sentence, Judge Cull asked Doc if he had anything to say. As Ben again made an effort to explain his philosophical position on the birth control issue and his reasons for risking jail to carry on his work, the judge cut him off, weary, he said, of such "filthy propaganda." With the judge mumbling about the carnal sins of the flesh and of living in sin without responsibility and ranting about sex hygiene and anarchist agitators, Ben thought of the Grand Inquisitor about to doom a heretic to the fire.

Although the laws of Cleveland didn't allow the stake as punishment for disseminating birth control literature, Dan Cull did his best: the maximum sentence of six months in the Cleveland workhouse plus a $1,000 fine and court costs. Compared to the recent mild sentences levied against Margaret Sanger, Emma Goldman, and other birth control advocates, the Cull decision was startling. Several months earlier Sanger had opened the first center for contraceptive instruction in the United States, a clinic in the Brownsville section of Brooklyn, where she and her sister showed women how to use pessaries and other contraceptive devices. She served thirty days on Blackwell's Island for a violation of the New York State law against the spreading of birth control information, a sentence that made Margaret Sanger a martyr. Ben Reitman now faced six months.

Through the early years of the birth control campaign the agitators had been harried, arrested, fined, and jailed. But those confrontations and punishments had been largely expected and were part of the price that most in the movement expected to pay. In many cases the arrests and publicity were invigorating to the protestors, fueling their determination, providing a mobilizing spirit, generating increased support. The Reitman verdict, however, was a sobering reminder that the birth control effort, as did so many other reform movements, had serious days ahead. The country was full of Dan Culls.

Reitman was released on $2,500 bail pending appeal and left Cleveland greatly burdened. He had been separated on the trip from the two most important women in his life, Emma Goldman and Anna Martindale, the English suffragist with whom he had been carrying on a secret affair. And his support from the radicals in Cleveland had been less than gratifying. "The great host of Free Speechers, Single-taxers, Birth Controllers, and Radicals, which Cleveland boasted of were conspicuous by their absence, although a splendid small group of women and Anarchist comrades stood by me. But somehow they did not touch my soul, and I did not reach their hearts or purses."[7] Realizing that he would never be a great rallying figure in the birth control fight, that the shock troops of the campaign identified much more closely with the women leaders, Ben faced a long jail sentence, isolated and disillusioned. Understanding his frustration, Emma wrote to the socialist Agnes Inglis, "I am really more concerned about Ben. In the first place, I am better known, and being a woman I get, by far, more support from everyone, which I think is foolish. Not so in the case of Ben. I find that women in Cleveland, who at first wanted to come to the rescue, have since changed their minds. Like all people who do not understand the principle of equality, they write me, 'Oh, if it were you or Margaret Sanger' as if that made any difference. When will people be big enough to have in mind an issue, and not the particular person?"[8]

Doc now headed to Rochester for another trial. On February 27, this time accompanied by Emma, Ida Rauh, Anna Sloan of the National Birth Control League, and attorney Harry Weinberger of the Free Speech League of New York, Ben and other birth control proponents spoke at a mass meeting at the Labor Lyceum, a gathering to protest, as a flyer announced, "the unjust, antiquated court rulings which send women and men to prison for teaching that which no one can deny will make the world a better place in which to live."

Infuriated by the Cleveland experience, emboldened by the presence of his anarchist comrades, Ben treated the Lyceum crowd to a virulent attack on Rochester's finest. Enough mud was thrown at the police, one of the papers reported, to keep them busy cleaning uniforms until Doomsday. Doc made all the rounds, denouncing the government, both state and national, the city officials, the law, society in general, and organized religion. "The trouble with Christianity," he boomed, "is that nobody believes in it enough to inconvenience themselves. They join the church and pray, but that doesn't help a hell of a lot. We have a wonderful government. They pass laws prohibiting the distribution of birth control literature, but if milk went up to 20 cents a quart today the government would not lift a hand to help the starving children get it." He vowed that he would not stop handing out the condemned leaflets. The birth control forces had distributed over a million pieces of literature in New York City alone, and no two-bit police force in Rochester was going to stall the movement. Emma also took the floor, adding her own inimitable invective: "The law is against birth control because it knows that if the working classes stop breeding, the parasites—the rich leeches on the bodies of the poor—will have to go to work."[9]

On February 28 the Rochester trial opened. With Emma in town, along with the entourage of other nationally recognized radicals, Ben drew a standing-room-only crowd. The *Rochester Union and Advertiser* raved over the "admiring throng" that pressed around Doc as he entered the courtroom and the large numbers of spectators who strained for glimpses of the infamous figures.[10]

Ben Reitman and the other radicals knew before the trial began that Judge Willis K. Gillet was of a different persuasion than Judge Dan Cull of Cleveland. Two weeks earlier Gillet had announced that he had read "What Every Girl Should Know" and "Limitation of Offspring" and had found in them nothing objectionable. Indeed, the two books could be purchased in several Rochester bookstores. Gillet earlier had dismissed the first charge against Reitman, that of selling the two publications; the trial was on the second charge—distributing the graphic birth control pamphlet "Why and How the Poor Should Not Have Children." As the trial now opened the judge delivered no strident attacks on the anarchists or on the birth control campaign they represented. Defense Attorney Weinberger later called Gillet a man of learning, fairness, and courtesy, an example for local courts across the country.

The Rochester trial was unique because, as Weinberger pointed out, the defendant came into court stating that, as an anarchist, he would not obey any law which, in his opinion, impeded human progress. Reitman had broken the law in the past, Weinberger told the packed courtroom, "and believes in breaking the law when the law interferes with human happiness." But in this instance, the lawyer argued, his client had not broken the birth control ordinance because he had not known that the offending pamphlet was inside the William Robinson book seized by the police. "Do you suppose, gentlemen of the jury, that if Dr. Reitman had any intentions of getting the pamphlet that has resulted in his arrest before the meeting on December 15th he would have sneaked one little pamphlet out in the audience?" That wasn't Doc's style, the counsel insisted. If he had wanted to distribute the pamphlet at the meeting, he would have done so with characteristic brashness and bravado and in great numbers.

Ben took the stand, declaring that the laws against the dissemination of birth control information were unjust and that he intended to defy them in cities across the country, including Rochester, not by sneaking solitary copies inside other books, but by openly handing them out. And he would first notify the police of his intentions! In the case of his arrest in December, Ben claimed that he had not known that the pamphlet was inside the book and was, therefore, innocent of the charge. Indeed, the meeting at which he was arrested was not a birth control rally but a lecture by Emma Goldman on drama and the lives of Ibsen and Strindberg. The birth control literature was merely lying on a table when seized by the police.

Before the jury retired to deliberate the case, Judge Gillet cautioned its members not to be prejudiced by the fact that Ben Reitman was an anarchist. "You must remember," he said, "that the defendant must be protected by our laws even though he may not believe in some of them." It took the jury less than an hour to acquit Ben, and as the courtroom crowd erupted with loud cheers and applause, Doc asked permission to say a few words. After thanking the jury members for their decision he turned to Judge Gillet and remarked,

"I have been arrested and tried many, many times but I have never, in any court in the country, had the fair, gracious treatment that has been accorded me by Your Honor in this case."[11]

The two trials in Cleveland and Rochester, exhausting and emotional, were now behind him. Although Ben planned to appeal the Cleveland verdict, he realized that several months in the workhouse would probably lie ahead. Cleveland, liberal Cleveland, the city of Tom Johnson, was also the city of Dan Cull, and as a result, Reitman faced jail. Rochester, the city of flowers and William Gillet, had been an unexpected surprise. The two trials illustrated dramatically the capriciousness of the courts on the highly charged and bewildering issue of birth control and the subjective treatment rendered by individual judges. If some magistrates regarded birth control agitation as threatening and symptomatic of a left-wing radical assault against American institutions, others regarded the issue as worthy of serious, constructive debate.

It would not be the anarchists, socialists, and other radicals who would finally drive a spike into the hearts of the moral crusaders and achieve large-scale social reform on birth control. Although masses of women in the United States were pleading for contraceptive information, the political climate was clearly evident from one of many letters written to the reformers: "I nearly had nervous prostration," one woman said, "after I had mailed you my letter asking for that 'information'. . . ."[12] There was just too much suspicion and animosity toward the radicals, too much apprehension that any cause promoted by these contemptible extremists must be anti-American. Although Ben Reitman and Emma Goldman and the others were understandably bitter over Margaret Sanger's move away from the radicals and her disavowal of the radical roots of birth control reform, her one-issue crusade, appealing to a larger segment of the American middle class including the medical profession, stood a far greater chance of success.

Ben was right when he looked back years later and wrote:

> Emma Goldman
> More than any one person in America
> Popularized B.C.
> She was Margaret Sanger's INSPIRATION
> No that ain't the word.
> Margaret imitated her and denied her.

Emma was the first person in America
To lecture on Birth Control
In one hundred cities.
And influence the NEWSPAPERS
To talk about B.C.
The Physicians, Social Scientists, Clergy & etc.
Became interested in B.C.
Only after the Radical had broken the ground.
And gone to jail.[13]

18. The Great Repression

These were grim days for America's radicals, the days of war mania, of red hunts, of phobic patriotism. The United States entered the war against Germany in April 1917, but to the radicals it quickly seemed as if the war were against them. A loosely worded Espionage Act passed that summer unleashed federal authorities as never before against all those who attacked the war. Socialists, Wobblies, anarchists—all were game and the hunting season was now open.

The tenor of this era was exemplified by an incident on the lonely dunes near Provincetown, Massachusetts. A local constable, prowling the beach in search of rumored German U-boat invasions, arrested Eugene O'Neill on suspicion of being a spy. Reporting on the startling arrest the following day, a local newspaper attempted to calm the rumors making such ominous waves in the Northeast. No, Gene O'Neill and a friend had not drawn revolvers against the arresting officer. No, he was not carrying drawings of the wireless station and nearby grounds. No, his typewriter was not a transmitting device. The Provincetown police, however, were not completely reassured, even after a long interrogation of the famous playwright. Convinced that O'Neill was indeed mapping invasion plans for the German government, the police continued on the hunt, shadowing O'Neill and steaming open his mail. "I was," O'Neill wrote later, "the victim of war hysteria."[1]

The biting winds of the winter of 1917–18, one of the coldest seasons recorded in New York, seemed symbolic to the remaining Greenwich Village idealists. The Great Repression was on. The communists, pacifists, and Bolsheviks found themselves on the run, in jails, their newspapers closed down, their offices ransacked, their spokesmen taunted and beaten, their philosophies ridiculed and made illegal. Some of the writers and artists of the Village still clung together, huddled from the cold and the Feds in their apartments, in club rooms and saloons. Others dropped their plans for the revolution and went on to something more respectable.

Federal and state officials stalked and arrested reds, labor organizers, and others on the political fringe for treason and antiwar activity. And the American people, at least most of them, marched to the same beat. The American Legion came out in favor of deporting all individuals who defamed American life. One minister called for the deportation of Bolsheviks "in ships of stone with sails of lead, with the wrath of God for a breeze and with hell for their first port."[2]

In his hometown of Terre Haute, Indiana, Eugene Debs saw a teacher fired because of her Socialist party membership, saw citizens attacking German-Americans on the streets and holding public bonfires of German-language books, saw a Socialist coal miner lynched for refusing to buy a Liberty Bond. In Cleveland an outraged observer reported on the handiwork of the local vigilance committee: "There is no longer civil law operating in Cleveland—at least so far as Constitutional rights are concerned. The American Protective League are holding up everybody, regardless of age, throwing them into jail, and taking them to the federal building the following day to put them through the 'third degree' . . . they arrest street speakers . . . they are waging an unremitting war. . . ."[3]

Spies rubbed elbows in radical organizations and at meetings. Emma Goldman hired several workers who, unknown to her, reported regularly to federal and state authorities. A secretary named Marion Barling sent chatty missives to her superiors on the Lusk Committee, a New York State body investigating subversion. Marion couldn't contain her right-wing, xenophobic predilections when, speaking of poet Lola Ridge, she wrote, "Let us hope someone will use his gun on her soon and put her out of the sight of mortal man. Let her go on with her great work of radical poems in Hell. There indeed will she find lots of fiery material." Of Harry Kelly of the Ferrer School, the anarchist institution founded by Emma Goldman and others several years earlier, Marion wrote, "I'm for hanging Kelly at once, no sunrise about it." Marion, incidentally, thought Kelly was from the "Free-Air School." Like so many other loyl Americans, Marion Barling was all for killing the damned Jews, Japs, and Huns, the treasonous scum who opposed the war.[4]

Another agent claimed that the apparent decrease in reported bombings by anarchist sabateurs was misleading. The bomb makers, he said, had seized upon an innovative, more heinous approach. The "skunks" had developed a phospherous-based substance that when wet was harmless but when dry was highly flammable. All the terrorists had to do, he said, was plant a good quantity of the wet stuff next to a target and leave. A few hours later, when the perpetrator was long gone, the now dry substance would ignite.[5]

Other agents talked of an imminent general strike by the workers, a prelude to a red revolution in America. Still others reported forebodingly on a supposed bomb squad recruited by Emma Goldman to exterminate public officials responsible for the arrest of prominent radicals.

The vehemence of government officials in Washington toward the radicals was no less contained than that of fieldworkers like Marion Barling. "Disloyal, un-American, anarchistic alien," one post office solicitor called Emma in 1918, "whose aim in life is to disobey and break all laws, incite strikes, riots, discord and dissatisfaction in the hearts and minds of foreign-born people." Foreigners, the official noted, were deficient in mental capacity and therefore easily led into acts of violence and barbarism. But ignorant foreigners were not the only dupes for Emma's unpatriotic venom, the solicitor continued. He pointed to an article in *Mother Earth* by none other than Helen Keller in which she lauded Emma Goldman for her speeches and acts in opposing conscription. Keller had written, "All the atrocities of impious war are committed in obedience to law and order . . . My heart aches for the people of all nations . . . they do not want war. They want peace and liberty to enjoy the fruits of their labor. . . ."

Emma Goldman, the solicitor concluded, had led this blind and deaf woman, one whose scope of knowledge was clouded by her physical deficiences, down the path of socialistic treason. Her drivel in *Mother Earth* was nothing short of German propaganda and was especially dangerous because of the sympathies Helen Keller could evoke in the public mind. "Coming, as it is supposed to, from the mind of a woman who is deaf and blind, who is given to read, by finger and lip reading, only such matter as those associated with her choose to give her, it is quite apparent that a printed statement of this character . . . will have served its purpose for there will be some people who will be influenced by it."[6]

The Post Office, not surprisingly, purged *Mother Earth* from circulation, an act which Ben Reitman protested:

> I understand that these are trying times and our Government is in no mood to temporize with radicals and theorists, and that America is in danger and needs the support and confidence of every publication and every man, woman, and child within its domain. We are anxious this should be, but, unless America and the Post Office Department especially, respects the rights and needs of millions of her inhabitants who are feeling, thinking, struggling, and desirous of maintaining constitutional democracy in a way which may be a little different from that desired by a small group of Senators, legislators, or officials, then America will have to suffer the experience of internal disturbances such as Russia is now having.[7]

The Washington files on Ben Reitman grew thicker as the suppression of radicals intensified.

In purges and trials across the country radicals faced hysterical judges, hysterical juries, and a hysterical press. As Wobblies left the Federal Building in Chicago after being charged with conspiracy, many glimpsed the message on a cheap movie theater marquee: "Special Feature—The Menace of the IWW," and in bright red letters, "THE RED VIPER." Ralph Easley, founder of the National Civic Federation, declared, "[Bill] Haywood and all that bunch should be 'hanged as high as Haman' if it were possible to erect a gibbet of that character."

Congressmen rushed to introduce bills making membership in red organizations a crime. The press ran lurid warnings of mythical plots of radicals to poison food, burn crops and cities, and spy for the Germans. The *Fargo* (North Dakota) *Forum* declared that IWW members "live by the stiletto, firebrand, and bomb." The *Tulsa Daily World* wanted "to strangle the IWW's. Kill them, just as you would kill any other kind of snake. Don't scotch 'em; kill 'em dead. It is no time to waste money on trials and continuances and things like that. All that is necessary is the evidence and a firing squad." In Centralia, Washington, the newsstand of blind Tom Lassiter was demolished and he was run out of town because he had the audacity to sell radical publications.[8]

An FBI agent arrested a forty-two-year-old Italian-American

named Angelo Macetta in Boston for selling the *Hobo News.* After a long interrogation in which Macetta seemingly demonstrated that he wasn't a mad bomb thrower, the agent reported to the Washington home office that he was "impressed with the cleverness and shrewdness of subject which is way beyond the innocent ignorance that he was trying to show before us."[9]

Bill Haywood wrote to John Reed from jail in 1918: "This big game is over . . . we never won a hand. The other fellow had the cut, shuffle, and deal all the time . . . Personally we didn't lose much, just a part of our life."[10] Haywood should not have been surprised. At a time of national crisis, many Wobblies, socialists, and anarchists had attacked the war and called the selective draft a rank, crude subterfuge of the capitalists to drag workers against their will into a war designed only to aid business interests. Under a mask of patriotism, the radicals cried, the government sought to compel young boys "to suffer privation and encounter death, diseases and mutilations on the blood soaked fields of France . . . in order that the capitalists in this country may amass fortunes. . . ." This was a war instigated by the "blood-puddlers of the Oligarchy" at the expense of the cannon-fodder workers, a war to crush Prussianism abroad while Prussianism reigned at home. One radical, denouncing the "river dog" Samuel Gompers and his AFL for their support of the war, said, "Gompers can no more speak for American Labor than a jackass could speak for a nightingale."[11]

Emma Goldman, an unrelenting critic of the war and its preparedness campaigns and national conscription, resolved to "speak against war so long as my voice will last." To Emma conscription was a totally repugnant regimentation of the individual by the state; the war itself a capitalist struggle over foreign markets. One of her favorite speeches during this period was entitled, "The Speculators in War and Starvation."[12] The radicals, of course, had played into the hands of the various "security leagues" and "committees of public safety" organized to sniff out traitors and disloyal citizens. These extralegal vigilante groups were more ready to act suddenly and violently against the radical menace than the government itself. For Ben Reitman the vigilantes of the war period brought back vivid memories of a few years earlier, of the antiunion leagues of San Diego, those real estate agents and bankers who escorted him, one night in 1912, into the desert.

The various federal laws passed during the war and the years immediately after, the state syndicalist laws, and the violence, both by the legal authorities and vigilantes, destroyed much of the American left. As Bill Haywood had said, the radicals never won a hand. For Ben Reitman the time had come to get out. Still burdened with the memories of San Diego, weary of the unrelenting political rancor, his boyish enthusiasm for the radical cause had collapsed in doubt. The revolution had gotten too serious. In the end he was too much the rakish blade, too much the man of simple pleasures, to make the ultimate commitment of the fanatic. Ben had lived the life of passionate dissent, had marched in the marches, made the speeches, mocked the judges, toyed with the law. Notoriety was one thing; oppression of this order was another, and he wanted out.

In July 1916 Ben had joined Emma in San Francisco just after the infamous bomb explosion at the Preparedness Day Parade. Nine people had been killed that day and scores maimed. The railroad operators in San Francisco who had formed the Law and Order Committee of the Chamber of Commerce and who had organized the parade were determined, as one said, to "show the sons of bitches where to get off." Tom Mooney and other radical unionists were sentenced to long prison terms on the most flimsy evidence. "Oh God," Ben wrote to Margaret Foley, "is there no rest . . . This city has been hell." He was exhausted, he said, and longed for the seaside and some peace.[13]

Ben Reitman had been with the anarchists for ten years, an extraordinary commitment given his irreconcilable personal conflicts with Emma Goldman and her comrades. A few years earlier, after another of the endless quarrels and reconciliations, Ben told his famous lover of the mountainous weight of frustration crushing him, of his feelings of inferiority around the anarchist intellectuals, of his need for respect. He called himself a janitor, a clown, valued in the anarchist community only as a circus barker. "You are a power," he wrote to Emma, "Berkman is a force and Reitman is a joke." He recalled again how Emma had questioned his resiliency and commitment in the struggle, had called him a coward.[14]

Added to his resentment of the anarchists was Ben's genuine longing for a permanent home and children, an absolute impossibility with Emma. "I always thought of Chicago as my home," he wrote, "as the one place where I could rest . . . with my feelings growing lukewarm toward the work into which I had been engaged so feverishly for ten years, there was only one termination." He decided to move back to Chicago for good and to take with him the suffragist from Bradford, England, with whom he had carried on a long affair—Anna Martindale.[15]

No man, not even Alexander Berkman, Emma Goldman wrote later, had so consecrated his life to her work as Ben Reitman had. With his Barnum and Bailey flair, his indefatigable energy, he had given inestimable service to her years of struggle. But most of all he had been a sustentative force in her life, opening her to a world of physical and emotional passion she had never known before, a world both compelling and devastating. Their temperaments and backgrounds hopelessly at odds, they nevertheless shared basic concerns for people in trouble, for the forgotten. But their relationship, they both now realized, had finally played itself out.[16] Although Ben occasionally returned to New York to chair Emma's Sunday night meetings and contributed articles to *Mother Earth*, the focus of his life was now Chicago and Anna Martindale.

In early 1917 Ben arrived at the train station he knew so well. "I felt the solemnity of the occasion," he wrote, "feelings of pain, regret, hope, joy and uncertainty. As the train passed Twenty-second Street, I saw many familiar sights of my boyhood days. The tracks where I first started to hitch on trains, St. John's Church, where I first went to school, Sixteenth and Clark, my first playground, Sixteenth and the track, where I was first arrested at eight. I closed my eyes and prayed."

Within a few weeks Ben had rented an office in the Bush Temple at Chicago Avenue and Clark, near the Newberry Library and the county jail, and resumed his medical practice. In the center of a modest vice area of gamblers, prostitutes, and pool halls, his natural clientele soon came calling. Doc treated scores of patients, but because of their chronic inability to pay he made little money.

Reitman soon contacted Dr. John Dill Robertson, commissioner of the Health Department, and asked for a job as a smallpox vaccinator. Although Robertson feared a public hailstorm of criticism, he hired Ben to work among the hobo population. Even though a number of patriotic organizations and social service groups, especially the Woman's Club of Chicago, were duly outraged that the notorious anarchist had been hired by the city, Ben trudged through the black and hobo wards of Chicago, his Health Department star glittering from his coat pocket. "I worked hard and conscientiously, had a good deal of aggression, some persuasion, and little tact, and carried a considerable air of authority." He later became a clinician in Chicago's first municipal disease clinic and was instrumental in starting the first VD clinic in the Cook County Jail.[17]

In early 1918 Emma Goldman entered the maximum security prison in Jefferson City, Missouri. Along with Alexander Berkman, Eleanor Fitzgerald, and Leonard Abbott, she had formed the No Conscription League several months earlier, an organization that sponsored a swirl of meetings and marches in the face of police and government intimidation. Convicted on charges of "conspiracy to induce persons not to register," Goldman and Berkman both received two-year sentences, she in Jefferson City, he in Atlanta.[18]

Ben visited Emma in prison and afterward wrote:

> It was strange to see my little-blue-eyed "Mommy" in her prison garb, with the pain of compulsory confinement and forced labor written upon her face. We could not say the things we felt; hostile eyes were upon us. Emma and I were conscious of my "desertion of her and her cause." It was a painful visit. I stood like a traitor before his confessor but could not confess. As I looked into her face I saw none of the reproach I felt for myself. As they led her back to her toil, I was heartbroken. I felt that if I had done my duty I should have been in jail with her. But I turned in to another path. I had been seduced by the ordinary man's desire for a home, a wife and a child.[19]

On February 22, 1918, Anna Martindale bore his child, a son they named Brutus. Ben wrote, "Many thrilling and wonderful experiences come into the life of a man—but I don't know of anything more glorious or spiritual than to kneel beside the woman you love, and hold in your arms a tiny son, a child of love and desire."

Although he had left behind the anarchist movement, Ben still had debts to pay. On March 15 he received a wire from Cleveland, Ohio: "The Appellate Court sustained the decision of Judge Cull. It is necessary for you to come to Cleveland immediately and begin your six month's sentence. . . ."[20] Three days later he entered the Warrensville Correction Farm to begin a six-month stay, the longest term meted out against any major radical in the United States for birth control agitation. Ben later described the Cleveland prison as something of a vacation spot. His friendship with the warden and his abilities as a physician gave him the run of the place. In return for assistance in the infirmary, the tuberculosis center, and the insane asylum, the famous radical doctor from Chicago was barely under lock and key and was even allowed to picnic with his wife and baby in the woods. He once bargained with the warden for a trip to see the Cleveland Indians play, an outing that was canceled at the last moment. Ben remembered the warden approaching him early on the scheduled day of the game: "Reitman, you'll excuse me if I ask you to do me a favor. Please don't go to the ball game. There'll be a number of city officials there who might recognize you. Here's a cigar; please take a walk in the woods."[21]

While in the Warrensville prison, Ben wrote a letter to his newborn son. He seemed more serene and contented with life than ever before. He talked of the security of home, the joy of being a parent, the enrichment of a loving, supportive wife, and of peace in his heart. "Oh my baby boy, I love you. I am so happy you are here in this wonderful world. Your Father loved life and lived life. I hope you will see and enjoy as much of the world as I did. I hope you will love men and women and have as much joy from loving as I did, and even more . . . I wish for you a beautiful, big life. I hope you will love people, all kinds—that you will especially love poor people, the tramps, the criminals and the outcasts. . . ."[22] Ben also wrote to Anna: "You are my honest to God wife and I love you with all my soul. I feel God gave you to me and I am proud of you and joyous about Brutus. I know myself, I know my needs. You are a beautiful part of my life and come what will you are MY ANNA."[23] Although they did not legally marry, they began to live together as man and wife.

Ben carried into his relationship with Anna the same kind of personal perplexities that had tormented Emma. He was soon apologizing for his womanizing and assuring Anna that his close attachment and devotion to his mother would no longer cloud their own life together. In one letter he wrote, "I promise you faithfully that as long as Mother is well you will never live with her again. There are some things I can learn, and I assure you that as far as I am concerned Your Mother in Law problem is solved." In another letter he alluded to his incessant hunt for women: "And the love that is mine for you makes it impossible to have utter abandonment with anyone else. You haunt me, you hold me. Yet the FORCES draw me, draw me, temporarily take me. But always and always I come back to you. . . ."[24]

Anna Martindale's allegiance and fidelity to Ben remained constant. She bore his outrageous philandering, gave him the home and family he craved, and buffered his ego against the assaults of detractors. She warmed to his outcast and bohemian friends in Chicago as Emma never had. A refugee from an English milltown sweatshop, Anna shared his concern for society's misfits. For all his foibles, Anna believed, Ben had the right instincts toward life. And so she stayed with him. He wrote to her, "You have been a great force and blessing in my life. And I am so glad you are my wife. I can understand now why a joylady has a pimp. She just has to have someone for spiritual security. And that is what you have been to me. Security, home, haven. You is my Mate and you is my joy."[25]

Shortly after Emma Goldman's release from prison in September 1918, Congress passed legislation authorizing the deportation of unnaturalized immigrants who belonged to organizations advocating revolution or sabotage. This was yet another terrifying spike to be driven into the heart of American radicalism. Emma had originally claimed citizenship through her early marriage to Jacob Kershner, but that claim had been negated years before. After Congress passed legislation in 1906 providing for the cancellation of citizenships obtained fraudulently, federal agents had unearthed information supposedly proving that Kershner had not met the five-year residency requirement when he applied for citizenship more than twenty years earlier. His citizenship was thereby revoked, as was Emma's. Of course, the entire investigation in 1906 had been conducted to denaturalize Emma Goldman. And now, in 1918, armed with this new deportation legislation, the federal government prepared at last to rid the country of one particularly undesirable alien.

America was witnessing official repression at its most strangling height, the period in which the U.S. Department of Justice, led by Attorney General A. Mitchell Palmer and his young, anti-red zealot in the General Intelligence Division, J. Edgar Hoover, launched a furious witch-hunt for radicals, invading private homes and union headquarters without warrant, arresting and detaining individuals upon the slightest whim, using agents provacateurs, editing evidence for use in court trials.

Hoover worked hard on the Goldman case. Emma was ordered to appear on October 28 at a hearing at Ellis Island to determine her immigration status. Before Hoover and other federal officials at the hearing she declared: "Ever since I have been in this country—and I have lived here practically all my life—it has been dinned into my ears that under the institutions of this alleged Democracy one is entirely free to think and feel as he pleases. What became of this sacred guarantee of freedom of thought and conscience when persons are being persecuted and driven out for the very motives and purposes for which the pioneers who built up this country laid down their lives?"

On November 26 immigration authorities ordered the deportation of Alexander Berkman. Three days later Assistant Secretary of Labor Louis Post, a single-taxer who had many years before defended Emma in his paper *The Public,* signed the order for her exile. Post later expressed regret over the deportation mania and his part in it. Harry Weinberger, lawyer for Goldman and Berkman, soon received orders to produce his two clients at Ellis Island on December 5.[26]

At Chicago's Morrison Hotel, on December 1, Ben Reitman joined Emma Goldman, Alexander Berkman, and other anarchists and radicals at a farewell banquet. In their speeches they each attacked the government and the imminent deportations. Ben went further, delivering a parting shot at the anarchists themselves. The frustrations and petty humiliations he had endured for a decade exploded that night in a startling attack on the radicals and their activities.

Doc started softly. Calling Emma Goldman the "greatest feminine force in America for a quarter century," he declared that the government's oppression against her was repugnant and shameful. Instead of deportation, Goldman and Berkman should be pensioned, Ben joked. But then he turned to other matters, saying that Emma had seduced him from religion, to which he had now returned. He spoke out against the revolution:

> You revolutionists, you radicals, you anarchists, go on with your petty talk and your petty ideas. But you'll never achieve the millennium in that manner. You may accomplish good and you may accomplish harm. I'm not a revolutionist, not an anarchist. I'm a reformer. I want to tell you that I expect to accomplish more on a platform of human brotherhood than you

> can with a platform of revolution. You can't lead men without being bigger, and better, and finer yourself. There is only one motto which you can follow, and, in following that motto, you will lose your present ideas and ideals and gain newer, bigger, and better ones. That motto—"Do unto others as you would have them do unto us."[27]

Those present were understandably aghast. Here was Ben Reitman, a man many of them considered a ten-year interloper in the anarchist ranks, standing up there lecturing to them on the golden rule, throwing Jesus at them. Ben was fortunate he wasn't tarred and feathered.

Even though she was outwardly perturbed, Emma was perhaps glad Ben had staked out so forcefully his own position. Defiantly, brazenly, he had that night declared his independence from his long-time intellectual oppressors, independence from a movement in which he never really belonged. His attachment to the anarchists had been rooted almost entirely in his attachment to Emma Goldman. For this powerful emotional bond with Emma, for this attraction to her personal magnetism, vision, and the world of excitement she offered, Ben had joined her anarchist crusade. If Emma had been a Wobbly, a socialist, a labor spokeswoman, a single-taxer, or a food faddist, he would probably have been as avid an ally. Her idealism, Ben knew, was directed toward the poor, the powerless. Her road had seemed to him an extension of his own, of his early efforts to ameliorate the lot of the American hobo, and he had traveled her road. But it had brought him much personal ridicule and antagonism. His attack on December 1 was not an attack on Emma, for he still admired her spiritual vigor and commitment. It was, instead, an attack on the intellectual arrogance of the group she represented. Ben had laid out his life's agenda and challenged theirs. Emma may have been embarrassed by his stance, but she most likely respected him for it.

Their tempestuous relationship, wracked with anger and jealousy, riddled with emotional and moral incompatibility, welded by sexual passion and also by a mutual concern for the underclasses, was very much on Emma's mind as she awaited deportation at Ellis Island a few days later. Although she and Ben had traveled different paths, nothing could diminish the ten years they had shared together. Her relationship with him had brought pain, she wrote on December 12, but also joy, ecstasy and much that made life full and vibrant. She did her most productive work during their years together and his devotion, his energy, was a significant force in her work. "I was glad to have been in Chicago and to see you again, dearest hobo. I never realized quite so well how far apart we have travelled. But it is all right, nothing you have done since you left me, or will yet do, can take away the 10 wonderful years with you . . . nothing in life can be achieved without pain. I am glad to have paid the price. I only hope I too have given you something worth whatever price you had paid for your love. I shall feel proud and glad."

Emma pensively wrote about her coming exile: "One does not live in a country 34 years, live as I have lived and find it easy to go. I found my spiritual birth here. All I know, I have gained here. All the turmoil of body and soul, all the love and all the hate that come to an intense human being in a lifetime, have come to me in this Country . . . I feel very deeply about the future of this Country. I have helped to sow the seeds, I hope to see their growth and their fruition even if I will be too far away to participate in the harvest."[28]

The two would write to each other often in the coming years. Just as in their days together, their moods still oscillated—bitterness, vindictiveness, respect, nostalgia, fear. They met briefly again, when Ben visited her in England in 1926 and in Canada in 1927, and during Emma's three-month lecture tour of the United States in 1934, the only time she was allowed to return. Ben tried at times to resurrect the romance with Emma only to be upbraided. Yet for the rest of his life she was never far from his thoughts.

Four days before Christmas, 1919, in the freezing early morning, Emma Goldman, Alexander Berkman, and 247 other immigrant radicals were awakened in their temporary quarters at Ellis Island and herded onto barges that carried them to an old army transport ship, the S.S. *Buford.* They sailed at dawn; their destination, Russia. J. Edgar Hoover, standing on the dock smiling, called the ship the "Red Ark."

19. Hobo College

Ben Reitman had come back to his Chicago, the Chicago of West Madison Street, the Chicago of the hobo, the prostitute, and the hustler. At the Madison Street bridge, the Daily News Building towered above the world of the transient. Up and down West Madison, with its bars, squalid missions, greasy spoons, and soup kitchens, men filled the street, mingling and jostling, staggering, staring at job bulletins, swapping rumors and stories. To the south on State Street was the amusement center of the hobo world, Bum's Broadway, with its bawdy burlesque, penny arcades, peep shows, lady barbers, and bookies. To the north, along Clark, was the homeless man's shopping district with its rows of pawnshops and secondhand stores advertising dollar suits and unclaimed laundry.

Throughout most of the year the hoboes, as Ben Reitman had done in his early years, spread across the country, their labor indispensable to many of the country's industries—in the spring taking hard-labor jobs in the industrial centers of the Midwest and planting jobs on farms from Canada to the Gulf; in July and August harvesting crops and picking berries from Oklahoma to the Far West; in September and October working the orange groves of California and the lumber camps of Washington and Oregon. As winter approached thousands returned to the big cities of the Midwest and East, especially Chicago, the hobo's mecca. Here, in the tenderloin district, they sought out the cheap rooming houses and restaurants and employment agencies catering to their needs.[1]

One young drifter described the lure of the West Madison corridor as "irresistible," an atmosphere both mysterious and telepathic, where derelicts brushed shoulders with crooks and gunmen, where the broken and battered found sympathy and understanding in mutual destitution. "All the old bums and human wrecks were my family," he said. "The brotherhood was made up of ordinary 'bos, pickpockets, panhandlers, petty thieves."

The jack-rollers were also there on the stem. Usually working in teams, the entrepreneurs of the alleys hung around the blind-pig saloons waiting for drunk laborers or other easy marks to stumble into a conveniently vulnerable spot. There, armed with billies, the thugs would pounce on the victim, beat him into an even greater stupor than that rendered by alcohol, and relieve him of money, watch, jewelry, and even clothes. Some jack-rolling squads lured homosexuals to hotel rooms with promises of affection and then administered the same treatment they meted out to the drunks.[2]

The Wobbly writer Ralph Chaplin remembered Chicago's hobohemia in these years, its "streets swarming with migratory workers resting up between jobs or ready to ship out—loggers, gandy dancers, lake seamen, harvest hands . . . every freight train that reached Chicago dumped jobless, odd-job workers on the already crowded 'skid road'." Chicago's "slave market" was the nexus for the country's migratory labor power.[3]

Terry Corbin, a raw-boned, booze-house philosopher who befriended Eugene O'Neill in Greenwich Village, spoke knowingly of the wanderers along the main stem. He once wrote Hutchins Hapgood that the life of the drifter was triumphant, full of hope, defiant of all odds and miseries. "I am very crummy," he said, "badly flea bitten, overrun with bed bugs, but, redemption of it all, I am free. . . ."[4] The hobo poet Harry Kemp wrote:

> Dogs tore my clothes, and in a woeful plight
> At many a back door for my food I pled
> Until I wished to God that I was dead. . . .
> My shoes broke through and showed an outburst toe;
> On every side the world was all my foe,
> Threatening me with jibe and jeer and chains,
> Hard benches, cells, and woe on endless woe—
> And yet that life was sweet for all its pains.[5]

Frank Beck, Episcopal minister and close friend of Ben Reitman, saw that the hobo life began by breaking ties, first with the family and then the community. It progressed, he said, by severing all associations with "static people and roving over the face of the earth. The hobo thus became not only a homeless man but a man without a cause, without a country, without, in fact, any type of responsible associations." This was the hobo's greatest need—a corporate existence and experience. To provide some semblance of that need, Chicago's Hobo College stood ready.[6]

As a drifter passed a ramshackle building a few blocks from the river, he might hear the strains of a favorite hobo ditty, sung to the tune of "America," coming from a second-floor window: "My Country, what of thee? / What hast thou done for me, / That I may sing?" If he climbed the stairs past the sign marked "Hobo College," the drifter might see Dad Crouch, a veteran stiff who had jumped freights on three continents. When Crouch was thrown from a boxcar a few years back, his right leg had been severed by the butcher-blade wheels underneath. With his wooden stub as a reminder to all road wanderers of the dangers of freight hopping, Dad Crouch was something of a permanent fixture at the college, greeting visitors, seeing that every hat was properly removed and cigarettes extinguished in certain rooms.

The drifter might see Joe Cheekla, the college's librarian, who maintained an extensive file of clippings, pamphlets, and original manuscripts which the hoboes referred to as the "Encyclopedia Hobocannia." Alongside the publications of noted philosophers, sociologists, and literary giants the hobo writers placed their own creations, some remarkably professional, others less so. One composition in the collection was a poem from an old hobo advising his fellows on the stem:

> If you meet Doc Reitman and you do not like him;
> Just go right on, go right on, go right on.
> If you meet him in the park just for a lark,
> put one hand in your pocket and the other on his locket,
> and go right on, go right on, go right on.
> At the end of your road and you happen to be broke;
> walk right up into his office and he will give you a bone
> and go right on, go right on, go right on.

Also among the assortment of reading materials in the "Encyclopedia" was the college's declaration of principles: "Since the world requires the labor of the migratory worker, he is entitled to its respect. The word 'hobo' should be a badge of honor, like the name of any other profession. We seek to make it so."[7]

During the years Ben Reitman had traveled the country with Emma Goldman, a well-known hobohemia figure named Michael C. Walsh and an Episcopal minister and noted Chicago socialist, Irwin St. John Tucker, took the lead in keeping alive the Chicago branch of the International Brotherhood Welfare Association that Ben had left behind in 1908. At the urging of Ben's old friend James Eads How, the "Millionaire Hobo," Walsh and Tucker reopened the Hobo College in 1913 on West Washington Street. Of several such colleges established and financed by How across the country, the Chicago branch, because of its location in the hobo capital, was the most visible and prestigious.

With his return to Chicago Ben again became one of the leading figures in hobohemia and the leading figure at the college. The ubiquitous hobo doctor kept the college moving, hustling local theaters for tickets and hitting up stores for clothing and food, collecting nickels and dimes from the men for the rent, planting stories in the press, lecturing. As he pressed forward through a packed college audience on a typical night, the swarthy Ben traded jibes and quips with his comrades. A student from the Art Institute remembered him holding forth with a kind of shabby majesty, decked out in slouchy gray suit, hair hanging over his ears down to his collar, a Buffalo Bill–style untrimmed mustache giving him the look of an old-fashioned professional gambler. "But there was that air about him," the student recalled, "that bespoke one of the believers in the brotherhood of man." Doc needed twenty dollars for the landlord on this particular evening and his announcement brought the usual catcalls. Dishpan in hand, he shoved through the crowd exhorting the men to come forth with coins. "I'm tired of looking into your ugly mugs," he boomed. "I'm going to leave for Europe." He reminded them of the free razors the college provided and the free meals and flops arranged for them. It took three trips through the audience to raise the needed cash. After speeches, both scheduled and spontaneous, after songs from Jimmy, the Caruso of Hobo Hall, the night ended with a lecture by John Loughman.

If Ben Reitman was the celebrity and front man of the Hobo College, John Loughman was, as one regular put it, the "silent soul."

Irish, a brilliant soapboxer, he moved easily among the hoboes and seemed to inspire a trust and confidence that no other individual, including Ben, could. The men never hissed Loughman as they did almost everyone else, even when he offered something like the following: "Dragstedt, your brain's so twisted it's like a corkscrew. Your soul is like the twisted and rusty nails you pull out of old boxes." Unlike the flambuoyant Reitman, Loughman was reluctant to talk of himself or his past. But when he did open up to those who had earned his confidence he spoke easily and brilliantly. He often talked of the importance of the work of the college and of the greatness of James Eads How and Ben Reitman. Doc called him a prophet, another "John crying in the wilderness."[8]

For the worker of the road, the Hobo College held out the promise of fraternity and community, pledging to raise his intellectual sights and prepare him to confront a hostile society. Night after night during the winter months, grizzled itinerants gathered at the college to hear Ben and other lecturers speak on such academic subjects as philosophy, literature, and religion and on such practical concerns as vagrancy laws and venereal disease. The college offered short courses in law, economics, public speaking, English composition, sanitation, and preventive medicine. In the law course, for example, the hoboes were made aware of their legal status in various states, especially on recent legislation affecting them. In addition to lectures the college offered various amateur theatricals, debates, open forums, and musical programs. The volunteer faculty roster included several outstanding writers, scholars, and teachers: Ernest W. Burgess, sociology; Herman Adler, mental hygiene; E. L. Schaub, philosophy; David Rotman, psychiatry; John Landesco, criminology; and Jim Tully, literature and philosophy of the road.[9]

In a chase with fire officials and unsympathetic neighbors and landlords, the Hobo College changed locations almost yearly—133 S. Green, 1118 W. Madison, 439 N. Clark, 913 W. Washington, 34 S. Peoria, 34 N. State, 641 W. Washington, 711 W. Harrison, 412 S. Halsted. Although the buildings varied the interiors remained pretty much the same: a large hall seating over 100, bookshelves lined with such volumes as *Totemism and Exogamy* and *Darwin and After Darwin* and old magazines discarded by local libraries, and oil portraits of Voltaire, Erasmus, Darwin, Whitman, Mark Twain, and Jack London.

In addition to guest lecturers and teachers the college had its own regulars, including "Professor" Paddy Carroll, who taught "How to Live Without Eating"; Yellow Kid Weil, America's "King of the Con Men," who taught finance; "Professor" Ohio Skip on geography (the best towns to hit and miss and the relative habits of the bulls and bulldogs in each); Slim Brundage, the college's walking encyclopedia of tariff rates and population figures, on statistics; and Jack McBeth, whom many considered the ultimate hobo egghead. "At the moment," Jack once declared, "I am mostly concerned with astronomy, prehistoric man and psychology of the non-conformist group."[10] On another occasion he gave a lecture on the glories of sunbathing and observed, "Out near the Nez Perce reservation in Idaho this summer I specialized in the influence of sunshine and am now qualified to teach a course of study in the physics and chemistry of light."[11] There was also the poet laureate of West Madison, A. W. Dragstedt, author of the following notable composition:

It takes very little for me to be happy;
The World has a smile for each day that goes by;
My diet of coffee and doughnuts so snappy,
Makes me very clever and mentally spry.

My shoes are but uppers, pants full of patches;
My stomach feels pleased when I fill it with soup;
When sleepy and tired my slumber I snatches,
In haystacks and hallways; sometimes in the coop.[12]

The Hobo College even had an athletic department of sorts: a Catholic cathedral opened its gymnasium doors to the hoboes, where they practiced anything from basketball to jiujitsu, a sport many wanderers picked up from the Japanese on the West Coast with whom they often worked side-by-side. The college also promoted the arts, once landing the opera star Mary Garden for an appearance. To a room bulging with hoboes, Garden gave a stirring concert. When the hoboes erupted during the finale with spirited foot stomping, Irwin St. John Tucker desperately implored the men to clap instead: although the ancient structure which housed the college had survived the Chicago fire, it now seemed on the verge of collapse. As Mary Garden left the stage one hobo graybeard took her hand and eloquently remarked, "By the eternal gods—Per deus sternus—eterni—etern—you're a damn good singer." Overwhelmed, the star exclaimed, "That's the finest compliment I've had this season. I'm coming to sing for you again next year."[13]

One female writer who paused for a few minutes at one of the Hobo College meetings after noticing its small sign was astonished at the bouyant eagerness of the thirty or so ragged men inside. They were far different, she said, than the usual picture of mission patrons, the supposedly stupid, flaccid loafers caricatured in cartoon strips and in burlesque skits. "With the sheepish, self-consciousness of twelve-year-old boys mixed with a passionate desire to express what burned within them, one by one these students of experience shuffled forward to the chairman's table and, as one member expressed it, 'gave vent to his thought'." The college, she concluded, had moved something deep in these men, had given them an outlet to express their individualism, "a desire to be something other than dull, sluggish machines."[14] As the letterhead of the college exclaimed, "The Hobo College is a service station, clearinghouse and Educational Institute for Homeless men!"

The Hobo College inevitably took on a comic-opera atmosphere. Like other fraternal organizations there was humor and mock ceremony; much of it was parody, both self-parody and parody of society's institutions. But because of the social conditions under which the college operated, the hoopla seemed especially ludicrous to outsiders. Ben and the other directors were often fending off snide editorials in the press that scoffed at the idea of hoboes in an educational institution. After one particularly annoying piece of satire by Jack Lait in the *Chicago Herald,* in which he managed to cram into a few paragraphs almost every stock stereotype of the hobo, Michael Walsh wrote:

> . . . migratory workers are victims of the most damnable outrages which any members of the human race must endure. When the free-born American citizen seeks employment in Louisiana, Alabama, Arkansas, Mississippi, Texas, and Kansas he is sentenced to eleven months and twenty day's hard labor in the convict camps for the crime of asking for work. He is forced to labor beneath the whip at building roads, hewing lumber and boiling turpentine. He attends a college in which the sheriff is chief instructor and with vicious men as assistant professors. They do their instructing with rifles as textbooks. The town constable gets $1 for the arrest of every migratory worker, the justice of the peace gets $1 for every conviction and the sheriff gets $1 for receiving the prisoner besides 20

cents a day which he makes on the garbage he compels his students to eat . . . we seek to teach these men the elements of law and to provide them with the means whereby they can protect themselves. Funny, isn't it? We seek to help them save untold agonies of suffering by giving them instruction in first aid to the injured and in relief to the suffering. Great joke, isn't it?[15]

From Loughman to Dragstedt to Ohio Skip the college provided a unique opportunity for sociologists and social workers. Here the academics could mingle with all types of social outcasts, ex-cons, addicts, and psychopathic vagrants in a setting that encouraged open discussion and stimulating interchange. Sociologists, philosophy professors, criminologists, psychiatrists—numerous students of social pathology spent many hours at the college listening to hobo orators expound and argue. E. A. Ross, a sociologist from the University of Wisconsin, wrote to Reitman in 1925: "After visiting the Hobo College with you and addressing the men there . . . I am impressed with the extraordinary opportunity that you have there for the study of personal traits and the adverse social currents which carry men downward."[16]

Nels Anderson often visted the Hobo College. The son of an immigrant Swede, Anderson spent his early years selling newspapers in the West Madison Street hobo hub and then hit the road as a skinner, worked the harvests and the mines; he later became a bridge snake, a structural iron itinerant. During his travels across the continent, with intermittent forays in and out of Chicago, Anderson became very friendly with members of a Mormon family in Utah; he later converted to the religion and went to college at Brigham Young. After a stint overseas in the army, Anderson ended up back in Chicago as a graduate student in sociology at the Univesity of Chicago.

During his early days at the university the vagabond-turned-student ventured forth one night to hear Ben Reitman lecture to a group of social workers. "Reitman was a man of middle years," Anderson remembered, "attractive physique, about six feet, stout but still trim, big head with a bushy haircut, black mustache, and he wore a Windsor tie, then the symbol of some intellectual type . . . One might get the impression he was a sloppy thinker, but all the while he was getting over his ideas."

Always trying to stimulate debate, a slightly devilish smile ever creasing his face, Ben began taunting the social workers that night with the bold assertion that their efficiency training tended to make them cold and impersonal in relations with the poor. His words, of course, provoked the desired stream of digs and insults. Among those who rose to challenge the flippant hobo doctor was Nels Anderson, and their half-hour exchange resulted in an invitation to retire to a coffee shop for further discussion. Ben, whose thinking seemed to go in "great leaps," began to talk of the need for a study of the homeless men in Chicago, why they gathered there, what kept them there, and how they survived.

At a subsequent meeting Doc announced to the young sociology student that Dr. William Evans, long-time head of Chicago's Public Health Department and a personal friend, had agreed to pledge enough money for Anderson to begin the study. Under the tutelage of Ernest W. Burgess of the University of Chicago, Joel D. Hunter, director of the United Charities, and Reitman, Anderson pushed ahead with the project, interviewing road wanderers in the slave markets, saloons, flophouses, gambling emporiums, and "leg-show" night spots. The chance encounter with Ben had sparked the beginning of the most detailed and pioneering study of hobohemia ever undertaken, Anderson's *The Hobo: The Sociology of the Homeless Man.*[17]

Ben Reitman remained the most important individual contact between those in the academic world and those on Chicago's main stem. Many professors and academics such as Ross and Anderson frequented the Hobo College; some became regular speakers. Doc remained the vital bridge between their world and his.

James Eads How often traveled to Chicago to check on the progress of the most notable branch college to which his International Brotherhood Welfare Association had given birth. In October 1920 he talked to reporters about the upcoming winter. "Professor Pittsburgh Joe has been appointed to be chair of culinary sciences. He has already learned that the thicker the coffee cups are made the less coffee they hold. The theory of relativity, you see." Ohio Skip, Ben's old rod-riding buddy, would hold down the chair of geography, How said, lecturing fellow hoboes on the best cities for panhandling and the habits and mental deportment of police, marshals, and sheriffs. Cincinnati Slim would speak on the vagrancy laws, a subject with which the old track rider and boodle-jail lodger was all too familiar. Ben, in addition to his other multifarious activities, would be in charge of health and fumigation.[18]

Many of the characters who passed through the college's doors were hobo legends. The deacon of American soapboxers often stayed at the college—"Professor Budman," spellbinder on main stems across the land. His favorite topic was the necessity for instituting a one-hour day, one-day work week.[19] A street-peddler intellectual named "Gabby," writer of articles on hobo life and dabbler in poetry, once delivered the most memorable verse on bedbugs in the annals of American letters: "They were crawling on the ceiling, on the sidewalls and the floor; / They were falling in the toilet singing 'Pull, boys, for the shore'."[20]

Justo F. de Lemos, a Puerto Rican who reportedly spoke eight languages, once wistfully declared at a college commencement program: "Hoboes . . . hope that in the future, social levels will be based on intellectual developments and achievements that will benefit humanity rather than upon political prestige acquired by the favorites of the industrial and financial captains of the present economic order. . . ."[21] His anticapitalist, antiestablishment refrain was heard often at the Hobo College, both from visiting professors and from students.

Rose the Buxom Blond, after six years on the road, told of riding the blind baggage in forty-four states without arrest. Playing the ukulele, writing poetry, Rose was a conspicuous figure in hobo gatherings from Chicago to New York. The *Chicago Daily News* noted that her gypsylike existence had not diminished her femininity: "She neither smokes nor uses a powder puff, but mostly because she doesn't need to do so. She has pink cheeks and cherry-red lips, which she says comes from a healthful existence, mostly in the open." Rose added, "Neither have I ever been in love. I am too much interested in all mankind."[22]

A reporter once asked some of the college regulars about their reading habits:

JOHN ROHN: "I read Charles Dickens, Hawthorne and Shakespeare. Karl Marx is my guide and I accept pragmatism as the final philosophy."

BERT FULTON: "Most of my reading is philosophy, psychology, psychoanalysis. The chief writers are Dewey, Fielding, William James. I get most of my psychoanalysis from Adler."

HERMAN GAUL: "My reading is very diversified but mostly biography and sociology. My aim is to understand man and men. The lives of the great interest me, Catherine of Russia, Napoleon, etc."[23]

A number of the hobo orators traveled to the South Side to deliver lectures at University of Chicago sociology classes. "Professor" Mike Smith of New York, known on water tanks as Chinatown Whitie, addressed students on the subject of unemployment, a field he had mastered. Frank Gibbons, alias Chicago Red, delivered entomological discourses on the customs of insects in the nation's lodging houses, a field to which he had been, unhappily, oft-exposed.[24]

The University of Chicago and the Hobo College also held debates which Reitman usually chaired. When the university's debating team faced a squad from the college in 1923, the university lads were in over their heads against the hoboes, masters of elocution, deduction, evasion, and quick wit. The formidable team included Boxcar Bernie, Larry the Loud, and Fred Fourdice. One of the Chicago boys remarked, "They are really good speakers at the Hobo institute; many of the men are college graduates; one I know is a graduate of Oxford University."[25]

Reitman took special efforts to ensure that the institution weeded out those from the street interested only in a warm flop. The large number of ancient but inviting easy chairs at the college were often havens for bums who had carried the banner the previous night and for whom even the most spirited debate was no match for much-wanted sleep. At the suggestion of offended hobo orators, the college replaced the easy chairs with austere, backless benches on which only sober, attentive individuals could sit. The hoboes called them "anti-booze, anti-snooze church pews."[26]

In all of this activity at the college—from chairing debates to recruiting lectures to hustling food and theater tickets—Ben Reitman was at the center. And, on a night at the college in April 1922, Ben, holding forth as usual, had a surprise that remained forever riveted in his mind. In the audience that night was a twenty-year-old journalism student from the University of Missouri who had hoboed to Chicago by way of New York. Trim, athletic, attractive, wearing a khaki soldier's uniform, she sat at the back of the room during the college meeting taking notes.

The following day the *Chicago Herald and Examiner* ran a critique of Ben Reitman's performance with the hoboes by Ben's daughter Helen, whom he had not seen in fifteen years. "Tonight I saw my father, Ben L. Reitman . . . The somewhat cynical and arrogant man whom I had disliked so heartily when I was a youngster, I found to be older, fatter, more grizzled, yet somehow mellowed, and fitting admirably into the atmosphere which the hazy room and the shabby audience lent to the place . . . I was, on the whole, quite agreeably surprised by him . . . he commanded my respect and admiration." She spoke of his strong intellect, his large physical presence in the hall, his attitude toward the men—concerned with their individual problems, not condescending, without cant, not there to peddle political gibberish but to encourage all the listeners toward idealistic visions for their own lives. "Vivid, alive, awake, tremendous in effect upon the men he talked to, sure of himself and of what he said, maintaining the utmost poise and remaining absolutely master of the situation, he talked interruptedly, impervious to the exclamations, the oaths of assent or disapproval which occasionally broke forth from the men he addressed." This was his world, she reported, and he was king in it.

Ben had a warm reunion with the daughter he had known only as a small child. Her mother was now in the Elgin Hospital for the Insane but was scheduled for release that week. He offered to take Helen home and do whatever he could for her, but she declined politely. "It must be in the blood—this wanderlust," Ben remarked. "It was just thirty years ago that I was first arrested, when I started out to travel. . . ."

Helen left Chicago after only a short stay and headed for the rail yards and an eastbound freight. "It happens to all the Reitmans, I guess," Ben said. "When they have a desire to see a new country or be in a new place, the lack of carfare to ride on the plush never stops them."[27] It certainly had never stopped Helen's father. And although his days on the road were now over, his wanderlust at least tamed, Ben still gloried in the kinship of those men who hadn't given up the life. He took great pride in knowing that his efforts had made the lot for some of them a bit easier.

In 1926 Doc Reitman talked to a *New York Times* reporter about the Hobo College. "Thousands of men have stopped a little while with us," he remarked, "and have been brought in contact with philosophy and psychology, with art and letters and music." It was not surprising to hear an animated discussion on economics or sociology from inside a boxcar.[28] The college had done its work well.

Each spring the hibernating main stem erupted as thousands of homeless men began drifting out on the freights. The annual parade of hoboes along the rows of employment offices was now in earnest, with the restless workers scanning the chalked signs and colored posters offering jobs, some offering a "ride on the cushions." The Hobo College closed its doors for the season. The men of the road were back on the road.

The college always held baccalaureate services, and at the 1926 event, 164 men, those who had faithfully attended the lectures throughout the winter months, received diplomas. Graduation day brought speeches, music, and food. At four o'clock Ben passed out slips of paper bearing these words:

> BE IT KNOWN TO ALL THE WORLD THAT ______________________
> has been a student at THE HOBO COLLEGE and has attended the lectures, discussions, clinics, musicals, readings, and visits to art galleries and theatres.
>
> He has also expressed a desire to get an education, better his own conditions and help build a world that will be without unemployment, poverty, wars, prostitution, ignorance, and injustice.
>
> He pledges himself to try individually to live a clean, honest, manly life, and to take care of his health and morals, and abstain from all habits that undermine his health and better nature. He agrees to cooperate with all people and organizations that are really trying to abolish poverty and misery, and to work to build a better world in which to live.

As they said their good-byes some of the men wept. With the coming of spring all of them faced the uncertain months ahead on the freights and in the jungles. For some of the weaker, the next winter, when the college would again open its doors, seemed a long way off. Before the meeting ended they all joined in the old Joe Hill favorite, "The Preacher and the Slave."

> You will eat—bye and bye,
> In that glorious land above the sky
> Work and pray—live on hay,
> You'll get pie in the sky when you die.[29]

20. "Outcast Narratives"

The lives of drifters held a special fascination for Ben Reitman. Behind every face at the soup lines, every stiff sprawled on the floor of a ten-cent flophouse, and every rouge-splashed streetwalker lay a deeper story. He composed short biographies—"Outcast Narratives" he called them—a chronicle of hundreds of misfits and unfits with whom he had shared mulligan, spent time in jail, and mooched, and with whom he had made love. He wanted the stories to offer an insight into the world of the underdog, the world of alley and gutter. This is a sample.[1]

Buffalo Slim

Buffalo Slim was a Tramp,
Twenty-two, and raised in the Buffalo Reform school.
He had a great passion for travel;
Had beat it from Coast to Coast in eight days.
He would deck it from Buffalo to Chicago in a night.
He was a member of the Lake Shore Gang.

Slim would steal a little; beg occasionally,
Work some and drink heavily.
Was on the road nine years, started as a punk
With Blinkey Morgan and Buffalo Fat.
When Blinkey was doing his bit at the Western Pen,
Slim kept him alive with his letters and gifts.

That night in the Jungle when he saw
Blinkey look at Skip's Punk,
He knew there was going to be trouble.
As Skip was reaching for his gat he knifed him.
When Slim lay dying with a bullet in his lung, he said:
"Kid please go see my mother, and tell her——."

Blinkey Morgan

Blinkey Morgan was a Bum,
Fifty-three years old hailed from Boston.
He knew all the saloon keepers
In every division town between Boston and Chicago.
He was a bird at finding "blind pigs" in dry towns.
He was a member of the Lake Shore Gang.

In his younger days he had been
A first class Dip and Gun,
But after he did the ten in the stir at Jackson,
And the five in the Big House at Pittsburg,
He thought he had better square it,
So he became an itinerant umbrella mender.

One night when the Gang was having a gump stew
With three half barrels and a gallon of white line,
Blinkey whispered to Slim: "Get Skip stewed.
We Will cop his Punk and make the Fair at Fostoria."
Skip shot Slim and Blinkey. As Blinkey died he said:
"Kid, if you want to see life, stick to the road."

Ohio Skip

Ohio Skip was a Hobo.
He was 37 and born in Columbus.
He used to work around Cleveland and Toledo.
His moniker was on all the water tanks,
On the B. & O., Lake Shore and Pensie.
He was a member of the old Lake Shore Gang.

The Lake Shore Gang had their headquarters
In the Jungle down near South Bend.
The Gang would often meet and feed and booze up.
Ohio Skip was a good painter.
He would work a little, travel a lot.
But seldom steal or beg.

One night Skip blew into the Jungles.
With a 15-year-old Punk that he picked up in Toledo.
Blinkey and Slim tried to snare the Kid.
They were all stewed and an awful fight started.
When Skip lay dying with a knife in his kidney.
He said: "Kid go home. This is how we all end."

Chi Kid

Chicago Kid was a tramp;
He was raised near the railroad tracks by the lake.
When he was eight he used to flip
On the slow-going freights and ride a mile or so.
At eleven he rode the fast freights
To the next division and back
When he was thirteen he beat the passengers
All the way to New York and back.

He started to bum all over the country,
Beat it to Mexico and back;
Stowed away on a ship going to Antwerp,
And came back by way of Paris.
He became an expert beggar,
A first-class panhandler.
He learned how to work the charity organizations,
And get the Country to give him transportation.

He often used to be picked up by the police,
But he was so young that they always let him go.
He wasn't lazy, but he never had time to work.
He always had some place to get to in a hurry.
He would ride the rods all night and deck it all day,
And start off in the morning without breakfast.
He just couldn't stay anywhere over a week.
He said: "I wonder if there is any cure for 'wanderlust'."

Tom

Tom was about forty-seven
And just crazy about kids.
He was forever giving candy and toys to children.
He used to spend hours sitting on the beach
With a bunch of children, telling them stories.
There was a peculiar sad look in his eyes.

He was sent to the workhouse for six months,
On the charge of annoying children.
They put him to work cleaning up the boy's cells.
He was helpful, intelligent and silent.
His own cell was plastered with children's pictures
And one photo of his parents, who were cousins.

Four months after he was released
He was arrested for killing a little girl.
He quoted: "All men kill the things they love."
The peculiar sad look in his eyes was gone
And resignation and hope were on his face.
"Help me get hanged quickly," was all he said.

Dick

Dick was a little blond artist;
Weighed 117, talked like a girl.
The vulgar called him a sissy,
The wise, a fairy.
He admitted he was a homo;
He painted well, made a good living.

One night he was walking in the park,
Met a "chicken"—a young fellow.
Dick began to monkey with him.
A bull who was hiding behind a bench grabbed Dick.
The "chicken" was a stool.
The police dragged Dick to a little house in the park.

A couple of park policemen beat him up and bawled him out.
Said: "We could send you to the pen and disgrace your family,
But if you've got any Jack we might let you go."
They took Dick's card, his watch and eighty-five dollars.
That he promised to pay forty dollars more in the morning.
That night Dick wanted to, but was too sick to kill himself.

The next day the stool collected the forty.
A few days later he trimmed Dick for another twenty-five.
Dick got so nervous he was unable to work.
The stool continued to shake him down,
So Dick left town and went to work in a town he hated.
He said: "Why did God make me so?"

Harry

Harry is a young fellow, twenty-four,
Born in Ohio of working-class family;
He is good looking, has a good eye and always smiles.
He never works except when in jail,

And then he never stays very long there.
Harry is a wonder with women.

He has more sweethearts, girls and lovers
Than any actor or banker in town.
It's true he doesn't go in for high-class women.
"Takes too much time to land them," he says.
"When a girl sees me for three times
And doesn't fall for me, I let her go to hell."

But he always has plenty of women wanting him.
Two of his most devoted girls were sick—
One had two diseases and the other three.
They were too poor to buy medicine,
But chipped in and bought him a twelve-dollar silk shirt.
He got so sick they put him in the hospital.

Everybody there knew what the matter was,
Yet two nurses and three patients fell for him.
He left the hospital in a cab with the janitor's wife.
A soldier's wife tried to kill herself because he wouldn't
   stay all night.
He had a Jew girl who was always weeping for her shame
And the fifteen dollars Harry promised to give the midwife.

Two waitresses over in the Greek's had a fight over him;
He patched it up, got three dollars from one,
And a ring and seventy cents from the other.
A constipated Christian Science lady tried to reform him.
She lost her virtue, religion and nearly one hundred dollars.
He said, "Anybody that goes after a woman can get her."

Arnold

Arnold was a varietist,
Thirty-five, born and educated in California;
Tall, good-looking, brown eyes;
Not much money, but made a good living;
Popular with women since he was fourteen.
When he married his habits did not change.

He explained to his wife—
Life is to live, love is to give;
Passion is to wake, sex to partake;
Lips are to kiss, just for bliss;

Bodies are to hold, so be bold;
Love is life; it is more than a wife.

One is not enough; it's no use to bluff;
Our greatest need no individual can feed.
Like a mad steed, no master it heeds.
Who can read, where passion will lead?
Oh! Who can tell;
His wife said: "Oh, hell!"

Moses

Moses was a powerful old man,
Seventy, grey-bearded and bent;
He was born and reared in Kansas,
Taught school, edited a newspaper,
And became a reformer.
He helped John Brown free the slaves.

After the war he worked for woman's emancipation.
Said: "Woman has a soul
And should have the vote;
She should have control over her own body."
They said he was crazy and put him in jail.
When he got out he was worse than ever.

He began to propagate free love and birth control
He said: "Love is enough. Marriage doesn't mean anything.
Children should not be born by accident,
Whether the parents are married or not.
Every child should be made welcome, healthy and happy.
That is the only way to have a decent society."

21. Hobo Kingdom

"The underworld," Walter Lippmann wrote, "lives by performing the services which convention may condemn and the law prohibit, but which, nevertheless, human appetites crave."[1] Nowhere, it seemed, could human appetites be better satisfied than in Chicago.

Open prostitution in the notorious levee district on Chicago's South Side was a thing of the past. Those days had seen everything from the twenty-five-cent cribs of black whores on Bed Bug Row and their staged sex circuses to the opulence of Mina and Ada Everleigh's mirrored mansion on South Dearborn, where amid the exotic shrubbery, damask-upholstered divans, mahogany stairs, and paneled rooms customers frequently paid out hundreds of dollars a night for fine wine, food prepared by a *cordon bleu* chef, and women renowned for their refinement, beauty, and sexual artistry.

The times had changed but prostitution still thrived in Chicago, run by the mob through payoffs to police, ward and precinct committeemen, state legislators, and state's attorneys. In February 1923 vice investigators tallied the profits—over $13 million a year, they estimated, flowed into the hands of resort owners, mobsters, and the city's civil servants. "Chicago's blood was hustlers' blood," Nelson Algren once wrote. In the 1920s, it was clear, much of the city was on the take.[2]

Ben Reitman traveled conspicuously in the world of organized vice. Al Kaufman, con man extraordinaire, said that Ben was acquainted with just about every hood in Chicago, including Al Capone, whom he introduced Kaufman to in a Chicago restaurant in the early 1920s. Reitman knew especially well mob whoremasters "Mike de Pike" Heitler and Jack Zuta, both of whom later met sudden but typical ends: Jack in a fusillade of tommy-gun bullets in a hotel dance hall in Wisconsin; Mike de Pike in a flaming farmhouse northwest of Chicago. Mike and Jack, two of Chicago's most noted panderers, were, for a time, Ben Reitman's employers.

Ben was a "line doctor," or house physician, for a string of notchhouses run by Heitler and Zuta. With his always rumpled suit, shabby black medical case, and walking stick, he was a frequent visitor to the houses and knew most of the joyladies by name. His inspection trips were always the occasion for lusty bantering and frequent caresses. Doc saw several hundred women a week and became so popular that many became his regular clients at his State Street office.[3]

"The fates have been kind to me," Ben once wrote. They had placed him in contact with many extraordinary individuals and in the center of stormy and momentous reform struggles. And now, in 1924, the fates—and the mob—gave him a kingdom.

The Granville Hotel, an imposing stone edifice at 3801 Grand Boulevard, had once hosted visiting dignitaries, industrialists, and scions of moneyed aristocracy at a time when the neighborhood was one of Chicago's most stylish. In 1924 the Granville Hotel still entertained a few dignitaries and scions, but they rarely stayed the night. The neighborhood had "changed," and the hotel changed with it. Chicago's Second Ward was now a middle-class black community, and the Granville was one of the city's best-known sporting houses, one of Ben's regular stops.

Run by another of the South Side's influential vice syndicates, a group of four men dubbed the "Four Horsemen"—Mike Hoffman, Sol Stearns, Abe Kress, and Phil Denman—the hotel thrived with about forty working girls charming several hundred men daily. In addition to its ladies the Granville offered gambling and drugs. Bookmakers, card sharps, and crap shooters swarmed around the hotel, as did the better grades of dope peddlers, always looking to set up expensive pipe parties. The small restaurant in the hotel's basement served as headquarters for a large number of pimps, most of whom were enjoying marked business success.[4]

But the Granville's days of fortune and prosperity were numbered. Mayor William E. Dever, elected on a promise to put a tight lid on Chicago vice, strove to be a politician of his word. In the summer of 1923 the Dever administration made numerous raids on the West Side's disorderly and gambling houses, netting in May alone over 100 arrests. Miss Jessie Binford, director of the Juvenile Protective Association, lauded the mayor's resolve: "There is no doubt that a sincere, energetic effort has been made to minimize commercialized vice in Chicago. Nightly raids . . . have played havoc with the vice ring and broken a majority of the more notorious resorts and driven others to cover." Although Miss Binford lamented an increase in street soliciting and indecent dancing in cafés, she remained confident that the city government would continue its assault on Chicago's carnality.[5]

In the fall of 1924 William Dever's vice siege reached the Granville Hotel. Newspapers, reform organizations, and neighborhood committees joined the police in a concerted campaign of harassment designed to encourage the undesirable occupants of the hotel to evacuate. Eighteen times in November police raided the hotel, arresting its guests on a number of charges and dragging its owners before the Chicago courts. Landlord Frank Thomas, when asked on the witness stand to explain the source of money used to purchase the hotel, said that he was a waiter on the Rock Island Railroad and that his only source of money for the hotel was his tips. "How much money did you pay for the hotel?" questioned the judge. "I paid $18,000 down," the landlord replied sheepishly.

The embarrassments mounted, as did police pressure. After one of the Four Horsemen was indicted for selling booze, and after Chicago police began standing in front of the hotel blocking suspicious women from entering, the syndicate decided that further commercial enterprise at the Granville Hotel was futile.

During this critical juncture, on the last Tuesday in November, a dark swarthy man carrying a tattered black bag sauntered into the Granville on his weekly visit. Ben found his friends, the Four Horsemen, and other gentlemen of the racket sitting around the lobby fireplace contemplating the future. Sol Stearns was spinning woeful tales: joy and gladness not seen in months; twenty pinches in thirty days; hard-earned money now in the pockets of morals court lawyers; threats of prison terms in the federal pen; even the ponies running backward.[6] The stories were not new to Doc. Having heard the plaintive howls of several vice lords over the years, he could appreciate the dilemmas that now threatened the Four Horsemen. Monkey Face Charley, for example, another Chicago whoremaster, had suffered the same kind of baneful treatment at the hands of the Chicago authorities. "This whorehouse business is a rotten racket," Charley had told Ben. "I was glad to get out of it . . . You have more trouble with competitors and with reform organizations and with the police." Monkey Face had made hundreds of thousands of dollars in the racket yet ended up being supported by his daughter.[7] Ben had also heard the laments of Mike de Pike, Jack Zuta, Solly Vision, and others, and he now listened sympathetically to the Four Horsemen.

Mike Hoffman complained that the syndicate faced three separate cases in the coming days in both morals and civil courts. Sol complained that hundreds of johns, begging for female attention, were being turned away by the police everyday. The whole business was just too depressing to face any longer. Mike then looked at Ben and suddenly declared, "Doc, don't you want a good hotel? I'll give it to you!" The flabbergasted Reitman was at first incredulous over the offer. When he discovered that the vice lords were actually serious about turning the hotel over to their friend the clap doctor, he began to talk of the thousands of homeless and shelterless men who could be helped in such a facility. Phil Denman assured him that the syndicate would provide the hotel rent free and also would throw in bellboys, a janitor, and even food for the hoboes. The scheme would relieve them of civic harassment, help Reitman, a loyal and faithful ally, and perform something of a public service to the homeless, thereby deflecting the stigma of numerous court appearances from the public image of the four syndicate members. Ben, always one to grasp opportunity by the throat, bounded into action. The vision was there unclouded, a coup of unmatched proportions in the history of derelict reform: "God's Kingdom for Hobos," he would call it.

The next day Doc hiked over to the United Charities and asked his friend Joe Hunter to send all his applicants to the Granville; he told other social agencies to spread the word too. But the indefatigable Reitman did most of the work himself. At Hogan's Flop and Muggsy's and the Hobo College he delivered the message: free flops and good meals; meet at nine o'clock at Green and Madison streets. At the Helping Hand Mission, the Cathedral Mission, the Bible Mission, at numerous other havens for the homeless, Ben heralded the glad tidings. After only a few hours he had assembled over 100 hoboes, led by the "King of the Soapboxers" and a Hobo College celebrity, John Loughman. After a few words of inspiration from Ben, the assemblage trouped to the el station, filled three cars, and rode triumphantly "on the cushions" to the Hobo Kingdom. Ben Reitman's reign was underway.[8]

At the Granville Hotel the Four Horsemen lounged in the parlor, still telling anyone who would listen their epic miseries. Suddenly, through the front door surged a motley army, wretched-looking denizens of West Madison led by their liberator, the clap doctor. The syndicate members, inured to daily raids by the police, were startled only momentarily. Never dreaming that Reitman could round up so many destitute men in so short a time, they were relatively unprepared for the first night of the Kingdom. Responding magnificently, however, they sent a number of hoboes to grocery stores and prepared for an organizational meeting, one which turned into a gala occasion. Ben introduced John Loughman, who gave his usual dazzling oratory, and Reggie Roberts sang. After a rousing rendition of the hobo's national anthem, "Hallelujah, I'm a Bum," Ben officially pronounced the birth of the Kingdom.

The benefactors and their guests prepared for the night as bellboys assigned hoboes to their rooms. Old Dad Spears, who had reputedly not slept in a bed for years and who had not had his clothes off in three years except for periods in the workhouse, drew room 203, the royal suite. When Dad saw the luxurious room with its mahogany bed, he was sorely intimidated. Not wanting to despoil the sheets, he spent the night on the floor, curled up on the thick Brussels carpet.

The Four Horsemen insisted that the hoboes receive free the same advantages afforded previous guests, except for the ministrations of the house ladies. Clean sheets, bath, bellboy service—it was all theirs. Everyone seemed in a state of bewilderment mixed with ecstasy. Only Chuck Connors, the junker, was unhappy. Chuck, once known as the "King of the Beggars," was a delightful, humorous Irishman, highly intelligent, but hopelessly addicted. He had been through twenty-five cures, jails, prison, insane asylums, and private sanatoriums. This night, given a chance to call the shots, Chuck became slightly imperious and phoned a bellboy to complain that the mattress was too soft. He preferred something more in the style of the beds of the House of Corrections. Chuck also asked for valet service to help him undress.[9]

In the early hours of the morning, with over 100 hoboes and outcasts asleep in the Granville, Ben gathered with his patrons. He could quickly see that the vice masters were genuinely affected by the sight of some of the derelicts. Sol Stearns told Ben that he had never seen anything so terrible in his life, men gulping food as if they were starved, young boys no more than eighteen years old with wasted looks. Some of them had shoes that barely covered the bottoms of their feet; many had no socks.

In the following days the Four Horsemen called together some of the area pimps and whores, enlisting their help to get the Kingdom off to a good start. Harry, a pimp who normally slept until four o'clock in the afternoon, took charge of the kitchen, a job that required morning hours. Ben and the mobsters set up a police committee to maintain a semblance of order and a commissary committee to canvass the neighborhood stores for donations of food. The lease on the hotel ran for over a year and the Four Horsemen vowed that the property would remain in the hands of the Kingdom for all of that time. The guests were required only to keep the place clean, in return for which they were given coffee and rolls in the morning, soup, bread, tea, and cake at night, and hotel facilities. The vice masters offered $500 a month for expenses to make the venture a success and even had a large sign painted—"God's Kingdom for Hobos—Free Lodging and Meals for Hobos."[10]

Word of the Hobo Kingdom spread quickly. One of the state's attorneys stalking the Four Horsemen charged that their sudden burst of altruism was motivated only by the legal clouds darkening their future.[11] But the hoboes didn't question the motives of the syndicate; they flocked to the Kingdom's door. The hotel quickly filled and by the fourth night most of the rooms housed at least five hoboes. Every afternoon, beginning at approximately four o'clock, a line of bedraggled men made the four-mile trek from the West Madison Street hobo corridor to the Granville Hotel, through the middle-class black neighborhood. In the morning, after dinner, a night's sleep, and breakfast, they would reverse the line of march. Reitman and a number of pimps and whores kept the place moving and syndicate men paid the bills.

On the first two Sunday afternoons the Kingdom held concerts. Ben especially remembered years later the community sings, hundreds joining in, hoboes, pimps and prostitutes, gamblers, even the policemen who were shadowing the Granville. A reporter from the *Tribune,* Maureen McKernan, remarked, "I never heard such singing in my life. This is the most impressive service I've ever attended." Doc agreed: "As the crowd sang it forgot that they were social outcasts. Song had united them into one great family. They sang for joy and were better for it."

Ben was moved by the Four Horsemen's sympathy for the transients. Although these syndicate men, calloused by years of running vice dens, were not logical proprietors of a charity house, they energetically tried to make it work. They not only put their money into the enterprise but spent large amounts of time at the Kingdom. The pimps and whores also enthusiastically joined in the effort. Reitman called the Kingdom after its first three weeks the most humanizing experiment in social reform he had ever seen. Many drifters told Ben how grateful they were for the Kingdom. A prostitute named Pauline came up to him with tears filling her eyes and said, "I wish Joe could go to the Hobo Kingdom every night. He isn't smoking the pipe any more, and he's very kind to me, and he wants me to stop hustling."

Ben turned the Kingdom into an expanded version of the Hobo College. The pimps and whores from the Granville sat around the lobby and meeting rooms joining the hoboes in discussions of philosophy, religion, and politics. Throughout most of the days and into the early morning hours, groups of men and women talked about the various issues they had argued and debated at the college. As Ben observed, "The Old Granville learned from the hobos something about economics and sociology." He called the Kingdom a "melting pot where hunger, poverty, misery and degradation of human lives were refined and transmuted into ideals for a better and useful life."[12]

But Doc's joy in the success of his reform endeavor was abruptly shattered. The Kingdom's black neighbors were outraged by what they saw as an influx of debased humanity making daily incursions into and out of their community. When the Granville had been a first-class house of harlotry, the citizens of the Second Ward had raised some protests. But when the hotel became a center for transients and derelicts, the howls could be heard all the way to West Madison Street. *The Whip,* a black newspaper, set the tone: "If the best that we have are unfit to dwell in the midst of the whites, by what course of reasoning can one Hoffman and his associates arrive at the conclusion that the lowest type of white humanity is fit to dwell in the most up-to-date residential section that we have?" The black press charged the Four Horsemen and their ilk with befouling the community with white trash, the slime and dregs of humanity. If the proper authorities failed to seal the doors of the hotel, the black editors railed, the place would be burned to the ground.

Black residents began calling the police to complain that hoboes were trying to hold them up. Black ministers thundered from their pulpits. Black aldermen approached the mayor, the Health Department, and the Fire Department. Alderman R. R. Jackson declared war against the ragged 300 of the Kingdom: "It's got to go. It's a disgrace to the neighborhood and, besides, it hurts property values."[13]

At the same time the battle over the Hobo Kingdom was being fought, the *Daily News* reported that the conditions at the Municipal Lodging House had deteriorated dangerously. With a desperate lack of funds at the Lodging House and an oppressively cold winter underway, many of Chicago's homeless men faced grim prospects. The Lodging House superintendent, T. W. Allinson, said that his facility could provide baths and disinfectant but few beds. At night the men must find one of the West Madison Street nickel flops or sneak into the back doorways of buildings, thereby running the risk of arrest for disorderly conduct. "Of course, some of the men find refuge for the night at Ben Reitman's Hobo College, but the College is more than filled now with H.B.A.'s (hobo bachelors of arts)." The Cathedral Shelter and other Christian missions, he reported, were also filled to capacity. The overflow of 300 residents at the Hobo Kingdom had much to lose in the upcoming legal struggle.[14]

The first courtroom salvos of the war against the Hobo Kingdom volleyed against Ben Reitman in mid-December. He faced arraignment on charges of conducting a disorderly house, a colossal irony considering the Granville Hotel's former business interests. The landlord of the hotel, besieged by his neighbors, sued for possession.

In a series of court appearances Reitman fervently defended the Kingdom. He brought Joe Hunter of the United Charities, Charlie Boyd of the Illinois Free Employment Agency, and a number of other heads of charitable organizations to testify in his behalf.

They spoke about the terrible unemployment in Chicago and the needs of the transient population. The Kingdom, they argued, was an innovative effort to combat the plight of the wandering population. Referring now to the Hobo Kingdom as "the Granville Hotel and Shelter for Homeless Men," a less grandiose and flamboyant title, Ben argued that the institution was performing a valuable social function, providing not only food and shelter to the outcasts and jobless but offering a haven for spiritual and emotional uplift.

One hundred residents of the Kingdom backed Doc up. On December 29 the hoboes formed a column of fours at the Grand Boulevard hostelry and prepared to walk to city hall in subzero weather to protest the attacks against the Kingdom. After briskly marching only a few blocks, the scantily dressed, shivering men opted for the nearest el station. Arriving at city hall they slowly filled the courtroom seats, prompting Judge Arnold Heap to order the services of three extra bailiffs. When some of the hoboes cheered at favorable testimony during the trial, Judge Heap bellowed at the wanderers, "Any further display of emotion and I'll have the place cleared. This is a court of justice, not a theater." The judge also declined a defense motion to hear testimony from some of the homeless men, regarding the attempt as a grandstand maneuver. The jury rendered a decision favoring the landlord, and the court issued an order dispossessing the Hobo Kingdom.[15]

When he looked back years later, Ben Reitman remembered the Hobo Kingdom as one of the most exhilarating episodes in his life. "I have had the opportunity of seeing many experiments in helping the unemployed and anti-social groups," he wrote, of "participating in the activities of religionists, reformers and revolutionists who were attempting to better the lot of social outcasts; but by far the most interesting, spectacular, and worthwhile effort to help men that I have ever witnessed took place in Chicago in 1924." The tragedy was that it lasted only a few weeks.[16]

The Hobo Kingdom closed with a jubilee concert, to which many men and women of the street trekked. The doors then were shut for good, and the flophouses and alleyways of Chicago had an increased population for the New Year.

22. Dill Pickle

Ben Hecht, in his inaugural issue of the *Chicago Literary Times* in March 1923, called Chicago "the pious, subnormal, fatheaded Rube town with the dirtiest streets in the world, the worst taste, the least manners, the most murderers on earth." But as Ben Hecht well knew, it also had been a city of cultural and artistic achievement, the city where Maurice Browne launched his Little Theatre; where an array of towering writers emerged at nearly the same time, men such as Carl Sandburg, Theodore Dreiser, Edgar Lee Masters, Sherwood Anderson, and Vachel Lindsay; where a remarkable assortment of writers, critics, and reporters matched wits over drinks and roast partridge at Schlogl's, the preeminent coffee house of the literati in the Midwest; where Harriet Monroe began to publish the likes of Ezra Pound and William Butler Yeats in *Poetry;* where Margaret Anderson offended literary circles by publishing in her *Little Review* the musings of Imagists and other modernists that baffled even Upton Sinclair. And, as Ben Hecht also well knew, Chicago was the city of the Dill Pickle Club.

The Dill Pickle was the brainchild of a wild, red-haired drifter named Jack Jones, former husband of the Wobbly orator and later Communist party leader Elizabeth Gurley Flynn, the "Rebel Girl." There were rumors when Jack hit Chicago that he had been one of a band of safe robbers with a specialty in handling nitroglycerin. The several missing fingers on his hands gave credibility to these rumors as well as to stories that he had applied his bomb-making skills in an IWW sabotage squad. Even after Jack had reportedly gone straight, the Chicago police were often at his door asking questions about the latest nitro jobs. With his mangled hands, long hair, green smoking jacket, and flowing black tie, Jack had the makings of a legend. "It was," Sherwood Anderson remarked, "a little like being in the presence of say Jesse James."[1]

Born in Canada, Jack Jones had tried numerous lines of work in his early days on the road—railroad construction, biscuit making, tunnel driving, printing, and diamond drilling. He had worked with and against several labor unions, mounted street-corner soapboxes in numerous tenderloins, and jumped countless freight trains. Active in the early days of the IWW, he married Flynn when she was only seventeen, and the two spent three years shuttling between assorted strikes and free-speech fights. Wearied from the constant roaming, Jack settled briefly in Butte, Montana, and later moved to Chicago. The indomitable Flynn, craving excitement, left him behind, complaining that he was boring, probably the only time in Jack Jones's life that adjective was attached to his name.

Jones joined the painters union in Chicago and got ten-day jobs in the building trades. Although he had settled down he still found the road and its characters compelling. He missed all the nuts and outcasts who had crossed his path—the hurdy-gurdy street dancers, the Irish revolutionaries, the barroom poets, and the ten-cent philosophers—and still wanted their company. There was no better city than Chicago to offer a bounteous supply, Jones knew, and no better way to gather them together than in a club that attracted all types of human miscellany. He probably got his cue from two small forums in which hobohemian reds and writers often mingled: the Radical Book Shop at 817½ N. Clark Street, run by a former minister turned rationalist named Udell; and the Open Forum, run by free-love anarchist Hilda Potter Loomis.[2]

Jones first opened a small coffee shop and debating forum on Locust Street and invited labor leaders, street-corner orators, and hoboes to share food and fellowship and to plot direct action and sabotage against capitalist swine. Slim Brundage, a soapboxer and early friend of Jones in Chicago, a man who often drank bathtub gin with James Farrell, told of the day in the barroom of the Turner Hall on Clark Street when Jones decided to use "Dill Pickle" as the name for the new club. Jim Larkin, a labor organizer from Dublin and a friend of Jones, had never eaten dill pickles until that fateful day. As the Irishman feasted on this new taste delight, he held up one of the pickles and proposed that the club be dedicated to this "noble piece of merchandise." Jones concurred but later worried that use of the name might bring a trade-mark infringement suit. To avoid such tribulation, the budding entrepreneur began to drop one of the letters from "Dill," and the club's name was sometimes spelled "Dil Pickle."

The little coffee house was not enough for Jones; visions of much more stimulated the retired bomb maker. In 1916 he moved his operation into a huge, barnlike brick structure at 18 Tooker Place, just off Washington Square on the Near North Side, close to the imposing Newberry Library. To many residents of Chicago the area had acquired a new name, "Bughouse Square." It was here where assorted curbstone philosophers, salty poets, labor pulpiteers, and evangelists of every philosophy and cult in the Western world gathered nightly in good weather to deliver their goods. This was intellectual manna to Jack Jones and offered the perfect spot for his emporium. He invited one and all.[3]

To young, struggling poets, to eager feminists, to sculptors and singers, playwrights and painters, to alehouse philosophers and esteemed intelligentsia, the Dill Pickle's open door beckoned. Actually, it was not so much a door as a speakeasy-like tunnel entrance flanked by trash cans. A green light cast a macabre glow over a sign bearing the words "Step High, Stoop Low, Leave Your Dignity Outside." Inside a long hall stretched through a series of rooms, their walls decorated with freakish drawings, autographed poems, clippings, posters, and caricatures. There was also a large cartoon of a man, mouth agape, shouting, "We gotta change the system."

This was a place, Jones said, where he wanted all ideas to be given a respectable hearing; no bizarre theory or dogma must fail to get an audience. Jones wanted the club not only to be a melting pot of ideas but of all classes as well. He brought together the tycoon, out for adventure and titillation, and the pickpocket, out for adventure, titillation, and the tycoon's wallet. He brought together writers and artists with hoboes and thieves, professors and politicians with hopheads and whores, gangsters and labor organizers with lawyers and social workers.

From its inception the Dill was never a stock bohemian bistro. Jones succeeded in attracting the celebrated literary figures of the Midwest—Sandburg and Anderson, Masters and Lindsay, Charles McArthur and Ring Lardner. Clarence Darrow stooped through the orange door, as did Harriet Monroe. And Max Bodenheim stopped by to smoke his corncob pipes and trade the latest iconoclastic musings with fellow intellectuals. Jones also managed to attract a mixture of bohemian poets, hard-muscled working stiffs, and thieves, all of which gave the Dill a curious character, one that perhaps was unmatched anywhere else. The club was clearly a reflection of its creator. Although it had its share of dreamers and dainty savants, the Dill Pickle was anything but a bohemian tearoom. The poet Kenneth Rexroth thought the mix a curious phenomenon. "A world less like Greenwich Village or Saint Germain would be hard to imagine," he wrote after sharing good times with this human mélange.[4]

Dill Picklers wrote and produced plays. Jack Jones acted, painted the scenery, and tended the electrical system. Some of Ben Hecht's earliest plays appeared first on the Dill stage. Although the acting was amateurish, the Dill players, directed by Earl Ford, put on Ibsen, Shaw, Strindberg, the early plays of Eugene O'Neill, even such ethereal productions as the drama plays of Yeats and Ezra Pound's translations of Japanese *Noh* plays. The cheap hotels along North Clark and Dearborn housed many burlesque queens and comics and stars of the Chautauqua circuit who acted on the Dill stage. Even strippers like Angela D'Amore performed in Dill Pickle plays, portraying Miss Julie and Hedda Gabler. Rexroth observed, "There is nothing whores like better than to play a whore on a Little Theater stage."[5]

The Dill Pickle became a refuge for indigent artists, a place where a painting could always pay a bill. Painters and sculptors sparred over and experimented with nascent trends in the arts. Impressed with Jones's determination to make the Dill a center for artistic achievement, Sherwood Anderson called the club and its creator "two bright spots in the rather somber aspect of our town."[6]

If Jack Jones brought serious culture to Tooker Alley he also brought revelry. He once told Anderson that the proletariat and working stiffs were just like the painters and poets—they would all think and reason and laugh if given half the chance. "Even a skinny, long haired poet will laugh," Jones said, "if you give him a hand and a warm place to sit."[7] Over 700 people sometimes jammed the grand lecture hall and ballroom to listen to the speakers recruited by the proprietor, who would often advertise innocuous subjects with lewd titles to ensure large crowds. One lecture on the theory of relativity was entitled, "Should the Brownian Movement Best Be Approached from the Rear."[8]

A ubiquitous figure at the Club was Dr. Ben Reitman. To the veteran clap doctor and anarchist spear-carrier the Dill Pickle was a choice forum from which to display his sweeping soapbox skills. Ben delivered perorations on an astounding variety of subjects: "Satisfying Sex Needs Without Trouble"; "The Form Divine"; "Can a Modern Man Be Happy Married with a Flapper?"; "Favorite Methods of Suicide"; "Red Lights and Trafficking"; "Social Outcast Clinics." He worked closely with Jones in lining up speakers and chairing meetings. During many of the weighty debates at the club Ben grimly held a stopwatch, cutting off the loquacious. He once said that at the Pickle they believed in everything. "We are radicals, anarchists, pickpockets, second-story men and thinkers. Anything to make the mind think! Some of us practice free love and some medicine. Most of us have gone through religion and tired of it—some of us have tired of our wives."[9]

Ben took on all comers at the Dill. He once debated Reverend Lewis Aronson on the subject of the existence of God and the holiness of the Bible. Doc prided himself on his dexterity in arguing all sides of a question. During his anarchist days in New York he had taught a Sunday school class in Emma Goldman's office; here, on this night at the Dill Pickle, he took the negative side of the question, arguing against the existence of the Almighty. In Aronson he faced a man who had also argued both sides; who in his earlier years had been a fervent atheist orator, stirring crowds of communists, socialists, and health faddists at the corner of St. Louis and Roosevelt; who would quote long sections of the Bible, refute its logic, and then defy the heavens to strike him dead (he had always survived). The Reverend Aronson who now stood before the Dill Pickle congregation to debate Ben Reitman was a reformed man. The former rebel atheist had become a Christian minister at a rescue mission on South State Street. With flashing eyes and dramatic gestures, his seedy clothing somehow adding power to his oration, he hurled biblical verses at the Dill audience with resounding sincerity. Ben was up against a formidable foe but did not hesitate as he opened his remarks with the usual references to his own greatness and so forth, then proceeded to make passing reference to the

Bible and its "Old Testicle." Reverend Aronson was aghast. "Blasphemy!" he shouted. As Ben continued to refer to the "Old Testicle" the mortified Aronson continued to shout "Blasphemy!" The audience roared. Ben was in his glory.[10]

Dadaism, Freud, and all the current -ologies then in vogue in America's learned institutions and lofty intellectual salons were open for inquiry at the Dill, and Jones invited respected professors and informed spokesmen to discuss their complexities. Some of the first open discussions on birth control took place at the Dill, as did meetings of the new American Communist party. William Z. Foster, who later became the party's national chairman, spent many evenings at the club. Any speaker, especially one inclined toward turgidness and pretension, faced an eager contingent of hecklers. Many in the crowd were crusty soapbox veterans, their quips and invective honed by years of confrontations in Bughouse Square and other forums. Few speakers, even the leading lights of artistic and literary Chicago circles, could successfully grapple with the vulgarity and sarcasm of Mike Sullivan, the Marxist logic of "Red" Martha Biegler, the rapier verbal assaults of Bert Weber, or the booming voice and biting wit of Big John Loughman, acclaimed by many as the greatest orator in America, greater even than William Jennings Bryan. This group devasted speaker after speaker who, either from innocence or masochistic tendencies, ascended the Dill's speakers' platform unprepared.

Lucy Page Gaston, president of the Anti-Cigarette League, a woman who claimed correctly that she looked like Abraham Lincoln, once took her antinicotine crusade to the smoky confines of Tooker Alley. After an hour of Lucy's lurid descriptions of the fate of those who succumbed to The Habit, Statistical Slim, resident mathematician, declared, "I never smoked a cigarette in my life. I've always been a snuff user. But after hearing this woman and looking into her face . . . has anybody got a cigarette?"[11]

The speakers marched to the Dill platform like fauns before slavering wolves. One unmercifully heckled woman who had dared preach patriotism to the cynical intelligentsia was reduced to foot stomps, shrieks, and threats that she would report them all to the authorities in Washington. An observer called her a "dowdy, fattish, impotent Joan of Arc, yet somehow splendid."[12]

On one day at the Dill Pickle it was General Coxey of the 1893 army; on another it was John Nicholas Biffel, leader of the Society for the Suppression of Baby-Talk among Women. One Spanish spiritualist appeared regularly before the Dill audience with a shaved head dyed green. Perhaps the largest mob ever to press into the club's auditorium savored a lecture by Magnus Hershfield on sexual abnormalities.[13]

During one memorable evening, with a poet ducking a variety of insults and innuendos, a distinguished-looking Englishman rose: "Would the speaker mind elucidating for the benefit of the company just what might be the curious source of his inspiration?" The speaker could only list God as his source. Amid the howls of the audience a thick-set German shoved his way to the rostrum to defend the poet, a man he judged to be of some promise. But the German, even in defense of the speaker, did object to the poet's use of the English language, which the German regarded as coarse and inelegant. "Take the great Shakespeare himself," the German pontificated. "He sounds so much better in German . . . take for instance how ugly that line sounds: Hark, hark the lark! Now listen to how soft it sounds in German: Horch, horch, die Lerch!"[14]

Cap'n George Wellington Streeter, who for over thirty years claimed squatter rights to the Near North Side adjacent to the lake, addressed the Picklers on July 15, 1919. The Cap'n's philosophical excursions ranged across a broad if shallow intellectual terrain: George Washington, class conflict, Ireland, Riparian rights, Prohibition, capitalists, crooked judges—he covered them all. On the issue of free speech, dear to all of the Dill Pickle regulars, Streeter declared, "People oughtn't to be dragged off to prison for arguin'! . . . That's what they done in Ireland, and what is the result? The Irish is just as bad as ever."[15]

The Dill Pickle held dances several nights a week in a large pavilion. Jones set up benefits and defense funds for assorted figures he felt had been denied justice and free speech. Sacco and Vanzetti were favorite causes. Jones even began to manufacture in his machine shop at the club toy ducks, which he called "Du-Dil-Duks." A boxlike contraption, the duck waddled on wooden wheels, opening an orange beak and moving its head from side to side when pulled by a string. Kenneth Rexroth claimed it looked something like Jones himself. Expecting to make a healthy profit on his enterprise, Jones manufactured hundreds of Du-Dil-Duks. Unfortunately, but not surprisingly, his clientele had little use for the toy. Jones even had competition from other duck makers on the Near North Side. One, Vincent Noga, his primary foe, claimed that Jones had stolen his idea. Another North Side habitué was also putting together drawings of a duck he called "Donald," but Walt Disney took his creation elsewhere.[16]

With Ben Reitman's help Jones also began to publish *The Dil Pickler,* a compendium of the latest stories, poems, jokes, cult gossip, and metaphysical ramblings from Chicago's literary and bohemian community. Some of the literary offerings in the magazine were respectable; most were not. The first issue offered this poetic effort by the "Reverend Dr. Reitman":

In Jail

Ain't it hell
To be in jail,
With no one
To come across
With the kale;
To go your bail.
It makes you feel
Like a tub of
Stale Ale—
I'll tell the world![17]

"Lowbrowism as well as intellectualism has its place with me," Jones wrote. "I run the world's greatest university where all isms, theories, phantasies and other stuff can have their hearing . . . Writers come here for inspiration, poets to dream, engineers to hear the latest wonders of mechanics and surgeons to learn the latest scientific methods in medicine."[18] The Dill Pickle was the most unique institution in the world, he boasted, where intelligent men and women from every field came to complete their education free from the bigotries of other institutions of learning. Although much of this was hype and bravado, the club did bring many individuals into contact with subjects they had never before explored or had long ago forgotten. Where else could bums and whores gather to hear Theodore Dreiser or Sherwood Anderson or Vachel Lindsay read aloud, or talk labor issues with Big Bill Haywood, or radical politics with John Reed, or almost anything with Jacob Loeb? What other forum could bring together such diverse figures as Frederick Cook, who claimed to be the first to reach the North Pole, and Eunice Tietjens, who did Oriental dances? Where else could laboring men fresh from the harvests mingle with playwrights such as Alfred Kreymborg? When Kreymborg brought to the Dill a small troupe of puppeteers called "The Merry Andrews," he opened to a house so full that he had to play his mandolin from atop a piano. Many in the crowd that night purchased Kreymborg's privately printed "Poem–Mimes." The author, no fool, had persuaded one of the greatest hawkers of them all to peddle the copies. During the intermission the hulking Ben Reitman jostled through the crowd waving a copy of the book, bellowing, "When you return to the bosom of the family, and the wife demands how and where you spent the evening—you won't be able to tell her how dull and harmless it was unless you take her one of these books to prove it." Astonished at Reitman's skills, the poet gushed, "The fantastic Anarchist . . . a masterful behemoth."[19]

The Dill Pickle was for many a bridge between cultural worlds. When upper- and middle-class businessmen from the Loop crossed the river for adventure, they often discovered at the club much artistic excellence and serious philosophical debate, mixed in, of course, with the presentations on subjects which could only be described as grotesque. The club was a kind of caricature of the intellectual ferment and social flux of postwar America. The Pickle's flat roof, where Jones hung his laundry, was a summer haven for lounging girls in bobbed hair and tortoise-shelled glasses discussing sexologist Havelock Ellis. Kenneth Rexroth remembered a girl from New York, who had recently hitchhiked to Chicago, as a perfect prototype of the beatniks of a later generation—torn blue jeans, sandals, sleazy satin blouse with no bra, and grasslike hair probably whacked off by pinking shears. The beats of the 1960s would have found the Dill Pickle a welcome sanctuary.[20]

Some of the club rooms housed transient writers, actors, and agitators, temporarily down on their luck but all preaching freedom—personal, literary, spiritual, and political. The club sponsored free-speech lectures and a series of talks on women's economic and sexual freedom. If a proscriptive Victorianism still warred in most of American society with Freudianism, atheism, raccoon coats, venereal prophylaxis, and anything red, the Dill Pickle embraced them all. At the Dill the Babbits always lost.

When members of Chicago's various clubs and organizations dedicated to law and morality ventured into Tooker Alley they were always duly outraged. Reverend T. R. Quayle, secretary of the Lake County Law and Order League, witnessed a play at the club on April 9, 1920, and reported its theme to city officials. In the third act a bum standing in the street is confronted by the form of Jesus Christ. The bum says, "Hello, it's old Jesus again. Didn't you get your belly full the last time you were here?" He continues, "It's no use of our going to the churches; they would kick us both out." The horrid scene closes, Quayle related, with the bum suggesting, "With your power why don't you make some wine and we would have a drink. It's a cold world. I know a woman down the street. She will be through for the night now. Let's both go and creep into bed with her and get a warm place."[21]

With its array of anarchists, Bolsheviks, free-lovers, and other sympathizers of social revolution, the Dill Pickle became from its beginning an institution much scrutinized by federal investigators. Informers from both the FBI and the War Department infiltrated the club. One such informant, P. J. Barry, once delivered to Washington an urgent report on the Dill's activities: "PLEASE HANDLE ALL THIS INFORMATION WITH GREATEST CARE, as I am travelling with some dangerous birds." Although Barry reported that the infamous anarchist Ben Reitman was uncharacteristically "very mild" and settled down with a new wife and his medical practice, the informer was not comfortable with Dr. Krishna, a Hindu orator who was criticizing foreign missionaries and extolling labor internationalism. Another informer concluded that the Dill Pickle was a free-love outfit. "They were there for anything that came. Girls were observed smoking cigarettes, one sat on a man's lap and there was much freedom."

The War Department feared that the Dill Pickle would spread its baneful influence to Milwaukee and other cities, a fear that Jack Jones attempted to soothe in a later interview with agent W. E. Rowens. Although sketches of radical leaders adorned some of the club rooms, and although Russian music and dancing were featured in Dill performances, Rowens concluded that the group was better able to wield pens and loud mouths than bombs. But even with these assurances the shadowing of the Dill by federal agents continued.[22]

The Dill Pickle Club did not spread to Milwaukee or other environs as the agents had feared. But the investigators, as well as other observers, did see a gradual change in the club through the 1920s. Its character changed as the cultural and political atmosphere in Chicago changed. And some very astute cultural analysts were slow to see the transformation of Chicago.

H. L. Mencken in 1920 claimed that the torch of literary greatness had passed from New York to the Windy City. Philistine, self-centered, and vulgar, New York was, Mencken claimed, only a wholesaler of ideas and art, not a connoisseur. He spoke of the eminent men of letters with Chicago roots—Dreiser, Anderson, Masters, Sandburg. He talked of the frenetic intellectual activity of Chicago in this period, the city's openness to innovation, its individuality. In the shadow of the stockyards, Mencken believed, a new literary vitality had taken sturdy root.

Mencken's vision of Chicago as the literary capital of the United States was premature, his words as much a slap at New York City as a christening of Chicago. All those writers of whom the sage of Baltimore had written, all the midwestern giants, finally did what others before them had done—they moved to New York. "There may be mountains more of talent at the end of Lake Michigan," one critic wrote, "yet when those mountains groan and flame, who knows it first?" New York knew. With its magazines, reviewers, publishers, editors, marketers, and distributors, with its money, New York continued to sound its siren call. It began to sap Chicago, and thus the Dill Pickle Club, of its towering figures: Dreiser, Anderson, Bodenheim, Masters. A steady procession of novelists, reviewers, playwrights, and newspaper reporters trekked eastward during the 1920s.[23]

The author and reviewer Harry Hansen had often chided his fellow literati on their migratory patterns, insisting that writers became sterile in Manhattan. And yet, by 1926 Harry Hansen sat at a desk in New York's Pulitzer Building and carried a latchkey to a white colonial house on Chester Hill. Harry Hansen had finally decided that the world of books and culture was only a diversion in Chicago; in New York it was a separate society, self-sufficient intellectually, exhilarating spiritually. In New York were volatile ideas, Hansen later wrote, as well as the massive audience for books, plays, and music. And in New York were all the other intellectuals who had followed the herd.[24] For a literary figure, Chicago in the mid-1920s became a lonely place. The exodus profoundly affected the character of the club in Tooker Alley.

When Prohibition ushered in Chicago's era of bootleg gin it spawned crowds of gangsters at the Dill. In the 1920s the sounds of guns often mixed with the sounds of jazz at the Dill Pickle's Saturday night dances, and fights were commonplace behind the orange door. When Ben Reitman jotted down a list of present and former Dill Pickle guests in the 1920s his roster contained several individuals "dead from gunshot."[25]

Lizzie Davis, queen of the hoboes and acid-tongued baiter at the Dill, once introduced to a club gathering "Wild Bill" Lovett, "the famous New York gangster that run Al Capone out of Brooklyn." Lovett, who had prospered by squeezing pennies out of the paychecks of Brooklyn dockworkers, should have stayed in Chicago. Shortly after his appearance at the Dill he was found mysteriously murdered in New York. He was one of a growing number of Dill guests who, as Doc Reitman found, died with their spats on.[26]

Symbolic of the Dill Pickle in the mid-1920s was the frequent appearance of Joseph ("Yellow Kid") Weil, perhaps the most ingenious con man and grafter in the history of American thievery. The Kid had a heart, however. "We never picked on poor people or cleaned them out completely," he would tell Dill Pickle guests. "Taking the life savings from a poor old woman is just the same as putting a revolver to her head." Of course the potential profit from a poor old woman was usually something less than the Kid wished to stalk. Weil sold phony racetrack concessions and imitation rings, hustled bogus stocks, and conned numerous victims with a fake medium setup, using a microphone hidden in a mystic's turban. A master impersonator, he posed at various times as a doctor, a mining engineer, a geologist, and an emissary of the German Imperial Bank. In one scam he took on the identity of J. P. Morgan. An avid reader of Nietzsche and Herbert Spencer, the Kid enjoyed hobnobbing with Jack Jones, Ben Reitman, and the others at the Dill Pickle, his splendid attire of winged collar, cravat and diamond stickpin, striped trousers, spats, and patent leather shoes always a subject of note. A man of cultivated tastes and refined nature, philosophical guru of shysterism, the Kid gained celebrity status, his sage words eagerly consumed by low-brows and intellectuals alike. Saul Bellow called him the "Dill Pickle Diogenes." The Yellow Kid estimated that 2,000 suckers fell for his schemes over a forty-year career and grossed the con king several million dollars. Unfortunately, Weil lost most of it to dubious real-estate investments. But to his Dill Pickle friends, the wily con man was the "High Financier" and always welcome.[27]

The early days of the Dill had oscillated between serious intellectual sport and the bizarre. As the years wore on the club tilted more and more toward the bizarre—Halloween parties honoring the best Adam and Eve costumes; talks on "Nymphomaniacs in Modern Literature," "Do the Charms of the Harlem Beauties Top Those of the Tiller Girls," and "Hormones as the New Enticer to Love"; visits from Mae West and her ensemble from "Sex"; proselytizing lectures on "The God Phtha and the Manner in which He Worshipped the Virgin"; and debates on "Resolved, That Perversion, Indolence and Drug Addiction are Unnatural." One newspaper reporter lamented that the club had deteriorated from an earnest, art-for-art's sake forum to a "sex-sideshow for gin-soaked collegiates and other perennial adolescents out for an intellectual jag."[28]

On August 2, 1931, the Dill Pickle reached perhaps the lowest point in its descent to sideshow. The focus of that night's activities was expected to be "Billie," female hobo, prostitute, friend of Dr. Ben Reitman, and pregnant. Jack Jones and Ben had persuaded Billie to discuss the subject, "What Shall an Unmarried Mother Do? Have a Child, an Abortion, or Commit Suicide?" As the crowd of 300 wedged into the lecture hall, the chairwoman for the evening, Roxy Hinkley, opened with a reading from Voltairine de Cleyre's poem "Bastard Born." After only four lines the place erupted. A shower of eggs whizzed to the front, along with vegetables in doubtful stages of maturity. Reitman was a favorite target, his black suit soon dribbling with a mucky egg salad. John Burns, a Dill Pickle regular, shouted above the din, "We've discussed queers and crooks, but this is too much, even for me, to take a woman about to become a mother and drag her through a lot of talk about it." Billie never gave the address. The Dill Pickle fare had become too tasteless even for its own insatiable audience.[29]

The Dill Pickle Club had survived disorganization, moralists' scorn, and an increasing exodus of literary figures. It did not survive a mob shakedown. A number of Chicago racketeers saw the club as a choice haven for bootlegging operations, a spot that would far outdistance the usual speakeasy in charm and profit. But the stubborn Jack Jones refused to turn his life's work over to a group of thugs, even for financial reward. Considering such defiance, he was lucky to escape the bottom of the Chicago River. Instead of physical violence the syndicate chose merely to put the Dill Pickle's helmsman in dry dock. Jones suddenly found at the Pickle door license inspectors, fire inspectors, and dance-hall inspectors, all carrying subpoenas. The club had, of course, violated numerous city ordinances for years with impunity. This time, however, Jones had violated a cardinal, unwritten city ordinance—the injunction to cooperate with the underworld.[30]

On March 18, 1931, Jones, nattily sporting a green beret and green slacks, faced Judge James Wilkerson on a charge of selling three pints of gin at the club to an undercover Prohibition agent. Although Jones beat this rap with the help of his friend Slim Brundage, who admitted selling the booze to the agent, he trudged to courtrooms often in the following months.[31] Jones faced a variety of judges on charges of operating without a food license, operating without an amusement license, maintaining a common nuisance, and violating a prohibition against operating a dance hall standing less than 100 feet from a church. After one of his court appearances he told a reporter, "I have had 150 arrest slips this winter, a distress warrant has been issued with the landlord, the police and the gangsters. I'll soon be without my old home, but I'll find a new one soon. I have had my club . . . for sixteen years and it won't take me long to find another spot."[32] Shortly after the interview the old brick barn on Tooker Alley was boarded up.

As the Dill Pickle suffered through its days of decline in the 1920s, the fortunes of its founder and guiding spirit had also withered. Jones had married a young painter named Ann Mitchell. Petite, aristocratic, Ann had worked very hard to help Jack make the club a center for the arts in its early years. In August 1920 the two visited Sherwood Anderson in the town of Ephraim, Wisconsin, where the writer had taken a home for the summer. The visitors had come across Lake Michigan in a small open boat constructed by Jones. On the return trip they encountered a severe storm, and when rescuers later found Jack and Ann floating on the splintered remains of the overturned boat, only Jack was still alive.[33]

The rakish impresario of Tooker Alley never recovered emotionally. Each year on the anniversary of Ann Mitchell's death, especially in the Dill Pickle's last years, Jones suffered strange fits of melancholy and madness. He attempted to reopen the club at several neighboring locations but was unsuccessful. Ben Reitman called him "a pastor without a flock." A reporter for the *Daily News* saw a grim-visaged Jones sitting under the Dill Pickle's cherry-red and lavender sign in 1933 slowly thumbing through a new book called *Garrets and Pretenders,* by Albert Parry. The book told of the passing of Chicago's great bohemian and literary era into the harshness of racketeer corruption and syndicate violence. A doleful Jones looked up at the reporter and began to recall the glory days of Sandburg, Anderson, Dreiser, and Masters; the days of giggling girls in horned-rimmed glasses who were deep into Freud and Nietzsche; the days of unshackled young men aroused by raw plays and the giggling girls. It was the passing of something stimulating, mad, gloriously decadent, debauching, important. Jones sadly sighed, "Gone, all gone." In 1940 he died. Some say it was his heart; others say he committed suicide.[34]

Ben Reitman and others tried to keep the spirit of the club alive. Van Allen Bradley, former literary editor of the *Chicago Daily News,* remembers a "cruddy, unkept" Reitman presiding over a meeting of the Dill Picklers above Riccardo's Restaurant in the late 1930s.[35] In 1944 some members of the old club briefly resurrected the Dill Pickle at its former location on Tooker Alley, but it closed after only a few months, on the order of Chicago's commissioner of buildings who declared it a fire hazard.

Other clubs and forums fleetingly appeared in Chicago: the Cheese Box; the Great Dane; the Mary Garden Forum, a women's club where men were invariably greeted with the words, "Mere man is always welcome"; the Temple of Wisdom; the Intellectual Inferno; the Lower Depths; and Ed Clasby's risque Seven Arts. Openly homosexual, Clasby once began a lecture on Oscar Wilde with these memorable words: "Oscar Wilde was a sodomist. A sodomist is one who enlarges the circles of his friends." The most notable forum after the Pickle was started by Slim Brundage. His College of Complexes outlived them all.[36]

But none of the clubs ever equaled the Dill Pickle. In the early 1940s John Schoenherr, a friend of Ben Reitman and frequent habitué of the club, called it a "rendezvous for geniuses and inventors, developing ideas into realities."[37] Red Terry, a tramp reporter from Greenwich Village, called it a true intellectual oasis. Terry had seen the philosopher T. V. Smith, the zoologist A. E. Emerson, and the Swedish physiologist Anton Carlson in spirited repartee with the fabled ozone orators of hobohemia. He had seen the spirits of down-and-out migrants and drifters roused by Dill Pickle debates and had watched the famous and lowly spar over fine points of philosophy.[38] Ben Reitman once said the Dill Pickle had even brought Shaw, Nietzsche, and Ibsen to the field of prostitution; numerous ladies of commercial virtue in Chicago could talk at length about these three writers after attending Dill Pickle presentations. "It might prove surprising, not to say downright disconcerting to any number (oh, say a few hundred thousand) of male Chicagoans," Doc said, if a prostitute should happen to mention one of the three at some odd moment. The greatness of the Dill Pickle, he noted, was that it brought about a synthesis, a coming together, "a great, comradely, joyous, free fusing in friendship and understanding of the imaginative and daring souls in every walk of Chicago life." The minister met the prostitute, the labor leader the editor, the sociologist the criminal, and all found a treasure of ideas.[39]

Jack Jones had told Sherwood Anderson that the working stiffs and forgotten of Chicago's streets were not much different than the esteemed painters and poets; they all just needed the chance to rise above the routine and the common. The Dill Pickle, to which the old hobo writer Bert Weber paid tribute, had taken them all on a wild ride.

> T'was a poor old barn in the alley,
> But gone is the dire disgrace
> The aristocrat must doff his hat
> To that Pickle of Tooker Place.[40]

23. Bughouse Square

The motley crowd presses together to hear from the man who would likely expound on some aspect of the world of sex—perhaps its techniques, or diseases of, or varieties and perversions in, or where and how to get it. There he stands, Byron roll collar, Windsor tie, and all, the notorious anarchist sex doctor. But tonight, friends, the oratory is off on another tack. Tonight he talks on "the rot that all men were created free and equal." A few of the crowd, disgruntled upon learning of the subject, edge away; most stay. Doc always draws a crowd at Bughouse Square, not because of oratorical virtuosity (other soapboxers can run circles around him); not because of profundity (other soapbox intellectuals are more seminal); but because old Ben Reitman is a mythic worthy in hobohemia, his exploits talked about in missions and bars and bohemian tearooms. Even with his fame and notoriety, his manner on the Square is still self-deprecatory; he still takes the insults and jibes of hecklers in stride and comes back for more. There he is, friends, where he is most at ease, on a box in Bughouse.[1]

Chicago legend says that in the city's infancy a well was dug on a cowpath in the North Side prairies. As people gathered at the well for water they often stayed to debate the great issues of the day. When Orasmus Bushnell and his friends donated the little tract of land to the city in 1842, they required that it forever be a public square. And so it has forever been—Washington Square, a.k.a. Bughouse Square.

Always a site for public oratory and debate, the Square flowered in the artistic and literary bohemia of the early twentieth century. Artists, trade unionists, socialists, prohibitionists, single-taxers, Druids, geologists who had proven the world flat, geologists who had proven that the earth's surface was inside a hollow sphere, atheists, suffragists, and people who had been in communication with inhabitants of Mars—they all congregated in the Square. Amid bookstores, studios, clubs, and all manner of bars and pubs the Square became the center for curbstone oratory. On Chicago's South Side many of the same types gathered in the grassy amphitheater in Washington Park, a forum known as the Bug Club. They also migrated to the Haymarket, to Municipal Pier, and to a couple of blocks on West Madison Street. But the mecca was always Bughouse Square, heart of hobohemia, stronghold of vagabond poets, revolutionists, writers, and intellectual hoboes, the thinkers, dreamers, and chronic agitators. They called the area "the village," and on every evening when the weather allowed it teemed with life.[2]

Several thousand at a time sometimes gathered to hear the rank tyros and sophisticated soapers expose their monomanias. Often, three or four large gatherings took place simultaneously along with several "beehives," arguments that drew small clusters of onlookers. During World War I the local authorities, worried about sedition, began to chase reds from the park, an action that prompted a petition from Clarence Darrow and 15,000 others to restore free speech. Darrow got his injunction restraining the police and the soaping continued.[3]

Many of the Square's regulars lived from hand to mouth in ramshackle, unkept hovels, their self-inflicted poverty relieved by binges of talk and sexual "varietism." The long hair, outlandish dress, obscene words; the discussions of Freud and syndicalism; the dabbling in the occult; the cynicism—it was all somehow so conventional in its unconventionality.

The poet Kenneth Rexroth, who spent countless days in the Square, called it a "ragamuffin bohemia" where the leaven of the underworld mixed with the crusty veterans of the labor movement, where petty crooks, whores, carnival performers, and bad, unpublished authors and penniless artists—in short, the losers—mingled with the winners—established editors, professors, writers, even clergymen. The Square, Rexroth insisted, was an important working-class educational institution, not only dispensing information but providing something of a decent wage for the stars. With plucky effort, some speakers could fill the hat with well over fifty dollars a weekend.[4]

Women's issues were favorite topics on the Square, Ben Reitman recalled, along with "prohibitionists, people from the Moody Bible Institute and atheists . . . I think atheists were made faster than Christians, however. It was a conglomeration of radicals and Christians, free thinkers and free lovers."[5]

No square block in America could have been surrounded by buildings, estates, and people representing such disparate elements in American culture. On one side was the solemn, dignified Newberry Library, center for sedate scholarly pursuits; just off the square was Tooker Alley's Dill Pickle Club; and on the rising-sun side of the Square was the majestic New England Congregational Church. Interspersed among the three were several aging mansions, their ritsy grandeur compromised by the collection of human miscellany usually milling about.

Bughouse was always on fire with the words of the prophets and philosophers: Morris Levin, the blind orator, who quoted Shakespeare at the drop of a nickel or dime or quarter and who knew the latest batting averages, not only of the Cubs and White Sox, but of every team in the majors; Herbert William Shaw, alias the "Cosmic Kid," a diminutive, pug-nosed veteran of the Boer War and many wars of words; James Sheridan, a bricklayer, and his sons Jimmy and Jack, who could recite poetry, debate Marxian dialectics, or argue ward politics; Jimmy Rohan, a former English professor with three teeth and a whiskey baritone voice. There was also Herbert L. ("Dad") Crouch, wooden-legged poet laureate of hobohemia who always mimeographed his speeches, perhaps hoping for a wider audience or for immortality. Dad Crouch's speeches, after all, should not have been favored only upon the cognoscenti of Bughouse Square. Ben Reitman's good friend Frank Beck, the most noted minister of hobohemia, was always fascinated by a smallish speaker who kept boasting that he once lived forty days on peanuts alone. "Forty days," he kept repeating. "The same number of days that it rained when Noah sought shelter in the Ark." The significance of this biblical allusion was forever lost to Frank Beck.[6]

Studs Terkel remembers hearing Frank Midney, known by many as the "Mayor of Bughouse Square," deflate one impudent heckler with the following: "If brains was bedbug juice, you couldn't drown a nit." Always savage in attacking the established institutions, Midney would heap scorn on the nearby YMCA, or "Young Magnolias Carefully Assorted." Terkel also remembered Ben Reitman in an Aristide Briant fedora and flowing cape, hawking at a dime a copy various treatises on sexual prowess. At Bughouse Square business was always lively for Chicago's eminent clap doctor.[7]

One of the soapboxers, a yellow-haired, moonshine-breathed former war resister, followed Reitman around like a mascot, a large quid of snuff wedged against his upper gum. This wizened stiff had only one subject on the soapbox: the pleasures of oral sex and its answers to all of the problems posed by Malthus and Marx. No wonder Ben Reitman was his idol.[8] Another orator, a huge Norwegian named Triphammer Johnson, former tool and die man with a proud walrus mustache and a rumbling voice, used to recite entire plays by Strindberg and Ibsen. He once spellbound the hoboes and smoke hounds on the Square with three weeks' worth of lectures on Kierkegaard and Nietzsche.

But the Demosthenes of the Square, the man who could make the best of the soapboxers cower, was the massive Irishman John Loughman, a figure James Farrell marched across the pages of *Studs Lonigan.* Six-foot-four, with a shock of black hair, dark-blue eyes, and Mephistophelian eyebrows, Loughman was not only the king of Chicago's soapboxers but was probably the best the country ever produced. A leading figure at the Hobo College along with Reitman, he was also a bloodied veteran of Wobbly wars at the Montana copper strikes. While handcuffed spread-eagled to the bars of a jail cell he was treated by a sheriff to a nightstick down the throat, which broke his jaw and most of his teeth and smashed his palate. Four months later Loughman returned to the strike. He never backed off. Once arrested for delivering a stinging antiwar speech, he was freed when his attorney, Clarence Darrow, showed that Big John had been reciting the words of Mark Twain. According to Jack Sheridan, Darrow himself once declared from a box in the Square, "There are few things I enjoy in this life—one of them is to come out here to the Square and discuss with you 'bugs' the reasons for living."[9]

Slim Brundage was one of the deans of Bughouse. He was born in Idaho in 1903 in the state mental hospital at which his parents worked. His father had various jobs as printer, day laborer, newspaper editor, and labor organizer and shuttled the family all across the country. He was a dedicated atheist and socialist, and the young

Brundage followed in that tradition. He hoboed from job to job in his early teens, spent time in chain gangs in Texas and Florida, and read voraciously, a habit inculcated by his father, who had a strong literary bent. Brundage landed in Chicago in 1922 and got a job as a housepainter, something he fixed on as a part-time career for most of his life. He soon gravitated to Bughouse Square, noting, "When I came to Chicago there were about 40 forums operating here. On a Sunday you could go from one to another, from 10 A.M. till midnight." In churches, in theaters, in the open, the forums were a principal source of intellectual stimulation and entertainment in the major cities before the thriving days of radio and television. This was also a period of social and intellectual ferment with women's rights, psychoanalysis, and a host of political and social ideologies drawing adherents and skeptics. The public forums, offering free platforms for proselytizing and scoffing, were valuable outlets for men such as Slim Brundage and thousands of others.[10]

Often after meetings at the Square, the speakers and many of their initiates would retire to the Penny Cafeteria or to the homes of one of the hobohemia residents to continue the discussion, most of which lasted all night. In Ben Reitman's book *Sister of the Road,* Box-Car Bertha Thompson remembered sleeping in at least two dozen different houses and halls during her first summer in Chicago after late-night buzz sessions with the Bughouse Square crowd.[11] Like the Dill Pickle Club and other forums, Bughouse Square acted as a powerful force in bringing together contrasting elements: hoboes with scholars, artists with political radicals, the religious with the irreligious, crackpot health faddists with doctors, eccentrics with other eccentrics. In all of this there was a kind of intellectual dynamism at work.

Kenneth Rexroth once remarked that the lunatic fringe of radical Chicago had taught him one fundamental lesson: the orthodox worldview on almost every matter, although often empirically sound, was accepted by millions of people only because of habit. If a ragged hobo in a gaslit room in the grime of West Madison Street or the night chill of Bughouse Square could work out a fairly respectable theory or worldview, it was clear that orthodoxy had only fed on itself, that even some of the musings from the soapbox had as much validity as those shibboleths blindly accepted by the multitudes. The lesson, then, of the Square was that of ceaseless exploration, of constant questioning and disbelief.[12] "Any way you look at Bughouse Square," Frank Beck wrote, "you will find it a part of the tolerance of democracy for free competition among opinions."[13]

For Ben Reitman, Bughouse Square was an oasis where he could mingle easily with con men and bohemians, whores and bums. He enjoyed their company with no fear of being misunderstood or manipulated or intimidated. He reveled in the stories and lives of these renegades of society and was stirred by their simple, human battles. Relationships among these people were on a more elemental level. He found mutual acceptance and could spar with the orators of the cultural underground and chide the curbstone scholars with none of the uneasiness that had burned him in his dealings with Alexander Berkman and some of Emma Goldman's anarchist friends. Chicago was his city; hobohemia his haunt. For many years to come the denizens of Bughouse Square would see the flowing cape, the walking cane, the fedora, and the Windsor tie.

24. In Mourning

At the door of an undistinguished North Clark Street chapel, Ben Reitman, making a supreme effort to maintain his usual breezy air, passed out handbills announcing the speakers for a funeral service. There were four: John Dill Robertson, Chicago's commissioner of Public Health; David Taumann, soapboxer from Bughouse Square; Clarissa Lansdale, singer of vulgar songs at a "men's only" playhouse; and Frank Beck, preacher. In the motley audience were the familiar types who walked with Doc—the pimps and prostitutes, panhandlers and radicals. They came to share his grief. The service was for Anna Martindale.

On April 23, 1930, at Henrotin Hospital, where she had given birth to a son twelve years earlier, Anna had succumbed to blood poisoning following an emergency operation. The most constant force in Ben's life was now gone. In one of his "Outcast Narratives" he had written of her:

Anna

Wife of My Soul
Mother of my hope.
Guardian of my faith.
Nurse of my moods.
Inspirator of my verse.
Satisfier of my needs.

The two had lived together for over thirteen years, her devotion to him unfailing, his affection for her deep. Life for any woman with Ben Reitman could not have been serene. Anna had to humor and mother him, bear the burdens of his miscreant womanizing, tolerate the excessive attentions he lavished on his mother, and subordinate her own independence to his needs and interests. She once wrote to him that the things that held them together through the years had been his work in the outside world and the extent to which she had been able to contribute to it. There was also the deep bond forged by their son, Brutus. Although Ben had not found in the relationship with Anna the kind of feverish passion he experienced with Emma Goldman and other women, there had been with her a spirit of personal comradeship and mutual caring of a kind he had never before known.

From her English milltown sweatshop to his world had been for Anna a great leap. She had come to America rebellious, defiant, hating the injustices she had experienced firsthand, caught up in the suffrage movement and other radical causes. Ben Reitman, dashing radical agitator, spokesman for hoboes and the underclasses with whom Anna identified, had been a fresh spirit. He was, she quickly discovered, boorish, aggressive, and crude, but he stood, in her mind, for the right people and the right worldview. The attraction to him had been magnetic and enduring. She enjoyed the company of the eccentrics and iconoclasts who made up his world; found pleasure in the Dill Pickle Club, Bughouse Square, and the other forums of which he was a part; and even became friends with his daughter, Helen.

Ben sacrificed little in his life with Anna. His close friend Frank Beck once said that Ben must have made Anna's life one of tragedy and pathos as he skipped from illicit bed to illicit bed. But she remained uncensorious, her own standards of right and wrong and common decency unaffected. "She was no puppet," Beck wrote. "She simply cared more for Doc than he was able to care for her."

Although he had come a long way in his emotional life from the days of May Schwartz, Reitman was still dominated by self-centeredness. He did care for Anna, but he remained unable to break out of the infantile sentimentality that marked his most intimate moments. In a darkly ironic letter Ben wrote:

> I want to spend all of the years of my life by your side.
> Then when life is over for me,
> I like to feel that it will be you that will fold my hands
> And for the last time straighten my hair.
> And let a tear drop in my face.
> And say he was my Man.
> He loved me the best he could.

He loved to hold me and to rest by my side.
He was so proud of the Son I gave him
His spirit and love will sustain me as long as I live.
And then maybe if there is some kind of a future life,
We will meet again.
That is what Ben hoped.

The relationship had forever remained one-sided, Anna the provider, Ben the object of attention and care. And now it was over. As the chapel service closed, as the preacher spoke about this woman's dogged honesty and dignity, Ben, his face red and saddened, uneasily shifted his bulk from side to side. With Brutus on one arm and his mother on the other he grimly followed the casket out to the street.[1]

Soapboxing in Chicago, 1920s.
Top: Cholly Wendorf, orator extraordinaire.
(Ben L. Reitman Papers, Special Collections, University Library, University of Illinois at Chicago)
Bottom: Washington Park, 1928.
(A. E. Holt, "'Bos," *Survey,* August 1, 1928)

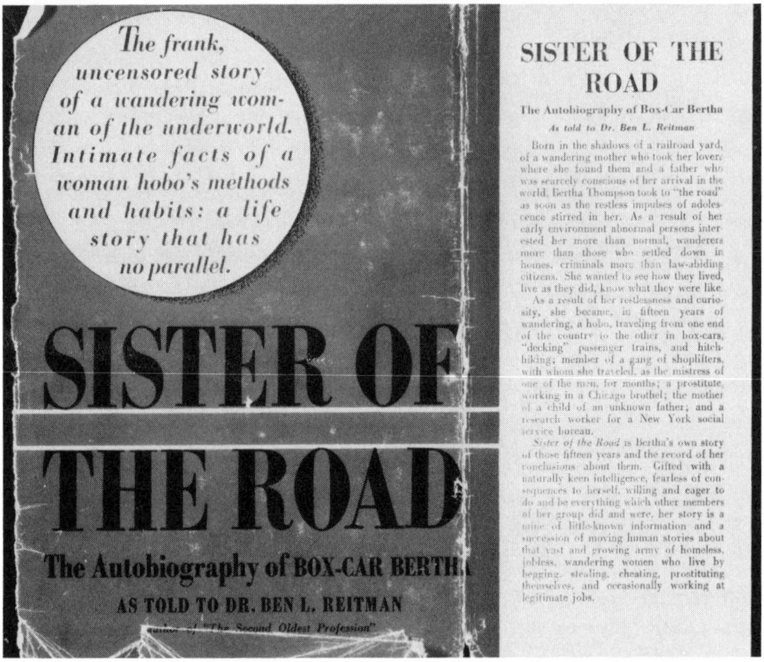

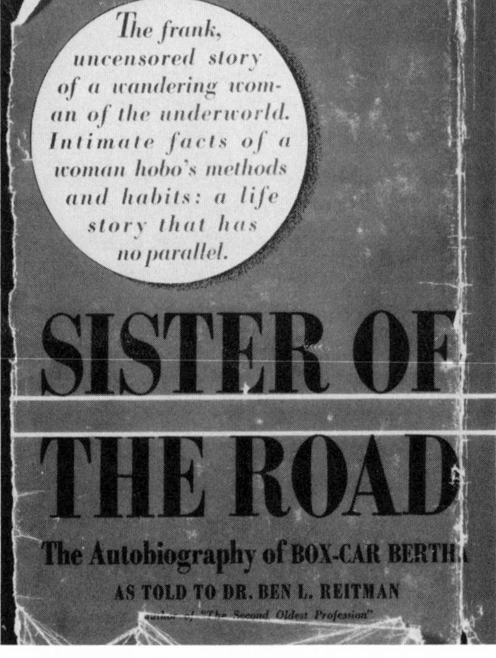

Ben Reitman, the "Hobo King."
Top: at a Hobo College gathering, with General Jacob Coxey on his right. (A. E. Holt, "'Bos," *Survey,* August 1, 1928)
Bottom: his principal literary offering.

DR. BEN L. REITMAN
Chicago's noted Physician and Social worker.

Tuesday October 2nd. At 9 p. m.

Satisfying Sex needs without trouble. Avoiding Venereal diseases practing Birth Control, sidestepping " jams, " experiencing joy and romance in love, finding variety in monogamy.

Sunday March 1st
Dr. Ben L. Reitman
"The 2nd Oldest Profession"
DILL PICKLE
858 N. State St.

Dr. BEN. L. REITMAN'S
Social Outcast Clinic
Dope Fiends Joy-ladies
Joy-men Pi's Ex-cons
Christians Atheists
and Racketeers

BIG DEBATE
at THE DILL PICKLE CLUB
Tuesday, September 25th. at 9 p. m.

Resolved that Perversion Indolence and Drug Addiction are Unnatural.

yes! Dr. Ben L. Reitman
no! John Laughman

A sampling of Dill Pickle lectures.
(Clippings from the *Dil Pickler,* courtesy The Newberry Library)

De Profundus. A photograph of Ben Reitman by Max Thorak, M.D., exhibited in Paris, 1931.
(Courtesy International Institute of Social History)

25. Still the King

It had been nearly thirty years since Ben Reitman, fresh from a tramping expedition, had walked into a ramshackle building on St. Louis's skid road to attend a meeting of the International Brotherhood Welfare Association. The gaunt, bearded man holding forth that day on the rights and dignity of migratory workers had changed Reitman's life.

Now, in early July 1930, James Eads How, the "Millionaire Hobo," had collapsed in a Cincinnati train station. His friend, attorney Nicholas Klein, remembered the scene: "There sitting on a bench, stooped, his head bowed, I found my friend. His face was haggard and seamed, his laborer's clothes shabby and torn. I scarcely recognized him." How died two weeks later at age fifty-six in a Staunton, Virginia, hospital of pneumonia, apparently aggravated by exhaustion and malnutrition.

Obituaries praised How's benevolence toward the underclasses. It would have been easy, the *Christian Century* remarked, for How to have lived in relative opulence, doling out his fortune to organized charities and gaining a reputation as a philanthropist. But he lived among the people he helped. "He gave himself," the magazine said, "with his gift."[1]

Thus, in the space of a few months Ben Reitman had lost two individuals whose influence on his life had been pronounced—Anna Martindale and James Eads How. How's work had gone a long way to give a large number of American itinerants a new sense of identity and a camaraderie with their fellow road workers. His hobo colleges had deeply affected the daily lives of thousands of men. His persistent lobbying of public officials and his publication, the *Hobo News*, had brought the problems of the migratories a new measure of attention. His work had also inspired others, some of whom by the 1930s had made their own mark as hobo benefactors and showmen. If Ben Reitman still enjoyed his self-proclaimed title "King of the Hoboes," there were now several others making their own claims to national sovereignty.

One was Jeff Davis. In 1906 Davis, then a brash road punk, met How in Cincinnati. Much like Ben Reitman, Davis fell under the spell of How and his IBWA. By 1908 he had formed his own organization, the Hoboes of America, Inc., a fraternity, Davis insisted, only for working stiffs—no bums, tramps, jungle buzzards, dingbats, moochers, fakirs, or geezers. He described the true knight of the road: "A hobo is not a hobo by choice—circumstances alter cases—and depressions alter circumstances. If because of reverses he must take to the road he keeps to the right of the road and does his best to keep out of trouble. In search of an opportunity he travels from place to place hoping to fit in somewhere. He is the greatest optimist in the world and believes the world owes him an opportunity."[2]

At the twenty-seventh convention held by his organization, on the roof garden of the Moose Temple in Pittsburgh, Jeff Davis was crowned monarch for life, King Jeff I, Emperor of the League of Hoboes of America. The official headquarters of the organization was in a small store in Cincinnati, where, sitting at his rolltop desk, Davis composed a remarkable aggregate of simple poetry and homespun philosophy proclaiming the dignity of the hobo and his moral and social superiority over the tramp and the bum. Over the years Davis lobbied for desert irrigation, highways, and flood control; spoke in schools warning children of the wanderlust; sold Liberty Bonds; assisted the Red Cross, the YMCA, and the Salvation Army in charitable work; and helped army and navy recruiters.

King Davis had under him an elaborate array of officers, including track walkers and jungle chiefs, a newspaper called the *Hobo News Review,* and a membership that included such honorary figures as Charlie Chaplin, William O. Douglass, Lowell Thomas, Jack Dempsey, Joe Louis, Harry Hopkins, and General Jacob Coxey.[3]

Jeff Davis once conferred on Ben Reitman the Hoboes of America's highest honor, the Order of Knight of the Road. A Chicago reporter observed, "Knighthood is in flower on the barren, sun-blistered, junk-strewn mesas which lie south of Van Buren Street between Canal and Clinton Streets. . . ." As cameramen from several newspapers, alerted to the ceremony by the publicity-seeking Davis and the likewise publicity-seeking Reitman, clicked their cameras in amusement, four squires knelt to begin the historic event. King Jeff sat on an oil-drum throne and dubbed knighthood on each of them. They delivered acceptance speeches, Sir Ben declaring, "The good people of society were meeting and asking 'what shall we do for the hobo?' Now the hobo is meeting to discuss what he is going to do with society. . . ." Ben's words were met with resounding cheers.[4]

But Doc's favor with King Jeff waxed and waned over the years as newspapers continued to refer to Ben as "King of the Hoboes," a title Jeff jealously reserved for himself alone. When the hobo doctor took no special pains to deny his own royal pretensions, he was summoned to a kangaroo court trial and Davis stripped him of his knighthood and put him on probation. Ben's reaction: "There is nobody fit for the title but me but I don't want it." Explaining that his natural modesty forbade him to list the reasons for his valid claim to the title, he listed them anyway: he had hoboed for more than forty years, had led a march of hoboes in 1906, and had started the Hobo College in Chicago. "I ask you, doesn't that entitle me . . . But remember, I don't want it. I've got some natural modesty."[5]

The same natural modesty characterized "Happy Dan" O'Brien, a man who claimed lineage from the ancient kings of the Emerald Isle. Even though modesty forbade, Dan O'Brien made it clear that he was "King of the Hoboes." He had found his true calling in hoboing, after teaching, boxing, railroading, soldiering, portering, writing, doctoring, sailing, and preaching. The road, with "its scenery, its vast lands, its salmon and trout brooks, babbling by the side of the hill . . . nature and all her charms," was the root of all true philosophy. All editors, he once chided the *New York Times,* should have advance schooling in vagabondage to give them a broader perspective.

Veteran of Coxey's Army, street-corner orator, poet, in 1930 O'Brien made New York to San Francisco by hopping freights. He was sixty-eight years old at the time, a diminutive, pink-pated Irishman who had organized a breadline in Washington, D.C., during the depression that, for a time, fed nearly 300 people a day. He attacked Jim Tully for slandering the hobo community in *Beggars of Life,* which O'Brien contended described yeggs and gay-cats and not honest hoboes. A hobo, he insisted, was the most optimistic soul alive, unlike the morose, sullen, and vicious caricatures so often portrayed in the press and in the writings of misguided souls like Jim Tully. Dan O'Brien, embattled warrior of the road, had broken nearly every bone in his body in a grueling fifty-year career on the freights. He narrowly escaped death several times; he narrowly escaped marriage on at least six occasions.[6]

Al Kaufman, another self-styled "King of the Hoboes," made very clear his attitude toward labor: "It is unconstitutional . . . hard work and I are enemies." Kaufman, who as a kid was derided by teachers and friends alike because of a severe speech impediment, escaped to the boxcar road at age twelve, panhandling, prizefighting, taking odd jobs at clubs. He once worked on a wheat farm for fifteen dollars a month, and it was this stint that convinced him to adopt the nonwork ethic. He became a con man, selling fake Chanel No. 5, selling land that wasn't his, even once selling a car that had no engine. He began to travel in style, making friends among movie stars and baronesses, his sartorial magnificence matching that of even Yellow Kid Weil, the most celebrated of the con men. Kaufman shuttled between New York, Chicago, Los Angeles, and Europe, frequenting the bohemian night spots, the left-wing speaking forums and bug clubs, attending hobo conventions. Jeff Davis accused Al Kaufman of being a colossal fraud in claiming to be a hobo. Hoboes were workers, Davis insisted, not cheap grafters.

Ben Reitman saw Kaufman differently. "For many years the newspapers and the hoboes have recognized you as an intelligent and worthy leader of the non-revolutionary hoboes," he wrote. "The type of hobo which you represent, and of which you are a worthy leader, is the poetic, rambling men of leisure who avoid all work and take life and anything else easy and are devoid of responsibility and attachment. . . ." To Doc Reitman, at least, Al Kaufman was one of the "romantic, poetic hobo spirits."[7]

At the annual conventions of the several hobo fraternal organizations, the election of a hobo king became a traditional rite. The tasteless whahoo surrounding the conventions offended many hoboes, who regarded such festivities as cruel burlesque on the plight of suffering migrant workers and a mockery to their dignity. But hundreds of legitimate hoboes over the years joined in the annual mayhem. For the hobo showmen the conventions provided the perfect setting. Here they could spin their stories of the road as eager reporters took it all down. Naturally Ben Reitman was at many such events, his cape and walking stick a swaggering trademark.

No gathering ever brought together all organizations or all individual claimants to the hobo throne. In the West, Jolly Joe Hamilton challenged the Reitmans and Davises; in Minneapolis, Joseph Leon Cohen Segal Lazarowitz, D. Mig., D. H-O. (Doctor of Migration and Doctor of Hobo-Ology), and head of the Rambling Hobo Fellowship of America, held forth. In the Midwest it was Jack Macbeth, dashing, debonair, speaker of three languages and student of ancient Greek. Widely traveled and read, Jack contended for many years that his name alone was sufficient reason for serious consideration. What better national emperor than King Macbeth![8]

And in New York it was Ben Benson, the "Coast Kid," ninety pounds of hobo dynamite, a map of the United States tattooed on his left arm, his monicker on his right. In 1937 Bennie made national headlines when he was dragged before a Manhattan court on charges of peddling his own *Hobo News* in Times Square without a license. The Coast Kid complained: "As a newspaper with a large circulation, containing all the features of a regular newspaper, we cannot understand how the judge's verdict can be upheld by a higher court . . . We intend to take our case to the highest court if necessary to uphold the Freedom of the Press. . . ." Founded in 1936, the tabloid quickly generated a circulation of 50,000. A mixture of quaint prose, line drawings, and advertisements for novelty items, the journal also featured valuable advice to the road weary: stay out of the South with its balls and chains and vicious train shacks; for a scenic, easy transatlantic jump hit the Pennsy, Chicago and Alton, Missouri Pacific, Union Pacific, Denver and Rio Grande, and Western Pacific; don't mix with tramps and yeggs. The Kid's publication thus joined the IBWA's *Hobo News* and Jeff Davis's *Hobo News Review* in a suddenly cluttered field.[9]

Ben Reitman, Jeff Davis, Dan O'Brien, Joe Hamilton, Joseph Lazarowitz, Al Kaufman, Jack Macbeth, Ben Benson—hobo kings all. The press loved the mock ceremonies and good-natured posturing of the hobo wags. The men themselves gloried in the public spotlight, savoring the bizarre notoriety. But behind the circus atmosphere of the hobo conventions, the hobo newspapers, and the kingly competition lay a serious attack on the image of the American hobo as a worthless, criminal scavenger. The birth of the fraternal organizations and the advent of the hobo celebrities and promoters gave further impetus to James Eads How's early dreams of improving the lives of America's itinerant workers. For the workers themselves, who debated and matched wits at the colleges, who carried membership cards of the organizations and voted for hobo kings at the conventions, who peddled the newspapers and contributed their own articles, there were now new outlets for their frustration and discontent.

Doc knew and respected these men, and his work and play among them remained the most compelling element in his life. But he felt a great personal emptiness after the loss of Anna Martindale. In July 1931 he married Rose Siegel of New York, a long-time friend and former pupil in one of his Sunday school classes. An English teacher in a junior college, Rose was thirty-eight years old when she wed the fifty-two-year-old Reitman. At Ben's home at 424 Aldine Avenue, Frank Beck, Methodist pastor and hobo college luminary, conducted the wedding service. Ben looked to Rose Siegel to fill his great need for companionship.[10] The relaionship, however, was short-lived and brought little comfort and much bitterness. The two soon separated.

In 1932 Ben gained a new measure of self-confidence and gratification: he published his first book, an exhaustive study of pimps. *The Second Oldest Profession* was not a conventional sociological study, although he made a determined effort to gather the kind of data generally found in such works. Accumulating information on the pimp population and its habits, constructing statistical tables, extrapolating the findings into general conclusions, Ben was not simply writing sensational exposé, as some might have assumed. He considered the study useful and important. Even though the validity of his statistics could be questioned and his conjectures challenged, the eminent University of Chicago sociologist Herbert Blumer considered the book a solid contribution. The noted Chicago writer Graham Taylor did too, calling it a "vividly realistic pathological study of a parasitic class. . . ."[11] The work complemented studies on the dynamics of the city then being produced by Blumer and his equally eminent colleagues Robert E. Park, Ernest W. Burgess, and others.

With the arrival of Park in 1916, the University of Chicago had become a center for the study of crime, ethnic groups, mental illness, poverty, juvenile delinquency, and other subjects which in their totality revealed the nature of Chicago, its cultures and subcultures, its pathologies. Such pioneering works as Nels Anderson's *The Hobo,* Frederick Thrasher's *The Gang,* and Louis Wirth's *The Ghetto* examined the structure of the city as no studies had previously done. One book built on another, each taking an individual perspective on specific social norms, cultural groups, neighborhoods, and institutions. Whether the researchers were gathering interviews or census figures or compiling life histories, they were all adding to an intimate portrait of the city. Perhaps no city was ever studied as exhaustively as was Chicago in the 1920s and 1930s. Ben Reitman's *The Second Oldest Profession* added to the mosaic constructed by Park and his colleagues.[12]

The *Chicago Sunday Times* once said of the hobo doctor, "You haven't seen (or known) Chicago until you have seen (or known) Ben Reitman."[13] The German writer Heinrich Hauser, who spent time with Ben in Chicago, saw clearly Doc's influence in the shrouded world in which he moved. Hauser once remarked that there was something almost pathetic about Reitman's unshakable hope and optimism, his vision of humanity marching forward toward freedom and equality. As the two trekked through the hobohemia and vice districts of Chicago, every policeman, panhandler, and streetwalker called the old anarchist "Doc." Like a mustached Mexican general reviewing his troops, Ben patrolled the streets, joking with the ladies, interrupting for a few minutes of conversation the booze-induced sleep of men bundled in newspapers on park benches, giving to almost everyone advice on sex, marriage, health, and politics. Sporting the usual slouch hat, wild-colored necktie, and large walking stick, he radiated a kind of infectious enthusiasm that seemed somehow out of place among these people. He could make them laugh as no one else could. Hauser remembered Ben wading into Lake Michigan, turning toward those on the beach, and delivering a spirited oration. The crowd loved it.

But even as Reitman played the part of hobo king showman, even as he continued the incessant jockeying for newspaper attention, he never lost respect for the troubled individuals who looked to him for help. Hauser remembered once seeing Ben deal with the problems of a black woman whose sixteen-year-old daughter had contracted syphilis; how he contacted the other youths involved, arranged for an examination of a baby who had apparently been cared for by the sick girl, and wrestled with numerous other difficulties surrounding the case. "Amazing, all quite amazing," Hauser wrote. Through Ben's medical office in the Reliance Building at 32 N. State Street marched an incredible assortment of homeless men and women, unemployed mothers, dope addicts, whores, pimps, pickpockets, and bootleggers, all displaying an array of personal problems sufficient to fill sociological volumes. Hauser encountered a streetwalker who had lost her leg in the blades of a motorboat propeller and had taken to the street to earn money for a prosthesis. For her and others of her ilk Ben was friend and counselor. In that medical practice on State Street he was making little more than a dollar per office visit. His clients paid when they could, which, in many cases, was never.[14]

Through the Hobo College, the debating forums, and his courtship of the press, Ben had remained one of the prominent figures in the world of hobohemia for more than three decades. In 1937, with the publication of his second book, *Sister of the Road: The Autobiography of Box-Car Bertha,* his stature was further enhanced. The Sheridan House publication was ostensibly an account of the travels and travails of one female road vagabond, an absorbing if implausible tale. But for those who knew anything of the life of Ben Reitman, the story had a ring of familiarity.

Bertha Thompson's first childhood playhouse was a boxcar. Before age twelve she rode the length of a railroad division and back. In and out of jails and bughouses and joints, stealing and hustling, mixing with dope fiends and pimps, labor skates and revolutionists, Bertha was drawn into the road underground. She mingled with tramps in hobo jungles; spent time in an anarchist colony in Washington State; listened to lectures in hobo colleges and labor halls; partied with lesbians in a North Dearborn Street apartment in Chicago; talked philosophy and politics with bohemian intellectuals and radicals at all-night, drunken soirees in New York City flats; did sixty days in Cleveland's Warrensville Workhouse for vagrancy; sampled the beds and beef stew in Manhattan's Municipal Lodging House; became the lover of a bandit later hung in Chicago; worked as a whore at Chicago's "Globe" on Erie Street near Clark; and gave birth to a child. Bertha was the philosopher quoting Ibsen; the reformer lashing out against society's abuse of the lower classes; the sociologist compiling information on prostitution. She met prominent figures including Jacob Coxey and James Eads How. She even took a job at Chicago's Polytechnic Pathological Laboratory and learned the rudiments of histological specimens and examining techniques. Truly, there was much of Ben Reitman in Box-Car Bertha. Ben never published his own autobiography, although he worked on it for a number of years, but this life of Bertha's came close.

The character of Bertha may have been inspired by an actual individual, one of the legion of wandering women Doc had encountered from his earliest days. But if Bertha was, indeed, one of that legion, Ben made her almost mythical. Battered by circumstance, driven by her own cravings, she tasted all of life, the wretchedness mixed with the jubilation. At the end of the running, a hell-bent lust for escape, she at last settled down with her child and lover, satisfied that her emotional house was in order. "I had achieved my purpose," she concluded; "everything I had set out in life to do I had accomplished." Looking back, she understood what the running had been about. "I had been trying to escape my own natural need to be responsible for someone, to live for someone else, some special individual person who belonged peculiarly to myself. For years I had told myself that I didn't want to be tied down, that I wanted to keep myself free to help others, to uplift the vast mass of struggling humanity." She now knew she had compromised much, had somehow, in all of the mad hustling, lost sight of primary needs that were "within reach of my own arms." This was not Box-Car Bertha; this was Ben Reitman. From the aging hobo warrior, through the words of a woman, this was a deeply personal confession.[15]

Most reviewers of the book were not generous. One said that it read like the work of a group of people imagining with all their power unspeakable degradation and lurid encounters and then weaving it all into a sick story. Another said that the life of Bertha seemed to be the prototype of a Hollywood creation, the "everything happens to me" syndrome.[16]

The allusion to Hollywood was prophetic. Thirty-five years later American International Pictures released *Boxcar Bertha,* a film produced by Roger Corman, directed by Martin Scorsese, and starring Barbara Hershey as Bertha and David Carradine as her sidekick. Like the reviewers of the book decades earlier, critics of the movie dismissed the production as an excuse to wallow in slaughter and filth and carnage. "Whatever sociological, political or dramatic motivations may once have existed in the story," one reviewer noted, "have been ruthlessly stripped from the plot, leaving all characters bereft of empathy or sympathy."[17]

But there had been sociological importance in Reitman's book. Herbert Blumer wrote in the *American Journal of Sociology,* "Students of social pathology and those interested in the more undignified undercurrents in modern life should find this volume to be informative and provocative."[18] Another sociologist, Donald Clemmer, credited Ben with exploring new terrain in the field of criminology. The secretary of the Chicago Academy of Criminology, Clemmer wrote to Reitman in 1940 that Doc had paved the way for the study of the white-collar criminal in America. Much of the credit for Edwin Sutherland's later work in the field, Clemmer insisted, should have gone to Reitman.[19] With no formal training in the field of sociology, generally seen only as a dabbler and an eccentric, Reitman had finally received recognition from individuals in the scholarly fraternity.

Throughout the 1930s, working as a part-time researcher for the Chicago Health Department, Ben carried on his investigations into the world of the outcast. He also continued his jocular swipes at the sociologists, most of whom did not share the views of Blumer and Clemmer. At a meeting in 1935 of the American Sociological Congress at the Commodore Hotel in New York, Ben declared, "My present work is to encourage citizens of the underworld to reform. I'm also trying to reform sociologists. I'm trying to teach them to concentrate less on research work and more on the application of their studies to the people I know."[20] Unlike most of those listening to him speak that day in New York, Doc had lived among the drifters and whores; his roots were in the sidewalk and alley culture, in the vice dens and the nickel flophouses, with the jockers and punks, and on the street corners with the soapbox philosophers.

One drifter who knew of Reitman's work firsthand wrote:

> He understands all—he knows all.
> All that they try to express, he
> already knows.
> Their lives he has lived, their deaths
> he has died;

Their loves he has known, their sins
he has committed.
And there he sits among them.

Holding them all, idealist and prostitute,
student and moron, conservative and
radical, the believer and the scoffer.
What is it that all these souls find in
this one man?

Against each other they would fight to
the death.
Yet in him they find a common
meeting ground.[21]

To this man, and to many others, Ben Reitman was still "King of the Hoboes."

26. Twilight of Hobohemia

In the 1920s Jacob Coxey, the aged general of the 1893 March on Washington, remarked to the sociologist Nels Anderson as they strolled the West Madison Street hobo district, "The old timers will not be here much longer." As Anderson looked back several decades later he realized that Coxey had been right. The traditional hobo, the migrant worker who came to Chicago because it was his center of transportation, employment, and recreation, was on his way out.[1]

In the 1920s the market demand for hobo labor had diminished. As the population had increased in the towns and cities of the West, the hobo jobs in the fields and mines and logging camps were sucked away by improved technology and new reservoirs of local home-guard labor. Also, increased mechanization now handled much of the work formerly done by transient, seasonal workers. The hobo, who had grown with the railroad and the expanding industries to which it brought life, found his economic world crumbling. He had become an anachronism.

Many of the migratories who once rode the rails now shook off the cinders and smoke and hit the highroad on mohair seats. The 1920s saw the age of the flivver bums, a new army of wanderers crisscrossing the country in dilapidated tin lizzies. If a guy could scrape together enough cash to buy a slightly used Ford, he could achieve a new independence of movement, free from skull-busting railroad bulls and the threat of the razor wheels of the freights. Thousands of gasoline gypsies coaxed their autos from town to town canvassing for odd jobs. A battered caravan laden with bedding and pots and other assorted household goods, the highway bums of the Twenties were a grim portent of the decade ahead, the western roads clogged by hollow-eyed Oakies and Arkies marching to the mournful beat of Depression America.

Ben Reitman had seen clearly the changing face of Chicago's hobohemia. West Madison Street, the teeming mecca for America's transient stiffs, was a far different place in the Thirties than it had been when Doc first launched his hobo crusade three decades earlier. On the main stem public relief agencies now absorbed many of the helpless vagrants who once staggered in the gutters. Hospitals, insane asylums, CC camps, and government-subsidized shelters housed many of the feebleminded, the epileptic, the tubercular, and the elderly. A casual visitor to a public lodging house in the 1930s would have been struck by the large number of men with one arm or one leg, men who were paralyzed or blind or very old or feebleminded. Before the advent of public assistance programs, many of these individuals would have perished in some alley or gutter—the nonsurvival of the unfit.[2]

Although the road was alive as never before with the refugees of the depression, entire families fleeing from poverty and despair, West Madison Street was not part of their lives. The ragged, unemployed men lining up for free soup in downtown Chicago were not, Reitman could see, the old seasonal workers who had made hobohemia a cycle of their lives, their oasis between jobs. These were not the jockers and punks and profesh of the rails he had known so well, the traditional freight-hopping, jungling, railroad migratories.[3] The old class was, as one road wanderer said a few years back, "in the sunset of hobo oblivion."[4] The old hobo propagandist Ben Benson mused, "If this was the beginning of the century I was talking to you boys, I would advise you all to 'hit the road'. For many men and boys who had the right stuff—sometimes called the American Rugged Individualism—made good. But, I regret to say, 'them days are gone forever'!"[5]

As the numbers of traditional hoboes dwindled on Chicago's main stem, many of the old-timers Ben knew so well also disappeared. Harry Batters was one. A Bughouse Square institution, few of Harry's comrades believed his stories about a friendship with Lenin and his tales of sacrificing fortune to serve the indigent. Most were willing to finance with an occasional quarter his street-corner ministry, a forlorn but unbridled call for liberty from human greed and exploitation and all the evils of insidious capitalism. Harry, the consummate soapbox red, distributed radical literature of all kinds, mounted park rostrums to proclaim a rich variety of ideas on the ills of American society and possible cures, defied the laws of the land as well as the laws of the Almighty.

The atheist, leftist radical was also a thief, a shoplifter of exceptional skill and daring. A friend remembered Harry dashing into his office one afternoon looking for refuge from pursuing department store detectives. Although Harry had been caught earlier that day swiping a pair of shoes, he had been permitted to leave the store without arrest on a promise to reform. The reformation had been shortlived; the bag now contained two pair of shoes.

When Alice Solenberger studied *One Thousand Homeless Men* for the Russell Sage Foundation, Harry Batters was among them, an outcast of spirit and ingenuity to whom Ben Reitman was understandably drawn. Doc often matched wits and insolence with Harry on the Square and at the Hobo College. His friends were friends of Harry.[6]

In December 1934 Harry met a tragic end. At a rooming house on West Chicago Avenue, Harry attempted to start a fire with what he apparently thought was kerosene. It was gasoline. Harry's wake in a dingy little chapel on North Clark Street was the subject of several articles in Chicago's dailies. Seventy-five mourners gathered to pay their respects and sing the old IWW marching song, "Hallelujah, I'm a Bum."[7] They also recited the Hobo's Prayer:

> Almighty God, heavenly father who has blessed us hobos with good health and avid appetites and made this world a bountiful and plentiful place for all of us bipeds with towering possibilities: Give us common sense enough to wander and roam the world, and make the freights warmer and safer to ride in. Make the "town clowns" more humane, sandwiches easier to get, and the chickens to come closer to the jungles that we hobos might have chicken-stew oftener. Abolish, O Lord, the lousy flophouses and ungodly vagrancy laws and their concomitants, the rock-piles. Send us, O Lord, more sunshine and less winter, so we can enjoy our leisure time more, and grant us the privilege to ride the cushions gratis. For these simple and elemental things we will forever praise thee, O Lord! Amen.[8]

Ben Reitman, master of ceremonies at the funeral services, implored that "everybody drink and be merry for that was Harry's wish just before he died." Strangely, the old drifter had left a will, a surprising act for a man so devoted to nonconformity. He had also carried a small insurance policy to cover the expenses for his burial and the wake. Ben announced that all mourners would receive, by order of Harry's will, free food and drink and twenty-five cents to purchase a night's lodging at one of the flophouses on the main stem. Several of Harry's friends spoke at the services. "He was a socialist agitator, a wobbly and a hobo," said one, "but what we liked in him was the fact that he was a good drinker and if he could look out from the casket now he would certainly enjoy this party."

After the wake Harry was cremated and his ashes spread on the dreary and frozen ground of Waldheim Cemetery. At the base of the anarchist monument, near the graves of the Haymarket martyrs, Ben Reitman now seemed a lonely figure. He softly spoke: "Dear Harry Batters, here where all the world is quiet, in this historic cemetery where rest the bones of our beloved Comrades and so many men and women who dreamed of a better world and tried so hard to establish justice and cooperative society—we commit your ashes to mingle with our unshed tear. We ask the spirit of freedom and justice to consecrate us anew." Doc would return many other times to the windswept fields of Waldheim.[9]

The wake of Harry Batters seemed to signal a spate of deaths among Chicago's hobo community in the following few years. In December 1936 Lena ("Mother") Greenstein was also laid to rest in Waldheim. Around the turn of the century, Lena and her husband, Morris, ran a barrelhouse on South State Street where she gained a reputation among Chicago's transient population as honest and square-dealing. After Prohibition they closed the saloon and opened a restaurant on the corner of Ninth and State streets, an establishment that became something of a legend in the world of the hobo.

The sign over the front door read: "Mother's Restaurant. Don't Go Hungry. See Mother." Thousands did over the years, social outcasts, hard-bitten drifters just off the freights with nothing in their pockets and an ache in their gut, aimless wanderers in need of a friend. Lena Greenstein, financially comfortable when she started the restaurant, certainly did not reap financial profit from it. Much of the home-cooked food went for nothing or a pittance; and in the hard days the homeless often lined up by the hundreds.[10]

Most hoboes got much more than food from Mother Greenstein. She ran a kind of informal referral service, sending the jobless to the Illinois Free Employment Office, the sick to the city's health clinics, and the homeless to various charities. And she encouraged them all to join their brothers at the Hobo College and the Dill Pickle Club. One of her circulars read: "Cheer up. Every day there are a thousand new jobs looking for men, and there are hundreds of men and women who want to serve God and Humanity by helping needy folks. Don't despair, don't hate, don't try and forget your misery in booze or crime. Be a man. Try harder. You can succeed. You can help build a world without unemployment, misery, hate and wrongdoing and avoid the human scrapheap."[11]

Each Thanksgiving and Christmas, Mother Greenstein and Ben Reitman threw a free dinner, which they called the "Feast of the Outcasts." Their guest list included just about everyone in the haunts and dark corners of Chicago's main stem—hoboes, reformed black-handers and white slavers, bootleggers and rumrunners, boozers and dopers, ex-cons and ex-gunmen, agitators, soapboxers, spittoon philosophers, gutter bums, and down-and-outs of every description.

"She was a great soul," Ben declared. "The hoboes didn't have to believe in Santa Claus; they believed in Mother Greenstein. At the Christmas banquet of 1936 a subdued Ben Reitman sat at the head table and dubbed the occasion the "Mother Greenstein Memorial Christmas Dinner." Several of the hoboes spoke at the banquet, including Billy Whiskers on "How the Bottle Made a Bum of Me" and the Cosmic Kid on "How to Live Grandiloquently on Nothing a Year." After much eating and drinking everyone had reached a consensus, an unusual occurrence among such a group: Mother Greenstein was always ready with a helping hand, treating them all with dignity and respect; she would, they lamented, be missed.[12] A poem found in the personal papers of Ben Reitman was dedicated to her:

> You gave your life, your every day,
> To help the poor, the weak astray.
> To build a world that only you
> Had faith it some day will come true
> A world where poverty and pain
> Will not be used to power again
> By cruel drones whose minds are set
> On gilded thrones of war and death
> A world where all shall live in peace
> Where all shall strive to others please

A life, you Mother Greenstein gave
Your work, that we this life may live.[13]

Only a few months after Mother Greenstein's death another pivotal figure of hobohemia passed away—Red Martha Biegler, keeper of the Martha Biegler Boarding House. A graduate of the University of Indiana, member of the church choir in a small midwestern village, schoolteacher for a time, typesetter—Martha Biegler left a life of convention and landed in Chicago's Near North Side. Trading in her protestant beginnings for the free-thinking spirit of radical bohemian protest, Martha took a job with the *Chicago Daily Socialist* and began to make appearances at Bughouse Square, her shapely body and flowing black hair inevitably an added dimension to her anticapitalist platform message. Brimming with confidence, her quick mind a good match for any street-corner philosopher, Martha Biegler became one of the most highly respected soapboxers on the Square.

But Martha gradually sank into destitution and became part of the class of men and women that had stirred her own humanitarian instincts—the drifters and loners and whores. Yet even in her despair Martha never lost her determination to help society's losers. Aided by a few others of the West Madison Street hobo district, she opened a rooming house on West Chicago Avenue for the truly desperate.[14]

It was common knowledge in hobo circles that, just as Mother Greenstein had never turned away a hungry stff, Martha Biegler never turned away a man or woman needing a night's flop. In Reitman's *Sister of the Road,* Box-Car Bertha Thompson said, "When any of us hobo girls were broke and or hungry, we always knew where we could get a meal and a bed, and no questions asked."[15] It was in Martha Biegler's rooming house that Harry Batters had lit his ill-fated fire.

In September 1937 another hobo legend departed the main stem for good. Herbert L. ("Dad") Crouch died at age seventy-two. Dad, a wisp of a man with a straggly gray mustache and a wooden leg, was quiet and self-effacing most of the time. But the gnarled veteran of the street corners and the jungles always experienced something of a metamorphosis when he mounted a soapbox. There he thundered and trembled and lashed out at capitalist insanity, his voice exploding with anger and rage. The hoboes spoke with reverance of Dad Crouch, a marcher in Coxey's Army, survivor of countless days on the rods and blinds. Dad gave voice to the frustrations and isolation of hundreds of younger men on skid road who clustered around to cheer on his frenzied oratory.

At Dad's funeral service Ben Reitman declared, "He came from somewhere to West Madison Street twenty-five years ago. He was fairly well educated and he spoke intelligently on economics. Dad became one of the professors in the Hobo College, and he traveled widely, through use of our nation's box cars, to spread his gospel of justice for the workingman." Ben also reminded the mourners of Dad's performance at one of the Hobo College's momentous confrontations with the University of Chicago debating team. The question posed for the night: Should all men strive for a college education? Arguing the affirmative were the ardent collegians, anxious to prove their mettle against their ragged elders. Marshaling persuasive evidence on the value of formal education in institutions of higher learning, the lads completed their arguments, beaming with confidence. Dad was not amused. Invective and profanity, sarcasm and wit, icy epithets filled the hall. Dad snarled. What did schoolroom learning have to do with higher education? What did curricula and turgid lectures and campus hoopla have to do with lessons for life? To his crusty comrades of the road who were in the audience that night, Dad was a stalwart soldier for their cause, a standard-bearer for those whose knowledge and skills had been gained mostly outside the touted halls of academe. His performance, Ben remembered, was one of the most magnificent demonstrations of soapbox oratory he had ever heard.

"I recall to you," Doc whispered sadly, "a few words from Robert W. Service, a poet you men can understand and appreciate: "There's a class of men / That don't fit in. . . ."[16] As perhaps no other central figure in Chicago's hobohemia, Ben Reitman had known its human miscellany. With characters such as Martha Biegler and Harry Batters and the others Reitman felt a close kinship, their spirit and humanity and foibles a strong bond. In the live years Chicago's hobohemia had been a place of fire and imagination, a bizarre mix of creativity and misery. Ben Reitman would miss it and its people.

27. Antisyph

Dr. Ben Reitman and the *spirochete pallida* had a long association. Doc, as most everyone in Chicago knew, was the city's best-known foe of the dreaded venereal disease organism. As a kid in the tenderloin section along Clark Street, Reitman heard the laments of the drifters and whores about the "syph" and the "running range." His first job was at the Cook Remedy Company, a manufacturer of Syphelene, a medicine for the hated malady. As a fledgling hobo on the freights and in the tramp steamers, he heard again the laments of the rough wanderers about the damned "pox." As a lab boy at Chicago's Polyclinic, he witnessed various pathological experiments on venereal disease. And as a student and instructor at the College of Physicians and Surgeons, he learned about and taught syphilis pathology. At his office on North State Street, Doc treated a stream of whores, pimps, racketeers, and even those of "polite" society with injections of Salvarsan, an organic arsenical compound introduced in Paris in 1911. In 1917 he established at the Iroquois Hospital the first municipal venereal disease clinic in Chicago, and later he began venereal clinics at the Cook County Jail and the Chicago House of Corrections. While in prison himself he started a clinic at the Cleveland House of Correction in Warrensville, Ohio. And as a line doctor in Jack Zuta's and Mike de Pike Heitler's notchhouses, he examined scores of prostitutes each week in the early Twenties. "Sing a Song of Salvarsan," went an underground tune hummed by some of those paying the price for ill-fated amorous adventures. Ben had heard countless renditions.[1]

In this field, as in so many others, Reitman played the antagonist, the gadfly. All through his medical career he called for broad public programs to spread the word that venereal disease was preventable. At a time when this subject, like the subject of birth control, was considered indelicate at best, Doc sounded a bull horn. He insisted that all the myths and superstitions surrounding the matter were not only ludicrous but tragic. Physicians and public health authorities who withheld information about venereal phophylaxis were charged by Ben with catering to a silly belief that knowledge of prevention would unleash a wave of licentiousness and moral decay throughout the land. The reluctance of the so-called experts on venereal disease to push prophylaxis was ruining the lives of thousands of people. Venereal disease could be conquered, not by cures, but by prevention.

"Venereal prophylaxis is a cinch," Doc once wrote. "The prevention of venereal disease is as absolute and as scientific as the prevention of infection in an abdominal operation. The procedure for prevention is unbelievably simple. Rubber preventives are fairly reliable when intelligently used by a sober person. And just as a man can put his finger in typhoid or tuberculosis germs and wash them off without ever any infection, so soap and water and immediate voiding after contact gives protection." But even though many public health authorities knew Ben was essentially correct in his call for a campaign of prevention, most remained intimidated by possible public reaction. The secretary of the Chicago Board of Health told Reitman, "I haven't any objection to you doing prophylaxis propaganda. I've been thinking about it a good deal, and we're going to do it, but we've got to be very careful . . . we're going to take it up some day, and do a lot of work along those lines, but for the present you be very careful and don't get us into trouble."[2]

By the mid-1930s venereal disease had become a national scourge. Dr. John Hinchman Stokes, a University of Pennsylvania professor, reported that the appalling growth in the number of cases had been accompanied by other chilling aspects. The causes of the disease, Dr. Hinchman said, lay not only in conventional intercourse between the sexes but in "sodomy and pederasty." He and many others now saw the disease as a formidable national threat that demanded national action.[3]

In 1937 that action came. Dr. Thomas Parran, Jr., surgeon general of the United States Public Health Service and a friend of President Franklin D. Roosevelt, assembled 600 doctors and social hygienists for a massive anti–venereal disease campaign and announced that he intended to fight syphilis and gonorrhea like other pandemic diseases such as tuberculosis. The Roosevelt administration launched an unprecedented attack on the syph and the president himself shocked even the national news media with a forthright endorsement of the campaign in a letter to a conference on VD control held in Washington. So taboo had been public discussion of the subject before Roosevelt's statement that *Time* magazine declared, "No President had ever said or written so frankly."

With Roosevelt's open support Thomas Parran moved swiftly. He pledged a much more liberal policy of distributing antisyphilitic drugs through federal agencies and encouraged a massive drive of diagnostic examinations. The U.S. Public Health Service stood ready, Parran promised, to help states and cities attack the frightening increase in venereal disease, a specter menacing the future of thousands of Americans. No longer would the subject be shrouded in infantile, head-in-the-sand prudery.[4]

The city of Chicago responded zealously to Thomas Parran's challenge. In a massive survey asking Chicagoans whether they wanted blood tests, a resounding 95 percent said yes. On a blustery August day in 1937, several thousand National Youth Administration youngsters marched through the Loop carrying huge banners bearing the slogan, "Friday the Thirteenth Is an Unlucky Day for Syphilis." Pictures of spirochetes plastered the city. Banners trailed airplanes circling above the city with the message, "Chicago Fight Syphilis." In the days following, a play called *Spirochete* opened in a theater whose lobby was given over to a crew of doctors and nurses armed with tubes and syringes. Led by Dr. Louis E. Schmidt, dean of Chicago's urologists, Dr. O. C. Wegner of the Public Health Service, and Chicago's health commissioner, Dr. Herman Bundeson, the drive to eradicate syphilis in Chicago surged forward. Dr. Reuben Kahn, who developed the Wasserman test to detect syphilis, left his University of Michigan post to direct the examinations. "Let the bloodbath begin," joked Dr. Wegner.

With the backing of the Chicago Medical Society, which bolstered the drive with 5,000 physicians, health authorities converted university laboratories and upgraded city labs. Ben Reitman, who had seen the days when the subject of venereal disease was reserved for whispers or for the low-life circles in which he moved, was somewhat astonished at the public response. Even his old associate Herman Bundeson joined the ballyhoo, having his own blood drawn during a public ceremony. Observing the Windy City's blizzard of anti–venereal disease activity, Thomas Parran said he was "agreeably astounded."

In the next two years the city of Chicago conducted more than one million blood tests. Pregnant women and newborn babies, workers, schoolteachers, prisoners, prostitutes—they all bared their arms to city clinicians. More than one-half of the city's elementary schoolchildren were tested for congenital syphilis. Approximately 5 percent of all the tests conducted in the city uncovered active syphilis, more than 42,000 previously unreported cases. Nearly 20 percent of those tested among the city's black population had the disease, over half in the infectious stage. In clubs, forums, and churches, in newspapers and magazines, the subject was discussed and debated. Families and friends talked openly about it. Numerous couples on the verge of marriage trooped nervously to clinics. Lay and professional lecturers spoke of the terrors of the disease. The whole venereal disease campaign was, Ben concluded, "honest and heroic." But, he insisted, it was at the same time futile and misdirected. Even after all the testing; even after the sufferers of the disease had begun the painful, prolonged treatment of arsenic and bismuth, treatment which some claimed gave as much misery as the disease itself; even after all the speeches and articles and the valiant efforts of the doctors, nurses, and other volunteers—after all that the disease still held the upper hand. It was still relatively easy for a man to go out on the town and pick up a case of syphilis, for as Doc Reitman said, the disease was still lurking in Chicago.[5]

Ben did what he could in the campaign. He established his own organization, the Chicago Society for the Prevention of Venereal Disease, which, except for a few volunteer typists, was a one-man show. It did give Reitman an air of authority, however. When he gave speeches about syphilis and about the campaign in Chicago, when he issued reports and wrote letters, he did it as director of a society, not as a maverick clap doctor.

Although wary of Ben's notoriety, the Chicago Syphilis Project hired him in 1937. As a special investigator, Ben was paid $150 a month and was charged with looking into Chicago vice and the origins of and possible solutions to the syphilis and gonorrhea problems in the red-light and skid-row districts. He submitted over 300 reports comprising nearly 2,000 pages during the first two years of the project. He went to the familiar haunts—to the lowest cabarets of North Clark Street, to the sin slums at Twenty-second and Wentworth, to the missions of West Madison. From the dope-sniffers around North Clark to the two-dollar crib whores in the tenderloin district, Doc interviewed people other researchers on the project preferred personally to avoid. He wrote reports on the conditions there, suggested programs, goaded officials, and pleaded for greater understanding of the lower classes and their enormous cultural disadvantages.

On a few occasions Reitman engineered syphilis slumming tours for some of the project officials. On August 5, 1937, he escorted four public health researchers along North Clark, talking to hoods and con men and exhibition dancers. He took them to Bughouse Square, where they mounted soapboxes to talk about the syphilis project. They met an abortionist on North State Street and later visited a pornographer by the name of Hard-On Slim. "Are your pants buttoned," Slim inquired of his guests as he darkened the room and rolled a movie showing two young men and a blond engaged in both heterosexual and homosexual sport. "Erotic movies are very common," Doc wrote later. "They are illegal, but very few people are arrested for showing them . . . that which is seen in movies and in photographs, men will practice . . . maybe some day some one will make a movie showing how the organs are washed with soap and water and how prophylactics are applied." The Public Health Service would later make Ben a prophet.

The group then traveled to South State Street between Thirty-first and Thirty-fifth. They went to the Cabin Inn, a hangout for female impersonators; to Wentworth Avenue, where black whores offered favors for a little change or a cold drink; to the cheap cabarets, where actresses put on sex shows backstage for select customers. One of the doctors remarked, "I could start a clinic down here in this district and do a lot of good, and give Salvarsan and Tryparsemide for fifty cents and gonorrhea treatments for twenty-five. . . ."

The health officials' tour moved to more encouraging environs: the Poro College for beauticians on South Parkway, which was hosting a WPA band concert. The college's owner later told the physicians that blacks in America now quested for beauty and culture, and confided that at the college they taught methods for removing the kinks from their hair and for applying makeup. "We teach our students cleanliness and health and our students teach their customers how to take care of their skins and their bodies and to avoid venereal disease . . . we are very much interested in this syphilis campaign." The publicity director of the Poro College expressed gratitude to Reitman for pointing out that blacks weren't more susceptible to syphilis because of their race but because of their poverty. "If you white people really want to help us, get our race jobs; get them out of these terrible slums. . . ."[6]

It was as if the physicians who toured with Reitman on that steamy August day had seen sights and people from another world, as if characters dreamed up by Jack London and Maxim Gorky, those from society's netherworld, had spoken to them. Thanks to Ben Reitman, a man with ties to both worlds, the researchers now had a clearer idea of the dimensions of the syphilis problem.

Just as he led researchers into the vice emporiums and slums, Ben also led those from the underside of Chicago out into the open to tell their stories. He had done the same thing for hoboes decades earlier in the sociological clinics. Now, one night in October 1937, to the staid, respectable old LaSalle Baptist Church, he brought a playgirl. "Sure, I'm happy at my business; I'm much better off than the women who work in the factories and in the kitchen . . . yes, I can justify myself for taking your husband's and your brother's money. Most of my customers are married men, and they talk to me about their wives. If there was anything good in good women, if they had any brains they'd be able to hold their husbands, and they wouldn't be patronizing us girls." Thus spoke a prostitute, friend of the director of the Chicago Society for the Prevention of Venereal Disease, before a large crowd. She breezily chatted about the glories of an active sex life, attacked puritan notions of virtue, and rhapsodized on the financial rewards of hustling. Ben's witty and audacious friend left the audience somewhat breathless. She also left Doc somewhat embarrassed. He had wanted her to present an accurate picture of the life of a professional prostitute, not an idealized fantasy. Prostitution, he was forced to interject to the audience, also had other aspects besides pleasure and profit. It had arrests, loneliness, poverty, and venereal disease. Indeed, the woman standing before them had once been a carrier of the disease. Ben's asides notwithstanding the playgirl was a hit. If those in the audience had gotten little information about venereal disease, the ostensible reason for holding the meeting, they at least went away with a new respect for the intelligence and charm of women in the hustling business.[7]

Scouting slum neighborhoods for possible clinic sites and interviewing assorted characters for his reports to the syphilis project, Reitman inevitably returned to the South Side. He later recalled standing in front of a bootleg joint at Thirty-first and State and being approached by several joyladies who mistook his look of investigative eagerness for passion. "We were accosted by twenty-seven women who wanted to know if we wanted 'to get a little pussy' and five men who were solicitous in inquiring if we wanted 'to get a little ass'. . . ." It was a procession, Ben said, leading not to pleasure but to clinics, hospitals, and insane asylums. He appealed to the project directors for greater understanding of and special consideration for the plight of the prostitute. The hospitals run by the Board of Health, he argued, were so inhumane and unfair to the ladies that many jumped bonds, bribed cops, left town, or even committed suicide to avoid hospitalization.[8]

In less than a year Reitman gave more than 100 talks on the subject of venereal disease. To radical groups, YMCA's, students, churches, American Legion meetings, labor organizations, police, and prisoners, Ben spread the word about the syphilis project and about prophylaxis. Fixing on the latter subject with crusading exhilaration, he struck up conversations about prevention not only in lecture halls but in paddy wagons, poolrooms, gambling houses, and bars. "Wash with soap and water!" "Use douches!" "Use condoms!" The old anarchist still had the blue fire of the agitator. Like birth control two decades earlier, prophylaxis was for Ben a noble cause worth sacrifice and dedication. He prodded doctors, badgered sociologists, needled clinicians and their patients.

As the syphilis project drew blood and began more injections of arsenic, Doc Reitman became louder and more offensive. He went to all sorts of meetings and conventions, deliberately injecting prophylaxis into the discussions. To crowds at Bughouse Square, to high school pupils and boys' clubs, to workers' organizations, he declared that they could have all the sex they wanted and never catch the syph. The secret, he said, should never have been a secret at all. Information about prevention should never have been withheld from the public. "I believe in cooperation," Ben wrote to Lawrence Linck, one of the directors of the project, "but do not think that the Surgeon General or the Health Commissioner, or the Secretary of the Board of Health has the right to soft-pedal prophylaxis."[9] His proposed program was simple: (1) to provide all syphilitics with prophylactic packages that could enable them to lead an active sex life without infecting their partners; (2) to teach the general public methods of prevention and offer prophylactic packages free through government programs.

Ben even approached the surgeon general and urged him to promote prophylaxis. Parran responded, "Please take it easy, Ben. I'm doing whatever I can. We've gone a long way in arousing the public to the importance of venereal disease. We agree with you that prophylaxis is important but there's a great deal of opposition to it in the clergy and the women's clubs and the educators, and so forth. We'll get to it eventually."[10] Ben pointed out that military physicians had long advocated prophylaxis. He cited a work by George C. Dunham entitled "Military Preventive Medicine" that had been published at the Medical Field Service School, Carlisle Barracks, in 1931: "Chemical prophylaxis prescribed by the War Department will prevent the development of venereal disease in more than 90% of actual exposures to infection. . . ." If the disease were so easy to prevent, why in the name of decency, Ben asked, was that fact being kept a secret. At swimming pools signs warned of athlete's foot. Drinking water was chlorinated to prevent typhoid. Restaurant workers were examined and taught how to prevent amoebic dysentery. Milk was pasteurized to prevent tuberculosis and undulant fever. Streams were sprayed to prevent malaria. Why, indeed, was venereal disease purposefully ignored?[11]

The directors of the syphilis project knew that the very idea of venereal prophylaxis raised in much of the public mind the fear of immorality and sexual promiscuity. Give the nation's youth prophylactics and the nation's youth would use them in orgiastic abandon. The concerns of the project leaders about public attitudes were certainly well founded. Several church organizations and women's clubs in Chicago launched a bitter campaign in 1938 against magazines carrying articles on prophylaxis. Several drugstores, including Walgreens and Liggettes, were raided and arrests made following the sale of condoms. In 1938 these were bootlegged items, sold by itinerant peddlers in poolrooms, cigar shops, and whorehouses. They were still, in other words, products from the world of Ben Reitman.[12]

Doc was fired from the Public Health Service on October 14, 1938, after he again publicly criticized the agency for not supporting prophylaxis. His visibility had long annoyed the officials of the Board of Health and others involved in the project; and his flair and hunger for recognition, his vulgar language on the stump and in reports, and, most of all, his incessant criticism of his superiors was finally too much. It was not the first time he had been fired, but it was perhaps the most poignant. Reitman, older and more concerned about steady employment, bitter about the project's continuing publicity without his name attached to it, pleaded with officials to allow him to continue. They refused.[13]

The control project did not, of course, end syphilis in Chicago. Although the open attack on the disease, involving various federal and state agencies, had been a monumental leap forward, although thousands who had before suffered the disease in shame now received treatment openly, syphilis remained a serious problem. In the coming years the use of a relatively new drug called penicillin would strike a powerful blow against the disease. But so would venereal prophylaxis.

In April 1942 Captain N. A. Angwin of the Medical Corps, U.S. Navy, wrote an article in *The Military Surgeon* entitled "Soap and Water as Venereal Disease Prophylactic." In the same year the U.S. Public Health Service produced a movie entitled *Know for Sure,* which related the prevention techniques Ben Reitman had been preaching for years. And when America's G.I.'s headed for Europe and Asia during World War II, they carried with them the kind of prophylactic kits Ben had so often recommended during the syphilis control project.[14] Doc, it turns out, had indeed known how to fight the *spirochete pallida* better than almost anyone else.

28. "Reveries at Sixty"

Reveries at Sixty[1]

by Ben L. Reitman

—Born January 1, 1879

It is a full half century
Since I sat on a platform by the side of the railroad tracks
Enjoying my first reverie.
The names on the box-cars—B. & O., Lake Shore, Santa Fe,
First stimulated my desire to see and know the world.

From ten to twenty I traveled in box cars, ships, walked along highways,
Thinking, dreaming, planning about building a better world.
I had never been educated, had read little, was without "religion," culture or a behavior pattern.
I developed as "Topsy," a natural Anarchist; had no standards, ideals or goal
Just wanted to live natural and learn how to help others do the same and be happy.

Forty years of studying, reading, investigating and living deeply have been my daily portion.
A little science, some philosophy, a smattering of history, a taste of culture
A distant view of art, a slight sound of music, a peep at the mystics;
A quarter of a century as an active physician, health officer and V.D. prevention advocate,
And a full decade as a full time anarchist and agitator taught me many things

The last quarter of a century I have "Intellectually" awakened; I hope "illuminated,"
And have been active in trying to solve LABOR, HEALTH, UNEMPLOYED, and SOCIAL PROBLEMS;
Have worked closely with the Unemployed groups, the Socialists, the Radicals and the Reformers,
Sociologists, Criminologists, Social Workers, Health Officers have been my daily companions.
In brief, I have been most intimate with those who make Social Problems and those who try to solve them.

And now at SIXTY I attempt to sum up "A Philosophy of Life,"
And to put down in a few brief paragraphs the most important things I've learned from living.
I have no standards, ideals, systems, formulas or rules of life to pass on.
I simply state what life did to me and for me, and how I reacted.
I was born in poverty and the slums, and my continued ambition has been to do away with them.
In my life time there have been more advances in Invention, Science, Industry, Transportation,
Aviation, Communication, Medicine, War, Government, and Education for the masses
Than there was in any previous century in the history of the world
And yet January 1, 1939, there is more unemployment, more lack of opportunity for success
More genuine ignorance, greater possibilities for wars and revolutions than there was January 1, [18]79.

There is nothing I ever learned, read or heard of that will help prevent or control
DISEASE, UNEMPLOYMENT, POVERTY, WAR, INTOLERANCE, LYING, STEALING, CHEATING, VANITY
And there is nothing I know of that will stop people from foolishness or disaster.
If I had never traveled a mile, gone to college, heard a lecture or read a book
I could not possibly know less about how to make people happy, comfortable

And yet, in spite of this I emphatically state that LIFE has always been wonderful and worth-while.
I am glad I am living; there have been very few hours in my life that I wasn't glad.
Nothing has been very difficult, or painful, or hard to bear.
Been in jail many times, hungry, broke, in debt, fired from jobs, tar-and-feathered, neglected,
But I always enjoyed life, never hated or envied any one and really never suffered.

I just lived every day, did what I wanted to do, never made any sacrifices for any one.
"Took what was on the platter." There was no "good" or no "bad"—everything was fine.
I have loved and enjoyed my family, friends and work and hated no one—not even Hitler.
What did I learn about life? That it is worth-while, it is fine; it is lots of fun.
Nothing makes much difference. You just live a natural life. That is all there is to it.

Ben Reitman and his son Brutus.
(Courtesy Medina Gross and Mecca Carpenter)

Anna Martindale, the mother of Brutus.
(Courtesy Medina Gross and Mecca Carpenter)

Medina Oliver, the mother of Medina, Mecca, Victoria, and Olive.
(Courtesy Medina Gross and Mecca Carpenter)

Ben Reitman at home on Bishop Street, with daughters Mecca and Medina.
(Ben L. Reitman Papers, Special Collections, University Library, University of Illinois at Chicago)

29. "De Profundus"

A Hasidic rabbi once said that every man should always carry two coins. In one pocket should be a coin with the legend, "I Am Dust and Ashes." In the other pocket should be a coin with the legend, "For Me Was the World Created."[1]

Ben Reitman had always looked critically at his own life. Behind the public bravado and the saucy confidence and brassiness were self-deprecation and doubt. In his letters and writings he never balked at exposing his own weaknesses and comic failures; indeed, he sometimes flaunted them. But he craved, more than anything else, respect and recognition. It never came easily. Even those close to the causes Doc espoused often had nothing to offer him but scorn and ridicule. Roger Baldwin, for example, thought him to be a totally vulgar man with few redeeming gifts. But others saw through the arrogance that masked his insecurity. The respected sociologist Nels Anderson called Reitman one of his greatest teachers: "What I learned from you was a degree of tolerance and understanding of people that was not taught either by precept or example in any of the classes I took . . . you do have the soul that encompasses all humanity."[2]

The hobo doctor from Chicago had lived through tremendous change in American society, had been close to artistic and cultural revolution, had touched the lives of influential radicals, had himself played a part in social protest and reform. Although Reitman flitted about in the world of letters and philosophy, although he wanted desperately to be accepted as a thinker, a man of ideas and intellect, he was, instead, often a target of contempt. But he kept trying, kept moving, driven by a compulsion to see and taste as much of life as he could. He was in all respects a man of enormous appetites. And because of his unquenched thirst for experience, the life of Ben Reitman was remarkable in its dimensions—the things he saw, the people he encountered, the causes for which he fought.

Ben's last years were spent with Medina Oliver, a woman he had met on a cold day in 1932 on the steps of a Chicago museum. When he invited her to warm her hands in his pockets, or so the family story goes, he soon had a new comrade.[3]

Born in Texas, in 1904, Medina had left home as a young teenager and attended the University of Texas. After teaching for a time, she went to a medical school in Galveston and later to the University of Chicago, where she earned a degree in microbiology. She later became a nurse. Ben's affair with Medina led to the birth of a child, Mecca, on December 8, 1936. Medina and the child moved into Ben's home on South Bishop Street, a house he had purchased from a woman abortionist and which was still equipped with a trapdoor leading to the room where the woman had done her work.

During those years on South Bishop, Ben was only a relic of that damned radical who had been dragged into the California desert three decades earlier. The old warrior now sometimes drew bemused glances, not hatred and hostility, as he walked the streets barefoot in the summer, hand in hand with Medina, like some aging flower child two decades before his time. Many of his neighbors knew little of Ben's celebrated past, of the days of marches and protests and violence, the days of Emma Goldman. Most of them gawked at the numerous ragged hoboes who often marched up the sidewalk to neighbor Reitman's house to cadger a meal and perhaps some coin. Family members sometimes complained that clothes they gave to Ben as presents ended up on the backs of West Madison Street bums.

If made uneasy by the presence of motley visitors in its quiet midst, Bishop Street nevertheless enjoyed Ben's wit, charm, ready smile, and his enthusiasm, which remained infectious. On some occasions Doc sported his best bohemian finery, transforming himself into the South Side's version of Oscar Wilde. Still the character; still seeking to shock and nettle; still the dandy. If the middle-class Irish-Catholics of Bishop Street didn't quite know what to make of their fellow resident, they could at least see that he radiated the aura of a celebrity.[4]

Medina's work as a nurse paid most of the bills. She took care of Ben through assorted illnesses, humored him, helped him stave off doubts about the usefulness of his life, encouraged him to remain as active and robust as he could in Chicago affairs. He still hosted reunions of radicals, a cultural lion of hobohemia with full beard and long hair. One night he stood in a shabby, smoky, second-floor hallway on North Clark Street, trying to muster up the energy of the live days, the fiery days of dissent, the days when large numbers of men and women sought to shake the world. "In the years gone by," Ben pensively recalled, "we used to have meetings that jammed the halls." A mere twenty-five people now listened as he told the story of the Haymarket martyrs, recounted the crusades of the anarchists, told of his own times of glory.

With a few of the onlookers lapsing into slumber, Doc Reitman, leaning heavily on the dusty rostrum, his white artist's tie as tattered as the spirit of his listeners, rambled from subject to subject—economics, Coxey's Army, atheism, jail. "I was born as an anarchist," he declared. "I was always against things. Sometimes, I guess, I was even against myself." He told of his years with Emma, "one of the greatest women of history," and the achievements of the labor movement. He read the last words of one of the Haymarket anarchists: "I hate your law and order . . . Hang me for it." As he had done so many times in the past the old showman and orator now called for a "religious function." "Slim," Ben shouted to the thin, bald piano player, "pass the collection box."[5]

In 1939 Ben Reitman's relatively sedate, mellowed existence on Chicago's South Side was powerfully invaded by old memories and passions. Once again the siren calling him was Emma Goldman. For the past few years the exiled anarchist had directed her work toward Spain, touring several European countries to make speeches and raise funds in behalf of Spanish anarchists fighting hopelessly against Francisco Franco's fascism. Later, after the collapse of the antifascist forces, she set up a committee to aid homeless Spanish women and children. In early 1937 Emma was on her way to Canada, still determined to assist war refugees.

Emma, in this later period of her life, was fighting great emotional burdens, too. She sorrowed over political developments in Europe—the degeneration of the Russian Revolution into Stalinist tyranny, the frightening ascendancy of Hitler's Germany, the events in Spain. She also sorrowed over a deeply personal loss: Alexander Berkman, her oldest and closest comrade of a lifetime, beset by illness, had committed suicide in France in 1936. Emma wrote, "I have lived long enough . . . Life holds nothing else. I feel like one drowning grabbing the air. . . ."[6] Arriving in Canada almost penniless, she survived financially through the help of some of her old friends in America, including Roger Baldwin, Leonard Abbott, and Harry Weinberger, who organized a seventieth birthday fund.

Another old friend also offered help. Ben had not corresponded with Emma for several years, but on May 2, 1939, he wrote to Eleanor Fitzgerald that he wanted to see Emma again.[7] The two old lovers exchanged a poignant series of letters, writing of the vibrant if stormy years they had shared, of the sorry state of world affairs, of the frustrations of advancing age. After a particularly warm letter from Emma, Ben wrote, "It's the letter I've been waiting for for years—to know that you feel kindly and somewhat appreciative of our work together and that you are sharing your troubles and your confidences . . . is all that I ever asked for. . . ."[8] Emma replied, "I admit they were for the most part very painful years for me, and no doubt also for you. But I would not have missed knowing such an exotic and primitive creature as you. And I have always told everybody what a worker you were, in fact, the only man of all the men I had known who had completely dedicated himself to the work and aims that were the strongest raison d'etre in my life."[9]

The two saw each other in Canada that summer. As they talked over old times and trials the comradeship was still evident; but so too were the antagonisms. When Ben revealed that he planned to write a book on their ten years together, Emma, fearful of what he might say, later appealed to a mutual friend to talk him out of it. "I realize," she remarked caustically, "that it will be a mess."[10]

Whatever plans Ben may have had were dashed in October 1939 when he suffered a stroke. True to the wild convulsions of their emotional bond, Emma was now sympathetic, writing to her former lover with understanding and uncharacteristic humor: "I know you still attract the ladies. But the heart is not so young any more, hence cannot respond to your affairs d'amour. Seriously speaking, dear Ben, you should make up your mind and sit back and invite your soul in wisdom and contemplation. Your old friend. Emma."[11]

Ben Reitman, ex-profesh of the rails, was now a physically battered man. The stroke had left him virtually unable to dress himself, and he was forced to begin insulin injections and a rigid diet, a horrifying prospect for a man whose overindulgence in food was almost legendary. "I have to begin life anew," he wrote. Forced to give up his office practice, confined much of the time to the house, Ben struggled with depression, his old ego and spirit withered. "I never realized my limitations and poverty so much before in my life," he confessed.[12]

Doc now had the haven of a family, however, and the support of Medina and his mother, who also shared the house on Bishop, and the joy brought by his children gradually began to sweep away the shrouding gloom. "I have a home, a delightful big son, a beautiful 3-year old daughter and a comrade," he wrote to Emma, "and I have a feeble will to go on."[13] She wrote back, "I rather think that with all your disappointments you still have reasons to be exceedingly glad . . . you are rich my dear, much more so than tens of thousands of people who have nobody and who are wanted nowhere. I am glad that you are not among them . . . One lives from day to day now. . . ."[14]

The words became hauntingly ironic, for less than three months later Emma Goldman suffered a paralyzing stroke and died on May 14, 1940, in Toronto. During her time in Canada, a friend remembered, Emma occasionally had gone to the United States border and, tears streaming down her face, looked toward the country that had meant so much to her.[15] America's most famous deportee, the woman whose image in the United States was that of a subversive instigator of revolution, had a deeply human side that was hidden from the public. Ben Reitman had seen that side, had known her passion, had appreciated her brilliance, had basked in her limelight, had suffered her rebukes, had shared her victories and defeats. On May 16 he wrote to Leroy Oberman, a man in prison with whom he often corresponded: "Emma came back to America today in a baggage car. She gave 50 years of her precious life trying to make America a better place to live in and to stop wars. And the the only way she could get back to America was in a steel casket."[16]

Ben joined a small group of comrades who met that casket at Chicago's Dearborn Station. Running his fingers through his shaggy hair he told reporters, "She will never die for me. She will live on."[17] He had earlier told Hutchins Hapgood, "She found me an intellectual ragamuffin and an exhibitionistic hobo. She gave me an intellectual horizon and a soul, showed me the beauty of poetry and the grandeur of literature, and the possibility of giving worthwhile service to humanity."[18]

The Japanese photographer and painter Sadakichi Hartmann, one of Emma's anarchist friends from the days in New York, wrote to Ben shortly after the funeral: "Emma was surely an exceptional character, a brave woman, a fighter who could deliver a message with flaming enthusiasm and keep it up for many years . . . Half of her success she owed to you, who were so loyal and owned the brutal ability to assist her materially through thick and thin. I am delighted to have met you both."[19]

"We are living day to day now," Emma had said. His energy drained, fighting off illness, Ben continued to correspond with prostitutes, criminals, and sociologists (their relative worth to society, in his eyes, probably in that order). He managed some speaking engagements, even presenting formal papers on criminology at the University of Chicago and the Chicago Academy of Criminology. He wrote lengthy letters on the implications of the war. Long rebelling against his Jewish ancestry, Doc startled even some of his closest friends with expressions of admiration for Hitler, both as a leader and a philosopher. The Jewish people, he declared, had brought much of the treatment on themselves. But as the war progressed, as the dimensions of the horror in Europe became manifest, Ben recoiled. "Darkness and despair filled the earth," he wrote.[20] He remembered his tramps through Germany many years before and the ingratiating character of the German people he met: "They were so tolerant, friendly and cultured. But that same people now have changed into sadistic brutes. I wonder if that's the norm for mankind."[21]

Now, for Ben Reitman, family became even more of a refuge. He mourned the loss of his brother Lew, a Chicago businessman with whom he had remained personally close. Ben's son, Brutus, graduated from the University of Chicago and joined the Air Corps Ferrying Command Service. And Ben and Medina celebrated the births of two more daughters, Medina in 1940 and Victoria in 1942. He wrote, "Victoria Regina will join her sisters . . . in a home of love, mutual respect and understanding, a family that reveres everything that is human, beautiful and loving, a family that fears no evil, trusts the future to take care of them, and has faith in the cosmos, that they will be given an opportunity to serve, be useful, self-supporting, industrious. . . ."[22]

These were days of reflection, of looking back and assessing. Writing of Theodore Schroeder, lawyer, philosopher, and gadfly psychologist, advocate of free speech and free love, Ben said that his life was one of valor, courage, intelligence, and colossal failure. Everything Schroeder loved and worked for was in a worse condition than when he started. Ben noted, "There are more wars & tyranny and despotism—there's less free speech—it's more dangerous to express an anti-governmental idea than it was when he started."[23] No doubt, Doc was writing about himself. With the terrible stories from Europe, with the death of many of his old radical and labor friends, with the dawning of much of bohemian life in Chicago, it seemed, at times, that all the protests and movements had changed little. Armies were again confronting armies, capitalists were still oppressing workers, society still sacrificed culture for profit, men and women still succumbed to the spiel of the demogogue and the tripe of the religious grafter.

But at other times it must have all seemed worth it. Ben recalled the victories in the birth control fight, his work among the hoboes, his books, the radical forums. The man left his mark, to be sure, not only in the annals of bombast and crudity, as some remembered him, but as one of America's most colorful reformers. He left his mark in the hearts of numerous outcasts, from the joyladies of North Clark Street in Chicago to the hoboes to the bohemian philosophers of Bughouse Square. He also left his mark as one of the country's most spirited, if unorthodox, radicals.

On November 11, 1942, Ben Reitman made his annual pilgrimage to Waldheim Cemetery. Accompanied by close friend Eileen O'Connor, Ben marched to the massive monument commemorating the martyrdom of the Haymarket anarchists. In former years such ceremonies in Waldheim would attract hundreds. This day, except for a couple of newspaper reporters, Doc and his friend stood alone, the wind whipping through the hundreds of gravestones and around the bronze and stone Haymarket statue bordered by black chains. Ben read verses from the works of an anarchist poet and softly recited the names of the anarchist martyrs. Later, pointing to a grave near the statue, he told a reporter, "Emma Goldman is buried there."[24]

Just six days later, on November 17, 1942, Ben Reitman died of a heart attack at the age of sixty-three. His body was laid to rest in Waldheim, close to Emma.

Nearly 700 persons crowded into Zimmerman's Chapel on South Ashland Avenue for the funeral services. As they had done throughout Doc's life, hoboes and radicals mingled with academics. From Professor Walter Alderton of the University of Chicago Theological Seminary to socialist attorney Seymour Stedman to Jack Robbins, director of the Boys' Brotherhood Republic, the mourners paid tribute. In the crowd sat men such as Herbert Shaw, alias the Cosmic Kid, who along with many others there that day had been a graduate of the Hobo College.[25]

In his will Ben bequeathed most of his small estate to his son, Brutus, but asked that a liberal contribution be made to those organizations fostering radical movements of which he had been a part in his lifetime. He also stipulated that "two hundred and fifty dollars shall be spent for food and drink for Hobos and unemployed who shall be invited by my son to a funeral dinner. I should like the service to be in a big hall, with food, drink, fun, and a happy time for all." Brutus carried out the request.[26]

Medina kept the family together on South Bishop. Another child, Olive, was born shortly after Ben's death, his fifth daughter. In 1943, Brutus, a second lieutenant in the Army Air Corps, was killed in a tragic air crash.

A decade before Ben's death, a photograph of him, taken by a Chicago surgeon and photographer named Max Thorak, won a prize at the Twenty-sixth International Salon of Photographic Art in Paris. It was entitled "De Profundus," or "Up from the Depths." Reitman had known the underside of American society as few knew it—the secrets of its vice dens; the lives of its raconteurs, pitchmen, and criminals; the hidden faces of its artists and bohemians; the frustrations of its reformers; the treachery and heroics of its poor; the fears and foibles of whores and drifters and all those who paid the grim price of failure. If there was much of the charlatan and opportunist in him, there was also a respect for the misfits and maltreated and a commitment to challenge injustice and snub entrenched convention. He hated the prigs and power-hungry and mocked them openly; he saw through the haughtiness and hypocrisy of white-collar shysters and fought them with conviction.

Of Ben Reitman the *Christian Century* declared: "Always a crusader, he made serious efforts to bring health to his footloose friends."[27] Yellow Kid Weil, king of the con men, said it another way: "Ben Reitman represented the type of philosopher that gives the sweet, intoxicating drink of hope to the weary, thirsty, starving pedestrian plodding down the dusty road of life."[28]

Perhaps the best assessment of Ben Reitman was made by old Ben Schultz, a hobo. Fumbling for words at Doc's wake at Zimmerman's Chapel, Schultz said that Reitman wasn't like the other clean-collar types who sometimes stooped to help the man on the bum. When Ben was handing out grub, Schultz said, he wasn't arrogant; it was as if you were doing Doc a favor by sitting down beside him to eat.[29] For that remark Ben would have handed the old hobo a five-spot.

Notes

Chapter 1: "Following the Monkey"

1. Unless otherwise indicated, information in this chapter is from Ben Reitman's unpublished autobiography, *Following the Monkey,* 1–185 (hereafter cited as *FTM*). The autobiography is in the Ben Reitman Papers, University of Illinois at Chicago (hereafter cited as Reitman Papers).

2. Stephen Longstreet, *Chicago: An Intimate Portrait of People, Pleasures, and Power: 1860–1919* (New York, 1973), 353.

3. Lloyd Wendt and Herman Kogan, *Bosses in Lusty Chicago* (Bloomington, Ind., 1967), 282.

4. Poem by H. H. Knibbes in Nels Anderson, "The Juvenile and the Tramp," *Journal of the American Institute of Criminal Law and Criminology* 14 (no. 2, August 1923): 292.

5. Harry Kemp, *Chanteys and Ballads* (New York, 1920), 90–91.

6. Quoted in Kenneth Allsop, *Hard Travellin': The Hobo and His History* (New York, 1967), 202–3.

7. William Aspinwall to John J. McCook, undated, John James McCook Papers, Antiquarian and Landmarks Society, Inc., Hartford, Conn. (hereafter cited as McCook Papers).

8. Richard Etulain, ed., *Jack London on the Road: The Tramp Diary and Other Hobo Writings* (Logan, Utah, 1977), 5.

9. Godfrey Irwin, *American Tramp and Underworld Slang* (New York, 1930), 201–2.

10. *New York Times,* Dec. 2, 1907 (hereafter cited as *Times*).

11. *Hobo News,* Dec. 1919, copy in RG 65, Records of the Department of Justice, FBI reel 67A, OG7342, National Archives.

12. Ben Reitman, "Prisons in My Life," *Phoenix* 19 (May 1937).

13. Ben Reitman, "Syphilis in My Life," *Phoenix* 18 (Feb. 1937): 7, 27–29.

14. RG 59, General Records of the Department of State, Passport Application, Ben Reitman, May 19, 1902, National Archives.

15. May Reitman to Brainard Warner, July 1902, RG 84, Records of Consular Posts, Leipzig, Letters Received, 1902–3, National Archives.

16. My appreciation to June Wozmik of the Loyola Medical College, Chicago, who unearthed this information in a volume listing 1904 graduates.

17. *Chicago Tribune,* Jan. 26, 1908 (hereafter cited as *Tribune*).

18. RG 94, Records of the Adjutant General, Office Document File #1332839, National Archives.

Chapter 2: Millionaire Hobo

1. Hollis Field, "Home for Own for Hoboes," undated clipping, McCook Papers.

2. Etulain, *Jack London on the Road,* 98–99.

3. See Josiah Flynt Willard, *My Life* (New York, 1908); *Tramping with Tramps* (Montclair, N.J., 1972).

4. *FTM,* 186–87.

5. *Times,* July 23, 24, 1930.

6. Ibid.

7. "How and the Hobo: Character Sketch of J. E. How, 'Millionaire Hobo,'" Ernest W. Burgess Papers, Document 126, University of Chicago Library (hereafter cited as Burgess Papers).

8. Roving Bill Aspinwall to James J. McCook, May 20, 1893, McCook Papers.

9. "How and the Hobo," Burgess Papers.

10. "All about the Entity of the Ego Is Taught at the Hobo University," *Literary Digest* 62 (July 12, 1919): 52–53.

11. *Times,* Aug. 19, 1923.

12. Ibid.

13. Ben Reitman to Henry Allen Moe, Oct. 31, 1938, Reitman Papers.

14. "How and the Hobo," Burgess Papers.

15. *FTM,* 186–87.

Chapter 3: The Banquet

1. *FTM,* 181.

2. Ibid., 188–89.

3. *Tribune,* May 20, 1907.

4. *Chicago Record-Herald,* May 21, 1907 (hereafter cited as *Record-Herald*); *Chicago Daily News,* May 20, 1907 (hereafter cited as *Daily News*); *Tribune,* May 20, 21, 22, 1907; *Chicago Inter-Ocean,* May 21, 1907 (hereafter cited as *Inter-Ocean*); *Times,* May 21, 1907.

5. Ben Reitman, "The Hobo Banquet," unpublished ms., Reitman Papers.

6. *Tribune,* May 21, 1907.

7. *Record-Herald,* May 21, 1907.

8. "Hobo Banquet," Reitman Papers.

9. *Record-Herald,* May 21, 1907; *Tribune,* May 21, 1907.

10. "Hobo Banquet," Reitman Papers; *Inter-Ocean,* May 21, 1907; *Tribune,* May 21, 1907.

11. "Hobo Banquet," Reitman Papers; *Tribune,* May 21, 1907.

12. "Hobo Banquet," Reitman Papers.

13. Ibid.; *Tribune,* May 21, 1907.

14. *Tribune,* April 25, 1907.

15. "Hobo Banquet," Reitman Papers.

16. *Tribune,* May 22, 1907.

17. *Times,* May 21, 1907.

18. *FTM,* 193–94.

19. *Daily News,* May 22, 1907.

20. "Hobo Banquet," Reitman Papers.

Chapter 4: King of the Hoboes

1. From "A Vagrom Ballad" by George W. Chadwick, 1896, courtesy of John Gruber, East Hartford, Conn.

2. Hamlin Garland, *A Son of the Middle Border* (New York, 1917), 174–75, 287–88.

3. Ben Reitman, "The American Tramp," unpublished ms., Reitman Papers.

4. Samuel Leavitt, "The Tramps and the Law," *Forum* 2 (1886): 190–200.

5. Washington Irving, *A History of New York* (New York, AMS Press, 1913), 255.

6. Clark Spence, "Knights of the Tie and Rail—Tramps and Hoboes in the West," *The Western Historical Quarterly* 2 (Jan. 1971): 5–19; Leavitt,

"Tramps and the Law"; *Times*, Aug. 2, 1909.

7. Reitman, "American Tramp."

8. Ibid.; Elbert Hubbard, "The Rights of Tramps," *Arena* 9 (1893): 593–600.

9. *The Railroad Gazette*, Aug. 31, 1894.

10. Orlando Lewis, "The American Tramp," *Atlantic Monthly* 101 (June 1908): 744–46; *Times*, Sept. 8, 1907; *Inter-Ocean*, Sept. 15, 1907; *Tribune*, June 16, 1907.

11. *Philadelphia Press*, July 14, 1907; *Times*, May 2, 1907; *Record-Herald*, July 31, 1907.

12. *Inter-Ocean*, May 26, 1907; *Tribune*, June 1, 1907.

13. *Record-Herald*, June 1, 1907; *Tribune*, June 1, 1907; *Daily News*, June 3, 1907.

14. *Daily News*, June 3, 1907.

15. Ibid., June 15, 1907; *Tribune*, June 15, 1907.

16. *FTM*, 195–99.

17. Lewis, "American Tramp," 746–47; *FTM*, 196–97.

18. *FTM*, 197–98.

19. Reitman, "American Tramp."

20. Unpublished review of Frances Bjorkman, "The New Anti-Vagrancy Campaign," Reitman Papers.

21. Ben Reitman, "Tramps and Charities," unpublished ms., Reitman Papers.

22. *FTM*, 207–8; *St. Louis Globe-Democrat*, Feb. 7, 1908.

23. *FTM*, 210.

24. Field, "Home of Own for Hoboes," McCook Papers.

25. *Times*, Dec. 2, 1907.

26. Ibid., Dec. 5, 1907.

27. Ibid., Dec. 15, 1907.

28. *FTM*, 205–6.

29. Report of the International Brotherhood Welfare Association, supplement 2, no. 7, Reitman Papers.

Chapter 5: To the Streets

1. *Times*, Jan. 24, 1908.

2. *Tribune*, Jan. 25, 1908; Leah Feder, *Unemployed Relief in Periods of Depression* (New York, 1936), 212.

3. *Tribune*, Jan. 2, 1908.

4. *FTM*, 273.

5. *Inter-Ocean*, Jan. 23, 1908; *Daily News*, Jan. 22, 1908.

6. *Inter-Ocean*, Jan. 22, 1908.

7. Ibid., Jan. 24, 1908; *Daily News*, Jan. 24, 1908.

8. *Daily News*, Jan. 23, 1908.

9. *Tribune*, Jan. 24, 1908.

10. Ibid.; *Record-Herald*, Jan. 24, 1908; *Daily News*, Jan. 24, 1908.

11. *Record-Herald*, Jan. 24, 1908.

12. *Tribune*, Jan. 24, 1908.

13. *Inter-Ocean*, Jan. 24, 1908.

14. Ibid.

15. Ibid., Jan. 25, 1908.

16. *Daily News*, Jan. 24, 1908.

17. Ibid., Jan. 28, 1908.

Chapter 6: Emma

1. Emma Goldman, *Living My Life* (New York, 1977), chaps. 1–31 (hereafter cited as *LML*); Richard Drinnon, *Rebel in Paradise* (New York, 1976), chaps. 1–13; Candace Falk, *Love, Anarchy, and Emma Goldman* (New York, 1984), chaps. 1–3; Alice Wexler, *Emma Goldman: An Intimate Life* (New York, 1984), chaps. 1–9.

2. John Perry, *Jack London: An American Myth* (Chicago, 1981), 122.

3. Frank Harris, *Contemporary Portraits* (New York, 4th ser., 1923), 247.

4. *Mother Earth* 12 (July 1917): 129.

5. "Emma Goldman's Faith," *Current Literature* 50 (Feb. 1911): 178.

6. Eugene Debs to W. S. Van Valkenburgh, Jan. 15, 1926, Tamiment Library, New York University (hereafter cited as TL).

7. *St. Louis Mirror,* Nov. 5, 1908.

8. *LML,* 413–14; *Tribune,* Mar. 3, 1908; *Daily News,* Mar. 5, 1908.

9. *Tribune,* Mar. 3, 1908; *Daily News,* Mar. 5, 1908.

10. *Tribune,* Mar. 6, 1908.

11. *LML,* 415.

12. *FTM,* 216.

13. *LML,* 415–16.

14. Ibid., 416.

15. *Daily News,* Mar. 14, 1908.

16. *Tribune,* Mar. 16, 1908.

17. Ibid., Mar. 17, 1908; *FTM,* 218; *LML,* 417–19.

18. Ibid.

19. *LML,* 417.

20. Ibid., 420.

21. Ibid.

22. Emma Goldman to Ben Reitman, Sept. 27, 1908, Reitman Papers (hereafter the initials EG and BR will be used in citing correspondence between Goldman and Reitman).

23. *LML,* 422.

24. Ibid., 422–23.

25. *FTM,* 219.

26. *LML,* 424–25.

27. *Tribune,* Apr. 1, 1908.

28. *LML,* 425; *FTM,* 220.

Chapter 7: On Tour

1. *Times,* Mar. 29, 1908; "A Review of the World," *Current Literature* 44 (May 1908): 461.

2. "Review of the World," 461–68; *Times,* Apr. 10, 1908.

3. *Portland Oregonian,* May 25, 1908.

4. *Mother Earth* 3 (May 1908): 133.

5. *Salt Lake Tribune,* Apr. 11, 1908.

6. Ibid.

7. Ibid., Apr. 13, 15, 1908.

8. *San Francisco Examiner,* Apr. 18, 1908.

9. *LML,* 426.

10. *San Francisco Examiner,* Apr. 20, 1908.

11. *Mother Earth* 7 (May 1908): 133–34.

12. *LML,* 426.

13. *FTM,* 243.

14. Ibid., 427.

15. Ibid., 428–29, 222; *Mother Earth* 3 (May 1908): 135–37.

16. *San Francisco Examiner,* Apr. 29, 1908.

17. *Los Angeles Times,* Apr. 29, 1908; May 3, 1908.

18. *Portland Oregonian,* May 24, 1908.

19. Ibid., May 20, 21, 1908; *LML,* 430; *Mother Earth* 3 (June 1908): 189.

20. *Portland Oregonian,* May 24, 1908.

21. *FTM,* 239.

22. *Mother Earth* 3 (July 1908): 225.

23. *FTM,* 241.

24. *LML,* 432–34.

25. Ibid., 434.

Chapter 8: "210"

1. *LML,* 516–17.

2. Alexander Berkman, *Prison Memoirs of an Anarchist* (New York, 1912), 10; *FTM,* 251–52.

3. *FTM,* 252; W. A. Swanberg, *Dreiser* (New York, 1965), 181.

4. Wexler, *Emma Goldman,* 126.

5. Ibid., 126–27; *FTM*, 252–53.

6. *New York Evening Post*, Feb. 24, 1912.

7. BR to EG, Sept. 12, 1914, Reitman Papers.

8. Interview with Elmer Gertz, Mar. 6, 1982.

9. *FTM*, 363.

10. Ibid., 257.

11. *LML*, 440.

12. EG to BR, Dec. 14 or 15, 1909, Reitman Papers.

13. EG to BR, Dec. 23, 1909, Reitman Papers.

14. EG to BR, July 21, 1910, Reitman Papers.

15. EG to BR, July 24, 1910, Reitman Papers.

16. BR to EG, Jan. 2, 1911, Reitman Papers.

17. EG to BR, July 21, 1910, Reitman Papers.

18. EG to BR, May 31, 1909, Reitman Papers.

19. EG to BR, 1914, Reitman Papers.

Chapter 9: Free Speech

1. *Mother Earth* 4 (Sept. 1909): 210–15.

2. Melvyn Dubofsky, *We Shall Be All: A History of the Industrial Workers of the World* (New York, 1969), 173–79; Mary Hill, "The Free Speech Fight at San Diego," *Survey* 28 (May 4, 1912): 192–94.

3. *Mother Earth* 3 (Feb. 1909), 421–23.

4. *LML*, 437–38; *Times*, Sept. 14, 27, 1908; *FTM*, 259; *Mother Earth* 3 (Sept. 1909): 273–75.

5. *Kansas City Star*, Nov. 4, 1908.

6. *Portland Oregonian*, Dec. 22, 1908.

7. *Mother Earth* 3 (Jan. 1909): 370–76; 3 (Feb. 1909): 403.

8. *San Francisco Examiner*, Jan. 15, 1909; *Times*, Jan. 16, 1909.

9. William Buwalda to Joseph Dickinson, Apr. 16, 1909, RG 94, Records of the Adjutant General's Office, General Correspondence, 1890–1917, #48140, National Archives.

10. *Mother Earth* 4 (Mar. 1909): 29–31.

11. Ibid., 3 (Feb. 1909): 411–17.

12. Richard O'Connor, *Jack London* (Boston, 1964), 125.

13. Charmian London, *The Book of Jack London*, vol. 2 (New York, 1921), 184.

14. *Times*, Apr. 9, 1909.

15. *Mother Earth* 4 (Apr. 1909): 51.

16. A sampling of editorial comment appears in ibid. 4 (June 1909): 103–7.

17. *New Haven Union*, May 15, 1909.

18. RG 60, Records of the Department of Justice, Central Files, #133149, National Archives; Drinnon, *Rebel in Paradise*, 127.

19. *Times*, May 24, 1909; *Mother Earth* 10 (June 1909): 103–6; *New York Evening Sun*, May 25, 1909.

20. *Times*, June 9, 1909; *LML*, 451–54; Drinnon, *Rebel in Paradise*, 128–29.

21. *Times*, July 1, 1909; *Mother Earth* 4 (July 1909): 146–51; *LML*, 454.

22. *Mother Earth* 4 (Sept. 1909): 210–15; *LML*, 455.

23. Ibid.

Chapter 10: Cradle of Liberty

1. Robert Rutland, ed., *The Papers of James Madison* (Charlottesville, Va., 1977), 297–98.

2. *Philadelphia Ledger*, Sept. 28, 1909.

3. Ibid., Sept. 27, 1909.

4. Ibid., Sept. 29, 1909; *Philadelphia Enquirer*, Sept. 29, 1909; *LML*, 457.

5. *Philadelphia Enquirer*, Sept. 30, 1909; Oct. 2, 1909.

6. *Philadelphia Ledger*, Sept. 30, 1909.

7. Ibid., Sept. 28, 1909.

8. Ibid., Oct. 3, 1909.

9. Ibid.

10. Ibid., Oct. 9, 1909.

11. Ibid., Oct. 16, 1909.

12. Ibid., Oct. 19, 1909; *FTM*, 290–91.

13. *Philadelphia Ledger*, Oct. 21, 1909.

14. Congressional Quarterly, *The Supreme Court and Individual Rights* (Washington, D.C., 1980), 20.

15. John W. Hales, ed., *Milton: Areopagitica* (London, 1949), 50.

Chapter 11: Village Sex

1. Justin Kaplan, *Lincoln Steffens: A Biography* (New York, 1974), 170. An excellent treatment of the circle of radicals among whom Emma and her friends moved is in Leslie Fishbein, *Rebels in Bohemia* (Chapel Hill, N.C., 1982).

2. Granville Hicks, *John Reed: The Making of a Revolutionary* (New York, 1936), 71.

3. Ibid., 94.

4. Ronald Steel, *Walter Lippmann and the American Century* (Boston, 1980), 50–53.

5. Kaplan, *Lincoln Steffens*, 196–98.

6. Sinclair Lewis, "Hobohemia," *Saturday Evening Post* 189 (no. 41, Apr. 7, 1917): 4–8, 121.

7. Fishbein, *Rebels in Bohemia*, 34.

8. Arthur Gelb and Barbara Gelb, *O'Neill* (New York, 1973), 298, 324.

9. Fishbein, *Rebels in Bohemia*, 99.

10. Ibid., 94–95.

11. Margaret Marsh, *Anarchist Women* (Philadelphia, 1981), 69–80; Drinnon, *Rebel in Paradise*, 149–52.

12. "Sex O'Clock in America," *Current Opinion* 55 (Aug. 1913): 113–14.

13. *FTM*, 270–71.

14. Dale Kramer, *Chicago Renaissance* (New York, 1966), 255.

15. *FTM*, 323–25.

16. Swanberg, *Dreiser*, 165, 196–97, 246.

17. Draft of a lecture delivered in San Francisco, July 1912, Reitman Papers.

18. *Times*, Nov. 18, 1910.

19. EG to BR, Jan. 23, 1912, Reitman Papers.

20. BR to EG, Jan. 2, 1911; Jan. 14, 19, 1912, Reitman Papers.

21. BR to EG, Jan. 1912; EG to BR, Jan. 17, 1912, Reitman Papers.

22. BR to EG, Sept. 15, 1910; EG to BR, Aug. 14, 1910; Nov. 29, 1910, Reitman Papers.

23. EG to BR, July 30, 1911, Reitman Papers; *Mother Earth* 5 (July 1910): 163; 6 (May 1911): 84–89; 6 (July 1911): 152.

24. *Detroit Journal*, Jan. 30, 1911.

Chapter 12: San Diego

1. Report of Alexander Lanier, "Industrial Workers of the World," RG 165, Records of the Military Intelligence Division, #4–10–10110–235, National Archives; Len DeCaux, *The Living Spirit of the Wobblies* (New York, 1978), 48–56; Dubofsky, *We Shall Be All*, 173–75.

2. A. E. Holt, "'Bos," *Survey* 60 (Aug. 1, 1928): 456–59.

3. Irwin, *American Tramp and Underworld Slang*, 41.

4. Dubofsky, *We Shall Be All*, 173–93; DeCaux, *Living Spirit*, 48–56.

5. *Industrial Worker,* May 1, 1912.

6. Ibid., Feb. 22, 1912; Hill, "Free Speech Fight"; Dubofsky, *We Shall Be All,* 189–90.

7. John L. Sehon to George Wickersham, May 3, 1912; F. C. Spalding to Wickersham, May 3, 1912; John Needham to Wickersham, May 4, 1912, RG 60, Records of the Department of Justice, Numerical File, #150139, National Archives.

8. *Times,* Apr. 5, 6, 1912; report of Harris Weinstock, May 1912, RG 60, Records of the Department of Justice, Numerical File, #150139, National Archives.

9. *LML,* 494–95; *FTM,* 278–79; *Times,* Apr. 8, 1912.

10. Ben Reitman, "The Respectable Mob," *Mother Earth* 7 (June 1912): 109–12; *FTM,* 280–84; *LML,* 495–501; Drinnon, *Rebel in Paradise,* 134–36; *Los Angeles Times,* May 15, 16, 1912; *San Diego News,* May 16, 1912; *Times,* May 16, 17, 1912; *Daily News,* May 17, 1912.

11. Reitman, "Respectable Mob"; *FTM,* 280–84; *LML,* 498–501; *Times,* May 16, 1912.

12. *Los Angeles Times,* May 16, 1912.

13. Ibid., May 19, 1912.

14. *Times,* May 17, 1912.

15. *Appeal to Reason,* May 25, 1912.

16. *FTM,* 285.

17. RG 60, Numerical File, #150139, National Archives.

18. William H. Taft to George Wickersham, Sept. 17, 1912, ibid.; *Los Angeles Times,* May 16, 20, 21, 1912; Dubofsky, *We Shall Be All,* 194–97.

19. Dubofsky, *We Shall Be All,* 196.

20. Elizabeth Gurley Flynn, *The Rebel Girl: An Autobiography* (New York, 1955), 178–79.

21. EG to BR, Weds., n.d. (1912), Reitman Papers.

22. BR to EG, Oct. 19, 1914, Reitman Papers.

23. Harry Kemp, *More Miles: An Autobiographical Novel* (New York, 1926), 49.

24. *LML,* 510–11.

25. *FTM,* 286–87; *LML,* 511–14; Drinnon, *Rebel in Paradise,* 136; *San Diego Sun,* May 12, 19, 20, 21, 1913; *Los Angeles Times,* May 21, 1913; *San Diego Union,* May 21, 1913.

26. *LML,* 514.

27. *San Diego Union,* May 21, 1913.

28. *Los Angeles Times,* May 22, 23, 1913.

29. *LML,* 557–59; George Edwards, "Free Speech in San Diego," *Mother Earth* 10 (July 1915): 182–85.

30. *FTM,* 288.

Chapter 13: Ludlow

1. Hicks, *John Reed,* 112–16, 134–37.

2. Ibid., 118.

3. Ibid., 139.

4. The most thorough monograph on the Ludlow coal strike is George McGovern and Leonard Guttridge, *The Great Coalfield War* (Boston, 1972).

5. *Rocky Mountain News and Times,* Apr. 26, 1914.

6. Ibid.

7. Leslie Marcy, "The Class War in Colorado," *The International Socialist Review* 14 (June 1914): 713–14.

8. Ibid., 717.

9. Max Eastman, "Class War in Colorado," *The Masses* 5 (June 1914): 1.

10. See two articles which discuss editorial reaction on the massacre: "Comment on Colorado by Those Who Know," *The Literary Digest* (May 16, 1914): 1163–65; "The Colorado Slaughter," ibid. (May 2, 1914): 1033–34.

11. Hicks, *John Reed*, 139.

12. Ibid., 140–44.

13. "Comment on Colorado," 1165.

14. Eastman, "Class War in Colorado," 1.

15. *Times*, Apr. 7, 1914.

16. *Times*, Apr. 29, 30, May 1, 1914: *Rocky Mountain News and Times*, Apr. 30, 1914.

17. Hicks, *John Reed*, 143–44.

18. *LML*, 533.

19. Ibid., 534; *Rocky Mountain News and Times*, May 3, 1914.

20. *LML*, 534; *FTM*, 248–49.

21. *FTM*, 249–50.

22. *LML*, 534.

23. *Rocky Mountain News and Times*, Apr. 27, 1914.

24. See petitions in RG 60, Records of the Department of Justice, General Classification File, #60–187–22, National Archives.

25. Emma Goldman to Margaret Sanger, May 1, 1914, Sanger Papers, Library of Congress (hereafter cited as Sanger Papers).

26. *LML*, 535–36; Drinnon, *Rebel in Paradise*, 175–76.

27. *LML*, 536–38.

28. Emma Goldman to Margaret Sanger, June 22, 1914, Sanger Papers.

Chapter 14: Billy Sunday

1. Karen Gullen, ed., *Billy Sunday Speaks* (New York, 1970), 5–7, 214; *Newark Evening News*, Apr. 14, 1915.

2. *Times*, Mar. 17, 1915.

3. Ibid., Apr. 4, 1915.

4. Ibid., Apr. 5, 1915.

5. Ibid., Apr. 17, 1915.

6. Ibid.

7. *Newark Evening News*, Apr. 14, 1915.

8. *Times*, Apr. 21, 1915.

9. Ibid.; *Newark Evening News*, Apr. 20, 21, 1915.

10. *Mother Earth* 10 (May 1915): 97–98.

11. *Newark Evening News*, Apr. 20, 1915.

12. Ibid., Apr. 20, 21, 1915; *Times*, Apr. 21, 1915.

13. *Times*, May 24, 1915.

14. *Mother Earth* 10 (May 1915): 95–101.

15. *FTM*, 46–48.

Chapter 15: The Poison Banquet

1. *Daily News*, Feb. 10, 1916.

2. Edward Kantowitz, *Corporation Sole: Cardinal Mundelein and Chicago Catholicism* (Notre Dame, Ind., 1983), 5–8, 10–11.

3. *Times*, Feb. 14, 1916.

4. *Tribune*, Feb. 11, 1916; *Daily News*, Feb. 11, 1916.

5. *Times*, Feb. 20, 1916.

6. *Tribune*, Feb. 13, 1916.

7. Ibid.

8. RG 165, War Department General Staff, Military Intelligence Division, #9684–19, National Archives.

9. *Daily News*, Feb. 14, 1916.

10. *Times*, Feb. 18, 1916.

11. Ibid.

12. *Daily News*, Feb. 14, 1916.

13. *Times*, Feb. 24, 1916.

14. Ibid., Feb. 23, 29, 1916.

15. *FTM*, 317–18.

16. RG 65, Records of the Federal Bureau of Investigation, Microfilm 1085, File OG1170, National Archives.

17. RG 165, Military Intelligence File, #9684–19, National Archives; *FTM*, 315–20.

18. RG 165, Military Intelligence File, #9684–19, National Archives.

Chapter 16: Birth Control

1. *FTM*, 233.

2. James Reed, *From Private Vice to Public Virtue: The Birth Control Movement and American Society since 1830* (New York, 1978), 6–7; *Mother Earth* 11 (Apr. 1916): 451–56.

3. The physician is quoted in ibid., 37–39; Fishbein, *Rebels in Bohemia*, 32–34; Hal Sears, *The Sex Radicals: Free Love in High Victorian America* (Lawrence, Kans., 1977), 70–74; Madeline Gray, *Margaret Sanger: A Biography of the Champion of Birth Control* (New York, 1979); Mary Ware Dennett, *Who's Obscene?* (New York, 1930), xix, 215; E. Haldeman-Julius, *Questions and Answers*, (Girard, Kans., 2d ser., 1935), 41–42.

4. Linda Gordon, *Woman's Body, Woman's Right: A Social History of Birth Control in America* (New York, 1976), 66–67.

5. *The Masses* 8 (June 1916): 27.

6. Gordon, *Woman's Body*, 136–41; Fishbein, *Rebels in Bohemia*, 101–6.

7. Drinnon, *Rebel in Paradise*, 166–67.

8. Gray, *Margaret Sanger*, 37–41; Gordon, *Woman's Body*, 213–15.

9. Reed, *Private Vice to Public Virtue*, 50.

10. Drinnon, *Rebel in Paradise*, 167.

11. *Mother Earth* 10 (Sept. 1915): 245–47.

12. Gordon, *Woman's Body*, 226; *The Masses* 6 (May 1915).

13. *Mother Earth* 10 (Oct. 1915): 269–70.

14. Swanberg, *Dreiser*, 203–4.

15. *Oregon Journal*, Aug. 7, 8, 14, 15, 1915; *Portland Oregonian*, Aug. 7, 8, 14, 1915.

16. *The Masses* 8 (Apr. 1916): 18.

17. *FTM*, 234–35.

18. Reed, *Private Vice to Public Virtue*, 97–98.

19. Drinnon, *Rebel in Paradise*, 170–71; Marsh, *Anarchist Women*, 111–12.

20. Emma Goldman to Ellen Kennan, Apr. 6, 1916, International Institute of Social History, Amsterdam (hereafter cited as IISH).

21. *Mother Earth* 11 (Mar. 1916): 426–30.

22. Ibid. 11 (Apr. 1916): 457; *Times*, Mar. 2, 1916.

23. William Sanger to Emma Goldman, Mar. 14, 1916, Sanger Papers.

24. *Mother Earth* 11 (May 1916): 504–7.

25. Fishbein, *Rebels in Bohemia*, 109.

26. *Times*, Apr. 28, 1916.

27. Emma Goldman to Alice Inglis, May 10, 1916, Labadie Collection, University of Michigan, Ann Arbor (hereafter cited as Labadie Collection).

28. Max Eastman, *Enjoyment of Living* (New York, 1948), 423–24; *LML*, 572.

29. *Mother Earth* 11 (June 1916): 508–16.

30. Ibid., 525–27.

31. Reitman, "Prisons in My Life."

32. *FTM*, 333–40.

33. *Mother Earth* 11 (July 1916): 546.

34. Emma Goldman to Alice Inglis, June 17, 1916, Labadie Collection.

35. *FTM*, 361–62.

36. *New York Post*, May 17, 1912.

37. Ben Reitman to Margaret Foley, Jan. 9, 1916, Foley Papers, Schlesinger Library, Radcliffe College (hereafter cited as Foley Papers).

38. Ben Reitman to Margaret Foley, June 27, 1916; Aug. 31, 1916, Foley Papers.

39. *Mother Earth* 11 (Aug. 1916): 586.

40. Ben Reitman, "American by Comparison," unpublished ms., Reitman Papers.

Chapter 17: Two Cities, Two Trials

1. Ben Reitman, "The 1915–1916 Tour," *Mother Earth* 11 (Oct. 1916): 647.

2. *Cleveland Plain Dealer*, Dec. 13, 1916.

3. *Rochester Democrat and Chronicle*, Dec. 16, 1916; Reed, *Private Vice to Public Virtue*, 51–52; Gordon, *Woman's Body*, 219–20.

4. *Cleveland Plain Dealer*, Jan. 12, 1917.

5. Ben Reitman, "The Cleveland Myth," *Mother Earth* 11 (Feb. 1917): 762.

6. Ibid., 762–63; Statement on birth control, May, 1917, Original Accession, #2, Reitman Papers.

7. Reitman, "Cleveland Myth," 762; *Cleveland Plain Dealer*, Jan. 16, 1917; *FTM*, 342–44.

8. Emma Goldman to Agnes Inglis, Jan. 1, 1917, Labadie Collection.

9. *Rochester Democrat and Chronicle*, Feb. 27, 28, 1917.

10. *Rochester Union and Advertiser*, Feb. 28, 1917.

11. *FTM*, 344; Reitman, "Cleveland Myth," 765; Harry Weinberger, "Reitman and Rochester," *Mother Earth* 12 (Apr. 1917): 44–45; *Rochester Democrat and Chronicle*, Mar. 1, 1917; *Rochester Evening Times*, Dec. 19, 1916.

12. Gordon, *Woman's Body*, 229.

13. Ben Reitman to Norman Hines, Feb. 13, 1937, Francis Countway Library of Medicine, Boston (hereafter cited as FCLM).

Chapter 18: The Great Repression

1. Gelb and Gelb, *O'Neill*, 327–28.

2. Drinnon, *Rebel in Paradise*, 211.

3. Nick Salvatore, *Eugene Debs: Citizen and Socialist* (Urbana, Ill., 1982), 288; RG 65, Records of the Department of Justice, FBI reel 647, OG234939, Tom Clifford to Newton Baker, Aug. 24, 1918, National Archives.

4. Investigative files, Box 4F1, Lusk Committee Records, New York State Archives, Albany.

5. RG 165, Records of the War Department General Staff, Military Intelligence Division, #10110–564, National Archives.

6. RG 28, Records of the Post Office Department, Records Relating to the Espionage Act, World War I, #46647, National Archives.

7. *Times*, Sept. 27, 1917.

8. DeCaux, *Living Spirit*, 130–32.

9. RG 65, Records of the Department of Justice, FBI reel 67A, OG7342, National Archives.

10. Salvatore, *Eugene Debs*, 289.

11. RG 165, Records of the War Department General Staff, Military Intelligence Division, #10110–235, National Archives.

12. Drinnon, *Rebel in Paradise*, 186.

13. Ben Reitman to Margaret Foley, Aug. 2, 1916, Foley Papers.

14. BR to EG, 1914, Reitman Papers.

15. *FTM*, 366–67.

16. Emma Goldman to Frank Heiner, Dec. 24, 1935, Goldman Papers, vol. 14, IISH.

17. *FTM*, 367, 370–73.

18. Falk, *Love, Anarchy, and Emma Goldman*, 262–66; Drinnon, *Rebel in Paradise*, 187–88.

19. *FTM*, 368.

20. Ibid., 375–76.

21. Reitman, "Prisons in My Life."

22. Ben Reitman to Brutus Reitman, May 6, 1918, Reitman Papers.

23. Ben Reitman to Anna Martindale, undated, Reitman Papers.

24. Ben Reitman to Anna Martindale, two undated letters, Reitman Papers.

25. Ben Reitman to Anna Martindale, undated, Reitman Papers.

26. Falk, *Love, Anarchy, and Emma Goldman*, 257–92; Drinnon, *Rebel in Paradise*, 112–20, 184–214; Wexler, *Emma Goldman*, 247–71.

27. *Tribune*, Dec. 2, 1919.

28. EG to BR, Dec. 12, 1919, Reitman Papers.

Chapter 19: Hobo College

1. Nels Anderson, *The Hobo: The Sociology of the Homeless Man* (Chicago, Phoenix Edition, 1975), 4–39; Holt, "'Bos"; "Chicago: Hobo Capital of America," *The Survey* 50 (June 1, 1923): 287–90, 303–5; Roger Bruns, *Knights of the Road: A Hobo History* (New York, 1980), 162–65.

2. Clifford Shaw, *The Jack-Roller: A Delinquent Boy's Own Story* (Chicago, Phoenix Edition, 1966), 80, 139–41.

3. Allsop, *Hard Travellin'*, 171; Ralph Chaplin, *Wobbly: The Rough-and-Tumble Story of an American Radical* (Chicago, 1948), 86–87.

4. Gelb and Gelb, *O'Neill*, 291.

5. Kemp, *Chanteys and Ballads*, 90–92.

6. Frank Beck, *Hobohemia*, (West Rindge, N.H., 1956), 76–77.

7. See various research documents on the American hobo in the Burgess Papers, boxes 126, 149.

8. Helen Bryant, "The Hobo College," term paper (History of Education, School of the Art Institute), 1926, Reitman Papers, 6–12.

9. Miscellaneous newspaper clippings, Irwin St. John Tucker Papers, University of Illinois at Chicago, Library (hereafter cited as Tucker Papers); Beck, *Hobohemia*, 73–75.

10. Ben Reitman, "Doctor of the Downtrodden," unpublished ms., Reitman Papers, 43–55.

11. *Daily News*, Sept. 24, 1932.

12. Anderson, *Hobo*, 213.

13. Clippings, Tucker Papers.

14. Dorothy Walton, "A Hobo College in Chicago," *Hobo News*, Jan. 1921.

15. Clippings, Tucker Papers.

16. E. A. Ross to Ben Reitman, Dec. 1, 1925, Ross Papers, State Historical Society of Wisconsin (hereafter cited as Ross Papers).

17. Nels Anderson, *The American Hobo* (Leiden, 1975), 162–64.

18. *Tribune*, Oct. 17, 1920.

19. *Daily News*, Apr. 11, 1941.

20. Anderson, *American Hobo*, 178–79.

21. *Daily News*, Nov. 20, 1931.

22. Ibid., Feb. 12, 1932.

23. Ibid., Mar. 6, 1929.

24. *Tribune*, Mar. 30, 1922.

25. *Daily News*, Mar. 20, 1923.

26. Holt, "'Bos," 456.

27. *Daily News*, Apr. 26, 1922; *Chicago Herald and Examiner*, Apr. 27, 1922.

28. *Times*, Mar. 25, 1926.

29. Bryant, "Hobo College," 14–16.

Chapter 20: "Outcast Narratives"

1. There are several folders of "Outcast Narratives" in the Reitman Papers. Among those reprinted here, "Moses" is about Moses Harman, the influential eugenicist and publisher of the free-thought periodical *The American Journal of Eugenics.* The "Chi Kid" is, of course, Ben Reitman himself.

Chapter 21: Hobo Kingdom

1. Francis Ianni and Elizabeth Reuss-Ianni, eds., *The Crime Society: Organized Crime and Corruption in America* (New York, 1976), 156.

2. Charles Merriam, *Chicago: A More Intimate View of Urban Politics* (New York, 1929), 44–45; John Landesco, *Organized Crime in Chicago, Part III: The Illinois Crime Survey, 1929* (Chicago, 1968), 34–41; Nelson Algren, *Chicago: City on the Make* (Sausalito, Calif., 1961), 56.

3. Interview with Elmer Gertz, Mar. 6, 1982; interview with Al Kaufman, Aug. 18, 1984.

4. *FTM,* 417–18.

5. Landesco, *Organized Crime,* 40–41.

6. *FTM,* 418–19.

7. Ben Reitman, unpublished ms., VDC #108, Reitman Papers.

8. *FTM,* 419–20; *Tribune,* Dec. 6, 1924.

9. *FTM,* 420–21; Ben Reitman, "Chuck Connors: A Famous Junker," unpublished ms., Reitman Papers.

10. *FTM,* 422.

11. *Tribune,* Dec. 6, 1924.

12. *FTM,* 422–25.

13. Ibid., 426; *Tribune,* Dec. 18, 1924.

14. *Daily News,* Dec. 22, 1924.

15. Ibid., Dec. 22, 23, 29, 1924; *Tribune,* Dec. 18, 1924.

16. Ben Reitman, *The Second Oldest Profession* (New York, 1931), 209.

Chapter 22: Dill Pickle

1. Ray L. White, ed., *Sherwood Anderson's Memoirs* (Chapel Hill, N.C., 1942), 125–26, 357; *The Dil Pickler* (no. 1), copy in the Newberry Library; *Daily News,* Mar. 9, 1932.

2. Les Sustar, "When Speech Was Free (and Usually Worth It)," *Reader* 13 (Oct. 21, 1983): 18; Chaplin, *Wobbly,* 170; Flynn, *Rebel Girl,* 84–87, 114.

3. *Daily News,* Feb. 29, 1964.

4. Kenneth Rexroth, *An Autobiographical Novel* (Garden City, N.Y., 1964), 135–40; Sherwood Anderson, "Jack Jones, 'The Pickler,'" *Daily News,* June 18, 1919; Albert Parry, *Garrets and Pretenders: A History of Bohemianism in America* (New York, 1933), 200–207; Sustar, "When Speech Was Free," 18.

5. Rexroth, *Autobiographical Novel,* 138.

6. Anderson, "Jack Jones."

7. Ibid.

8. Rexroth, *Autobiographical Novel,* 136.

9. *Chicago Sun,* Mar. 14, 1944 (hereafter cited as *Sun*); *Tribune,* Mar. 16, 1919.

10. Irving Meyers to Editor, *Chicago Magazine,* June 25, 1981.

11. *Chicago Sun-Times,* June 17, 1951 (hereafter cited as *Sun-Times*); *Chicago Sunday Times,* Aug. 22, 1937 (hereafter cited as *Sunday Times*).

12. Parry, *Garrets and Pretenders,* 203.

13. *Sunday Times,* Aug. 22, 1937; *Sun,* Mar. 14, 1944.

14. Alfred Kreymborg, *Troubadour: An Autobiography* (New York, 1925), 345–46.

15. *Tribune,* July 14, 1919.

16. Rexroth, *Autobiographical Novel,* 136; Chaplin, *Wobbly,* 361; Sustar, "When Speech Was Free," 24; Flynn, *Rebel Girl,* 333.

17. Copy in the Newberry Library.

18. *The Dil Pickler* 1 (no. 2), copy in the Newberry Library.

19. Kreymborg, *Troubadour,* 344–45.

20. Rexroth, *Autobiographical Novel,* 269.

21. Minutes of the Chicago Law and Order League, Oct. 13, 1920, Chicago Historical Society.

22. RG 165, War Department General Staff, Military Intelligence Division Files #10110–551, National Archives.

23. "Chicago as the Literary Capital of the United States," *Current Opinion* 69 (Aug. 1920): 242–43.

24. "From Chicago to New York," *The Bookman* 64 (Dec. 1926): 452–54.

25. Ben Reitman, "Highlights in Dill Pickle History," unpublished ms., Reitman Papers.

26. *Chicago Times,* Aug. 22, 1937.

27. Saul Bellow, "A Talk with the Yellow Kid," *Reporter* 15 (Sept. 6, 1956): 41–44; Joseph Weil (as told to W. T. Brannon), *"Yellow Kid" Weil* (Chicago, 1948); *Chicago Times,* Mar. 14, 1940; *Milwaukee Journal,* July 12, 1974.

28. Miscellaneous clippings and advertisements, Newberry Library.

29. Ben Reitman, *Sister of the Road: The Autobiography of Box-Car Bertha* (New York, 1937), 210–11; *Tribune,* Aug. 3, 1931.

30. *Sunday Times,* Aug. 22, 1937.

31. *Daily News,* Mar. 18, 1931; Sustar, "When Speech Was Free," 24.

32. *Chicago Herald and Examiner,* Mar. 13, 1933 (hereafter cited as *Herald and Examiner*).

33. White, *Sherwood Anderson's Memoirs,* 356–58.

34. *Daily News,* Mar. 3, 9, 1932; Rexroth, *Autobiographical Novel,* 137.

35. Interview with Van Allen Bradley, Oct. 21, 1982, Phoenix, Ariz.

36. *Sun,* Mar. 14, Aug. 15, 1944; *Daily News,* Mar. 18, 1944; Sustar, "When Speech Was Free," 26–32.

37. John Schoenherr, "Dill Pickle Memories," unpublished ms., Reitman Papers.

38. *Daily News,* Feb. 29, 1964.

39. *Chicago Times,* Aug. 22, 1937.

40. *Daily News,* Feb. 29, 1964.

Chapter 23: Bughouse Square

1. Beck, *Hobohemia,* 68.

2. *Sun-Times,* June 17, 1951; Rexroth, *Autobiographical Novel,* 105; "Hobo Capital of America," 289–90.

3. *Daily News,* Feb. 29, 1964.

4. Rexroth, *Autobiographical Novel,* 138.

5. *Chicago Daily Times,* Sept. 24, 1940.

6. *Sun-Times,* June 17, 1951; Beck, *Hobohemia,* 68–69.

7. Studs Terkel, *Talking to Myself* (New York, 1973), 49.

8. Rexroth, *Autobiographical Novel,* 140.

9. Ibid., 141, 183; *Sun-Times,* June 17, 1951; Sustar, "When Speech Was Free," 20.

10. Sustar, "When Speech Was Free," 14, 16; *Sun-Times,* Aug. 10, 1967.

11. Reitman, *Sister of the Road,* 68.

12. Rexroth, *Autobiographical Novel,* 119.

13. Beck, *Hobohemia,* 71.

Chapter 24: In Mourning

1. Beck, *Hobohemia,* 40–45; *Tribune,* Apr. 24, 1930; *Herald and Examiner,* Apr. 24, 25, 1930. The undated letters from which the quotes were drawn are in the Reitman Papers.

Chapter 25: Still the King

1. *Times,* July 23, 1930; "Millionaire Hobo Is Dead," *The Christian Century* 47 (Aug. 20, 1930): 1020.

2. Hoboes of America, Inc., 1940 Yearbook, copy in Reitman Papers.

3. Ibid.; "Hobo Hegemony: Convention to Decide among Rival Kings of Road Knights," *Literary Digest* 123 (Apr. 10, 1937): 10–12.

4. "Doctor of the Downtrodden," unpublished ms., Reitman Papers, 75–79.

5. Edwin Lahey, "Ben Reitman Pushes into Field of Social Pathology," clipping, FCLM.

6. "Hobo Hegemony," 10–12; *Times,* Nov. 28, 1926; *New York Sun,* Dec. 30, 1935.

7. Interview with Al Kaufman, Aug. 18, 1984; Ben Reitman to Al Kaufman, May 3, 1933, in the possession of Al Kaufman.

8. "Hobo Hegemony," 10–12; *Daily News,* Sept. 12, 1932.

9. "For Hoboes: Hobo News," *Time* (May 17, 1937): 68–69; Allsop, *Hard Travellin',* 226–30.

10. Clipping, July 18, 1931, Reitman Papers.

11. Interview with Herbert Blumer, Aug. 14, 1981; *Daily News,* Aug. 15, 1931.

12. Anderson, *Hobo,* xxiii–xxvi; Shaw, *Jack-Roller,* v–xviii.

13. *Sunday Times,* Aug. 22, 1937.

14. Henrich Hauser, *Feldwege Nach Chicago* (Berlin, 1931), 11, 191–92, 197–98; Ben Reitman to Anna Martindale, undated, Reitman Papers.

15. Reitman, *Sister of the Road.*

16. *Books* (July 25, 1937): 17; *Survey* 74 (Mar. 1937): 95.

17. *Variety,* May 31, 1972.

18. *American Journal of Sociology* 43 (Jan. 1938): 370.

19. Donald Clemmer to Ben Reitman, Sept. 23, 1940, Reitman Papers.

20. *New York Sun,* Dec. 30, 1935.

21. Adolph ——— to Ben Reitman, Feb. 7, 1934, Reitman Papers.

Chapter 26: Twilight of Hobohemia

1. Anderson, *Hobo,* xxi.

2. Ben Reitman, "The History, Types, and Characteristics of the Hobo," unpublished ms., Reitman Papers.

3. Thomas Healy, "The Hobo Hits the Highroad," *American Mercury* 8 (July 1926): 334–38; Lowell A. Norris, "America's Homeless Army," *Scribner's Magazine* 93 (May 1933): 316–18; Howard Bahr, *Disaffiliated Man* (Toronto, 1970), 19.

4. Quote by Lord Open Road, Hobo Convention, Aug. 1978, Britt, Iowa.

5. Allsop, *Hard Travellin',* 45.

6. Beck, *Hobohemia,* 46–50.

7. *Daily News,* Dec. 19, 1934; *Tribune,* Dec. 19, 1934.

8. Beck, *Hobohemia,* 77.

9. *Tribune,* Dec. 19, 1934; *Daily News,* Dec. 19, 1934.

10. Anderson, *Hobo,* 183–84.

11. Circular, Reitman Papers.

12. *Tribune,* Dec. 18, 21, 1936.

13. Anonymous poem, Reitman Papers.

14. Beck, *Hobohemia,* 51–56.

15. Reitman, *Sister of the Road*, 60.

16. Beck, *Hobohemia*, 68; *Daily News*, Sept. 27, 1937.

Chapter 27: Antisyph

1. Reitman, "Syphilis in My Life," 7, 27–29. For a comprehensive social history of venereal disease in the U.S. see Allan M. Brandt, *No Magic Bullet* (New York, 1985).

2. Ibid., 28; Ben Reitman, Venereal Disease Reports, Reitman Papers, 550.

3. "Venereal Disease Campaign," *Time* 29 (Jan. 11, 1937): 38–39.

4. Ibid.

5. Paul deKruif, "Chicago Against Syphilis," *The Reader's Digest* 38 (Mar. 1941): 23–26; "Fighting Syphilis," *Literary Digest* 124 (Sept. 18, 1937): 7; Ben Reitman to *Millar's Chicago Letter*, Dec. 15, 1939, Reitman Papers; *Tribune*, Jan. 6, Mar. 3, 1939.

6. Reitman, Venereal Disease Reports, Reitman Papers, 523–26.

7. Ibid., 680.

8. Ibid., 278.

9. Ben Reitman to Nels Anderson, Nov. 15, 1938; Ben Reitman to Lawrence Linck, Nov. 13, 1938, Reitman Papers.

10. Ben Reitman to Nels Anderson, Nov. 26, 1938, Reitman Papers.

11. Ben Reitman to unknown, Dec. 4, 1937, Reitman Papers.

12. Reitman, Venereal Disease Reports, Reitman Papers, 1419.

13. Ben Reitman to Lawrence Linck, Nov. 13, 1938, Reitman Papers.

14. Ben Reitman, "Soap and Water as a Venereal Disease Prophylactic," unpublished ms., Reitman Papers.

Chapter 28: "Reveries at Sixty"

1. This two-page, typewritten manuscript, dated Jan. 1, 1939, is in the Reitman Papers.

Chapter 29: "De Profundus"

1. Quoted in Milton Kanvitz, "America: An Inheritance or an Achievement," *Bicentennial Convocations at Sage Chapel* (Ithaca, N.Y., 1976).

2. Nels Anderson to Ben Reitman, Nov. 26, 1938, Reitman Papers.

3. My appreciation to Medina Gross, Mecca Carpenter, and Ruth Highberg for information about the Reitman family during Ben's last years.

4. John Dellorto to Allen Keison, Editor, *Chicago Magazine*, June 5, 1981.

5. Clipping, "Faithful Nap at Haymarket Riot Reunion," Reitman Papers.

6. Falk, *Love, Anarchy, and Emma Goldman*, 479–91.

7. Ben Reitman to M. Eleanor Fitzgerald, May 22, 1939, TL.

8. BR to EG, June 23, 1939, quoted in Falk, *Love, Anarchy, and Emma Goldman*, 495–96.

9. EG to BR, June 29, 1939, Reitman Papers.

10. Emma Goldman to M. Eleanor Fitzgerald, July 24, 1939, TL.

11. EG to BR, Oct. 6, 1939, Reitman Papers.

12. BR to EG, Nov. 13, 1939, quoted in Falk, *Love, Anarchy, and Emma Goldman*, 503–5.

13. Ibid.

14. EG to BR, Nov. 22, 1939, Reitman Papers.

15. Falk, *Love, Anarchy, and Emma Goldman*, 512.

16. Ben Reitman to Leroy Oberman, May 16, 1940, Reitman Papers.

17. *Daily News,* May 16, 1940.

18. Ben Reitman to Hutchins Hapgood, Feb. 27, 1940, Reitman Papers.

19. Sadakichi Hartmann to Ben Reitman, June 2, 1940, Reitman Papers.

20. Ben Reitman to "My Dear February Children," Feb. 19, 1942, Reitman Papers.

21. Ben Reitman to "Obie, Dave, Adolph, et," Nov. 11, 1938, Reitman Papers.

22. Ben Reitman to "My Dear February Children," Feb. 19, 1942, Reitman Papers.

23. Ben Reitman to Theodore Schroeder, Nov. 23, 1940, in Joseph Ishill, *Theodore Schroeder: An Evolutionary Psychologist* (Berkeley Heights, N.J., 1940), in the Library of Congress Rare Book Room.

24. *Daily News,* Nov. 11, 1942.

25. *Daily News,* Nov. 20, 1942; *Tribune,* Nov. 20, 1942.

26. *Daily News,* Nov. 18, 1942. See a certified copy of the will in Reitman Papers, as well as numerous clippings about his death.

27. *Christian Century* 59 (Dec. 2, 1942): 1499.

28. Clipping, "Hoboes Pay Way, and Cheerfully, to Hail Reitman," Nov. 1942, Reitman Papers.

29. Clipping, Nov. 1942, Reitman Papers.

Hobo Glossary

angel food mission-house sermon

barrelhouse combined rooming house, saloon, and whorehouse

blind baggage favorite spot for train jumpers, between the mail and express coach by the tender

boodle jail small-town jail that profited from arresting hoboes and illegally using money provided by the town for their care

bridge snake structural ironworker who usually carried hand tools for work on bridges, culverts, etc.

bull policeman

cadger to panhandle

con tuberculosis

ding-bat tramp beggar

dip pickpocket

flip to hop freights

flophouse a cheap rooming house

gandy dancer one in a gang of track workmen on a railroad

gay cat a hobo tenderfoot

geezer an old-timer

home guard town worker who did not travel

hoop-chisler peddler of worthless rings and watches

ice harvester worker who helped clear frozen lakes

jack-roller town thief who fleeced migratory laborers

jerkwater small-town

jocker road kid's "foster parent" and teacher

joylady prostitute

jungle hobo camp

jungle buzzard low-life of the jungle

main stem principal city street catering to hoboes

mission stiff vagrant whose profession was to get "saved," and thereby receive a flop and a meal

monicker assumed name

moocher beggar

mulligan stew

mushfakir itinerant umbrella mender

nickel flop all-night moving picture show

notchhouse whorehouse

pete man tramp safeblower and expert on the use of nitroglycerin

profesh upper-class professional hobo

punk bread; young tramp

rattler freight car

road knight veteran hobo

rot booze cheap alcohol

shack train brakeman

shark employment agent

skid road city area with employment agencies for hoboes

sky pilot preacher

spiel story

stew bum bum who remained in one city or town

stiff hobo

tenderloin city area of low-class dives, whorehouses, etc.

throwing the feet panhandling

timber beast itinerant forester

vag vagrant

yegg itinerant burglar and safeblower

Selected Bibliography

The principal manuscript collection used in the preparation of this volume was the Ben Reitman Papers, located at the University of Illinois at Chicago. The collection is extraordinarily rich, not only for the correspondence and writings of Reitman, but for the dynamics of underclass and bohemian life in Chicago through the 1930s.

The National Archives in Washington, D.C., has extensive investigative files on Reitman as well as on Emma Goldman, Alexander Berkman, James Eads How, and other radicals. These are located in Record Group 65, Records of the Federal Bureau of Investigation, and Record Group 165, Records of the War Department General and Special Staffs, Records of the Office of the Director of Intelligence.

Other repositories holding important manuscript collections of materials relating to Reitman and his work are Boston University; the International Institute of Social History, Amsterdam; and the University of Michigan, Labadie Collection. Scattered items are in collections at Radcliffe College, Schlesinger Library; University of Chicago, Regenstein Library; New York University, Tamiment Library; State Historical Society of Wisconsin; Countway Library, Boston; and the Newberry Library, Chicago.

The selected bibliography that follows lists articles and books consulted in the writing of this book.

"All about the Entity of the Ego Is Taught at the Hobo University," *Literary Digest* 62 (July 12, 1919): 52–53.

Allsop, Kenneth. *Hard Travellin': The Hobo and His History.* New York: New American Library, 1967.

Anderson, Margaret. *My Thirty Years' War: An Autobiography.* London: Alfred A. Knopf, 1930.

Anderson, Nels. *The American Hobo.* Leiden: E. J. Brill, 1975.

———. *The Hobo: The Sociology of the Homeless Man.* Chicago: University of Chicago Press, 1923; Phoenix Edition, 1975.

———. "The Juvenile and the Tramp," *Journal of the American Institute of Criminal Law and Criminology* 14 (no. 2, Aug. 1923): 290–312.

———. *Men on the Move.* Chicago: University of Chicago Press, 1940.

Bahr, Howard. *Disaffiliated Man.* Toronto: University of Toronto Press, 1970.

Beck, Frank. *Hobohemia.* West Rindge, N.H.: Richard R. Smith Publishers, 1956.

Bellow, Saul. "A Talk with the Yellow Kid," *Reporter* 15 (Sept. 6, 1956): 41–44.

Berkman, Alexander. *Prison Memoirs of an Anarchist.* New York: Mother Earth Publishing, 1912.

Bjorkman, Frances. "The New Anti-Vagrancy Campaign," *The American Review of Reviews* 27 (Feb. 1908): 206–11.

Brandt, Allan M. *No Magic Bullet: A Social History of Venereal Disease in the United States since 1880.* New York: Oxford University Press, 1985.

Broun, Haywood, and Margaret Leech. *Anthony Comstock: Roundsman of the Lord.* New York: Literary Guild of America, 1927.

Browning, Frank, and John Gerassi. *The American Way of Crime.* New York: G. P. Putnam's Sons, 1980.

Bruns, Roger. *Knights of the Road: A Hobo History.* New York: Methuen, 1980.

Chaplin, Ralph. *Wobbly: The Rough-and-Tumble Story of an American Radical.* Chicago: University of Chicago Press, 1948.

"Chicago: Hobo Capital of America," *The Survey* 50 (June 1, 1923): 287–90, 303–5.

"Chicago as the Literary Capital of the United States," *Current Opinion* 69 (Aug. 1920): 242–43.

"The Colorado Slaughter," *The Literary Digest* (May 2, 1914): 1033–34.

"Comment on Colorado by Those Who Know." *The Literary Digest* (May 16, 1914): 1163–65.

DeCaux, Len. *The Living Spirit of the Wobblies.* New York: International Publishers, 1978.

Dedmon, Emmett. *Fabulous Chicago.* New York: Random House, 1953.

de Ford, Miriam Allen. *Up-Hill All the Way: The Life of Maynard Shipley.* Yellow Springs, Ohio: Antioch Press, 1956.

deKruif, Paul. "Chicago Against Syphilis," *The Reader's Digest* 38 (Mar. 1941): 23–26.

Drinnon, Richard. *Rebel in Paradise.* New York: Harper and Row, 1976.

Dubofsky, Melvyn. *We Shall Be All: A History of the Industrial Workers of the World.* Chicago: Quadrangle, 1969.

Duffey, Bernard. *The Chicago Renaissance in American Letters.* East Lansing: Michigan State College Press, 1954.

Eastman, Max. "Class War in Colorado," *The Masses* 5 (June 1914): 1–4.

———. *Enjoyment of Living.* New York: Harper and Brothers Publishers, 1948.

Edge, William. *The Main Stem.* New York: Vanguard Press, 1927.
"Emma Goldman's Faith," *Current Literature* 50 (Feb. 1911): 176–78.
Etulain, Richard, ed. *Jack London on the Road: The Tramp Diary and Other Hobo Writings.* Logan: Utah State University Press, 1977.
Facciolo, Jay. *The Wobs and the Bos: The IWW and the Hobo.* Master's thesis, Hunter College, 1977.
Falk, Candace. *Love, Anarchy, and Emma Goldman.* New York: Holt, Rinehart and Winston, 1984.
Feder, Leah. *Unemployment Relief in Periods of Depression.* New York: Russell Sage Foundation, 1936.
Feied, Frederick. *No Pie in the Sky.* New York: Citadel Press, 1964.
Fishbein, Leslie. *Rebels in Bohemia.* Chapel Hill: University of North Carolina Press, 1982.
Flynn, Elizabeth Gurley. *The Rebel Girl: An Autobiography.* New York: International Publishers, 1955.
"For Hoboes: Hobo News," *Time* (May 17, 1937): 68–69.
Garland, Hamlin. *A Son of the Middle Border.* New York: Macmillan Company, 1917.
Gelb, Arthur, and Barbara Gelb. *O'Neill.* New York: Harper and Row Publishers, 1973.
Goldman, Emma. *Anarchism and Other Essays.* New York: Mother Earth Publishing Association, 1911.
———. *Living My Life.* New York: Meridian Books, 1917.
———. *Red Emma Speaks: Selected Writings and Speeches by Emma Goldman.* Compiled and edited by Alix Kates Shulman. New York: Random House, 1972.
Gordon, Linda. *Woman's Body, Woman's Right: A Social History of Birth Control in America.* New York: Grossman Publishers, 1976.
Gray, Madeline. *Margaret Sanger: A Biography of the Champion of Birth Control.* New York: Richard Marek Publishers, 1979.
Gullen, Karen, ed. *Billy Sunday Speaks.* New York: Chelsea House Publishers, 1970.
Hapgood, Hutchins. *Types from City Streets.* New York: Funk and Wagnalls Company, 1910.
———. *A Victorian in the Modern World.* New York: Harcourt Brace and Company, 1939.
Hansen, Harry. "From Chicago to New York," *The Bookman* 64 (Dec. 1926): 452–54.
———. *Midwest Portraits.* New York: Harcourt, Brace and Company, 1923.
Harris, Frank. *Contemporary Portraits.* 4th ser. New York: Brentano's, 1923.
Hartgrove, Dane. "Alexander Berkman: The Question of Revolutionary Methods." Unpublished ms., author's files.
Hauser, Henrich. *Feldwege Nach Chicago.* Berlin: S. Fischer Verlag, 1931.
Healy, Thomas. "The Hobo Hits the Highroad," *American Mercury* 8 (July 1926): 334–38.

Hicks, Granville. *John Reed: The Making of a Revolutionary.* New York: Macmillan Co., 1936.

Hill, Mary. "The Free Speech Fight at San Diego," *The Survey* 28 (May 4, 1912): 192–94.

"Hobo Hegemony: Convention to Decide among Rival Kings of Road Knights," *Literary Digest* 123 (Apr. 10, 1937): 10–12.

Hoffman, Victor, *The American Tramp, 1870–1900.* Ph.D. diss., University of Chicago, 1953.

Holt, Arthur. "'Bos," *The Survey* 60 (Aug. 1, 1928): 456–59.

Hubbard, Elbert. "The Rights of Tramps," *Arena* 9 (1893): 593–600.

Ianni, Frances, and Elizabeth Reuss-Ianni, eds. *The Crime Society: Organized Crime and Corruption in America.* New York: New American Library, 1976.

Irle, Walter. *Chicago Uncensored.* New York: Exposition Press, 1965.

Irving, Washington. *A History of New York.* New York: AMS Press, 1913.

Irwin, Godfrey. *American Tramp and Underworld Slang.* New York: Sears Publishing Company, 1930.

Kantowitz, Edward. *Corporation Sole: Cardinal Mundelein and Chicago Catholicism.* Notre Dame, Ind.: University of Notre Dame Press, 1983.

Kaplan, Justin. *Lincoln Steffens: A Biography.* New York: Simon and Schuster, 1974.

Kazarian, John. "The Starvation Army," *The Nation* 136 (Apr. 12–26, 1933): 396–98, 443–45, 472–73.

Kemp, Harry. *Chanteys and Ballads.* New York: Brentano's, 1920.

———. *Tramping on Life.* Garden City, N.Y.: Garden City Publishing Company, 1922.

Kobler, John. *Capone: The Life and World of Al Capone.* New York: G. P. Putnam's Sons, 1971.

Kornbluh, Joyce, ed. *Rebel Voices.* Ann Arbor: University of Michigan Press, 1964.

Kramer, Dale. *Chicago Renaissance.* New York: Appleton-Century, 1966.

Kreymborg, Alfred. *Troubadour: An Autobiography.* New York: Boni and Liveright, 1925.

Landesco, John. *Organized Crime in America, Part III: The Illinois Crime Survey, 1929.* Chicago: University of Chicago Press, 1968.

Leavitt, Samuel. "The Tramps and the Law," *Forum* 2 (1886): 190–200.

Levine, Louis. "The Development of Syndicalism in America," *Political Science Quarterly* 28 (Sept. 1913): 451–79.

Lewis, Orlando. "The American Tramp," *Atlantic Monthly* 101 (June 1908): 744–53.

———. "Concerning Vagrancy," *Charities* 21 (Jan. 23, 1909): 713–17.

Lewis, Sinclair. "Hobohemia," *Saturday Evening Post* 189 (no. 41, Apr. 7, 1917): 3–6, 121–22, 125–26, 129–30, 133.

London, Charmian. *The Book of Jack London,* vol. 2. New York: Century Company, 1921.

Longstreet, Stephen. *Chicago: An Intimate Portrait of People, Pleasures, and Power: 1860–1919.* New York: David McKay Company, 1973.

Luhan, Mabel Dodge. *Intimate Memories, Vol. 3: Movers and Shakers.* New York: Harcourt, Brace and Company, 1936.

Mabley, John, and Bill Ballance. "King of the Con Men," *American Mercury* 52 (June 1941): 695–702.

Marcy, Leslie. "The Class War in Colorado," *The International Socialist Review* 14 (June 1914): 709–21.

Marsh, Margaret. *Anarchist Women.* Philadelphia: Temple University Press, 1981.

Mayer, Harold, and Richard Wade. *Chicago: Growth of a Metropolis.* Chicago: University of Chicago Press, 1969.

Merriam, Charles. *Chicago: A More Intimate View of Urban Politics.* New York: Macmillan Company, 1929.

"Millionaire Hobo Is Dead," *The Christian Century* 47 (Aug. 20, 1930): 1020.

Minehan, Thomas. *Boy and Girl Tramps of America.* New York: Farrar and Rinehart, 1934.

Nash, Jay Robert. *Hustlers and Con Men.* New York: M. Evans and Company, 1976.

Norris, Lowell. "America's Homeless Army," *Scribner's Magazine* 93 (May 1933): 316–18.

O'Connor, Richard. *Jack London.* Boston: Little, Brown and Company, 1964.

O'Neill, William. *The Last Romantic: A Life of Max Eastman.* New York: Oxford University Press, 1978.

Parker, Carleton. "The California Casual and His Revolt," *Quarterly Journal of Economics* 30 (Nov. 1915): 110–26.

Parry, Albert. *Garrets and Pretenders: A History of Bohemianism in America.* New York: Covici-Friede Publishers, 1933.

"The Philadelphia Tramp Conference," *Charities* 11 (Nov. 28, 1903): 514–15.

Preston, William. *Aliens and Dissenters: Federal Suppression of Radicals, 1903–33.* New York: Harper and Row, 1966.

Reckless, Walter. *Vice in Chicago.* Chicago: University of Chicago Press, 1933.

Reed, James. *From Private Vice to Public Virtue: The Birth Control Movement and American Society since 1830.* New York: Basic Books, 1978.

Reitman, Ben. "Prisons in My Life," *Phoenix* 19 (May 1937).

———. *The Second Oldest Profession.* New York: Vanguard Press, 1931.

———. *Sister of the Road: The Autobiography of Box-Car Bertha as Told to Dr. Ben L. Reitman.* New York: Sheridan House, 1937.

———. "Syphilis in My Life," *Phoenix* 18 (Feb. 1937): 7, 27–29.

"Relentless War Against Vice in Chicago," *The Survey* 38 (June 9, 1917): 249.

Revolutionary Radicalism, Its History, Purpose and Tactics. Report of the Joint Legislative Committee Investigating Seditious Activities. Albany, N.Y.: J. B. Lyon, 1920.

Rexroth, Kenneth. *An Autobiographical Novel.* Garden City, N.Y.: Doubleday and Company, 1964.

Salvatore, Nick. *Eugene Debs: Citizen and Socialist.* Urbana: University of Illinois Press, 1982.

Sanger, Margaret. *My Fight for Birth Control.* New York: Farrar and Rinehart, 1931.

Scherill, James. *Sherwood Anderson.* Denver: University of Denver Press, 1951.

Sears, Hal. *The Sex Radicals: Free Love in High Victorian America.* Lawrence: Regents Press of Kansas, 1977.

"Sex O'Clock in America," *Current Opinion* 55 (Aug. 1913): 113–14.

Shaw, Clifford. *The Jack-Roller: A Delinquent Boy's Own Story.* Chicago: University of Chicago Press, 1930; Phoenix edition, 1966.

Shulman, Alix Kates. *To the Barricades: The Anarchist Life of Emma Goldman.* New York: Thomas Y. Crowell, 1971.

Sochen, June. *Movers and Shakers: American Women Thinkers and Activists, 1900–1970.* New York: Quadrangle, 1973.

Solenberger, Alice. *One Thousand Homeless Men.* New York: Charities Publications Committee, 1911.

Spence, Clark. "Knights of the Tie and Rail—Tramps and Hoboes in the West," *The Western Historical Quarterly* 2 (Jan. 1971): 5–19.

Steel, Ronald. *Walter Lippmann and the American Century.* Boston: Little, Brown and Company, 1980.

Steffens, Lincoln. *The Autobiography of Lincoln Steffens.* New York: Harcourt, Brace and Company, 1931.

Sustar, Lee. "When Speech Was Free (and Usually Worth It)," *Reader* 13 (Oct. 21, 1983).

Sutherland, Edwin. *The Professional Thief.* 12th ed. Chicago: University of Chicago Press, 1972.

Sutherland, Edwin, and Harvey Locke. *Twenty Thousand Homeless Men.* Chicago: J. B. Lippincott Company, 1936.

Swanberg, W. A. *Dreiser.* New York: Charles Scribner's Sons, 1965.

"Tent Colony of Strikers Swept by Machine Guns," *The Survey* 23 (May 2, 1914): 108–10.

Terkel, Studs. *Talking to Myself: A Memoir of My Times.* New York: Pantheon, 1973.

"This Is a Primer for Hobo 'Gaycats'," *Life* 3 (Oct. 4, 1937): 14–17.

Thrasher, Frederic. *The Gang: A Study of 1,313 Gangs in Chicago.* Chicago: University of Chicago Press, 1927.

Turner, George. "The City of Chicago: A Study of the Great Immoralities," *McClure's Magazine* 28 (Apr. 1907): 579–87.

"Venereal Disease Campaign," *Time* 29 (Jan. 11, 1937): 38.

Weil, Joseph (as told to W. T. Brannon). *"Yellow Kid" Weil.* Chicago: Ziff-Davis Publishing Company, 1948.

Wendt, Lloyd, and Herman Kogan. *Bosses in Lusty Chicago.* Bloomington: Indiana University Press, 1967.

Wexler, Alice. *Emma Goldman: An Intimate Life.* New York: Pantheon, 1984.

White, Ray. *Sherwood Anderson's Memoirs.* Chapel Hill: University of North Carolina Press, 1942.

Willard, Josiah Flynt. *My Life.* New York: Outing Publishing Company, 1908.

———. *Tramping with Tramps.* Montclair, N.J.: Patterson Smith Publishing Company, 1972.

Zorbaugh, Harvey. *The Gold Coast and the Slum.* Chicago: University of Chicago Press, 1929; Phoenix edition, 1976.

Index

A Note on the Author

Roger A. Bruns is Director of Publications for the National Historical Publications and Records Commission at the National Archives in Washington, D.C. He has written for *Smithsonian*, the *Los Angeles Times*, the *Washington Post*, and the *Chicago Tribune*, among others. Bruns is coauthor, with Arthur Schlesinger, Jr., of *Congress Investigates: A Documented History*, and author of *Am I Not a Man and a Brother: The Antislavery Crusade of Revolutionary America, 1688–1787*, and *Knights of the Road: A Hobo History*. He has also written juvenile biographies for the Chelsea House series on world leaders.